# Electing Peace

MW00411930

Settlements to civil conflict, which are notably difficult to secure, sometimes contain clauses enabling the combatant sides to participate as political parties in post-conflict elections. In *Electing Peace*, Aila M. Matanock presents a theory that explains both the causes and the consequences of these provisions. Matanock draws on new world-wide cross-national data on electoral participation provisions, case studies, and interviews with representatives of all sides of the conflicts in these cases and others (including with former combatant leaders). She shows that electoral participation provisions, nonexistent during the Cold War, are now in almost half of all peace agreements. Moreover, she demonstrates that these provisions are associated with an increase in the chance that peace will endure, potentially contributing to a global decline in civil conflict, a result which challenges prevailing pessimism about post-conflict elections. Matanock argues that electoral processes and democracy promotion programs pave the way for international actors to help secure settlements by detecting and sanctioning noncompliance. Matanock's theory and evidence also suggest a broader conception of international intervention than currently exists, identifying how these inclusive elections can enable external enforcement mechanisms and provide an alternative to military coercion by peacekeeping troops in many cases.

Aila M. Matanock is Assistant Professor of Political Science at the University of California, Berkeley. Her research addresses international intervention, civil conflict, and weak states. Her Stanford University dissertation, on which this book is based, won the 2013 Helen Dwight Reid Award from the American Political Science Association for the best dissertation from the previous two years in international relations, law, and politics.

# Electing Peace

*From Civil Conflict to Political Participation*

Aila M. Matanock

*University of California, Berkeley*

CAMBRIDGE
UNIVERSITY PRESS

# CAMBRIDGE
UNIVERSITY PRESS

University Printing House, Cambridge CB2 8BS, United Kingdom

One Liberty Plaza, 20th Floor, New York, NY 10006, USA

477 Williamstown Road, Port Melbourne, VIC 3207, Australia

314-321, 3rd Floor, Plot 3, Splendor Forum, Jasola District Centre, New Delhi - 110025, India

79 Anson Road, #06-04/06, Singapore 079906

Cambridge University Press is part of the University of Cambridge.

It furthers the University's mission by disseminating knowledge in the pursuit of
education, learning and research at the highest international levels of excellence.

www.cambridge.org
Information on this title: www.cambridge.org/9781316638811
DOI: 10.1017/9781316987179

First published 2017
First paperback edition 2018

*A catalogue record for this publication is available from the British Library*

ISBN 978-1-107-18917-1 Hardback
ISBN 978-1-316-63881-1 Paperback

# Contents

# Figures

# Tables

# Acknowledgments

When I began this project, I did not realize exactly what writing a book would entail; I also did not know how much assistance I would receive along the way. In conducting the research, I greatly appreciate several sources of funding and institutional support that made this book possible. These include grants during graduate school from the Eisenhower Institute, the National Science Foundation, the National Consortium for the Study of Terrorism and Responses to Terrorism at the University of Maryland, and, at Stanford, the Freeman Spogli Institute for International Studies, the Graduate Research Opportunities Fund, and the Stanford Center on International Conflict and Negotiation. They also include funding through the Institute on Global Conflict and Cooperation for final fieldwork and from the Scowcroft Institute of International Affairs for final archival research.

In addition, I am grateful to the many individuals who were willing to speak with me about their experiences leading rebel groups and governments through these transitions from battlefield to ballot box or their experiences supporting these processes as international policymakers – we covered much more detail from many cases than could be corralled into the pages of this book. I also thank those who provided initial contacts, including Alfonso Cuéllar and Marta Ruiz in Colombia, Mike McDonald in Guatemala, and Erika Murcia in El Salvador; Brenna Powell did the same and so much more in Northern Ireland. All who gave their time were invaluable to developing my thinking.

Many students with whom I have had the pleasure of working have contributed to the research for this project, which required tremendous data collection, and some also provided comments on various pieces of the project. I appreciate this outstanding assistance from Ben Allen, Katie Beall, Caroline Brandt, David Dow, Natalia Garbiras-Díaz, Chelsea Johnson, Adam Lichtenheld, Andrew Reddie, and many others, including those who helped collect data for the Rebel Group Electoral Participation (MGEP) dataset.

I am also indebted to those who helped this research become a book. Comments from John Haslam at Cambridge University Press and the anonymous reviewers have considerably strengthened the manuscript at the final stages; Teresa Lawson and Bridget Samburg similarly contributed at earlier stages.

Pieces of this project appeared as a stand-alone article, "Bullets for Ballots,"[1] and paper, "External Engagement,"[2] presenting parts of the theory and empirics from this book. The journal editors and anonymous reviewers' comments on these also provided useful advice that I greatly appreciate.

My colleagues have been crucial in my writing this book. The University of California, Berkeley provides an intellectual community that is both engaging and supportive. My colleagues here have offered excellent advice on all dimensions of this book, from the ideas to the evidence. I am especially grateful to Sarah Anzia, Leo Arriola, Pradeep Chhibber, Thad Dunning, Ron Hassner, Michaela Mattes, Bob Powell, and Jason Wittenberg for reading and providing crucially insightful feedback on much of the manuscript. Susan Hyde, even before she came to Berkeley, Katerina Linos, and Alison Post deserve special thanks for reading sections multiple times and offering invaluable advice. My colleagues, together with four from other universities, Jon Pevehouse, Jack Snyder, Beth Simmons, and Barbara Walter, attended a "book bash" in October 2014, which was generously funded by the Institute of International Studies. That conference and the written comments from the participants significantly improved this book, and I so appreciated their time and thoughtfulness. Other colleagues, including Mike Allison, Dinorah Azpuru, Laia Balcells, Emily Beaulieu, Ana Bracic, Dawn Brancati, Jessica Maves Braithwaite, Inken von Borzyskowski, Sarah Bush, Erica Chenoweth, Sarah Daly, Christian Davenport, Daniela Donno, Michael Doyle, Nisha Fazal, Tom Flores, Page Fortna, Scott Gates, Anita Gohdes, Caroline Hartzell, Reyko Huang, Stathis Kalyvas, Judith Kelley, David Lake, Roy Licklider, Desireé Nilsson, Irfan Nooruddin, Nicholas Sambanis, Mimmi Söderberg Kovacs, Paul Staniland, Abbey Steele, and Libby Wood, also gave freely of their time in ways that greatly contributed to this book, in some cases even reading many chapters of my manuscript. I am grateful for their kindness, and I consider myself lucky to be a part of the wonderful community of scholars working on these topics.

[1] Matanock 2017. I appreciate *International Security* for allowing me to use material from "Bullets for Ballots" in this book.
[2] Matanock 2016b.

I have had the opportunity to present pieces of this project, and each has made this book stronger, due to the incisive comments provided by discussants and audience members, who number too many to name here. These presentations took place at national conferences of the organizations that foster our political science and peace science communities, as well as at seminars at Columbia University, Duke University, the Elliott School at George Washington University, Emory University, the Gerald R. Ford School of Public Policy at the University of Michigan, the Naval Postgraduate School, the Peace Research Institute Oslo, Stanford University, Universidad de Los Andes, University of California, Berkeley, University of California, Los Angeles, University of California, Merced, University of California, San Diego, the University of Chicago, University of Texas, Austin, Uppsala University, Yale University, the Conflict Consortium's Virtual Workshop, and more.

I am grateful to the Hoover Institution at Stanford University, where I was a W. Glenn Campbell and Rita Ricardo-Campbell National Fellow and the Arch W. Shaw National Fellow during 2015–2016, for allowing me to be on research leave during the final revisions of this book. I especially appreciate Eli Berman and the Institute on Global Conflict and Cooperation for providing a postdoctoral fellowship with funding from the Department of Defense's Minerva Research Initiative, which allowed me to turn my dissertation into a manuscript. I am also grateful to the Center for International Security and Cooperation (CISAC), to other funding sources at Stanford University, and to the Miller Center for Public Affairs at the University of Virginia for providing stipend funding as I wrote my dissertation.

This project formed while I was at Stanford University, and I could not be more appreciative of those who helped me develop it, shaping what would become this book. My dissertation chair, Jim Fearon, encouraged me to find interesting questions and advised me on how to answer them more clearly and persuasively. His suggestions immensely improved every aspect of this book. The other members of my dissertation committee, Martha Crenshaw, Steve Krasner, David Laitin, Ken Schultz, and Steve Stedman, were also outstanding. They were devoted to the details when needed, they provided new perspectives at turning points in this project, and they were above all consistently enthusiastic about it through the entire process. These incredible political scientists – and wonderful people – have provided more than I could have asked for in terms of guidance and support. I also benefited at Stanford from advice and encouragement on this project from Lisa Blaydes, Gary Cox, Tino Cuellar, Alberto Díaz-Cayeros, Lynn Eden, Justin Grimmer, Karen Jusko, Beatriz Magaloni, Scott Sagan, Mike Tomz, Barry Weingast, and Jeremy Weinstein. In addition, I am grateful to the other graduate students with whom

I attended Stanford. For this particular project, Andrea Abel van Es, Dara Cohen, Luke Condra, Jesse Driscoll, Desha Girod, Jessica Gottlieb, Bobby Gulotty, Danielle Harlan, Ruth Kricheli, Melissa Lee, Nicholai Lidow, Avital Livny, Ollie Kaplan, Bethany Lacina, Maggie Peters, Lauren Prather, Bryan Price, Amanda Robinson, Rachel Stein, and Chris Warshaw contributed significantly by reading sections, providing comments, and making the process more fun for their friendship.

My interest in this subject began, even before I entered graduate school, while I was working at the RAND Corporation and studying at Harvard; Nora Bensahel, Jasen Castillo, Kim Cragin, Mike Hiscox, and Andy Kydd, in particular, encouraged me to explore these ideas while also pointing me toward PhD programs. I remain deeply indebted to them for putting me on the path toward this book. A special thank you to Sarah Harting, my best friend since our neighboring cubicles at RAND, who has spent considerable time listening to these ideas.

I have been very fortunate to have a wonderfully supportive and encouraging group of friends and family who have made the years working on this book wonderful. I appreciate my friends who have feigned interest in the minutia of civil conflict and elections over the years, while continuing to invite me to go places despite that I often declined to work on this book. My family is owed a deep debt of gratitude. They have been unwaveringly behind me in all that I choose to do, inspiring me in many different ways. Jason Stevens has endured the most during the course of my writing this book, and yet he remains the most enthusiastic about it and all my endeavors. I could not ask for a better partner. This is for him.

*Part I*

# Introduction and Theory

# 1  Credible Transitions from Civil Conflict
## Provisions for Combatant Participation in Post-Conflict Elections

International attention focused on the Nepalese leaders as they strode onto a stage in 2006 to sign a settlement and end a decade-long civil war. The conflict began in 1996 when a Maoist group attacked the government, aiming to replace the monarchy with a communist state. The war had devastated the country, killing thousands, including civilians as well as combatants on each side. Two previous rounds of negotiations accompanied by ceasefires had failed. But this time, Pushpa "Prachanda" Kamal Dahal, head of the Maoists – a terrorist organization according to the U.S. Department of State and other observers – and Girija Koirala, Nepal's prime minister, signed a peace agreement. The country's hopes for ending the conflict were pinned on this settlement.

Negotiators had carefully designed the settlement with the goal of producing durable peace. In contrast to some previous conflicts with leftist insurgents in other states, whose settlements provided for power-sharing based on fixed formulas or dividing control of territory based on combatant strongholds, the 2006 Nepalese settlement provided for the Maoists to transition from a rebel group to a political party. Despite the institutional challenges in such a transition, this settlement was thereby based on peaceful competition by each side's political parties in elections to distribute political power.

Since 2006, international attention has frequently returned to Nepal, especially in 2008 for the first elections, when the Maoists won, and again in 2013 for the next elections, when the Maoists slipped to third place. Remarkably, despite tension over drafting a new constitution, the former combatants have continued to run candidates and to comply with the other provisions of the settlement. International pressure has helped: the United Nations, the United States, and other external actors have not only monitored the elections, but have also provided incentives for compliance. These external actors have leveraged these incentives, including a trust fund for the Maoists, to help prevent a return to fighting during the difficult 2013 elections. Peace has persisted in Nepal when many worried it would fail.

The death toll of civil conflicts dwarfs the casualties caused by wars between states in the modern era, and, like the Nepalese case, peace may be precarious even when settlements are signed. Civil conflicts have produced millions of deaths since 1945, five times as many as wars between states in this modern era.[1] Many casualties come after periods of peace: for example, more than 90 percent of all civil conflicts since 2000 have been recurrences of earlier conflicts.[2] Settlements to end fighting are especially hard to secure.[3] Historically, they have tended to fail, giving way to additional fighting.[4] The evidence in this book shows, for instance, that conflict recurred after 40 percent of settlements signed in civil conflicts between 1975 and 2005. Constructing settlements that combatants will sign and sustain has been one of the most difficult challenges in ending civil conflicts.

Some settlements hold, however, such as the one in Nepal. This book identifies electoral participation provisions as a crucial component of why settlements succeed. Peace agreements are increasingly based on provisions that establish former rebel groups as political parties set to participate alongside government parties in post-conflict elections – and, compared to other settlements, these provisions are associated with an 80 percent increase in the chance that a settlement will produce enduring peace. These results emerge from this book's examination of the causes *and* consequences of electoral participation provisions in new cross-national data on 122 peace agreements and 388 civil conflicts (Chapters 3, 4, and 6) and case studies of civil wars that cross the end of the Cold War and that are resolved through peace agreements (including in-depth discussion of Guatemala and El Salvador in Chapters 5 and 7).

This book develops a theory that electoral participation provisions facilitate external engagement to monitor and enforce combatant compliance with negotiated settlements, and, in doing so, produce less precarious settlements and more enduring peace between signatories. Electoral participation provisions may even have contributed to the global decline in civil conflict that has occurred since the end of the Cold War. Successful settlements are now signed more frequently,[5] often with these provisions, reducing the persistence and recurrence of fighting.

---

[1] Fearon and Laitin 2003: 75.    [2] For example, see Collier et al. 2003.    [3] Fearon 2004.
[4] See Collier et al. 2003; Walter 2004; Toft 2009.
[5] Evidence on peace agreements is shown in Chapter 3. Extended data are available in Fazal 2015. Mack 2014 discusses similar evidence on peace (17–18) and explains it in part by the rise of an international security administration broadly conceived that can secure bargains (47).

## Electoral Participation Provisions

This book is fundamentally about peace, as well as how international intervention works, but its subject is post-conflict elections. Post-conflict elections are a divisive issue. Combatants and democracy activists at times push for elections when negotiating settlements,[6] while intergovernmental officials often supervise elections when they operate in post-conflict contexts.[7] But many studying post-conflict contexts show that elections on the whole do not increase the probability or durability of peace,[8] and some even suggest that elections in which ex-combatant parties participate can reduce the chances for a stable settlement,[9] arguing that, to the extent that post-conflict elections contribute to rapid democratization under weak institutions, they may trigger political violence as they introduce competition.[10] Policymakers and academics alike have focused on the difficult cases of Afghanistan and Iraq, however, and, in doing so, they fail to account for important terms or circumstances of post-conflict elections that may produce different causes or consequences.[11] Many "post-conflict" elections, such as those in Afghanistan in 2009, are held hastily during conflict by incumbent governments – rebel parties do not participate as part of a peace agreement, and they typically do not produce peace. But pessimism is not warranted across cases. There is variation in the causes and – most importantly – the consequences of types of post-conflict elections (as Chapter 6 shows empirically).

This book posits that one particular type of post-conflict elections, those produced by participation provisions in peace agreements, warrant optimism in terms of their effects on peace. *Electoral participation provisions* are defined in this book as clauses in peace agreements that enable both rebel group and government parties to participate in post-conflict

---

[6] For example, in one of the earliest cases, the founders of the Umkhonto We Sizwe, the armed wing of the African National Congress in South Africa, demanded in 1985 that the government "treat us like a political party" and provide for open participation in the constitution; see Zartman 1995: 152.

[7] Peacekeeping missions coincide with post-conflict elections so often that some scholars suggest that elections are part of the United Nations' standard operating procedure; see Collier 2009. Others, however, have noted that international actors' procedures evolve across cases; see Ottaway 2003.

[8] Collier et al. 2008; Flores and Nooruddin 2012; Brancati and Snyder 2013.

[9] For example, see Walter 1999.

[10] Snyder 2000; Paris 2004; Cederman et al. 2010; some empirical evidence, however, counters the recurrence argument, as shown in Licklider 2006.

[11] One difference that has been examined is timing: those held later seem to be less dangerous than those held immediately after conflict termination (see Flores and Nooruddin 2012; Brancati and Snyder 2013).

elections.[12] *Peace agreements*[13] are deals signed between two or more opposing sides in civil conflicts to solve, regulate, or outline a process to solve the differences over which the signatories were fighting.[14] During peace agreements, combatants must often disarm and demobilize while also finding a way to distribute power between them, which is risky compared to ceasefires and other mechanisms that reduce but do not end conflict. Rather than employing fixed-formula power-sharing arrangements or territorial divisions between government-held and rebel-held areas, peace agreements increasingly distribute political power among ex-combatant parties through electoral participation provisions.

Peace agreements with electoral participation provisions reflect consensus between the opposing sides in which they agree to hold elections and to allow each side to participate as political parties. In almost all peace agreements, governments conduct post-conflict elections, and so the settlement must legalize the rebel groups as political parties or otherwise establish them as such. In many cases, these provisions are explicit: for example, the 1994 settlement in Djibouti stated that "once the present

---

[12] I use the term "combatants," "combatant sides," or just "sides" to refer collectively to the rebel group(s) and the government in conflict with each other. I continue to use these names, as well as "ex-combatant parties," for the actors even after the settlement for simplicity.

"Rebel groups" are defined here as all non-governmental organizations using violence to achieve a political agenda. The groups are non-governmental in that they are not legally paid by the state to use arms to achieve the political agenda they seek. (However, a group may be pro-state in its aims or even affiliated with some part of the government, such as an elected party.) The group must use violence that seeks to destroy property and/ or harm people, and the violence also must have a professed political aim, or it is merely common crime (a criterion used in many definitions of civil conflict; see Gleditsch et al. 2002). Terrorist, insurgent, and other rebel groups sometimes use different specific tactics, but each uses a violent strategy not at the legal behest of the state to pursue their political aims. In initial data collection, I examined electoral participation by all rebel groups, but post-conflict electoral participation was limited to rebel groups that had engaged in at least a "minor" civil conflict (meaning one that resulted in 25 or more battle deaths annually); see Matanock 2016b. The data analysis therefore focuses on these groups.

"Governments" are the actors that rebel groups oppose. In most cases, where there was an established state before the civil conflict began, it is clear which side is the government. The incumbent or, where none exists, the side that has more control and recognition is considered the "government."

I generally treat both rebel groups and governments as unitary actors, although they may have different factions with different preferences, and extensions to this work should consider revising this assumption. Indeed, multiple rebel groups may also compose the side that opposes the government, which may change some of the dynamics; empirically, most settlements have a single rebel group, and just splinters outside of it (see Chapter 4), but extensions to this work should also study whether the dynamics are different with multiple rebel groups (signing or not signing onto settlements).

[13] A term used interchangeably in this study with *settlements*.

[14] The concept is described in more depth, and coding choices noted, in Chapter 3. Please also refer to the Online Appendix at https://dataverse.harvard.edu/dataverse/matanock.

Peace agreement has been signed, [the rebel group] will become a legal political party."[15] The expectations that each side will run candidates, and that their electoral participation emerges from the peace agreements, differentiate these elections from other post-conflict elections.

While normatively appealing, the transformation toward participatory elections to secure and stabilize peace agreements is somewhat surprising for several reasons. First, electoral uncertainty can complicate the problem of balancing power in a post-conflict settlement, potentially producing lopsided outcomes that might lead an electoral loser to anticipate greater gains by returning to conflict.[16] But electoral participation provisions only rarely establish fully free and fair contests open to all opposition parties competing for each citizen's equally-weighted vote. Instead, most of these provisions engineer or otherwise constrain the results of elections (using ethnic quotas for example) and thereby distribute power commensurate with combatants' expectations. Because of this, elections may not overcome cleavages that result from conflict, nor enhance democratization. The inclusion of electoral participation provisions should therefore be thought of as distinct from democratization.[17]

Electoral participation provisions were first included in settlements negotiated for seemingly intractable conflicts after the end of the Cold War, including in El Salvador (1992), Mozambique (1992), and Bosnia and Herzegovina (1995). These peace agreements have held, even though the extent to which the subsequent post-conflict elections are democratic is debatable (for example, quotas giving shares of seats to specific ethnic groups were at times employed). In contrast, a peace agreement with electoral participations provisions in Angola failed, and combatants returned to the battlefield after the polls closed in 1992 (see discussion of this case in Chapter 7). Both combatants and the international community seem to believe, however, that electoral participation provisions can help produce peace in many cases, and such provisions continue to be included in settlements. Nepal (2006) is an example, and despite moments when one side or the other fell short of full implementation, but settlement held and peace has endured for at least a decade. This is just one recent example of many in which electoral participation provisions are included to help foster enduring peace between former combatants.

---

[15] Chapter 3 discusses how to identify these provisions in more depth and also provides a list of all cases.

[16] See Walter 2002.

[17] Electoral participation provisions emerged only after the end of the Cold War with the spread of external engagement, and thus do not appear to be associated with the third wave of democratization, which began in the 1970s.

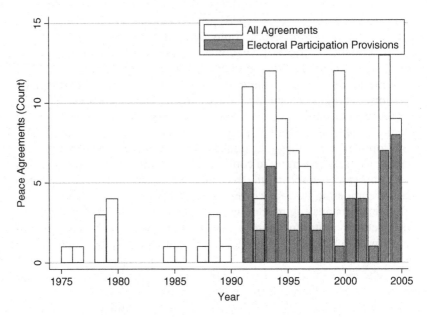

Figure 1.1 Electoral Participation Provisions and Peace Agreements over Time

Overall, electoral participation provisions have been incorporated into peace agreements to end some of the most dangerous civil wars. The number of peace agreements has increased since the end of the Cold War, and the share with electoral participation provisions has soared. Prior to 1989, not a single peace agreement included electoral participation provisions. Since then, almost half of all signed peace agreements have been based on these provisions (Figure 1.1). This book focuses, first, on the causes of electoral provisions, and, second, on the consequences of these provisions for peace. In particular, what explains the patterns in the inclusion of electoral participation provisions? Do settlements that include electoral participation provisions produce more enduring peace than other settlements, and, if so, why?

## External Engagement Theory

Electoral participation provisions are negotiated into settlements by combatants seeking to overcome a central obstacle to end civil conflicts: how to ensure that each side will comply with the terms of a mutually beneficial settlement even as power shifts, making combatants' commitments less credible. I argue that these provisions engage international actors to monitor and incentivize compliance,[18] facilitated by the benchmarks and milestones of electoral cycles that feature ex-combatant parties, especially as democracy promotion programs spread (see Table 1.1). (The theory is developed in more depth in Chapter 2.)

Commitment problems constitute a crucial constraint on securing and sustaining peace agreements. Combatants must first identify a bargain that benefits all sides, which is often possible relatively soon after fighting starts because bluffing is difficult during war, and conflict is costly in many cases, so combatants should then be able to settle. The risk that one combatant side will become temporarily stronger during the implementation of the peace agreement, giving it an incentive to try to grab more power than was initially allocated, however, can derail plans for peace.[19] Such a power grab may provoke renewed conflict. Or, if any side grows concerned that any other may make such a power grab, it might refuse to sign or return to fighting preemptively or as punishment after signing. These fears, called credible commitment problems, can be resolved by arrangements that reduce the benefit of noncompliance, so that it is not greater than the benefit of compliance. Rebel groups, even more so than governments, may be concerned about their opponents' noncompliance because governments have the advantage of working within state institutions. However, once the combatants can identify a mutually beneficial bargain, all sides have incentives to make noncompliance sufficiently costly to secure the settlement. The question is how to do so.[20]

[18] The term "international actors" (also "external actors" and "outsiders" interchangeably) refers in this book to the foreign states, intergovernmental organizations, and non-governmental organizations involved in international intervention, either with or without force. The United Nations does the largest share of this international intervention by deploying peacekeeping troops, but also by observing elections and in other ways assisting post-conflict states. Regional intergovernmental organizations, such as the European Union, the Organization of American States, and the African Union also serve some of these functions, often those that do not involve troops, as the case studies show. While these intergovernmental organizations operate most of these missions, the major powers – especially the United States, but also regional powers and former colonial powers – are also important actors. In addition to occasionally leading operations themselves, they hold influence in these organizations (especially those with veto power in the U.N. Security Council) and provide funding, particularly in the form of reconstruction, democracy, and good governance assistance. The International Monetary Fund and the World Bank are also important actors in these contexts. Finally, while intergovernmental organizations monitor many of the first elections that occur post-conflict in these states, a number of non-governmental organizations either assist them or run their own operations. Most notably, these include the Carter Center, the National Democratic Institute, the International Republican Institute, and others that are not based in the United States, such as the Norwegian Helsinki Committee (Hyde 2011b; Kelley 2012).
[19] Fearon 1995; Walter 1997, 1999, 2002.
[20] Enforcing compliance without a central authority is also tackled by the literature on international law and treaties (see Keohane 1984; Simmons 1998; and, on human rights, for instance, Simmons 2009; Hafner-Burton 2005, 2013).

Table 1.1 *Essential Steps of External Engagement Theory*

**CIVIL CONFLICTS ARE DIFFICULT TO END WITH SETTLEMENTS:**
Government and rebel group(s) seek peace agreements to stop fighting that **distribute power between themselves** based on their relative strength.

BUT can each side trust the other not to take advantage of the settlement as it is implemented? Combatants on all sides face **credible commitment problems:** each has incentives to grab more power when, during implementation, that side become relatively stronger – and each will be concerned about complying given the other side's incentives for noncompliance. Rebel groups may be most concerned.

**OUTSIDERS CAN HELP:**
**Outsiders with sufficient information and credible leverage can enforce compliance.**
Otherwise, combatants may refuse to sign settlements, or settlements may fail with potential noncompliance, and conflict may resume. Outsiders are often needed, but how do they engage?

**Electoral participation provisions** in a peace agreement facilitate outsiders' involvement because:
- **Coordination cycles** produced by elections' unambiguous benchmarks and milestones **increase information and leverage** at moments of power distribution, thereby allowing all actors to signal noncompliance and apply sanctions effectively;
- **After the Cold War,** major powers became more willing to get involved with ending civil conflicts, and **democracy promotion programs spread** in many regions of the world, further **facilitating external engagement through these electoral processes**. Election observation and conditional incentives, including funds for political parties, for example, provided mechanisms with sufficient information and credible leverage to enforce compliance by each side.

**Armed actors using military coercion** after a peace agreement can similarly solve the commitment problem as long as they stay.

BUT a armed intervention **can be costly for outsiders,** as it involves threat of force or use of force, which risks casualties and expends resources.

THUS **expectations of outsider enforcement based on electoral participation provisions are credible**, because such involvement is low-cost for outsiders, for instance compared to armed intervention, and therefore this mechanism is likely to help overcome combatants' commitment problems.

THUS peace agreements that depend on armed intervention by outsiders alone are relatively rare, and they may fail as credibility of armed interveners falters, weakening prospects of enforcement for combatants.

The theory thus implies that peace agreements should be more likely to include electoral participation provisions **only after the Cold War, spreading by region, and still not in states with special relationships to enforcers**, as international involvement through democracy promotion programs became available gradually.

The theory thus also implies **more enduring peace** after peace agreements with electoral participation provisions, particularly when they also have clear expectations of external engagement.

A typical solution suggested for combatants to overcome commitment problems is to engage external actors to detect noncompliance with the settlement and sanction it with force,[21] but armed international intervention set to punish with force is infrequent because the personnel, arms, and materiel required to guarantee a settlement are costly. Such peacekeeping often does not occur at all. Moreover, even in the rare cases in which peace is enforced by semi-permanent armed peacekeepers, most mandates do not allow for restitution or retribution in the event of a violation, leaving the seizure unchecked by force. Because armed international actors can rarely credibly threaten or use force to punish noncompliance with peace agreements, especially over the implementation period, including when political power is distributed among combatants, many settlements require other mechanisms to secure and sustain them.

This book offers a different conception of enforcement, in which external actors, without using force, change the cost calculation of noncompliance by former combatant groups.[22] Once combatants have assessed the cost of continuing conflict and their opponents' capabilities through fighting, and have identified a mutually beneficial settlement, they still need enforcement to overcome commitment problems. Punishment need only be greater than the power or resources that the temporarily stronger side can grab at any particular moment, and it needs to be balanced enough that all sides expect enforcement. But enforcement must cost little enough that the commitment by the international actor to engage is credible. External enforcement is more credible if there is a low-cost, long-term mechanism to detect and sanction noncompliance (which armed peacekeeping often does not provide).

This book argues that electoral participation provisions can enable this low-cost, and therefore credible, external enforcement over time. The provisions establish cycles whose culmination is to distribute political power between participating ex-combatant parties. Noncompliance can be difficult to detect because ex-combatants can often find ways to subtly alter institutions to gain an advantage while implementing the multiple pieces of most peace agreements. The public benchmarks tied to regular milestones in these cycles clarify what is and is not compliance – and enable multiple actors to coordinate to provide information and condition incentives on the

---

[21] Walter 1997, 1999, 2002.
[22] Some of the mechanisms described in this section are also employed by armed peace-keepers (see Fortna 2008).

ex-combatants' compliance. Such coordination, especially at crucial moments when political power is distributed between the sides, raises the expected cost of noncompliance for each side. This combination of benchmarks and milestones to which former combatants are bound, and the coordination of external actors around them, makes it possible for monitoring and sanctioning to be effectively administered. International actors – typically the U.N. and other intergovernmental organizations as primary observers, and foreign donors as primary suppliers of conditional incentives – are needed to administer this enforcement because domestic actors are often weak and polarized in post-conflict contexts.

This book also argues that the systemic changes that began at the end of the Cold War have reduced the costs for international actors to enforce peace agreements through electoral participation provisions, especially as international democracy promotion programs rapidly proliferated. While these systemic changes have also importantly increased the incentives for international actors to help end civil conflicts by increasing the security concerns emanating from civil conflicts relative to other threats, they also crucially established conventions and institutions that facilitated external enforcement. Electoral participation provisions began to be seen as a legitimate mechanism to distribute power after a civil conflict – and to draw much greater levels of international involvement. International actors, primarily intergovernmental organizations and representatives of democratic governments, become involved in enforcing election-related provisions in post-conflict contexts because they were now able to do so at lower costs than they would incur by sending armed peacekeepers. Once in a country, these external actors could use democracy promotion programs to provide international election observation and other monitoring, and conditional incentives, especially material assistance including foreign aid and assistance for political parties. External engagement through electoral participation provisions is not possible in all post-conflict settings: for example, pre-existing special or strategic relationships between a potential enforcer and a combatant side may make unbiased enforcement appear not credible – and thus make it less likely to be employed because it is more likely to fail to resolve commitment problems. (Chapter 4 shows lower rates of these provisions across such cases, while Chapter 7 explores this issue in Cambodia where international actors had such pre-existing relationships that could not be overcome.) However, there are many cases in which such external enforcement is both possible and effective at producing enduring peace.

### Illustrations: How These Dynamics Work

Examples abound of how, once adopted, electoral participation provisions combined with credible external engagement have facilitated enforcement and maintained peace. In El Salvador, for instance, the demobilization of government forces was delayed during implementation. The ex-rebel party, as well as members of El Salvador's civil society, voiced concerns about the delay, which could have produced a substantial change in power over time. As the elections approached, the United Nations issued public statements about the government's slow progress to pressure the government into complying. These efforts were accompanied by specific threats from the United States and other international actors to withdraw aid, which would have been unpopular. The government then moved quickly toward compliance. Noncompliance with other terms of the settlement existed beyond disarmament – usually impeding efforts to redistribute power – and external engagement in the electoral process again enforced the agreement. For example, when the government failed to issue voter registration cards in a timely manner – many likely rebel supporters had not previously voted – the United States froze funds, producing an increase in the pace of voter registration (described in Chapter 7).

Much of the international pressure around these post-conflict elections is on the government, because it is often more able to renege subtly due to its advantage in terms of standing and control of formal state structures. Rebel groups, however, are also sometimes subject to punishment for violations. In Mozambique, for instance, the rebel group, Mozambique National Resistance (Renamo), moved to renege on the settlement after faring poorly at the polls, but a combination of international actors had established a trust fund for party development conditioned on compliance, which created a substantial incentive that induced Renamo's political party to continue to participate and build peace (see Chapter 7).

In Macedonia, the incentives for each side's compliance included not just aid, but also Macedonia's eligibility for membership in NATO and the European Union, intergovernmental bodies that were very popular with Macedonian voters. International election observation was also essential for monitoring compliance with the agreement's electoral provisions, as European intergovernmental organizations sent more than 800 monitors to cover the first post-conflict election. Success in Macedonia hinged on this international involvement (see Chapter 6).

In some cases, all sides have been closely monitored for compliance, even decades after any armed peacekeepers have left. In Bosnia and Herzegovina (described in Chapter 2), the E.U. monitors for the 2010 elections continued to assess compliance with rules set in the 1995 Dayton Accords. Such monitoring has thus ensured that elections based on quotas – a component of the participation provisions for a country divided by ethnicity – were maintained even 15 years after the peace agreement. While the E.U. might have been expected to criticize the elections for failing to meet the organization's own democracy standards, instead it worked to assure that power-sharing was still taking place as it was supposed to.

International enforcement is far more difficult when settlements are based not on electoral participation provisions, but on, for instance, fixed formulas for power-sharing. In Chad, for example (see Chapter 2), external actors did not attempt to engage, and even if they had, they would have lacked sufficient information about compliance and credible leverage to enforce the settlement.

Chapter 2 elaborates on the causes and consequences of external engagement theory, explaining how electoral participation provisions, alongside international democracy promotion programs, can provide low-cost mechanisms to credibly detect and sanction noncompliance, enhancing the prospects for enduring peace – and the rest of this book offers much more evidence on electoral participation provisions and external engagement.

## The Motivation in Context

This book matters for several reasons. This book offers a mechanism for engaging external actors to enforce peace agreements that, when available, can stabilize settlements. Electoral participation provisions, when included in peace agreements, can reduce the cost and thereby increase the credibility of external engagement. Electoral participation provisions can thus help all sides in a conflict overcome the most persistent obstacles to peace agreements. This book suggests a new understanding of the role, manner, and prospects for post-conflict elections and, more broadly, for international intervention.

This book contrasts prevailing pessimism and presents an important corrective to current thinking about post-conflict elections.[23] The central empirical finding – that settlements based on electoral participation provisions can produce more enduring peace than other settlements can – counters concerns that elections themselves are conflict inducing. Including electoral provisions in peace agreements may appear counterintuitive, because the distribution of power between combatants through elections can be uncertain, but the mechanism theorizes that elections created by participation provisions specifically can stabilize settlements by easing external enforcement. In explaining how this particular type of post-conflict election contributes to peace, this book highlights the importance of distinguishing between different types of elections in post-conflict settings.

Electoral participation provisions help overcome persistent obstacles to peace, but other outcomes may not be as positive. They may involve trading some dimension of democracy for stability. Arranging elections that share power between all sides so as to prevent the emergence of a "loser" that is ready to return to conflict, typically requires some electoral engineering such as ethnic quotas, resulting in an elite deal.[24] The problems of limited democracy have been well documented in these contexts: post-conflict elections have been shown to sustain wartime cleavages, lead to low levels of openness, and even result in international election observation that does not focus on democratic standards.[25] This raises questions about the norms – collective beliefs about behavior – that surround these electoral processes in post-conflict contexts. Elections receive significant international attention in part because of the idea that they advance democracy.[26] Electoral participation provisions rely on external engagement, but the goal is stability, not democracy: post-conflict elections may be better at producing peace than democracy.[27] While the focus of this book is peace, the conclusion, Chapter 8, suggests that future work should address this potential stability-democracy trade-off in priorities explicitly.

[23] Collier et al. 2008; Collier 2009; and, particularly for elections held soon after the conflict, Flores and Nooruddin 2012; Brancati and Snyder 2013. Broader literature also links elections to violence, such as through coercion for votes (see Dunning 2011; Steele 2011; Staniland 2015; Balcells and Steele 2016), not to mention the many studies on electoral violence.
[24] Shugart 1992.
[25] See, for example, Snyder 2000; Lyons 2002a; Paris 2004; Reilly and Nordlund 2008.
[26] For example, see Diamond 2006.
[27] Some existing studies focus on democracy, perhaps producing some of the pessimism surrounding these elections. Lyons (2005) evaluates early post-conflict elections with regard to both peace and democracy.

This book's central contribution is an expanded understanding of international intervention in enforcing settlements to end civil conflicts. International involvement can be much broader than armed peace-keepers. Military coercion is not always needed. Elections can work in post-conflict settings through external monitoring and enforcement using a broad array of rewards and punishments, mainly tied to aid and other material assistance. Military coercion, in contrast, is often not a credible mechanism for peacekeepers to use, because international interveners will be tempted to withdraw some or all of their forces due to costs and domestic pressures, rather than to punish noncompliance with force. As this book makes clear, when electoral participation provisions are included in settlements, force may not be needed to enforce them. Another form of international intervention, specifically engagement through elections, is often more effective alternative enforcement mechanisms.

If this book is correct about the mechanism, it may also assist in solving other domestic political problems. This book thus ties to larger ideas about compliance and enforcement broadly conceived, and it suggests a much-expanded role for global governance. External engage-ment to monitor and incentivize compliance, using aid and other nonmilitary mechanisms, can help solve combatant commitment problems in these contexts. The same could be true of a number of other domestic political problems as diverse as political repression and other potential human rights violations, fraud in leadership transitions, and even corruption.[28] The external engagement mechanism could be used to exact compliance in these cases, given the right conditions, in a credible way due to its relatively low cost compared to other interven-tion. These conditions under which the mechanism may work are expli-cated over the course of this book and discussed explicitly in the conclusion.

Post-conflict elections created by these participation provisions encom-pass many of the most dangerous, and the most successful, cases of conflict termination from recent decades. They are the subject of this book. This book's most important implications, however, are about international intervention. In particular that troops are not always needed to solve domestic problems like combatant commitment problems. In the concluding chapter, I return to the questions of how policymakers can recognize when electoral participation provisions may work and can

---

[28] The mechanisms relate to those in some existing studies, including, for example, Simmons 2009; Hafner-Burton 2005 2013; Donno 2013.

encourage their inclusion in peace agreements. I also discuss how these mechanisms can be applied to solving other domestic problems.

## Empirical Evidence, Research Design, and Book Plan

External engagement theory has implications for both the causes and the consequences of electoral participation provisions. The first two chapters of this book establish the theory. In Chapter 2, I explain the logic behind external engagement theory and offer illustrations of the mechanism at work. That chapter generates sets of implications on both the causes and consequences of electoral participation provisions based on this theory and alternative theories. The rest of the book tests those implications. I briefly overview the evidence, design, and plan for the book in this section.

The book draws on quantitative and qualitative data to evaluate the proposed theory and alternatives. For the quantitative analysis, I collected data on electoral participation provisions by analyzing the full text of each peace agreement for the period from 1975 to 2005, a period that covers settlements during the Cold War and afterward. I also used a new cross-national data project, called the Rebel Group Electoral Participation Dataset (MGEP), which identifies the implementation of these provisions.[29] I used two comparison sets in the analysis: all peace agreements in the Uppsala Conflict Data Program (UCDP) Peace Agreement Dataset and all conflicts in the UCDP Conflict Termination Dataset. I compiled additional variables reflecting, for example, expectations of external engagement through the electoral process. Using these data, I assess when electoral participation provision were included in peace agreements, and the outcomes associated with their inclusion, especially in terms of enduring peace.

Because these statistical tests can show only cross-national correlations on the causes and consequences of electoral participation provisions, I use case studies to understand the underlying mechanisms. I selected cases that provide clear variation over time – before and after the end of the Cold War – in expectations of external engagement appropriate to enforce a settlement. Among the set of cases crossing the end of the Cold War, I focused on the Central American cases, which provide a clear test of my theory: during the Cold War, international actors had involved themselves in supporting the fighting in these conflicts, on one side or the

---

[29] MGEP also identifies all national legislative electoral participation by armed non-state groups from 1970 to 2010, both during and after conflict, as is described in much more depth in Matanock 2016b.

other, and they then sought, after the Cold War, to intervene in a nonpartisan way for peace. This required a considerable change in perceptions from the combatant sides about bias of the proposed external enforcers of compliance. The cases thus offer an opportunity to examine if it was the shifting conditions in the international system that facilitated the expectation of external actor engagement through elections to help overcome combatants' commitment problems – and if the electoral participation provisions helped to secure peace.

Ten cases were actively fought across the end of the Cold War and then ended in peace agreements with electoral participation provisions. After testing some implications across these ten cases, I used process-tracing in the two Central American cases among these that include electoral participation provisions and that produce enduring peace, "positive" cases, to examine the mechanism through which these provisions are included in settlements and through which they succeed in sustaining peace. Aside from providing especially clear tests at the end of the Cold War, and featuring sufficiently detailed data, these cases also differ on rebel group dimensions that alternative theories predict to be important, allowing a test of those mechanisms between the two cases. These cases are Guatemala and El Salvador. I drew on other cases from among the ten, especially Angola and Cambodia, which are outliers, to understand how these provisions sometimes fail and what that means for the theory. In addition, I examined the contrasting case of Bangladesh, a "negative" case that does not include electoral participation provisions and must employ alternative provisions in its settlement, to better understand the mechanism.

Data collection for the case studies drew on my interviews with former leaders of rebel groups, governments, and civil society who were involved in decisions about the electoral participation provisions and their implementation, as well as individuals who led international missions in these post-conflict states. I also consulted the presidential records for the period of the initial Central American negotiations (which began in 1989) at the George H.W. Bush Library, and I located other primary sources on these conflicts and intervention through various outlets, including websites of the U.S. State Department and the United Nations, and the archives of organizations devoted to documenting these rebel groups. Further evidence came from historical records in a variety of secondary sources.

The quantitative and qualitative evidence show that electoral participation provisions are more likely to be included in settlements in which systemic characteristics allow combatants to expect credible external enforcement of compliance, and that including such provisions fosters more enduring peace than alternative arrangements do. I preview these findings below along with the book's plan.

### Causes: Characteristics that Signal Expectations of External Engagement

The first set of observable implications from this theory relate to the idea that provisions for rebel groups and governments to participate electorally will be more likely to be included in peace agreements when combatants expect international actors to engage through the electoral process to enforce compliance. International actors – including the United Nations and other intergovernmental organizations who monitor these elections, and the United States and other (primarily Western) donors who condition assistance on information about compliance – should be more likely to engage as international democracy promotion programs spread. Such programs only became widespread after the end of the Cold War, but did not extend uniformly to all regions in the world. Instead, there were regional waves of democracy promotion programs that provided for election observation and associated aid. This variation suggests differing levels of international involvement in specific regions at specific times; for example, Latin America began to receive these programs even before the Berlin Wall fell, and Eastern Europe was among the first to receive them afterward (these waves are described in more depth in Chapter 3).

Where democracy promotion programs were not proffered by international actors, or where states had strategic or other special ties to potential external enforcers that made them less credible, we should expect to find combatants to be less likely to expect effective nonpartisan enforcement of compliance (because a partisan international actor might be more lenient toward the side with which it has strong ties) and therefore less likely to include electoral participation provisions in a peace agreement.[30] These systemic and state characteristics affect the expectation of availability of credible international enforcers and, therefore, the inclusion of electoral participation provisions.

The theory also implies that, while all combatants need to bind themselves to settlements in order to gain the dividends of peace, rebel groups in particular should push for external enforcement because they may not trust state institutions to not favor incumbent governments. We should see, then, that rebel groups should be more likely than incumbent governments to advocate for the inclusion of electoral participation provisions in peace agreements when external engagement is available.

---

[30] Girod 2011; Donno 2013.

The evidence presented in Chapters 3, 4, and 5 is consistent with these implications. Chapter 3 provides a brief overview of patterns of international involvement across post-conflict contexts. The end of the Cold War produced some armed peacekeeping missions in post-conflict contexts, but they typically have lacked resources to threaten force and have been relatively rare. The Cold War's end also produced other types of external engagement, especially international election observation and other democracy promotion programs, although these varied systematically by region and state, as discussed.

Chapter 4 uses quantitative evidence to test when electoral participation provisions are included among all peace agreements and among all conflicts. The cross-national analysis shows that electoral participation provisions became more common after the Cold War and then were correlated with the spread of democracy promotion programs regionally. Electoral participation provisions are also negatively correlated with strategic or other special ties between governments and international actors.

Chapter 5 examines crucial cases of civil conflict that began during the Cold War and ended after it with peace agreements that included electoral participation provisions; the chapter assesses all ten such cases before focusing on Guatemala and El Salvador. The ten cases together illustrate that it is rebel groups, rather than incumbent governments, regardless of their ideology, that push for electoral participation provisions in peace processes. The process-tracing in Guatemala and El Salvador then shows how commitment problems blocked a peace agreement prior to 1989, and then how settlements with electoral participation provisions were signed in each case when the end of the Cold War changed external actors' strategies in these contexts and, as a result, also changed combatants' expectations. The "negative" case of Bangladesh, which unlike these "positive" cases did not achieve a settlement based on electoral participation provisions, demonstrates what happens when such expectations of external engagement do not shift.

These results are consistent with combatants who are more likely to push for the inclusion of electoral participation provisions when they expect credible engagement by external actors.

*Consequences: Enduring Peace*

The second set of implications of external engagement theory arises from the idea that electoral participation provisions should improve the chance of stable conflict resolution. They should enable an external actor to detect and sanction noncompliance at a sufficiently low cost so that it can provide effective enforcement. With credible external enforcement, the signatories should be less likely to renege on the settlement and return to conflict either preemptively or as punishment. Peace agreements with electoral participation provisions should thus be less likely to fail and cause conflict recurrence. However, peace agreements with electoral participation provisions should only be more durable than other power distribution arrangements if combatants expect that an external actor will engage in a nonpartisan way through the electoral process to enforce compliance. The theory also has implications for the extent of international involvement in post-conflict elections produced by participation provisions (and for some other features of these elections).

The evidence in Chapters 6 and 7 is consistent with these implications. Using cross-national analysis, Chapter 6 shows that electoral participation provisions are associated with more enduring peace – in these data, settlements with these provisions succeed 80 percent more frequently than those with alternative provisions – but the pacifying effect only exists where combatants had expectations of external engagement in the electoral process. Chapter 6 also explores the nature of international actors' involvement in post-conflict elections, and it shows extensive election observation and democracy assistance, as well as clear conditionality of these incentives on compliance with the terms of the settlements around the elections. Moreover, this chapter tackles the potential for selection problems with several strategies, which include using potentially exogenous proxy measures for expectations of external enforcement, and these relationships hold (see Chapter 6).

Chapter 7 returns to the same set of case studies and, again focusing on Guatemala and El Salvador to provide detailed process-tracing, shows how international actors engaged through the electoral process and generated incentives for signatories to comply with the peace agreement: they threatened punishments, or even removed benefits, when potential non-compliance was detected. The chapter also examines instances of the failure of these provisions, such as in outliers Angola and Cambodia, to better understand the limits of their contribution to enduring peace. It also explores how tenuous a settlement can be without provisions by returning to Bangladesh.

This book concludes in Chapter 8 with implications for future research and for policy. I examine how the theory and evidence expands the conception of international involvement in peacekeeping, and what that might mean for successful intervention. I discuss the tradeoff between peace and democracy in these post-conflict elections and argue that an overemphasis on democracy in these contexts may come at the expense of peace. I posit that international organizations should consider engaging through post-conflict elections with the explicit goal of stability in more conflicts and that states may need to strengthen international organizations to do so.

## Considering Alternative Arguments

The evidence described above helps distinguish external engagement theory from alternative explanations and, in doing so, further clarifies the mechanism.

It is difficult to prove arguments that depend on beliefs, perceptions, or information – of former combatants and interveners in this case – because it is hard to acquire systematic and reliable data on what these actors think and know. No one piece of evidence on its own can prove or disprove external engagement theory, but the results of multi-method tests of different implications of this theory and alternative explanations taken together offer persuasive support. Chapter 2 has a comprehensive discussion of alternative explanations, but I outline them briefly here.

The most significant challenge to the argument that electoral participation provisions lead to more peace is that conflicts in which combatants agree to these provisions were already easier to settle for other reasons. I call this the *ease explanation*. It implies that electoral participation provisions are more likely to be included in settlements when conflicts are easiest to solve – for instance, in smaller conflicts in states that have stronger institutions.[31] If so, then proper identification of easy cases should make any correlation with peace disappear. However, it could very well be that, even if combatants are selecting these provisions only in easy cases, they do so because they anticipate causal effects from the provisions; otherwise, there would be no reason not to include them even in hard cases.[32] The selection effect represented by the "ease" explanation does not have much explanatory power on observed dimensions, as Chapter 4 shows; in fact, electoral participation provisions tend to be included in somewhat harder cases to solve more often than easier cases. Still, I use multiple methods and seek plausibly exogenous variables in the cross-national analyses to provide the most rigorous tests possible given the potential for selection on unobserved dimensions.

Most studies have little to say about why electoral participation provisions would be included in settlements, or what relationship these provisions should have with peace. Institutional explanations suggest that elections engineered to power-share through a settlement may also help

---

[31] See, for example, Fortna 2008.
[32] Schultz (2010) makes this general point about selection effects.

maintain peace,[33] although the mechanism leading to peace is not clear. According to such explanations, elections may be seen as a type of institution that reconciles *de jure* and *de facto* power better than other institutional types. Reallocating positions within the government by a fixed formula, for instance, could also change power in line with an agreed settlement. But perhaps elections are easier if the vote reflects popular support for each side and if fighting capability is also a function of the same factor. This could produce another selection effect – one in which combatants choose to include electoral participation provisions when it is easier to rely on elections than on other arrangements. However, it is unlikely that the results of such post-conflict elections will tend to match the distribution of popular support for each side. These elections are frequently characterized by electoral engineering and low levels of openness to the outcome of the vote,[34] and they are monitored primarily to prevent further fighting – based on standards set by peace agreements – rather than to spur democracy.[35] The institutional logic, then, does not seem to explain why elections would be favored over other institutional arrangements for fostering a stable power distribution in a settlement, although I test some of its implications.

The best-developed alternative theories explaining the inclusion of post-conflict elections, and potentially their impact on peace, focus on the demands or desires of international actors. What I call the *escape explanation* suggests that outside interveners will impose elections when they wish to withdraw their own troops that have been extensively engaged on the ground; this may be especially true in unstable contexts.[36] The motivation for the interveners to impose elections may be either to create a legitimate government to contract with, as a partner rather than a subordinate, or, more cynically, to leave some nominally legitimate government in place as they exit altogether.

However, evidence for the escape explanation suggests that it is unlikely to explain electoral participation provisions. Much theorizing about post-conflict elections has been based on recent dramatic failures, and empirical testing in these studies often conflates distinct types of post-conflict elections. The most prominent examples of "escape" cases, the elections in Afghanistan in 2009 and 2010, were hasty elections arranged by an international intervener to legitimate a selected government so that it could withdraw from the unstable context as soon as possible.[37] In such

---

[33] On power-sharing, for instance, see Walter 2002.
[34] See Snyder 2000; Lyons 2002a; Paris 2004; Reilly and Nordlund 2008.
[35] Hyde 2011b; Kelley 2012.
[36] See especially Kumar 1998; Lyons 2002b, 2005; Collier 2009; Hansen 2014.
[37] See Collier 2009: 80.

cases, it is often clear that the international actors prefer a particular outcome, so they would have little incentive to encourage opponents' participation in elections, especially if it entailed extended settlement negotiations. In contrast are post-conflict elections meant to resolve conflicts in Bosnia and Herzegovina, Burundi, Macedonia, Mozambique, South Africa, Sudan, and elsewhere, where elections emerged from peace agreements that feature provisions for rebel groups to participate in government-run elections. The result of conflating these two types, and focusing on recent failures among the first type, gives a negative view of elections implemented to resolve conflicts that may be unwarranted. Nonetheless, escape is the best-established alternative explanation in the literature on post-conflict elections, and it has implications for the causes and consequences of electoral participation provisions, so I evaluate it.

Another explanation in the literature on post-conflict elections suggests that the United States and Western allies – dominant after the Cold War – favor assisting post-conflict regimes that hold elections. Before they will provide aid or other assistance to domestic actors in post-conflict contexts, external actors will demand at least a façade of democracy.[38] While it could be the case that international actors will impose their preference directly on combatants, it is also possible that combatants anticipate this and therefore preemptively include elections in settlements. This *enjoinder explanation* is similar to external engagement theory in some ways: both are driven by the idea that the United States and other involved international actors find it preferable to engage through elections but for different reasons. Chapters 4 and 6 distinguish between these arguments, based on when electoral participation provisions are included and how they are then used, although the two arguments are closely linked together.

Another explanation, which I call the *emulation explanation*, suggests that elections may be chosen due to the diffusion internationally of the norm of democracy. This explanation implies that we should see electoral participation provisions included in more and more peace agreements. Provisions for participatory elections would thus reflect a desire by domestic actors to ensure conformity with socially defined norms, as parties, rather than consideration of the consequences. Rebel groups or governments, or external actors, see embracing elections as what they *should* do. I find, however (as shown in Chapters 3 and 4), that the spread of electoral participation provisions does not map evenly to the spread of democratic norms. Normative conventions certainly underpin external

[38] See Driscoll 2008.

engagement theory as well, but focusing on expectations of external engagement around elections (democracy promotion) rather than just elections, which are somewhat different, and the spread of electoral participation provisions matches the former better than the latter.

This examination of alternatives reveals no especially convincing explanations for the cases examined in this book, in which the rebel group and the government agree to settle a civil conflict that distributes power through electoral participation provisions. However, the alternative explanations are developed in more depth in the Chapter 2, where their implications are detailed, which also helps clarify the mechanisms at work.

This overview also reinforces how much we do not understand about post-conflict elections – and how little theoretical and empirical progress has been made toward understanding their causes and consequences. Scholars have begun to explore variation in timeframes and power-sharing rules in post-conflict elections,[39] but significant variation across types of elections remains unexplored. This book enriches our understanding by examining post-conflict elections established by electoral participation provisions.

[39] Reilly and Reynolds 1999; Reilly 2002; Brancati and Snyder 2011, 2013; Flores and Nooruddin 2012.

# 2    Electoral Participation Provisions
## A Theory of External Engagement

When voters went to the polls in Bosnia and Herzegovina in 2010, international election observers watched closely for compliance with the institutional arrangements that had been negotiated in the peace agreement with the Republika Srpska a decade and a half earlier. The 1995 Dayton Accords had provided for the combatants to form parties and established a complex electoral system engineered to guarantee representation by the three major ethnic groups that reflected the balance of power among them at the end of the conflict. The settlement thus distributed political power through electoral participation provisions and, in doing so, set public benchmarks and regular milestones around which to measure and incentivize compliance with the peace agreement.

Engagement by international observers and foreign donors through this participatory electoral process created a means to enforce the settlement throughout the implementation period, even after other international involvement had ended. Long after peacekeeping troops drew down, the international community remained engaged in monitoring and providing incentives for compliance with the peace agreement. For instance, international observers for the October 2010 general elections – a core team of 20 long-term observers along with 300 short-term observers – assessed the elections against the criteria established by the 1995 settlement.[1] Although the observers conceded that the ethnic quotas did not meet European democracy standards, the final report from the mission measured the elections primarily against the terms set in the peace agreement and concluded that they had been generally conducted accordingly.[2] International actors have conditioned aid, movement toward membership in intergovernmental organizations, and other benefits on compliance. The settlement has, since 1995, maintained peace among the combatants, despite some discontent over the slow process toward democratization among the population.

---

[1] Söderberg Kovacs 2008: 134–156; Kelley 2012: 63.
[2] Organization for Security and Cooperation in Europe 2010.

Contrast Bosnia and Herzegovina and other settlements based on electoral participation provisions and external actors' engagement with alternative settlements. In Chad, for example, throughout the late 1980s, the government pursued a power-sharing strategy in which it distributed cabinet positions to rebel groups that signed peace agreements. New appointments were met with displeasure by rebels who had previously been placed in cabinet positions as a result of their settlements with the government. As the number of cabinet positions ballooned, less power and fewer resources were available for those who had signed on earlier and for those in the president's inner circle. Interior Minister Mahamat Itno became so concerned about the resulting reduction of his power that, when another rebel was made foreign minister, he attempted a coup.[3] In this case, not only were external actors not expected to engage to stabilize the settlements, but, even if they had, they would not have known whether and to what extent the government had failed to comply with its private agreements, and so could not have effectively sanctioned noncompliance.

Why was the peace agreement in Bosnia and Herzegovina designed around provisions that allowed both sides to participate as political parties in post-conflict elections? Examples from El Salvador, Macedonia, and Mozambique, described in Chapter 1, beg the same question, as they were similarly based on electoral participation provisions, even without the substantial armed peacekeeping mission that Bosnia and Herzegovina had. And, why was the Chadian settlement not? And, most importantly, does this design choice affect long-term prospects for enduring peace? Each settlement involved shared power between combatants, but in the first cases through electoral quotas and in Chad through promised cabinet positions. The electoral participation provisions are, of course, not the only difference between these particular cases, but the provisions seem to be systematically important. This chapter posits that electoral participation provisions facilitate effective international involvement to enforce a settlement and thus make enduring peace more likely.

Existing literature largely neglects the study of peace agreements based on electoral participation provisions, which is the term this book uses for clauses in peace agreements specifying post-conflict elections in which both sides are to participate as political parties. I argue that such provisions increase the ability of combatants to secure stable agreements. External actors can reduce combatants' concerns about their opponent's commitment to a settlement by engaging to detect and sanction noncompliance by each side, provided external actors have sufficient information

---

[3] Atlas and Licklider 1999: 43–46.

and credible leverage. Electoral participation provisions lower the cost and thereby increase the credibility of such enforcement by enacting cyclical coordination devices and, as democracy promotion programs spread, establishing strong institutions and conventions through which external actors can engage. External actors typically use international election observation and associated aid in these contexts. The theory thus posits a method to help enforce settlements.

This external engagement theory has observable implications for the causes and consequences of electoral participation provisions. Electoral participation provisions offer a mechanism to efficiently engage external actors, but outsiders who are willing to help stabilize settlements and who are seen as nonpartisan by each side do not always exist. So, I argue, combatants are most likely to include such provisions when interested but nonpartisan outsiders are available. Typically, the rebel group, which might be concerned that the incumbent government can more effectively manipulate state institutions that distribute political power in the settlement, will be most likely to demand electoral participation provisions to secure this external enforcement. Moreover, including electoral participation provisions in settlements should then produce more enduring peace because external actors can more easily enforce the settlement.

In this chapter, I develop the theoretical claims of the book. I first identify why electoral participation provisions are not necessarily an obvious choice for peace agreements, and I discuss some obstacles to effectively settling civil conflict. Next, I argue that international actors need sufficient information and credible leverage to overcome these obstacles and enforce a settlement. I then argue that electoral participation provisions facilitate external engagement that is low cost and therefore credible in this enforcement. In doing so, I explain how electoral institutions and the international actors together can foster enduring peace. Finally, I formulate empirical implications from this external engagement theory, and I contrast them with implications from alternative explanations.

## Electoral Participation Provisions as a Puzzle

Existing theories suggest that electoral participation provisions may make peace agreements harder to design, and alternative forms of power distribution may provide more certain payoffs at lower costs to the combatants than elections typically do. Why then would combatants base settlements on electoral participation provisions? This section outlines why previous studies would not predict that peace agreements would be based on electoral participation provisions, one of the puzzles that motivates this study. The next sections then explain the emergence of electoral participation provisions and address the puzzle.

Any negotiated settlement to a civil conflict requires a bargain that benefits all sides. Because conflict typically destroys resources, or is otherwise costly, there are often a number of bargains from which all sides would benefit more than continued fighting.[4] The "peace dividend" created by preserving resources by ending conflict can be divided between the two sides during negotiations. There are many ways, besides elections, to allocate power and this peace dividend, such as power-sharing based on a fixed formula or dividing control over territory.

Elections have several drawbacks as mechanisms for power distribution in such settlements when compared, for example, to fixed formulas. First, elections are expensive to implement due to costs of registering candidates and voters, campaigning, and organizing the vote.[5] Elections may thus increase the cost of a settlement to such an extent that it is no longer a more beneficial option for combatants than continuing to fight. Second, compared to other power-sharing arrangements, elections provide less flexibility because outcomes are constrained by institutional rules that allow only for certain divisions of power, not just any division of power.[6] Elections may then make it difficult to design a deal in which each side benefits from power and the peace dividend to an extent commensurate with its expected payoffs from fighting.

Finally, elections may produce a losing side that is worse off than it would have been fighting. Free and fair elections are, by design, uncertain, so votes may not distribute power at the ballot box according to expectations from the battlefield. Moreover, in post-conflict contexts, institutions backed by civil society are not often not sufficiently strong to ensure repeated elections,[7] which is the usual mechanism underpinning democracy and providing even losing parties incentives to keep participating.[8] The outcome of these elections then may provide one side with fewer benefits than it expects from fighting, constituting an incentive for that combatant to return to conflict. For elections to secure

---

[4] On this point, see Fearon 1995.

[5] Post-conflict elections in relatively new democracies are particularly expensive. These are the costs just to hold the elections; they do not include campaign spending by the parties. The first elections in Cambodia in 1993, for example, cost $45 per voter, although the cost had declined to $2 per voter in 2003, according to the ACE Electoral Knowledge Network.

[6] Governments may be somewhat able to alter institutions to gain a wider range of options, such as changing electoral rules in ways that allow greater representation for a particular group's supporters or that make it easier for a new party to participate, but they are still constrained.

[7] Walter 2002.     [8] Przeworski 1991, 2006.

peace, all sides must expect to get *at least* as much influence through the settlement as they expected to secure through conflict; otherwise the side that is short may restart the fight. Fixed formulas and territorial bargains, by contrast, might yield more stability due solely to the certainty of resource distributions.

The design of electoral participation provisions can minimize this final drawback, but doing so reduces other strengths of elections, raising the question of why combatants include these election provisions at all. Dividing or sharing power commensurate with combatants' strength is necessary for peace agreements to be sustainable.[9] Elections can be engineered to avoid uncertainty by institutionalizing a deal among particular combatant leaders to match combatants' expectations in terms of the power distribution,[10] thus dividing power in much the same way as fighting was expected to,[11] for example through ethnic quotas. In Burundi, for instance, the peace agreements signed in 2000 and 2003 required that the National Assembly and other government bodies be 60 percent Hutu and 40 percent Tutsi, and that the Senate and armed forces be 50–50.[12] The agreement protected the ruling minority Tutsi by ensuring that the group's influence would be greater than it would have been if it participated in a free and fair election but, presumably, at least equal to what it could have expected to secure through conflict. Electoral deals in other conflicts, including Bosnia and Herzegovina, Lebanon, and South Africa, similarly sheltered ruling minorities. Such elections are based on elite deals, designed to match *de jure* power to *de facto* power.[13] Civil society may demand more open contests later,[14] but initially, at least, "elections in a postconflict setting are fundamentally different."[15]

Establishing some certainty about the outcome of elections through such an elite deal may, however, reduce the normative appeal of elections, which raises questions of why combatants would use electoral participation provisions to distribute power at all. Why not simply distribute power according to, say, a fixed formula (if, perhaps, to be followed by elections at some later point)? Allowing voters to hold leaders accountable for their policies is the foundation of elections' normative appeal and of democracy. Decreasing uncertainty through the design of these elections in the peace agreement reduces these advantages.

---

[9] Walter 2002; Wantchekon 2004; Durant and Weintraub 2014; Hartzell and Hoddie 2015.
[10] Schumpeter 1942; Lijphart 1968; Norris 2008.    [11] Shugart 1992.
[12] Article 164 of Burundi's constitution; on this, see Hartzell and Hoddie 2015.
[13] For example, see Reilly and Nordlund 2008.
[14] Walter 1999; Brancati and Snyder 2013.    [15] Garbar 1998: 1.

Post-conflict elections have often been criticized for these undemocratic characteristics, particularly by those excluded from these processes, because they permit the cleavages and power structures from the conflict to persist.[16] International actors often do not push strongly for open democracy in these contexts, focusing instead on stability and referring back to the settlement signed by the combatants.[17] In other words, such elections may produce a democracy-stability tradeoff, favoring stability.

If not to develop democracy, then, why are electoral participation provisions increasingly included in peace agreements? In other words, if these elections just mimic direct power-sharing provisions in allocating government positions and resources among the combatants, why would they be preferred over other mechanisms?[18] No systematic explanation of this puzzle exists.[19] Existing studies hint at two salient features of these post-conflict elections: the undemocratic arrangements in many of these elections and the international involvement they attract.[20] I draw on these factors to develop a theory in this chapter – that these provisions are better at securing enduring peace than alternative means of distributing power – and I present empirical evidence in Chapters 6 and 7.

## Persistent Commitment Problems

In settlements, combatants have reasons not to trust their opponents to comply, creating commitment problems that are a common source of conflict recurrence. Success therefore can depend on overcoming commitment problems. In this section, I draw on existing work to show that commitment problems can involve both informational and incentive issues, and that combatants seek to overcome both of these issues when conflict is costly, so that they each can secure a share of the resulting payoff from peace. Rebel groups are more likely to seek a mechanism beyond the state structures to overcome these issues because of their concerns that governments might be able to manipulate these institutions surreptitiously for an advantage. The question that emerges from this

---

[16] See Snyder 2000; Lyons 2002a; Paris 2004; Reilly and Nordlund 2008.

[17] Hyde 2011b; Kelley 2012.     [18] See, for example, Walter 1999; Walter 2002.

[19] Most of the existing studies that describe these cases attribute the electoral deals to factors that would produce "ripeness" for *any* settlement, such as war weariness or identifying a mutually beneficial deal. For example, see Irvin 1999; Zahar 1999; De Zeeuw 2008; Söderberg Kovacs 2007. They do not, however, explain why peace agreements would center on electoral participation provisions rather than other provisions. Weinberg et al. (2009) confirm that there is significant variation in the inclusion of electoral participation provisions in post-conflict agreements, through a cross-national study of terrorist organizations (21–22).

[20] For example, see Jarstad 2008.

section, then, is what mechanism the combatants will use to overcome their commitment problems.

A bargaining perspective posits that, because fighting is often costly, combatants should always be able to settle on a deal that provides both sides more benefit than they would have received from combat.[21] There are cases in which fighting is not that costly for leaders – for example, heads of hierarchical states sponsored by foreign states – and combatant sides are unlikely to settle in such cases.[22] Contexts that are "ripe" for a settlement, due to withdrawal of foreign sponsors, for instance, are a scope condition for peace agreements.[23] However, combatants still may be unable to settle either because they cannot identify a deal or because they cannot credibly commit to a deal. Information asymmetries that make identification of mutually beneficial bargains difficult are likely to be resolved soon after fighting begins, because bluffing about capabilities and resolve is difficult during conflict that calls on and thus reveals those resources.[24] Identifying such a settlement is, however, another scope condition for peace agreements. Even with both of these scope conditions in place, often early in a conflict, commitment problems are likely to persist.

Commitment problems have derailed many potential peace agreements in civil conflicts, even when the other problems preventing combatants from settling have been resolved.[25] Research on peace agreements suggests that they have been relatively rare and, when reached, fragile.[26] In the data that I have collected for this book, about half of all settlements fail as fighting resumes among signatories. In an assessment of all conflicts, those that end in settlements experience a 27-percentage-point increase in conflict recurrence compared to cases in which fighting gradually ends (while those that end in definitive victories experience a 24-percentage-point decrease in conflict recurrence).[27] These difficulties are especially present in conflicts with multiple rebel groups.[28] Settlements, however, are becoming more common compared to other types of termination, and, when they include electoral participation provisions, settlements are more likely to succeed, as Chapter 6 shows.

Commitment problems occur when one side becomes relatively weaker, or is expected to become relatively weaker, during a peace

---

[21] See Fearon 1995; Powell 2002; Reiter 2003.

[22] Mason and Fett 1996, for example, explore when combatants will choose to continue conflict rather than settle, which is in part due to these costs.

[23] Zartman 1985.

[24] Most theorists hold this view. See Blainey 1988; and on civil conflict, for example, see Powell 2006; Fearon 2007. Some are more skeptical, such as Mattes and Savun 2010.

[25] Walter 1997, 2002.     [26] Walter 2002; Cronin 2009.     [27] Toft 2009.

[28] Cunningham 2006.

|  | Rebel Group (R) Honors | Rebel Group (R) Reneges |
|---|---|---|
| Government (G) Honors | G share<br><br>R share<br><br>*(Compliance)* | G share – power grabbed<br><br>R share + power grabbed<br><br>*(R noncompliance)* |
| Government (G) Reneges | G share + power grabbed<br><br>R share – power grabbed<br><br>*(G noncompliance)* | G share – cost of fighting<br><br>R share – cost of fighting<br><br>*(Conflict resumes)* |

Figure 2.1 Settlement Payoffs to Combatants Depending on Compliance

process, providing the other sides incentives to renege on the peace agreement, even if doing so derails a mutually beneficial bargain.[29] The commitment problem can be formalized by making a set of simplifying assumptions to produce a widely explored interaction known as the "prisoner's dilemma." (The formal model is presented in the Appendix.)

Consider two strategic actors: a government and a rebel group.[30] Each seeks to control as large a share of power or policy influence as possible. The government offers the rebel group some share of power to avoid costly conflict, and the rebel group decides whether to accept. If they sign a negotiated settlement, each side then decides whether to honor or to renege on the deal (see Figure 2.1 below). Because of commitment problems, compliance by both sides is not an equilibrium solution in the prisoner's dilemma, due to commitment problems. Each side could gain more from seizing additional power compared to what it would be allocated under the settlement, and so it has an incentive to renege.[31]

Commitment problems can arise throughout implementation. Any settlement terms, as part of demobilization or during subsequent political

---

[29] On the commitment issue in civil conflicts, see Walter 1997, 2002; Fearon 2004; Fearon and Laitin 2007.

[30] See Chapter 1 for definitions of these actors.

[31] Noncompliance as a rational choice only requires that the amount of power that the reneging side can grab is positive compared to compliance – a benefit from grabbing additional power – and it does not depend on any other dimension of the interaction between the two sides, such as their relative power. The idea of a cost of conflict is central in producing any mutually beneficial bargain, but, once it exists, the crucial idea in this model is the commitment problems that work against compliance. (Again, the formal model is in the Appendix.)

processes, can change the balance of power, and then the incentives for combatants. The first demobilization phase often poses a clear risk to peace, as a temporarily stronger side, in relative terms, can attack its opponent more successfully.[32] If a government, for instance, withdraws from certain regions, it may leave its civilian supporters more vulnerable to a surprise attack by a rebel group. If the rebel group then kills or intimidates these civilians, support for the government weakens. The rebel group can then use its position of increased strength to demand a better bargain for itself through threat of further force.[33] In many cases, however, combatants may implement stepwise demobilization and integration of force structures to avoid some of these risks. Noncompliance may occur further into implementation, too. A change in the political rules, or in the timing of their implementation, could diminish power differentially for each side. For example, a government may delay in integrating a rebel group into the state's power structure to allow the government to maintain more power, perhaps passing laws favorable to its platform before integrating the legislature. While political provisions may sometimes be easier to implement than demobilization,[34] if one side fears losing out at a late stage due to its opponents' noncompliance, it may refuse to sign or to stay committed to settlement at an earlier stage.[35]

At any of these stages, the commitment problem is an informational issue and an incentive issue. It is an informational issue because each side lacks knowledge about whether its opponent will comply with complex deals and yet must be confident that a minimum level of compliance is maintained; it is an incentive issue because each side must anticipate that it and its opponent will benefit from the settlement and face costs for noncompliance. The obstacle is not just that one side will choose not to comply in order to gain more power in an obvious way. Even perceptions of noncompliance can cause a settlement's failure. For instance, a rebel group might interpret a slight delay or deviation by a government in integrating the rebel group into the state's power structures as a signal that the government intends to back out of the deal. But the government may have delayed intentionally to gain more power, or it may have

---

[32] A surprise attack is the common interpretation of reneging, often based on the models in Walter 2002.

[33] Such a situation could even produce genocide; see Licklider 1995.

[34] Walter 2002: 28.

[35] The model (see the Appendix) suggests that there are some circumstances under which continuing to comply while the other side opts for noncompliance can be a better option, depending on the cost of conflict, so there may be some leeway on what level of compliance the actors need to commit to in order to sustain peace. This may explain some of the dynamics in the Guatemalan case presented in subsequent chapters.

delayed inadvertently due to low capacity to implement, or it may have simply gone slower than expected because it had a different understanding of the timeline for compliance. If the rebel group perceives such a delay in this situation, however, it may expect that the government is trying to place it in a position of decreased strength from which it would have to accept a worse bargain. Whatever the truth is, one side or the other may threaten or actually return to fighting to prevent any perceived effort by the other side to gain an advantage or increase its own relative strength. The pathways through which combatants return to conflict are thus (1) noncompliance by reinitiating fighting; (2) noncompliance by altering aspects of the deal, accidentally or intentionally, which leads the opponent to return to fighting; or (3) concerns by one side that its opponent is engaging in either type of noncompliance, which again leads that side to return to fighting.[36] The combatant sides may even have foreseen these problems and refused a settlement in favor of continued fighting.

Rebel groups are often more vulnerable to noncompliance by governments than governments are to noncompliance by rebel groups. Some scholars have noted that this is because most deals demand more disarmament by the rebel group than the government.[37] However, the issue is actually more complicated. *De jure* power favors the government (by definition because the government is the side in power when civil conflict starts), so institutions must change in a settlement to match *de facto* power. Moreover, the government is the stronger combatant side in most cases. The institutions in place are, therefore, biased toward the more powerful actor, and provide opportunities for it – the government – to resist changes to the status quo distribution of power. These opportunities also may not be obvious to its opponent: the government can, for example, take more than its share of power through institutional mechanisms that initially reflected its dominant position. In a case like Chad, the government may change rules preserving more power for the president in foreign policy, even as it agrees to a rebel as the foreign minister. Indeed, manipulation of institutions, electoral or otherwise, can encompass both legal and illegal actions in governmental attempts to grab more power for the incumbent.[38] For these reasons, rebel groups may be more vulnerable under state structures alone than established governments.

All sides nevertheless have incentives to commit themselves credibly to peace agreements in order to gain a share of the peace dividend when a mutually beneficial compromise exists. Each side therefore must find a way to make noncompliance detectable and subject to sanctions in

---

[36] Similarly categorized by Fortna 2008: 82–85.   [37] Fearon and Laitin 2007.
[38] For example, Beaulieu 2014: 4.

order to secure the settlement that provides the benefits of peace. Peace processes inherently weaken the enforcement mechanisms held by combatants during the conflict, their threat to use force, and so they must have other mechanisms to hold each side to compliance with the settlement. A rebel group, in particular, may seek a mechanism beyond the state structures, given its concerns about how a government might use these institutions, perhaps surreptitiously, to its own advantage.[39] The question is what mechanism the combatants will use to do so.

### Commitment Problems Are Difficult to Overcome

Scholars have identified few mechanisms for overcoming the dual challenges of detecting noncompliance and increasing its cost. Guaranteed power-sharing arrangements alone, for example, rarely resolve the commitment problem. Such arrangements provide the mutual benefits necessary to secure a bargain that is better than fighting, and they can reduce the marginal gains from reneging.[40] Power-sharing in some form – integrating each sides' forces into a single force, for instance – may enhance each side's ability to sanction noncompliance by the other.[41] When all sides are incorporated into the state structures by guaranteed power-sharing arrangements, none will have exclusive control of the military, government, or economy of a state. Such arrangements, therefore, reduce the benefit to each side of trying to seize complete control. Peace agreements designed to include these institutions that share power, especially control over multiple aspects of the state, have been shown to reduce conflict recurrence.[42] Nonetheless, such arrangements are most useful when the balance of power is relatively equal between all sides: equality provides a mutual veto that is enough to block or significantly sanction noncompliance.[43] However, if one side is weaker than the other, it may not be able to win sufficient power through fighting to obtain such a mutual veto, so providing it with such a veto in a settlement may meet objections from its opponent.[44]

Even in balanced settings, the implementation of power-sharing provisions ignite commitment problems. Moments of shifting strength

---

[39] On this point, for example, see Fortna 2008: 22.

[40] For example, see Walter 2002; Hartzell et al. 2001; Hartzell and Hoddie 2003, 2007; Mattes and Savun 2009.

[41] See Hoddie and Hartzell 2003; Fortna 2004.

[42] See Hartzell and Hoddie 2007, but all of the studies just cited to some extent as well.

[43] Walter 2002: 37.

[44] Aspects of this argument are presented in different circumstances in Boix and Svolik 2013: 302–303; also see Cox et al. 2013, for example, on less-than-fully democratic states holding elections.

accompany even incremental alternation by side of disarmament, demobilization, and integration of state apparatuses; simultaneity and precision in
these processes of change are profoundly difficult to arrange or
implement.[45] If using a mutual veto, then mutual vulnerability at each
moment must be maintained.[46] Any misalignment changes incentives and
again produces concerns about commitment. While incremental alternation is essential because it reduces the amount of power that either side
could seize at any stage by reneging, such arrangements do not prevent
reneging (or concerns about reneging) that could lead back to conflict.

Retaining arms is another mechanism that allows each side to maintain
its ability to enforce a settlement. Many settlements without electoral
participation provisions provide, or allow tacitly, for arms retention,
particularly alongside bargains based on increased autonomy. In territorial conflicts, such divisions are a natural solution, and it may make sense
to allow each side to maintain its ability to protect itself through the threat
of force, at least temporarily. Even in non-territorial conflicts, these
provisions have been used on occasion. For example, in Colombia
in 1998, the government demilitarized a zone the size of Switzerland,
which came to be known as Farclandia, allowing a rebel group, the
Revolutionary Armed Forces of Colombia (FARC), to control a secure
base (at least during the peace negotiations). The problem with using
separate zones of control is that when demobilization and disarmament
do not occur, which they often do not, future power imbalances or
perceived threats can escalate to conflict recurrence easily. Even full
settlements of this sort, especially without complete secession, often
manifest as pauses in the fighting rather than mechanisms to terminate
fighting.

The path to a peace agreement is thus plagued by both informational
and incentive issues that result in persistent commitment problems.
Power-sharing agreements, including engineered or otherwise "fixed"
elections, can result in a mutually beneficial settlement that at least
matches *de jure* power to *de facto* power at the time of the settlement.
But these arrangements provide mechanisms for overcoming concerns
about noncompliance after implementation only in balanced conflicts.
Agreements with territorial divisions at best establish an uncertain
mechanism to overcome commitment problems in some secessionist
conflicts. During implementation, and beyond in many conflicts, combatants need another mechanism through which noncompliance can be
detected and sanctioned, ensuring a minimum level of compliance by
each side.

[45] See, for example, Fortna 2008.    [46] Bekoe 2008.

## External Engagement Theory

Many combatants overcome commitment problems through external engagement, signing and implementing peace agreements, because it increases the likelihood that noncompliance will be detected and sanctioned to an extent that it does not produce net benefits. In short, rather than having to trust its opponents, each side trusts outside enforcement. In this section, I argue that international actors need credible leverage and sufficient information to threaten a cost for noncompliance by both sides over time and therefore to provide external enforcement. I then argue that electoral participation provisions enable this very mechanism cost-effectively and, thus, credibly.

### Enforcing Compliance Broadly Conceived

This book develops ideas about compliance and enforcement broadly conceived. Consistent with literature on international law and treaties that focus on "management," under which noncompliance is typically viewed not as deliberate violation but rather as a problem of ambiguity, capacity, or a shift in conditions that is outside of the actor's control, information alone can overcome some issues.[47] However, given incentives to grab more power during implementation processes due to intentionally changing institutional design, enforcement is also necessary.[48] The form of enforcement is where this book makes much of its mark. In the enforcement literature, there is the possibility of self-enforcement with reciprocation or reputational costs providing the mechanism;[49] however, these mechanisms work best when repeated interactions under a stable institution are established or when actors risk retaliation in kind (for example, if relatively balanced sides can both access military force), which are rare in these shaky post-conflict contexts.[50] Civil society can also be mobilized under the right conditions to threaten costs for noncompliance,[51] but these do not function well if civil society cannot overcome collective action problems,[52] which is often difficult with weak and polarized civil society following conflict as the next sections discuss. The most likely mechanism in these contexts is external enforcement, although other mechanisms involving civil society and self-enforcement may develop over time.[53] This book extends compliance and enforcement

---

[47] Chayes and Chayes 1995; Simmons 1998.    [48] Downs et al. 1996; Simmons 1998.
[49] Keohane 1984.    [50] Simmons 2010: 276, citing Morrow 2007.
[51] For example, see Simmons 2009.    [52] Simmons 2010: 276, citing Guzman 2008.
[53] Also cited as crucial to human rights enforcement, for instance; see Hafner-Burton 2005, 2013; Carter 2016.

| | Rebel Group (R) Honors | Rebel Group (R) Reneges |
|---|---|---|
| Government (G) Honors | G share[a]<br><br>R share[a] | G share – power grabbed<br><br>R share + power grabbed<br>**– international sanction** |
| Government (G) Reneges | G share + power grabbed<br>**– international sanction**<br><br>R share – power grabbed | G share – cost of fighting<br><br>R share – cost of fighting |

[a] Shares now include any incentives offered by the international community, which can be withdrawn with noncompliance (see Table 2.1).

Figure 2.2 Settlement Payoffs to Combatants Depending on Compliance and External Enforcement

concepts from international law and treaties to the context of domestic conflict settlements, details how international actors can aid enforcement in these contexts at a low cost, and identifies some scope conditions for when they can do so.

Theoretically, then, international actors can impose a cost for noncompliance, potentially negating the benefit either side could seize through noncompliance. If the sanction outweighs any benefit that the rebel group or government would receive from reneging, then each side should have incentives to sign and to comply with a settlement.[54] Consider again the prisoner's dilemma that underpins the theory on commitment problems: it illustrates how international involvement can increase the changes that both sides will honor the peace agreement (see the Appendix).

The mechanisms through which international actors help combatants overcome the commitment problems inherent to settlements, however, are not well understood.[55] Common wisdom, consistent with mechanisms suggested in some studies, is that peacekeeping operates by threatening or using military force.[56] Armed peacekeepers, for example, can in theory detect and then sanction noncompliance by reducing the existing resources of either side, which they could do militarily by, say, bombing camps or bases. The *threat* of force, rather than its actual use, may often be sufficient

[54] This assumes that the combatants have identified a mutually beneficial deal, as discussed in the previous section, and as formalized in the Appendix. See Walter 2002. Bekoe (2008) also makes a similar point about "mutual vulnerability" produced both by the timing of implementation and by international actors.

[55] Fortna and Howard 2008: 292.     [56] E.g. Walter 1997: 340–341.

to exact compliance.[57] But if deterrence fails, the threat must be followed by punishment with military force.[58] Indeed, the international actor's commitment to use force if needed must be credible to deter noncompliance.[59]

Potential casualties and financial costs, however, call into question the likelihood of the continued presence and persistence of peacekeepers who can credibly threaten military coercion.[60] Peacekeeping troops are rarely sent, and, when they are, their action is often limited.[61] Among U.N. missions dispatched to post-civil war states from 1946 to 2012, only 51 percent were authorized to employ any military force. [62] Regardless of whether they are authorized to use force, peacekeeping troops are rarely deployed throughout the full implementation period, even if actors do not anticipate violence. In Guatemala, for instance, U.N. military observers deployed for six months in 1997 but left before many settlement deadlines around the elections in 1999.

When missions are authorized to use force, they often elect not to apply it for military coercion. For example, a U.N. study of eight "enforcement" missions found that peacekeepers intervened in only 20 percent of reported combatant attacks on civilians, despite being authorized to do so, and when peacekeepers did respond, "a show of force to deter" was rare.[63] Troops also tend to retreat in the face of noncompliance in the form of surprise attacks.[64] Missions may be hesitant to risk casualties or provoke combatants, may see military force as disproportionate punishment for the noncompliance, or may focus on civilian protection rather than combatant punishment.[65] In general, high costs can diminish military coercion's credibility in many cases. Even armed peacekeepers, when deployed, sometimes use other mechanisms that do not entail threatening or using force.[66] Only in unusual post-conflict contexts, such as in Sierra Leone, do sufficiently motivated armed peacekeepers credibly use military coercion.[67] All other post-conflict cases require other mechanisms of

---

[57] Ruggeri et al. 2013: 389.     [58] Walter 2002.

[59] Schelling 1966; Hultman et al. 2014 argue such resolve is needed in peacekeeping, specifically, but others suggest it is rare in these settings; see Fortna 2008: 88.

[60] On this, see Fortna 2008; Gilligan and Sergenti 2008; Beardsley 2012, 2013.

[61] For instance, see United Nations 2008. Part of the reason may be that it is difficult to recruit troops from member states – see Hillen 2000 – but Chapter 3 describes more broadly how the end of the Cold War produced changes that encouraged international actors to engage more often as guarantors, and, at the same time, why military coercion has remained rare.

[62] Matanock and Lichtenheld 2016.     [63] U.N. General Assembly 2014: 8, 21.

[64] Fortna 2008: 87–89.

[65] Missions authorized for force are often restricted to civilian protection; see Hultman et al. 2014; 2016.

[66] Matanock and Lichtenheld 2016; more examples of cases also can be found in Fortna 2008: 89–102.

[67] Fortna 2008: 88.

international involvement to enforce settlements and overcome commitment problems.[68]

### *International Involvement Requires Sufficient Information and Credible Leverage*

Settlements are difficult to enforce because noncompliance can be hard to detect and sanction. I argue external actors must obtain *sufficient information* to monitor combatants' adherence to a peace agreement, and *credible leverage* – military or, more likely, nonmilitary rewards or punishment – to make noncompliance marginally more costly than compliance. For the mechanism to be credible, international actors must be interested in ending conflict rather than backing one combatant side in the conflict, and they must face low costs to commit to staying involved throughout the settlement's implementation process. In this section, I demonstrate the importance of each condition and describe how they are commonly met through electoral cycles.

First, enforcing compliance requires *sufficient information*. Combatants must be able to trust that monitors can detect noncompliance. Outsiders need information to tell when one side is reneging so that they can threaten sanctions and, if necessary, employ them. Monitors must obtain sufficient information to confirm or refute combatant concerns that the other side seeks to renege or alter the deal, subtly or not and intentionally or not. Some noncompliance may occur during peace processes: even if both sides remain committed to the settlement, small factions may engage in skirmishes or seek to steal more power than they were allotted in the agreement. Whether such incidents are limited or not, and accidental or not, monitors' clear communication can increase the likelihood that transgressions will remain localized: if a monitor investigates a complaint, for example, judges it to be merely an isolated incident, communicates its judgement effectively to both sides, then conflict may be less likely to resume. Beyond preventing uncertainty and minimizing effects of accidents, however, a central role of information is to detect noncompliance in order to sanction it. Even with local incidents, international actors must at times sanction the relevant actors to appease all sides. External actors may even be able to detect combatants planning coordinated noncompliance and threaten sanctions to make it less beneficial.[69]

The information must be sufficiently detailed to detect even subtle noncompliance. International actors can bring resources to bear in collecting information. Intergovernmental organizations may provide innovative technology and send many observers. Intergovernmental organizations

[68] Walter 2002.     [69] Some of these functions are also discussed in Fortna 2008: 93–98.

often cannot obtain all the information that they need without others, however. International actors may therefore need to coordinate to obtain sufficient information. Domestic actors can help identify compliance and augment accountability: they may provide information that the international actors could not acquire on their own, such as reports about violations in remote regions of a post-conflict country. Even combatants may have opportunities to send signals of their own compliance, as well as to raise concerns about their opponents' compliance.

The information, however, must cover noncompliance by all sides to be sufficient for these functions. International actors must commit to detect, and sanction, noncompliance with the terms of the settlement by each side. If international actors cannot, or will not, monitor the compliance of both sides, commitment problems remain. For example, if international actors visibly favor one side, then the favored side will know that it can renege without consequence. Interveners may be effective if they are somewhat partisan toward whichever side is weaker, but not toward the stronger side.[70] For example, a weak rebel group would need to know that aid would be revoked should a strong government fail to redistribute funds to its supporters, but that government would not necessarily need the same assurances for the terms applying to that rebel group. In general, however, nonpartisan monitors may be most effective for resolving commitment problems.

Part of an international actor's role is therefore to arbitrate, in addition to collecting evidence and coordinating among actors, in order to obtain sufficient information. Domestic actors such as elements of civil society are often weak and cannot sanction parties, in part because peace processes can vitiate their threat of rebellion,[71] but they also may be polarized at the end of a civil conflict. They are thus typically unable to monitor, or incentivize, compliance without strong partisanship, even bias. In Central America, for example, domestic actors were more likely to be seen as "politically ill informed, alienated, and manipulated" than international actors were.[72] Partisanship can lead actors, particularly former combatants, to complain about actions that may not constitute noncompliance. Outsiders may be especially crucial in interpreting information, in addition to obtaining information, to examine both sides' compliance. In these contexts, international actors are needed, at least initially, to monitor, and incentivize, compliance in a less partisan manner in many

---

[70] This insight is important in several other studies of armed intervention; see, for example, Betts 1994; Walter 1997. Certain kinds of bias have also been found to be helpful in mediation, although for slightly different reasons (e.g. Kydd 2003; Svensson 2009).
[71] Wantchekon 2004: 27.     [72] Stanley 2013: 289.

cases.[73] While not every international actor is seen as nonpartisan, many may be less partisan than domestic actors in these scenarios, sometimes systematically so as coming sections discuss.

International actors can often obtain this information. A set of tools for that purpose that is becoming more widely adopted, as described in Chapter 3, is international election observation.[74] International election observers provide information about parties' compliance with the rules of the electoral process, as well as standards of democratization, human rights protection, and law and order.[75] These rules and standards match many aspects of peace agreement compliance, particularly when participation provisions bring combatant parties from both sides into elections. In post-conflict states, in fact, international observers typically base their assessment of compliance on the terms of settlements, privileging them over any other standards.[76] In Bosnia and Herzegovina, for example, the European Union measured the 2010 elections against the benchmarks of the 1995 Dayton Accords. Similar instances abound. The E.U. report on the 2010 elections in Burundi acknowledged that its assessment of the electoral process was based on the constitution "referring explicitly to the [2000] Arusha Agreement for Peace and Reconciliation in Burundi," and it rated that election as good, notwithstanding electoral engineering that contributed to what it termed a lack of choice. I return to the potential trade-off between democracy and peace in later chapters,[77] but these are processes by which international actors at times can obtain sufficient information to detect compliance with a settlement, and then help overcome commitment problems and secure peace.[78] These missions are often conducted by the United Nations, building on its peacekeeping monitoring missions, but at

[73] Over time, the elections also may offer the possibility of incremental change by gradually allowing more input from citizens as they become more effective in this role. This point is made by Wantchekon 2004, also, and is mentioned elsewhere, including Beaulieu 2014: 132.

[74] For example, see Donno 2013; Beaulieu 2014.

[75] Carothers 1999; Bjornlund 2004; Hyde 2007; Kelley 2008.

[76] Kelley 2012; Hyde and Marinov 2014.

[77] Researchers sometimes note that post-conflict states are held to a different set of standards than other states, potentially problematically for democracy (see Hyde 2011b; Kelley 2012), and publics in both states just described have recently shown some frustration with these quota systems because of the lack of democratic choice.

[78] Others have suggested international election observation can serve a role in promoting peace; see McCoy 1993: especially 131–133; Elklit and Svensson 1997; Carothers 1999; Bjornlund 2004.

a lower cost to collect information since the organization need not send troops to do so.[79]

Second, enforcing compliance requires *credible leverage* so that each side expects a cost for noncompliance that, at a minimum, offsets the benefit that it could receive from reneging. The threatened sanction must be punitive enough to make compliance more beneficial than noncompliance. International actors can sanction noncompliance by reducing the existing resources of either side by seizing assets, withholding aid, or terminating membership in trade and intergovernmental organizations. They could also provide new resources that could later be revoked, such as trade deals, development assistance, or party-building aid. Most interventions and external involvements use leverage that involves material incentives, sometimes augmented through normative incentives, such as international shaming.[80]

As with information, leverage must be maintained against each side, and the mechanism must be sustained over the course of implementation so that the commitment problem will not be exacerbated. Nonpartisan external enforcement, as with information, is also crucial for leverage. In fact, the incentives of international actors must be aligned with ending conflict, rather than backing one side or the other. While this is not always the case, the sections below describe conditions under which it is systematically likely.

Cost is also crucial in credibly maintaining leverage throughout a peace process' implementation period. But such leverage need not always be extensive; in fact, well-designed peace agreement can reduce the amount of leverage that an international actor must employ. The extent of the sanction can be less if, for instance, both sides draw down their forces in increments under a peace agreement, decreasing the value of reneging at each stage. With that settlement design, neither side is as comparatively weak as it would be if one drew down completely before its opponent did. Such incremental steps are included in almost all modern peace processes. By reducing the value of noncompliance, such settlement design makes it less expensive for the international actor to threaten or impose sanctions.

---

[79] In later elections, regional organizations such as the Organization of American States often assume the lead on observation. A number of non-governmental organizations are also involved at times, including most notably the Carter Center.

[80] See, for example, Matanock and Lichtenheld 2016. The book usually refers to these as "conditional incentives." Conditionality can refer to the strategic use of foreign aid to induce governments to undertake structural adjustments and economic reforms, but I use it more generally to mean that the incentives are tied to the behavior of targeted actors, and specifically compliance by combatants during the implementation period of a peace process. Others similarly use the term applied to aid and other forms of leverage used in this way; see Girod 2011; Donno 2013.

Coordination can also help reduce the cost. The United Nations handles the distribution of some post-conflict resources – and does much of the monitoring, through peacekeepers and international election observers in post-conflict contexts – but donor states and organizations (including the International Monetary Fund and the World Bank) often provide significant resources. For example, post-conflict states receive foreign aid at higher rates in the first six years after the onset of peace compared to those that have not experienced conflict.[81] Rebuilding conflicted states has historically been seen as a central obligation of the international community.[82] These resources, as described below, are often conditioned on combatants' compliance with terms of a settlement.

Adding conditionality if not already applied to this aid is not inherently costly. It could, of course, become costly if former combatants fail to correct their violations, leading to prolonged periods without aid on which citizens depend; this could produce transnational costs such as increasing refugee flows, too. However, adding conditions is likely to make such prolonged periods very costly for those trying to hold power, so each side will likely be strongly incentivized to comply with the bargain they signed. Moreover, recurring conflict itself would probably produce similar costs, such as refugee flows, for international actors. Most of the cost of such a mechanism, then, is already borne by the international actors, and adding conditionality is low cost compared to alternatives.

Leverage – particularly if it can be reasonably sized and coordinated among multiple actors and, indeed, not too costly for international actors so that it is credible – can encompass all sorts of mechanisms of enforcement by international actors. A set of tools used to provide leverage that are also becoming more widely adopted, as this book will describe (Chapter 3), is democracy assistance. The international community supplies substantial development aid and, increasingly, democracy and governance assistance in post-conflict contexts and elsewhere. Programs providing this assistance began in the 1980s, significantly expanded in the 1990s, and have been conditional on compliance with constitutional rules and procedures.[83] The information from international election observation is used for "unlocking foreign aid or loans,"[84] and general conditionally around compliance with electoral rules seems to apply to democracy and governance assistance narrowly, but also foreign aid (and loans and the like) more broadly.[85] Some standards for this aid are case specific, especially in post-conflict contexts, and others are applied across cases, such as those prohibiting

[81] Collier and Hoeffler 2004: 1136.    [82] For example, see Call with Wyeth 2008.
[83] Carothers 1999: 6, 85; Bjornlund 2004: 24.    [84] McCoy 1993: 133.
[85] Dunning 2004; Levitsky and Way 2010: 14, 17–18, 31–32; Hyde 2011b: 143–144.

coups, even if these are not always stated formally.[86] Many peace
agreements with electoral participation provisions also rely on international programs to support political parties; in such cases, even small
reductions in resources can have effects.[87] These deals may include
trust funds or other aid for the former rebel groups to form political
parties. Conditional benefits for compliance with settlement terms
range beyond aid, although they are often related to elections.
Sanctions include removing assistance directly from the state or parties;
delegitimizing a party so that foreign donors withhold assistance and
domestic supporters consider switching candidates (or parties, or even
sides); or barring a party from participation in activities, such as campaigning, that may mean a loss of power and resources.[88] Intermediate
steps, such as threats, pressure, or promises, are also possible. While
threats may be common (as in the Mozambique and El Salvador cases,
described in the Chapter 1), actual punishment should be relatively rare
if the threat is sufficient to deter noncompliance.[89] These incentives
may be provided to the state as part of the settlement, or they may lie in
existing resources. Examples of leverage are in Table 2.1.

For external enforcement to work, international actors must detect and
sanction noncompliance with settlement terms. They need sufficient
information and credible leverage. To obtain both, international actors
must be committed to ending conflict, rather than partisan to a combatant side, and this enforcement must be low cost. While military mechanisms, such as reducing the existing resources by bombing camps or bases,
may be employed in some cases, that leverage will often be too costly
to be credible. Even peacekeeping troops or other armed interveners
often operate through another mechanism.[90] As the examples above
show, elections – particularly those resulting from participation provisions – can be effective in this role. In fact, existing evidence begins to
demonstrate that international actors use these mechanisms against noncompliance by any combatant party by evaluating them rigorously and

---

[86] Carothers 1999: 6, 85; Azpuru et al. 2008; Youngs 2008; McFaul 2010: 20.
[87] Carothers 1999.
[88] Some of these mechanisms are discussed in Bekoe 2008; Fortna 2008: 89–93,
98–102.
[89] These mechanisms have been used to punish occasional violators; see Chapter 7.
[90] Again, see the discussion in Fortna 2008: 89–93, 98–102. Armed missions that have
limited mandates can sometimes be effective at reducing the risk of conflict recurrence
using sanctions involving material incentives, rather than threatening force; see
Matanock and Lichtenheld 2016. Leaders of some such limited missions have extolled
the use of these nonmilitary sanctions for noncompliance; see De Soto and del Castillo
1994; Arnault 2001. Some scholars also recognize the importance of such non-forceful
leverage with or without peacekeeping troops; see Bekoe 2008.

Table 2.1 *Examples of Leverage*

| Economic and Political Rewards | Signaling and Pressure | Economic and Political Punishments |
| --- | --- | --- |
| Foreign aid, including democracy and governance assistance, party funds, and election aid; development assistance; and military aid | Praise for compliance, through resolutions, declarations, and official statements | Removal of material rewards provided or promised: withdrawal of aid, delay in acceptance to or suspension of membership in intergovernmental organizations, beneficial treaties, or preferential trade agreements |
| Membership in intergovernmental organizations | Promise of rewards for compliance, or continued compliance | |
| Accession, or negotiations toward accession, to other beneficial treaties; inclusion in preferential trade agreements | Criticism for noncompliance in resolutions, declarations, and official statements | Removal of other economic benefits, and imposition of sanctions |
| | Calls for or threat of punishment for noncompliance unless improvements are made | Removal of other political benefits, including breaking diplomatic ties, visa bans |

Note: These examples draw on the work of Simpser and Donno 2012; Donno 2013; and Nielsen and Simmons 2015 on conditionality around elections and human rights protections.

enacting sanctions, including withdrawing aid and other benefits,[91] and this book evaluates this claim further: Chapters 6 and 7 present significant evidence of responses to noncompliance with settlement terms where, for example, benefits are threatened or temporarily frozen.[92] These institutions provide a particularly low-cost mechanism for this type of enforcement, and coincide with external actors becoming more interested in ending civil conflicts in a nonpartisan manner, which allows international actors to effectively monitor and incentivize compliance.

---

[91] Even though actual punishment should be rare because the threat thereof should often deter noncompliance. See Kelley 2009: 7, 15; Boulding and Hyde 2005; von Borzyskowski and Vabulas 2014. These measures, of course, rely on counterfactuals, and it is hard to "accurately measure the difference in the amount of aid received from the amount of aid that might have been received under different circumstances" (Boulding and Hyde 2005: 22). Case evidence is also clear in Suhrke and Buckmaster 2005; Frerks 2006; Emmanuel and Rothchild 2007; Manning and Malbrough 2010.

[92] Data on conditionality and pressure – punishments or rewards, and "mediation, diplomatic missions, and shaming," conditioned on abiding by the rules of the game – show that 77 percent of post-conflict elections after settlements with electoral participation provisions have been subject to this type of sanction (Chapter 6).

*Electoral Participation Provisions Provide a Mechanism for External Engagement*

I posit that electoral participation provisions can reduce the enforcement costs for external actors and thereby provide a credible mechanism to detect and sanction noncompliance.[93] I argue that electoral participation provisions are effective because they establish cycles that coordinate information and leverage and then facilitate international involvement through institutions designed for democracy promotion.

I define electoral participation provisions in peace agreements as those that legalize political parties from all sides of a conflict to compete in scheduled elections, as discussed in Chapter 1. The participatory elections produced by these provisions, and particularly their internationalization, are important to stabilizing settlements, as I will argue; however, notably, these elections need not be "free and fair," or even particularly democratic, to establish cycles coordinating information and leverage to facilitate external engagement. The elections produced by such provisions are typically institutionalized to avoid uncertainty so that power distribution from the polls matches the expected power distribution from continued fighting.[94] For example, weak groups in Colombia received just one special seat in the legislature and a share of public campaign financing. Strong groups in Burundi were provided a quota that set aside the majority of seats for their own ethnic group. In many cases, sometimes just through a small tweak to the elections, state institutions provide at least a minimum guarantee of power for each side. Any mutually-beneficial agreement requires such payoffs in the arrangement, and each sort of settlement can appropriately distribute power among elites, perhaps minimizing the role of the mass vote.[95] Electoral participation provisions still may be preferable to

---

[93] The rare case studies on post-conflict rebel group electoral participation mainly focus on whether rebels become *effective* politicians in functioning democracies. See Irvin 1999; Zahar 1999; Manning 2004, 2008; Lyons 2005; Deonandan et al. 2007; Söderberg Kovacs 2007; De Zeeuw 2008. In concurrent studies to this one, Acosta 2014 and Manning and Smith 2016 examine in cross-national data when rebels are successfully incorporated into party politics, broadly across different conflict outcomes: both show that rebels that sign settlements are significantly more likely to participate, which is the specific set of cases that this book seeks to explain.

[94] Consociationalism, as described by Lijphart 1968; Norris 2008; and, in these post-conflict contexts, see Walter 2002; Wantchekon 2004; Durant and Weintraub 2014; Hartzell and Hoddie 2015.

[95] Also described in "pacts"; see O'Donnell and Schmitter 1986. More work examining differences in post-conflict elections, including examining their institutions, but also turnout, citizen organization, and campaign duration would make an instructive extension to this study, although the combination of these factors produces less than clear implications. This point also ties to a larger literature on the purposes of elections in authoritarian and

alternatives, perhaps for normative reasons, but, I argue, also because they provide such an efficient mechanism to enforce compliance with settlements in post-conflict contexts.

*Coordination Cycles* Agreements with electoral participation provisions establish cycles around public benchmarks and regular milestones, which culminate in power distribution between ex-combatants according to the terms of the settlement. Their benchmarks and milestones help clarify and bolster consensus on compliance, and – in combination with the culmination points when power is distributed – encourage substantial attention from and accountability to a variety of actors. The cycles coordinate actors to send signals about compliance *and* allow those actors to react to those signals with sufficient punishment of any noncompliance. Electoral processes act as "focal points," devices that coordinate multiple actors' attention,[96] but their institutional design also allows them to foster accountability to these actors, as I will discuss in more depth below. These *coordination cycles* thus assist in providing both information and leverage at a low cost.

Electoral participation provisions are useful in establishing benchmarks and milestones for implementation that are endorsed by all parties and observable to external actors, and that thus increase clarity and consensus on compliance. Such provisions require specifying *publicly* who is eligible to run for office, the resources that will be made available for their campaigns, how winners will be chosen, the resources and policy areas that winners will control, and how winners will exercise that control procedurally. When and how the government will be selected thereby becomes a specific public process to which all sides agree before implementation. In contrast, other provisions for power-sharing may include backroom promises of appointments and resource sharing, making these more private agreements opaque and difficult to enforce. Electoral participation provisions also produce public leaders who may have strong incentives to comply, given that their reputations and their jobs are tied to their promises of compliance with the peace agreement. They may have the capacity and incentives to mobilize their followers to comply, too.

In addition to public benchmarks, electoral participation provisions also establish *regular* milestones: initial post-conflict elections are not isolated events consisting of the vote alone, but rather an ongoing timetable of events scheduled for specific dates. Electoral commissions can set

other less-than-fully democratic states, which is discussed further in Chapter 8; see reviews by Gandhi and Lust-Okar 2009 and Brancati 2014. Beaulieu 2014 also identifies elections as a mechanism to engage international actors in these contexts (10, 18).
[96] Schelling 1960: 54–58.

deadlines that regulate voter registration, party and candidate declaration, campaign periods, and concessions of defeated candidates. Other processes can be linked to these milestones, such as disarming prior to registering candidates for elections and allowing campaigning to begin.[97] Linked steps can also be designed to benefit different parties by, for example, requiring that the rebel group turns in its weapons *and* that the government forces downsize before each party can register candidates and begin campaigning. Implementation requires many simultaneous steps under any conditions, but the regular timing of electoral processes ties these steps together transparently. These timetables clearly delineate when parties must enact elements of power-sharing. They allow multiple points at which observation can determine compliance unambiguously, both with the electoral terms of a peace agreement and the non-electoral provisions that are pegged to elections. As elections recur over time, the cycles also allow for continued monitoring of the deal's implementation, while also sustaining shifts in the distribution of power based on rules specified in the peace agreement (and, indeed, Chapter 6 shows that almost all of these elections recur as expected).

Electoral participation provisions work more fundamentally because they facilitate coordination on these compliance cues. Elections have been identified as domestically useful in other contexts because they increase the ability to observe collectively and respond effectively if rulers fail to comply with the agreed-upon arrangement: "the institution of *publicly understood rules for regular elections*" is a signal that all actors can use to observe and coordinate their behavior.[98] The publicity and regularity of these institutions allow each actor to observe how well others believe that the leader is complying with its terms; this provides more accurate observation and, more crucially, allows multiple observers to simultaneously sanction or threaten sanction for noncompliance.[99] It is

---

[97] All of the peace agreements with electoral participation provisions examined empirically in this book tie some non-electoral milestones to the electoral calendar.

[98] Fearon 2011: 1662.

[99] See Fearon 2011. Coordination is a crucial element in this argument; it can be accomplished through institutions that establish standards for what constitutes noncompliance with a deal and that coordinate a response; see Weingast 1997. Electoral processes may work best for coordinating multiple actors to provide information on and respond to noncompliance with their bargain, but other institutions may also serve some of these functions, such as constitutions, according to Weingast 1997. This same idea explains much of the importance of elite pacts during developing democracy: these elites are agreeing on the limits beyond which they will sanction one another. See O'Donnell and Schmitter 1986; Karl 1990.

Others make similar claims about international agreements or treaties (e.g. Keohane 1984; Simmons 1998, 2009), which can also gain a high degree of legitimacy both domestically and internationally (e.g. Claude 1966; Franck 1990), a point to which this chapter returns when discussing the cost of such coordination.

not just information that changes the expected behavior, but also the accompanying incentives. If incentives can be coordinated on broadly agreed information, the impact of threatening to remove those incentives is more credible – because the multiple signals make information on noncompliance more likely to be accurate – and more substantial coming from multiple actors.

During post-conflict elections established through participation provisions, external actors are able to observe signals from various constituents about parties' noncompliance, but they are also able to apply sanctions at moments of maximal impact. The electoral participation provisions require that power will be distributed at the culmination of these cycles, which provides a point at which stronger sanctions could be imposed should either side fail to comply. The risk of losing resources and even power at these moments becomes a particularly important incentive.[100] Officials competing in elections and those elected typically profit directly from benefits provided to their parties, both domestically and internationally, in the form of salary, funds for logistical support, and the like. In addition to the direct cost of losing some resources for noncompliance, they may face consequences in terms of power distribution. If they lose what they need to provide patronage or effective governance, then those in their elite coalitions or their constituents may turn against them, potentially ousting them from their positions within their parties and regimes. Even in a state with ethnic quotas, where candidates are elected within an ethic group, power brokers and voters could turn away from failing candidates or parties, favoring their competitors within the same ethnic group. Unless constrained by the rules of highly engineered contexts, such as ethnic quotas, they might even turn to the opposite side. Because power brokers or voters are hard to mobilize after a conflict to sanction their own side, any initial signals of less support for these candidates or parties are particularly strong signals, and they can then be reinforced by sanctions such as revoking international aid, as I discuss further below. Because ex-combatants are invested in maintaining their

---

[100] Through the linkages designed into settlements and beyond them, as described above, these cycles can increase accountability directly. A peace agreement may specify that, for instance, campaigning may not begin until disarmament and demobilization have taken place. Maximizing benefits often requires full participation in the electoral process, which incentivizes any prerequisite steps that are supposed to be taken. Campaigning late means fewer party funds from external actors, as well as fewer contributions and less time to court voters, so former combatants may be more careful to ensure timely compliance with disarmament and demobilization provisions. Delays in implementation can revive commitment concerns and derail a peace process, either during initial disarmament and demobilization, or later during the distribution of political power, so timely compliance is crucial.

positions and possibly gaining more power within their parties and regimes, the pressure and threat of sanction by international actors can outweigh their incentives to violate the agreement. Candidates and elected officials are thus especially vulnerable to shaming and to the threat of withdrawal of international assistance. Coordination cycles culminate in moments of power distribution, at which time external actors can more easily and effectively detect and punish noncompliance by election participants.[101]

These coordination cycles are especially useful when international actors, who typically have less information than domestic actors, engage to enforce a settlement. When coordinated through the campaign and voting process, signals to the international community become clearer, and international actors can then take action, when noncompliance is present, to sanction the noncompliant side so that it does not gain a strategic advantage. International actors can use these cycles – the benchmarks and milestones leading up to culmination points – to identify what is and is not compliance. They then also can coordinate their responses at moments of maximal impact, pooling the sanctions of any available domestic actors with international actors including intergovernmental organizations monitoring compliance and foreign donors providing additional conditional incentives (as described in the previous section).

In short, provisions establishing electoral processes with participation by both combatant sides allow external actors to detect and sanction noncompliance with a settlement at a low cost (see Figure 2.3).

*Democracy Promotion Programs*    The argument about enforcement through electoral participation provisions is based on the importance of enabling efficient external engagement, which is low cost and thus credible. Part of the efficiency comes from establishing coordination cycles that focus attention and accountability on benchmarks and milestones that lead up to power distribution – as described above – and part comes from changes in the international system that facilitate international involvement in particular around elections through institutions designed for democracy promotion.

After the Cold War, the international system became more interested in efforts to end civil conflict, but also in other types of involvement, especially

---

[101] These culmination points might also become flashpoints for political violence, but existing work suggests that contenders refrain from threatening or using force in periods outside of elections, which reduces it overall (Harish and Little 2016) – and, in these post-conflict contexts, makes it easier to observe and sanction as well by consolidating it to particular moments with the most attention and accountability.

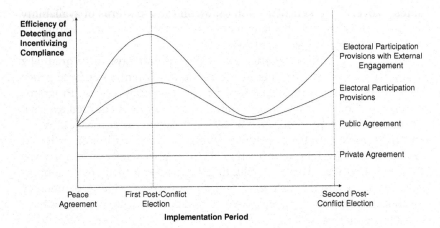

Figure 2.3 Electoral Participation Provisions Establishing Coordination Cycles

in elections.[102] (Discussed in much more depth in Chapter 3.) In brief, during the Cold War, the major powers often used civil conflicts as proxy wars to compete among each other. But afterward, their priorities changed as civil conflicts were a clear remaining threat to systemic peace. External involvement in enforcing settlements became more likely in many cases. These changes made armed peacekeeping more widespread,[103] but neither consistently nor persistently present.[104] Much increased external involvement took the form of expansive promotion of democracy.[105]

Democracy promotion programs spread with the end of the Cold War.[106] However, democracy promotion programs, like other forms of international involvement did not become uniformly available. Democracy promotion developed in regional waves after the end of the Cold War. Even once a region gained many such programs, however, the presence of strategic or other special relationships with the target state of interest sometimes weakened international actors' willingness and ability to enforce agreements through this mechanism, or through any other as

---

[102] Levitsky and Way 2010: 14; Hyde 2011b.
[103] Walter 2002; Doyle and Sambanis 2000, 2006; Fortna 2008.
[104] E.g. Fortna 2008; Gilligan and Sergenti 2008; Beardsley 2012, 2013.
[105] McCoy 1993.
[106] The role of these tools in conflict termination has been recognized since the end of the Cold War; see McCoy et al. 1991.

noted above.[107] (The next section draws on these patterns of availability to derive hypotheses, and Chapter 3 discusses the historical availability of these institutions in more depth.)

However, as these institutions spread in these ways, they gradually began to provide new means of external engagement to enforce peace agreements. Indeed, they established normative conventions. Programs such as election observation and conditional incentives engaged external actors in electoral processes in non-conflict contexts after the Cold War – and they proved useful in conflict contexts. These institutions allowed external actors into the coordination cycles established by electoral participation provisions, further facilitating external enforcement of compliance, as the examples in the section above suggest. These democracy promotion programs coupled with electoral participation provisions have three particular benefits.

First, electoral processes attract international involvement more easily and cheaply than alternative provisions due to the cultural salience once democracy promotion increased. The cultural salience of electoral processes increased due in part to the win for liberalism with U.S. hegemony after the Cold War, producing an internationally recognized normative convention for distributing power and monitoring that distribution. Normative conventions became important devices that helped culturally align relevant actors.[108] In adopting this convention, combatants could also add legitimacy to their settlements in this international context. These are additional advantages of electoral processes, beyond establishing specific moments and clear standards to examine what constitutes compliance before distributing power in each cycle.

These conventions coordinate international attention on these moments, and so facilitate the work of international actors to assess compliance.[109] In the modern era, elections garner more coverage in

---

[107] See, for example, Donno 2013.

[108] On the United Nations, for example, see Voeten 2005. The cultural dimension to this argument relies on the dominance of the West; an alternative to consider would be if the Soviet Union had won the Cold War. Something else, say May Day, for example, could have been established as the moment in which any changes in power would occur. Assuming that these May Day celebrations had all of the same characteristics of elections that produce coordination cycles – if they established public benchmarks and regular milestones, drew in all different actors at a culmination of each cycle to monitor and condition incentives on compliance at the point in which power is distributed, and they thus generated attention and accountability – they would facilitate this external engagement. But they would need to have these characteristics, and then the international community would have to focus on them, in order to serve the functions of electoral processes.

[109] From my interview with Former Secretary of State Condoleezza Rice at Stanford University, 2013.

the foreign press than any other nonviolent event.[110] Through this
mechanism, external actors know to what standards to hold both sides
at set times, and they can coordinate among themselves (drawing domestic actors in as well) to identify and incentivize compliance.

The second advantage of democracy promotion programs is that they
allow for international involvement in a way that is less often viewed as
a violation of state sovereignty. Democracy promotion programs have
emerged as a mechanism through which external actors can engage in
domestic politics with legitimacy. The special standing afforded to
international election observation and the conditional incentives that
accompany it are premised on acceptance by domestic actors. One mainly
normative argument is that a new conceptualization of the state, which
developed in the Americas, allowed leaders to request intervention from
peer states to certify the elections through which they took power, without
impinging on their own perceived sovereignty.[111] Other explanations
have both normative and instrumental components, suggesting that
benefits accrue at both the domestic and international levels from the
certification of the state's "good" power distribution practices.[112] In any
event, this type of involvement emerged with the end of the Cold War in
regions nearest to the West and then spread to neighboring regions.
The legitimacy of this type of intervention – seen as less of a violation of
sovereignty than others due to the consent of the state – may over time
also make it a more cost-effective mechanism for intervening.[113]

The expanding democracy promotion regime finally generates a third
benefit of using these processes: as institutions promoting democracy
became available region by region, they made it easier and more efficient
for post-conflict states to set up systems for engaging external actors.
Those institutions, and the structures underpinning them, eventually
converged on a standard model. In it, the United Nations led these
missions, especially up to the first elections, supported by regional
organizations (which at times replaced the United Nations as they
developed expertise in monitoring and conditioning incentives).
Foreign donors, working with these intergovernmental organizations,
provided incentives to be conditioned on compliance.

Diffusion mechanisms of learning and emulation likely explain some of
the spread of these institutions, as well as these conventions, informing
this theory about electoral participation provisions as a low-cost mechanism. Combatants, as well as the external actors with whom they partner in

[110] Golan and Wanta 2003.    [111] Santa-Cruz 2005, 2013.
[112] Hyde 2011b; Kelley 2012.
[113] This argument is made about legitimacy in the context of broader intervention in
Krasner and Risse 2014; Matanock 2014.

peace processes, learn from experience with engagement and elections in their own state, and from the experiences of neighboring states, about how this type of intervention may work to help them overcome commitment problems. I do not posit a fully functionalist argument, but the function of these institutions certainly seems to help explain them.

As the case studies in Chapter 5 demonstrate, a positive experience enforcing a deal with electoral participation provisions in El Salvador, for example, influenced the design of a deal in Guatemala. International actors first demonstrated to the rebel group in Guatemala that they would intervene with sanctions to punish government violations of the electoral process after a 1993 irregularity. Additional evidence from similar international involvement in neighboring states, especially in El Salvador, corroborated that information. Both direct learning and diffusion were important in leading both sides in Guatemala to sign the 1996 settlement with electoral participation provisions.

International organizations also update their approaches based on earlier missions. For example, the United Nations created a Lessons Learned Unit, and, based on both failures and successes, it changed its recommendations over time on elections and other institutions.[114] Like other diffusion theories that focus on the demand for international election observation, there seems to be some expectation that governments seek to use these mechanisms to reap benefits associated with adoption (and avoid costs associated with nonadoption).[115] The underlying idea is that the information that the combatants and their partners have about the available policy options, especially regarding costs and benefits, change with diffusion.[116]

As democracy promotion programs spread, external actors became able to engage effectively through the coordination cycles established by electoral participation provisions to enforce agreements. Compared to alternative forms of intervention, such as armed U.N. missions like neotrusteeships, this type of external engagement is clearly less costly. Many, including U.N. peacekeepers, can employ this mechanism to detect and enforce compliance with a peace agreement. The coordination cycles, and the consensus on involvement through institutions for democracy promotion programs, just described, produced that low cost. It is difficult to separate the effect of coordination

---

[114] Howard 2008: 336–337.    [115] Hyde 2011b.

[116] Such arguments are developed, for instance, in the context of neoliberal policies and democratization and liberalization in Simmons and Elkins 2004; Gleditsch and Ward 2006; and more generally conceptualized in Elkins and Simmons 2005; Simmons et al. 2006.

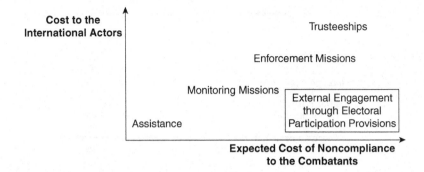

Figure 2.4 Efficient Mechanism for External Enforcement

cycles from the effect of democracy promotion programs. I theorize that both components together provide better information and leverage for interested international actor than aid or observation alone around a traditional agreement (see Figure 2.4).[117]

### *Settlements without Electoral Participation Provisions*

Electoral participation provisions are advantageous because they lower the cost of enforcement for external actors – both through their institutional advantages and through their systemic advantages after the end of the Cold War – but combatants also sign peace agreements without them. How do peace agreements work to overcome commitment problems without electoral participation provisions to engage external actors? Sometimes combatants simply may not be able to overcome them, and so they may not sign an agreement but rather continue the conflict until a victory is achieved by one side or until the conflict simply fades (see Figure 2.5).

Governments and rebel groups may also at times employ other mechanisms besides electoral participation provisions to raise the cost of noncompliance. First, many have tried alternative power-sharing arrangements, such as through a fixed formula, with some sort of military coercion to enforce compliance. But success using such mechanisms is rare: the international community is typically not

---

[117] I can show that international actors are necessary by examining an interaction (see Chapter 6), so the low cost is not solely from the inherent characteristics of elections, but I cannot test the relative importance of each component in involving international actors, although I show aspects of each in the qualitative evidence.

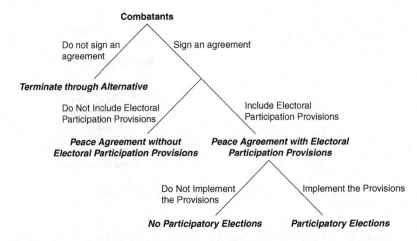

Figure 2.5 Set of Choices Producing Electoral Participation Provisions

sufficiently committed to help enforce a deal through costly long-term peacekeeping employing forceful coercion. Even in when it is sufficiently committed, however, electoral participation provisions can provide a mechanism to enforce a settlement that is less costly for these external actors.

Second, without armed peacekeepers, alternative mechanisms, such as published demobilization deadlines or schedules for truth and reconciliation processes, could produce useful information and could even be linked to conditional incentives or similar leverage. But they are not as efficient and inexpensive as electoral participation provisions, due to the coordination cycles produced by electoral participation provisions and external engagement in the cycles through the democracy promotion programs spread after systemic shifts. Many aspects of existing settlements, however, are complementary to electoral participation, and the coordination cycles they establish allow for these provisions (demobilization, disarmament, and reconciliation and security sector reform, reestablishing the rule of law, for example)[118] to be better enforced because they typically are pegged to the electoral calendar to ensure that external actors have information and leverage to sanction any noncompliance.

---

[118] E.g. Doyle and Sambanis 2000, 2006; Walter 2002; Hartzell et al. 2001; Hartzell and Hoddie 2003, 2007; Paris 2004; Humphreys and Weinstein 2007; Mattes and Savun 2009; Toft 2009, 2010; Gilligan et al. 2013.

In any of these cases, interaction between the former rebel group(s) and the government may be useful in providing each side with more information about the legal institutions that make distribution of power more transparent. This process may reduce misperceptions about compliance.[119] No mechanism other than electoral participation provisions, however, continues to draw in external engagement over time and at such low cost.

Territorial divisions can leave each side armed and thus able to enforce a settlement through the threat of force. This mechanism may be especially available to combatants in secessionist conflicts. In many cases, however, particularly where the territorial division requires the parties to interact frequently, the possibility or threat of future imbalances may drive the combatants back to conflict. Such commitment mechanisms are thus potentially more prone to failure than those featuring electoral participation provisions backed by external engagement.[120]

Overall this theory makes two main points: first, combatants facing commitment problems may benefit from international engagement to detect and increase the cost of noncompliance (even without force). Second, electoral participation provisions provide a mechanism for enforcing peace agreements that have a number of advantages over other possible solutions to the commitment problem. These advantages are generally due to the characteristics of electoral participation provisions – the coordination cycles they establish produce information and permit leverage at a low cost – and their context – in that they facilitate external engagement through existing democracy promotion institutions. When combatants sign settlements that include electoral participation provisions, they may renege before employing them. However, the evidence is that they generally do not, and that these institutions help produce enduring peace. This mechanism is most likely to be available and used in conflicts where expectations exist that international actors are willing and able to monitor and coordinate enforcement.

## Hypotheses

External engagement theory has observable implications for when electoral participation provisions will be included in peace agreements, and what relationship these electoral participation provisions will have with enduring peace. Many aspects of this theory are difficult to test

---

[119] Aspects of this argument from other institutional contexts are presented in Boix and Svolik 2013: 301.

[120] Lake and Rothchild 2005 make a similar point about decentralization, which is often a component of territorial divisions, unless the state fully splits into new states.

directly because, in part, actors may have incentives to hide instrumental motivations for their activities (like participating in elections), and because, in part, actual punishment should be rare: the theory implies that compliance is a better option than noncompliance and sanctions, so deviations that draw punishment should not be common. Threats of sanction sometimes occur, however, and I use qualitative evidence to examine these cases, among others. Other aspects of implementation are also difficult to measure quantitatively: if the theory is correct that electoral participation provisions help identify noncompliance, for example, comparisons may seem to indicate that peace agreements with electoral participation provisions produce more instances of noncompliance (such as slow demobilization), but it may actually be the case that those provisions simply help identify these incidents. The quantitative and qualitative analyses must adapt to these challenges. Based on the theory, as well as these challenges, I generate two sets of testable implications (hypotheses). I then also generate implications from alternative explanations.

### Causes of Electoral Participation

The first set of hypotheses concern the causes of including electoral participation provisions in peace agreements. Broadly, when available, electoral participation provisions should be chosen by combatants to make noncompliance more costly and thus commit both sides more firmly to an agreement. The availability of the mechanism depends on whether combatants expect an international actor to engage through the electoral process in order to monitor and hold both sides accountable for noncompliance.

The end of the Cold War resolved problems among the great powers and made it easier for them to work together to assist in civil conflict termination: it decreased their partisanship in these conflicts so that often they could be expected to monitor and sanction both sides for noncompliance; and, it coincided with the emergence of institutions of democracy promotion that provided mechanisms for less costly intervention through elections. Together, these developments increased expectations of nonpartisan external engagement through the electoral process that would be sufficient to detect and sanction most instances of noncompliance by either side. In quantitative summary statistics, the post-Cold War period is associated with more electoral participation provisions (see Figure 1.1 in Chapter 1). In quantitative and qualitative tests throughout this book, then, electoral participation provisions should be more prevalent after the end of the Cold War, and, to the extent that

I can measure the mechanism (especially through the case studies in Chapter 5), its end should also increase combatants' expectations of relatively nonpartisan external engagement (see summary of hypotheses in Table 2.2).

Expectations of international engagement should also vary systematically beyond the end of the Cold War. Regional rates of democracy promotion should be associated with increased expectations of nonpartisan external engagement through the electoral process, while strategic or special partnerships with potential interveners should decrease such expectations (potential interveners need to be somewhat interested in peace but nonpartisan in the conflicts, a "Goldilocks" aspect of the argument).

These hypotheses build on literature on the diffusion of democracy promotion, suggesting that the spread of these institutions indicates an increased supply of this less costly mechanism for external enforcement: if similar states have experienced external monitoring, for example, this will likely increase expectations of engagement through this mechanism in the state of interest, unless its government happens to have an especially close relationship with these external actors. Electoral participation provisions should be more prevalent in regions with higher rates of democracy promotion, but less prevalent where governments have strategic or special relationships with engaged international actors. These correlations can be tested quantitatively by comparing peace agreements and also by comparing all conflicts. The proxy variables for these expectations precede, and are plausibly exogenous to, strategic decisions by combatants to design their settlements to include electoral participation provisions, thereby providing some support for a causal effect. This is discussed further in Chapters 4 and 6.

Finally, the theory does not imply that international actors force combatants to accept the mechanism, but rather that the combatants themselves see a mutually beneficial settlement to which they choose to bind themselves in order to overcome commitment problems. Derived from this secondary expectation is the final implication in this set: combatants – especially rebel groups given their greater concern that the institutions of the state might be co-opted by the government to allow subtle noncompliance – should request electoral participation provisions in most cases. These provisions will be sought by the combatants to achieve a deal.

### Consequences of Electoral Participation

The second set of hypotheses concerns the idea that electoral participation provisions are stabilizing because they help overcome commitment

Table 2.2 *Empirical Implications for Causes and Consequences of Electoral Participation Provisions*

| | *Variation of Interest:* Inclusion of electoral participation provisions | Actor requesting inclusion of provisions | Conflict recurrence |
|---|---|---|---|
| External Engagement Explanation | Increases with the end of the Cold War (H1)<br><br>Increases with higher regional rates of democracy promotion (H1a)<br><br>Decreases with governments that have strategic or special relationships with international actors (H1b) | Combatants – more often the rebel group (H2) | Decreases after peace agreements with electoral participation provisions more than other agreements (H3)<br><br>And, pacifying effect of electoral participation provisions increases with the expectation of external engagement to enforce the peace agreement (H3a)<br><br>(International election observation, democracy aid, and conditionality on compliance also increases) |
| *Alternative Explanations*<br>Escape Explanation | Increases with the presence of peacekeepers, or other armed interveners<br><br>Increases with the number of troops<br><br>Not clear that any of the other determinants implied by external engagement theory should hold | International intervener | No clear prediction, but may increase if these are particularly contentious conflicts |

| | | | |
|---|---|---|---|
| Enjoinder Explanation | Increases with the end of the Cold War<br>Increases with higher regional rates of democracy promotion<br>Increases if governments have strategic or special relationships with international actors | International intervener | No clear prediction, but may decrease if international involvement generates conditions for peace (e.g. through development or another mechanism)<br>(International election observation and democracy aid, *but not* conditionality on compliance, also increase) |
| Emulation Explanation | Increases with the end of the Cold War<br>Increases with higher regional rates of democracy promotion<br>*Increases* if governments have strategic or special relationships with international actors | Combatants – more often the government | No clear prediction, may decrease if emulation also applies to norms of peace |
| Ease Explanation | Increases with more settled cases (longer, larger conflicts with stronger governments)<br>Not clear that any of the other determinants implied by external engagement theory should hold | No clear prediction | Decreases in peace agreements with electoral participation provisions more than other agreements<br>Does not depend on expectations of international engagement to enforce the deal increasing |

problems. Compared to peace agreements with alternative provisions, those with electoral participation should see less conflict recurrence between signatories. External engagement theory posits that electoral participation provisions generate information to monitor compliance and mechanisms to incentivize compliance, so each side should expect marginally greater cost and less benefit for its own noncompliance. Once both sides are encouraged to comply, they are less likely to return to conflict, preemptively or as punishment for the other side's noncompliance. Thus, peace agreements with electoral participation provisions are associated with a lower likelihood of conflict recurrence than are peace agreements without such provisions.

External engagement theory actually posits a more specific implication: electoral participation provisions are stabilizing *when* international actors are expected to engage. A peace agreement that includes electoral participation provisions with expected engagement from international actors should be more successful in stabilizing than one that does not. The prior implication should hold because external actors may be anticipated to enforce when electoral participation provisions are included, but testing the moderating variable directly helps assess the theory. The theory implies that electoral participation provisions will only act as commitment mechanisms, and thus decrease the risk of conflict recurrence if an external actor is likely to engage in the electoral process. In advance of the peace agreement, the exogenous regional democracy promotion rates serve as proxies for these expectations. Therefore, the pacifying association of peace agreements with electoral participation provisions exists with the expectation of international engagement to enforce the deal.

The theory also has implications for the resulting electoral processes, although they are difficult to assess. This is due both to a lack of reliable data and to challenges identifying an appropriate comparison group. For example, the elections may have higher rates of international election observation and democracy aid, and they may receive more enforcement around these electoral processes (both through conditionality and other less coercive mechanisms such as mediation, diplomatic missions, and shaming), than other post-conflict or otherwise emerging elections. I test this dimension of the theory through summary statistics (which should be treated cautiously) and examination of implementation in the case studies (Chapter 7).

## Alternative Explanations

Few studies have focused on electoral participation provisions, and clear competing theories do not exist. However, the existing literature on international involvement, on selection of elections and settlement terms, and on these institutional structures suggest underlying logics that can be used to develop alternative explanations. These alternative explanations also help clarify my proposed causal mechanism. (Implications of each are summarized in Table 2.2.) Elections potentially play many different roles in fostering peace, and in general may simply be normatively appealing, but electoral participation provisions may circumscribe the number of potential roles. These are not just any elections: they are formed as part of a peace process, feature extensive international involvement in many cases, and frequently reduce the level of competition and thus uncertainty. Their characteristics must be taken into account in considering alternative explanations.

### International Involvement

External engagement theory, of course, fits in this category, but broader theories on international involvement in establishing elections can be modified to explain why electoral participation provisions are included in peace agreements, too. Each also has implications about the impact of these provisions on peace. First, what I call the escape explanation holds that international actors impose elections so that they may withdraw from interventions quickly, perhaps especially when interventions are costly and in unstable situations.[121] The motivation for establishing post-conflict elections may be to create a contracting partner with whom foreign powers can work to strengthen the state after formally exiting the conflict. In a more cynical version of the argument, an elected leader may be established to provide some illusion of such a partnership, which might then be abandoned. This explanation may apply when international actors have an engagement from which to escape; they may be involved to produce a regime change or to force an end to fighting. Most interventions in these contexts are the latter, such as peacekeeping or neo-trusteeship missions that the United Nations is operating.[122] Larger engagements, with a greater investment of troops and costs, may provide more incentives for the interveners to escape, especially should unexpected expenses occur (although such engagement may also signal deeper commitment).

---

[121] See especially Kumar 1998; Lyons 2002b, 2005; Collier 2009; Hansen 2014.

[122] While some think there must be troops present for this argument to hold, a more nuanced version holds that international actors considering such missions will not commit forces unless the peace agreement in the proposed state includes elections to set a fixed date for such escape (e.g. Lyons 2002b). I test both forms of the theory and show the results in Chapter 4.

The escape explanation envisions elections that are likely to be qualitatively different from those that are produced by electoral participation provisions. As these elections are a quick means of escape, involving the rebel group as a new political party may be an unnecessary complication. Interveners may impose these elections on governments, potentially with promises that they will be helped to win, while simply ignoring the rebels. Recent examples invoking the escape argument, such as Afghanistan especially in 2009, do not include any peace agreement with electoral participation provisions for the rebel groups; instead these are the hasty elections that produce the expected government win.[123] Inclusion of opposition parties and even the rebel groups might be more prudent in establishing such a government, but it is also likely to add many additional costs in time and resources, even just for negotiations.[124] It is also not clear that international actors seeking escape could leverage rebel groups into this type of arrangement or would want to expend the effort to do so. The differences between these elections and those produced by electoral participation provisions are striking: Afghanistan in contrast to Burundi, Macedonia, Mozambique, South Africa, or Sudan. Much of the theorizing about escape has been based on the recent dramatic failures in cases such as Afghanistan, and the empirical testing often conflates all post-conflict elections, but such elections differ from those conceived of as mechanisms for conflict resolution.

The escape explanation has implications for the causes and consequences of electoral participation provisions, despite initial evidence suggesting that it is unlikely to be consistent. Most obviously, the escape explanation implies that missions are costly for the intervener, and so the intervener should be more likely to impose elections in order to withdraw from conflicts in which they have intervened or at least agreed to intervene. The predictor of such elections should be that peacekeepers are in place or planned. The number of troops may matter, because more troops increase costs, both in terms of funding and potential casualties. If the escape explanation holds, it should be the interveners, not the rebel groups, who demand these electoral provisions in peace agreements. Missions in especially unstable scenarios that are likely to produce the most cost in blood and treasure should be most concerning to the interveners, who seek to escape before collapse. Thus, rather than a positive correlation with peace, the escape theory implies that electoral participation provisions should have no correlation with peace, or

---

[123] For example, see Collier 2009: 80.
[124] Finnemore 1996; Lyons 2002b; Paris 2004; Diamond 2006.

perhaps even correlate with conflict recurrence, if they are seen in particularly costly peacekeeping operations for the interveners.

While the escape explanation is the best established in the literature on
post-conflict elections more broadly, two other explanations can be
drawn from the idea of international involvement in these processes.
The second perspective is one that I call the enjoinder explanation. It is
based on the idea that external actors may simply prefer to engage
through elections over any other mechanism. Such a claim is made to
explain the emergence of elected presidents in warlord-dominated states
in the Caucasus and Central Asian regions. Although this argument has
not been directly tested empirically, the theory is that foreign
donors demand a figurehead and a façade of democracy before they will
provide aid.[125] While it could be the case that these international actors
will directly impose their preference on the combatants, it is also possible
that the combatants may anticipate that preference and will preemptively
establish elections with their agreements. Unlike the escape explanation,
this explanation is not predicated on the presence of intervening troops,
but it similarly reflects the idea that international actors may have
a preferred form of involvement that they impose on the states in which
they will become involved. Like the escape explanation, this explanation
does not seem to claim that a peace agreement or electoral participation
provisions are necessary. Nonetheless, it is more plausible under this
explanation than under the escape explanation that international actors
may be willing to wait for a peace process to conclude, because they are
not seeking quick exit but rather an entrance.

This alternative mechanism is very close to external engagement theory's mechanism, and their similarity makes it difficult to definitively test
between the two, but defining each helps clarify both. Both are based on
the idea that the United States and its Western allies, which have dominated the global system since the end of the Cold War, have had a general
preference for elections. The enjoinder explanation, however, in contrast
to external engagement theory, does not imply that the resulting democracy promotion programs are used by international actors to help enforce
the peace agreement. Both explanations imply that electoral participation
provisions should be more likely with external engagement, but only the
enjoinder explanation implies that this will be *especially* likely in cases with
strong relationships to the West, such as colonial ties. The explanations
also differ on whether the provisions foster enduring peace. Existing
scholarship suggests that external actors enjoining states to adopt elections so that they can provide foreign aid may be too invested in these

[125] Driscoll 2008.

cases to condition incentives on compliance, as would be implied by external engagement theory.[126] That need not inherently be the case, however. Just having international actors involved may increase development, for example, which may reduce the risk of further fighting. The explanation thus has no clear implication for peace. In addition, while both explanations may anticipate more international election observation and democracy aid, the enjoinder explanation does not imply that assistance is conditioned on compliance with the specific terms of a settlement, as external engagement theory does. To some extent, though, the struggle to separate these theories reflects the similarity of their underlying logics: both are driven by the idea that international actors find it preferable to engage through elections. The tests reported in Chapters 4, 5, 6, and 7 seek to distinguish these arguments, but cannot entirely differentiate between them.

The third perspective based on international involvement is one I call the emulation explanation. Electoral participation provisions may merely reflect a desire by any actor to ensure conformity with socially defined roles: these provisions are chosen only because of normative trends. Rebel groups or governments, or external actors see these behaviors as what they *should* do. This explanation is highly compatible with external engagement theory, except that the latter posits that elections are chosen in part because of their consequences; however, the normative aspects of elections produce mechanisms for generating attention and accountability.

This emulation explanation would imply that we should expect these provisions to be included when certain organizational characteristics are present, internationally or domestically. For example, they should be seen in peace agreements for conflicts in which groups are fighting over state structures, or states with existing elections and established democracy, or in regions or time periods that emphasize democratic governance. This final element is the one that emerges most directly from democratization theories: as elections increase around the world, electoral participation provisions should be increasingly included everywhere, perhaps especially when international actors are involved regionally in elections. Governments that have significant ties to other governments through trade and other organizations should be more likely to feel this pressure, and so they should push more for electoral participation provisions. It is not clear what impact the provisions should have on conflict recurrence, as these states are already violating norms of peace, although they may be more likely to emulate those norms as well. Given that electoral

---

[126] Driscoll 2008: 3.

participation provisions emerged after the Cold War, international involvement may explain their rise, but other mechanisms may underlie that explanation.

## Selection

It is possible that electoral participation provisions are selected simply for reasons related to why states select any elections or any settlements, and that these selection patterns also have potential implications for peace. A selection explanation could be similar to the emulation explanation. Based on the literature about democratization, as well as about elections in nondemocratic contexts, we might posit that some circumstances encourage this form of governance over others. Some of these conditions are described above: conflicts that contest the structures of the central state, or states that have conditions facilitating democracy (perhaps existing elections and established democracy, or permissive conditions such as a high level of development), or regions and time periods in which many others are turning toward this type of governance. I test these hypotheses under the emulation explanation, although they could follow other logics (asking which conditions make elections more appealing from a domestic rather than international perspective). This selection explanation does not necessarily have any implications about conflict recurrence but, as with the emulation explanation, it is possible that preferences for peace accompany these preferences for elections.

Another logic emerges from work on settlements. It is also possible that electoral participation provisions are included just for show in "easy" cases for fostering peace: perhaps rebel groups and governments select many provisions in settlements that are likely to hold for other reasons. The ease explanation posits that some conflicts are easier to resolve, or are thought to be more fully settled, and so peace is likely to stick regardless of what provisions are included. There are several implications of this ease explanation. First, electoral participation provisions should be more likely to be included in conflicts that are more easily settled, especially smaller conflicts involving stronger states.[127] It is not clear which side should push for these particular provisions, although neither side should resist, because the provisions are not posited to have a causal effect on peace or any other aspect of the settlement. If included only in these easy cases, the provisions should be correlated with peace due to selection rather than due to a causal effect. Thus, their presence may simply indicate peace, rather than causally contribute to it. Properly identifying similarly easy

---

[127] See Fortna 2008.

cases, then, should make any correlation with peace disappear. In terms of the explanation, however, even if these provisions have selection effects due to their strategic inclusion, it is likely that combatants or other actors anticipate that they also have causal effects, because otherwise there would be no reason not to include them.[128] If these provisions are included in peace agreements that are expected to be easy, they should correlate with many other provisions as well, because any number of them can be added when the deal is expected to stick anyway for endogenous reasons.[129] Neither of these selection stories is borne out by the evidence presented in Chapters 4 and 6. In fact, electoral participation provisions tend to be included in the slightly harder cases for peace.

### Institutional Structure

Two additional logics about the institutional structures of elections do not provide such clear competing theories in this set of cases, but they are still useful to consider. First, elections provide an opportunity for *de jure* power to change to match *de facto* power. So elections in which the outcome is expected to match the power distribution could be especially good candidates for electoral participation provisions. The change in institutions and institutional participation provided through electoral participation by both sides certainly shifts *de jure* power, but any peace agreement also makes these changes by, say, reallocating government or rebel positions. In fact, any deal that will be agreed to by both sides must change *de jure* power to match *de facto* power. If elections are a representation of popular support for each side, and fighting capability is also a function of the same factor, then it may be easier to match *de jure* power to *de facto* power through elections than through other institutions.

The elections produced by these provisions, however, are consistently characterized by high levels of engineering and low levels of openness.[130] This suggests that the elite deal is not simply produced through an open vote, because popular support is not a direct match to the power distribution in the conflict. Electoral participation provisions establish elections that are typically intentionally insulated from the mass vote to remove the uncertainty that might otherwise produce an unexpected outcome that could cause the loser to return to conflict. If elections always produced a close match anyway, such insulation would be unnecessary. This logic thus does not seem likely. Nonetheless, the explanation plausibly implies

---

[128] This general idea is in Schultz 2010.    [129] Hartzell and Hoddie 2015.
[130] E.g. Snyder 2000; Lyons 2002a; Paris 2004; Reilly and Nordlund 2008.

that certain types of groups – those that are stronger, for instance – may be better able to compete in elections and thus more likely to agree to electoral participation provisions.

The second logic, also discussed earlier, is about power-sharing. Elections specifically designed to share power may be used in certain cases of peace agreement design, presumably in place of other arrangements such as fixed formulas. A theory that electoral participation provisions are simply equivalent to other arrangements as long as both produce power-sharing does not tell us anything about which cases should be more likely to include electoral participation provisions, which actor should push for them, or whether the electoral participation provisions will have any impact on peace that differs from those of any other provisions. We might see something that, like the emulation theory, predicts increasing inclusion due to normative pressure for this type of power-sharing over any other, but this idea is that there is no instrumental reason to prefer this institution over any other for power-sharing.

As part of this explanation or alternative explanations, particular characteristics of systems, states, actors, or others may correlate with the inclusion of electoral participation provisions. These factors, such as group strength and conflict intensity, relate to the selection explanations. The empirical chapters assess many of these characteristics, and, in general, it is almost certain that some of these additional factors will relate to the causes or consequences of electoral participation provisions.[131]

Each empirical chapter tests aspects of external engagement theory against these alternative theories. There is no single conclusive analysis that can determine whether external engagement theory outperforms these other theories, but, taken together, the set of analyses can nicely distinguish between them. The implications of external engagement theory and these alternative explanations are summarized in Table 2.2.

## Conclusion

Electoral participation provisions in peace agreements provide a mechanism through which international actors can monitor and incentivize compliance. These provisions provide coordination cycles that facilitate external intervention to collect information and provide credible conditional incentives at these moments, under the right conditions. Electoral participation provisions thus help combatants overcome commitment problems by increasing the chances that external actors will

[131] Additional theorizing on the domestic factors, in particular, would be a welcome extension to this study. Huang 2016 takes a step in such a direction.

detect and sanction settlement noncompliance, making it more costly. Over the long term, the cost is low for international actors, especially when democracy promotion programs enable them to engage in those elections. This chapter elaborated on the mechanism by briefly reviewing the difficulties of overcoming commitment problems, examining the aspects of international engagement needed to assist combatants in doing so, and exploring the ways in which electoral participation provisions facilitate this external involvement. The next chapters empirically test the theory.

# 3     International Involvement over Time
## Changes with the End of the Cold War
## and Patterns Thereafter

The Jana Samhati Samiti/Shanti Bahini (JSS/SB), a rebel group fighting the government of Bangladesh over a long-standing dispute about autonomy for the Chittagong Hill Tracts (CHT), faced rounds of failed negotiations between 1985 and 1989.[1] The JSS/SB had repeatedly requested external engagement during this period to guarantee the terms of a settlement and to protect the rebel supporters in its event.[2] However, external actors did not engage,[3] and no bargain was reached.[4]

During the Cold War, many combatants in states across regions faced limited availability of credible settlement enforcement by external actors. Even after it ended, availability increased slowly, spreading region by region. It reached Asia last and provided less engagement than in other regions, due to the preferences of major regional powers, especially China and India.[5] During these 1980s negotiations in Bangladesh, incentives did not exist to enforce deals through external engagement around electoral participation provisions, in part because those elections were "not particularly susceptible to influence by international monitors."[6] The leader of the rebel group there, Shantu Larma, said, "We appealed to the international community, but the response was not enough to get a third-party role. We didn't get very positive responses."[7] However, opportunities for external engagement around the world, including Asia, eventually increased: rebel groups have been able to engage external actors through electoral participation provisions, in such cases as Nepal's in 2006, which is described in Chapter 1.

This chapter shows that patterns of external engagement have changed over time, producing a dramatic increase in peace agreements and a transformation in their design, and, alongside this, a shift in the mechanisms of international involvement that can enforce them. These changes correlated with a global decline in civil conflict over the same years.[8] The end of the

---

[1] Mohsin 2003.  [2] Ghosh 1989.  [3] Fortna 2008: 61.  [4] Mohsin 2003.
[5] Discussed broadly in, for example, Carothers 1999: 43; Legro 2005: 174.
[6] Kelley 2012: 218.  [7] Fortna 2008: 62.  [8] Mack 2014.

Cold War changed the global system in ways that allowed for and encouraged international intervention to secure and enforce settlements in post-conflict contexts. The institutions allowing this increase in the availability of enforcement spread by region, beginning in the regions geographically closest to the Western powers. As the standoff between the United States and the Soviet Union eased, international actors began to coordinate on this type of engagement. Western hegemony also permitted the diffusion of democracy promotion programs. The previous chapter made the argument that these institutions became, in the post-Cold War period, an efficient and acceptable form of external engagement that could enforce settlements, at least as long as settlements include electoral participation provisions. This chapter describes some of the historical changes, demonstrates the growth of peace agreements and electoral participation provisions, and then shows the spread of broader democracy promotion programs across regions over time. It also describes in more detail mechanisms that may underlie the diffusion of these institutions and norms. In doing so, this chapter provides the context in which the theory is situated.

### Ending Hegemonic Competition Created a Context for Ending Civil Conflict

The end of the Cold War increased the incentives in several ways for international actors to involve themselves in ending civil conflicts. First, the end of the Cold War permitted the major powers – the veto players in the system – to coordinate among themselves on certain objectives. Rather than fighting one another in proxy wars, it became possible for the United States and other international actors to call for engagement to enforce compliance with settlements to civil conflict in the expectation that other veto players – particularly Russia – would not impede these efforts. A trend of coordinated crisis management through the United Nations began after the end of the Security Council's paralysis in the late 1980s. Second, the threat of civil conflicts loomed large in comparison to other threats in the relatively stable post-Cold War era. Finally, norms likely played a role as liberalism dominated. Taken together, the United States and other international actors had reason to be concerned about civil conflicts and, with the end of the threat of the Cold War and the rise of liberalism, they could intervene.[9] Intervention, however, was not typically that peacekeeping troops were sent to threaten military coercion. I describe the mechanisms in more depth first, and then I turn to the question of what type of involvement occurred.

---

[9] For more in-depth coverage on this, see Feste 2003.

Under the bipolar system of the Cold War, the United States and the Soviet Union had competed for hegemony, including through proxy wars, which produced and prolonged many civil conflicts. Aside from intervention by major powers to win influence, state strength and state sovereignty were the central principles of foreign policy. States signed new treaties, such as the Universal Declaration of Human Rights, but they were largely alone in deciding how they would implement these and other commitments.[10] The end of the Cold War meant that the United States and its allies no longer needed to maintain principles of nonintervention to have an argument for excluding the influence of their rivals.

Without the competition for hegemony, interested international actors could now coordinate to back settlements to civil conflicts in war-torn countries, among other initiatives. The United States and other countries that had composed the Western Bloc – which now led the international system through a set of intergovernmental organizations, including the United Nations, the North Atlantic Treaty Organization (NATO), and, eventually, the European Union – no longer faced continual opposition to this type of involvement. After the dissolution of the Soviet Union, Russia no longer sought to proselytize for communism in opposition to U.S. capitalism and had lost international influence, and so it no longer stood in the way of Western peacekeeping efforts.[11] As Russia was no longer competing for dominance with the United States, attempts at international intervention no longer held the zero-sum strategic importance that they had held during the bipolar Cold War.

No other state emerged in Russia's place seeking substantial revisions to the international system. Rather than challenging the system, China, for example, has sought integration into the international system,[12] even as it has sought to check U.S. involvement in Asia.[13] China's emergence, then, has implications for Western external engagement in the region, and perhaps in certain countries in which China has strategic interests – for instance, it may make imposing sanctions on oil in Sudan more difficult[14] – but it has not opposed enforcing settlements to civil conflict as a uniform policy. Moreover, at least until recent conflicts, other states also largely have not tried to impede these peacebuilding missions.[15]

The systemic change encouraged a trend of "internationally coordinated efforts at crisis management" through the United Nations, as veto players

[10] Mayall 1996: 5.
[11] Lebow and Risse 1995; Brooks and Wohlforth 2000; Legro 2005: 143, 146, 150–151.
[12] Legro 2005: 173.   [13] Legro 2005: 174.   [14] Alden 2005, Tull 2006.
[15] Most, in fact, have not interfered with U.S. security policy at all, although that may be changing; see Mastanduno and Kapstein 1999; Brooks and Wohlforth 2005; Brooks and Wohlforth 2008.

in the Security Council could call for action in conflict states and expect assistance (or at least minimal resistance) from the other veto players.[16]

Termination of civil conflicts came to be the focus of many efforts after the end of the Cold War. During the Cold War, civil conflicts were often proxy wars fought between the United States and the Soviet Union that led to high rates of battle deaths, and, while the outcome was important to the global balance, the Cold War often overshadowed concerns about these conflicts themselves.[17] After the Cold War, the relative threat of these civil conflicts increased. The death toll from civil wars in the modern era – 16 million, according to a 2003 estimate – is much higher than from interstate wars – 3 million – and they tend to last longer and reoccur more frequently.[18] Now in a relatively peaceful world in terms of interstate conflict, potential interveners could turn their attention to these intrastate conflicts. Contagion from these conflicts is a threat, for instance, fostered in part by leaders seeking to influence the outcome, even externalizing fighting, during civil conflicts.[19] Even if a conflict remains largely within a single state, it can draw other states into supporting roles or spread new civil conflicts to its neighbors.[20] Civil war has also frequently arisen in weak states, which were a concern for potential interveners at the end of the Cold War and which prompted renewed concern after the terrorist attacks of September 11, 2001. Former United Nations Secretary General Kofi Annan has cautioned that "no challenge in international relations today is more pressing or more difficult than that of supporting weak states."[21]

Norms that developed about responding to civil conflict may have contributed to changing international involvement.[22] The American foreign-policy preference for interventionism of some sort can be traced back to the era of World War II – when the United Nations was created and the Bretton Woods agreement was signed – and it largely remained constant with the end of the Cold War.[23] Norms seem to have played a role in humanitarian intervention in certain conflicts.[24] At a minimum, norms affected Western rhetoric about intervention to secure settlements to civil conflict.[25]

The new role for the United States, as well as its Western allies, emerged after the Cold War in terms of engagement. The U.S. Department of

[16] Mayall 1996: 2.    [17] Dobbins 2003; Lacina et al. 2006.
[18] For example, see Walter 1997; Fearon and Laitin 2003 (they provide these estimates); Collier and Hoeffler 2004.
[19] For example, see Gleditsch et al. 2008.
[20] For example, see Brown 1996; including, on U.N. involvement, de Jonge Oudraat 1996.
[21] Quoted in Dobbins et al. 2007: n.p.    [22] Finnemore 1996, 2003.
[23] Legro 2005: 74, 77, 167; Leffler and Legro 2011: 69.    [24] Finnemore 1996, 2003.
[25] Like the "responsibility to protect," for example; see Evans and Sahnoun 2002.

Defense's 1992 Defense Planning Guidance draft recognized that the American military should shift its aim from the former Soviet Union to potential regional threats: "while the U.S. cannot become the world's 'policeman,' by assuming responsibility for righting every wrong," it would assume "the preeminent responsibility for addressing selectively those wrongs which threaten not only our interests, but those of our allies or friends, or which could seriously unsettle international relations."[26] The constraints on intervention are a central concern in this document, but it shows an expanded function in terms of enforcement. The United States decided to continue this commitment now that the main motivation was terminating conflict rather than furthering it, doing so primarily through intergovernmental organizations. The first Bush and Clinton administrations focused on expanding NATO in response to the new threats to international security.[27] They also increasingly relied on the United Nations to send armed forces into civil conflicts.

States, when they intervene, typically operate through intergovernmental organizations designed to reduce both costs and risks of casualties. The United Nations helps to legitimize interventions and, crucially, also shares costs across states,[28] although the United States still pays much of the U.N.'s peacekeeping budget.[29] The United States has often proven the most willing to absorb the cost of peacekeeping, perhaps rivaled only by France when supporting peacekeeping in its former colonies. Casualties remain a large concern: the loss of life abroad constitutes a political risk for politicians at home. The United States intervened in Somalia and elsewhere in the early 1990s using its own troops, but the political costs of a few catastrophes, such as downed U.S. helicopters in Mogadishu in 1993, made the Clinton administration much more cautious.[30] Other states also became more cautious.[31] Even the United Nations, influenced by the reluctance of its member states, limited its armed peacekeeping missions.[32]

While the United States typically was not motivated to deploy troops in conflicted states, it did engage in a number of cases after the Cold War. Peacekeeping missions certainly increased, but they did not become ubiquitous.[33] The United Nations led 33 peacekeeping missions in the 1990s, compared to six in the 1980s.[34] Armed international interventions

---

[26] Quoted in Gellman 1992: A1.
[27] Legro 2005: 74, 77, 167; Leffler and Legro 2011: 69.
[28] For example, see Fearon and Laitin 2004.     [29] Mayall 1996, Kreps 2011.
[30] Dobbins 2003.     [31] Levite et al. 1992.
[32] United Nations 2008. Soliciting adequate troops from U.N. member states is always difficult and usually results in insufficient forces; see Hillen 2000.
[33] Walter 1997, 1999, 2002; Fortna 2004, 2008; Cronin 2009; Weinberg et al. 2009.
[34] For many examples, see Dobbins 2003, 2008; Dobbins et al. 2005, 2008; Fortna 2008.

tend to occur in the most difficult civil conflicts to terminate – those that last the longest and cause the most deaths[35] – although international interveners also consider the likely cost and probability of success for the mission.[36] Armed intervention remains rare, but this is likely because of interveners' concerns about material costs and casualties, particularly after significant incidents, rather than strategic calculations in the particular cases.

## Patterns in Peace Agreements before and after the End of the Cold War

After the Cold War, peace agreements became much more prevalent, perhaps due to external engagement by major powers to enforce them, which potentially take a variety of alternative forms aside from relatively rare peacekeeping troop deployments using credible military coercion. The theory is detailed in the theory chapter that precedes this one, and the comparison across the end of the Cold War is tested more rigorously in the empirical chapters that follow, so this chapter provides the context in which the theory is situated.

To examine trends over time, all peace agreements in civil conflicts from 1975 to 2005, drawn from the UCDP Peace Agreement Dataset, constitute the universe of cases.[37] That dataset contains settlements between at least two opposing sides in conflicts that resulted in 25 or more battle deaths per year. To be counted, a peace agreement must "concern the incompatibility" over which the signatories were fighting, and must solve, regulate, or outline a process to solve it.[38] I cluster continuous peace processes to treat sets of negotiations ending with a single solution together.[39] These peace agreements differ from cease-fires, or from conflicts where the fighting simply petered out, in that these

---

[35] De Jonge Oudraat 1996; Fortna 2004, 2008.

[36] Jakobsen 1996; Gilligan and Stedman 2003: 48.

[37] The list of peace agreements is in the Online Appendix at https://dataverse.harvard.edu/dataverse/matanock, and the coding rules are available from the author.

[38] Harbom et al. 2006; Högbladh 2012. The updated version of this dataset includes more agreements than other datasets, such as the Peace Accord Matrix, and encompasses almost all of the peace agreements in those sets (except Lebanon in 1989). The Peace Accord Matrix is quite similar to the data I use once accords are clustered into peace processes.

[39] Clustered peace processes include, for example, the negotiations in El Salvador that were guided by the United Nations (1990–1992). In other cases – in Georgia and Guinea-Bissau, for instance – earlier accords that become part of an agreement are mentioned in some press coverage but not recorded in these datasets, so clustering also reduces bias. I control for peace processes that had provisions calling for some sort of later negotiations that did not take place, and the main results hold.

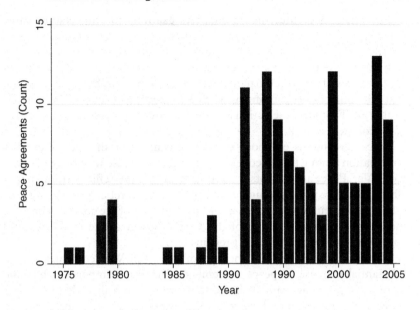

Figure 3.1  Peace Agreements over Time

seek to resolve – not pause – the conflict. The time period covered by these data allows examination of the "third wave" of democratization, which began in 1974, creating a comparison among cases that experienced normative pressure to hold elections.[40]

I examine each dyadic peace process between each signing rebel group and the government. I analyze the data at the dyadic level for several reasons: first, different rebel groups participating in the same peace process can implement different terms of an agreement; second, much of the data now available on conflicts are at the rebel group level, such as size of the rebel forces, so the dyadic level allows this variation in the analysis; finally, external engagement theory only implies that *dyadic* participation increases enforcement. Most of the comparison in the analyses in practice is across agreements, even when the data are on a dyadic level, because only 12 agreements have multiple dyadic signatories. The results throughout the empirical chapters, then, also hold when data are examined on the agreement level.

Figure 3.1 shows the number of peace agreements over time. The end of the Cold War is associated with a substantial increase in the likelihood of a peace agreement. The pattern is similar in a longer data range.[41]

[40] Huntington 1991; Levitsky and Way 2010: 14.    [41] Fazal 2015.

The analyses in the coming chapters examine the universe of cases composed of peace agreements and assess causes and consequences of the inclusion of electoral participation provisions. This focused comparison reduces heterogeneity across cases by conditioning on the ability of the two sides of a conflict to negotiate a settlement. It is, however, possible that selection could occur in terms of which conflicts ever achieve a signed deal at all. To address selection effects, I conduct analyses on the universe of all conflicts as well.

Peace agreements compose a small percentage of all types of conflict termination among these active cases, but they increase with the end of the Cold War. Peace agreements as a subset of all dyadic conflict terminations – which may take place through government victory, rebel group victory, or other conflict outcome, such as a slow petering out of the conflict – became more frequent after the end of the Cold War, at a rate of 45 percent, compared to 15 percent in the previous era.

This evidence shows that the end of the Cold War correlates with a substantial increase in peace agreements. But more important than the increase in peace agreements is the transformation in their design – from traditional arrangements for power distribution to electoral participation provisions. The coordinating effect of the end of the Cold War generates more peace agreements, although it is insufficient alone to produce the transformation in settlement design that also takes place, showing even when controlling for the number of peace agreements. Rather, the book argues that the change in design is due to new low-cost, long-term mechanisms for external enforcement. The next subsection reviews this sea change in design, then the following section offers evidence on the new mechanisms.

### Changing Terms of Peace Agreements: Electoral Participation Provisions

A transformation in the approach to crafting peace agreements took place at the end of the Cold War. Previous studies have neglected the study of electoral participation provisions in favor of other dimensions of settlement design and post-conflict elections. But electoral participation provisions can make the difference between enduring peace and conflict recurrence as this book shows. Beyond coding whether post-conflict elections followed a civil conflict, this project examines whether the deal specified this transition "from bullets to ballots" for both sides, as well as whether it was implemented.[42]

---

[42] Electoral participation provisions, by definition, require a deal between the combatant sides. However, it is possible that such provisions could be included under a "ceasefire"

Electoral participation provisions consist of agreement on two components: agreement to hold elections and to allow participation by the rebel group as a political party. I gather evidence on these two components by analyzing the text of the agreements, through which I identify whether each deal includes (1) clear expectations to hold elections by setting a date – or by already having held elections regularly for two cycles that are not revoked by the deal – and (2) clear expectations that both sides will run candidates.[43] In almost all peace agreements, governments conduct the elections, and so, in order to include rebel groups, the deal must (a) legalize them as political parties; (b) create a transitional government that includes them as parties; or, occasionally, (c) include groups already participating on their own or through established alliances with political parties. It is possible that electoral participation provisions created following the establishment of transitional governments, rather than direct legalization, for example, could have different consequences.[44] Chapter 6 tests this empirically. Both ultimately produce this transition from the battlefield to the ballot box, however, so I code both categories of peace agreement as including electoral participation provisions.

Electoral participation provisions are usually easily identifiable. The 1992 agreement in El Salvador, for example, set an election date and provided for "legalization of [the rebel group] as a political party." Cases that are not as clear may include provisions in peace agreements that legalize multi-party competition broadly, such as in Zimbabwe in 1979, or where parties participate in elections prior to the conflict but then are not directly brought back into the process in the peace agreements, such as in the Republic of the Congo in 1999. Such cases are not included in the initial coding because monitoring and incentivizing compliance with the negotiated settlement for both sides was not necessarily set through the elections. They also include instances when rebel groups are brought into regional but not national transitional governments as

---

rather than a "peace agreement." The peace agreement data are quite inclusive, but, as I will discuss in Chapter 4, I also use a dataset on all civil conflicts (Kreutz 2010). That coding even includes a few more peace agreements. Coding these cases for electoral participation provisions, through this secondary analysis, is also useful in overcoming any bias that could result from selection into provisions falling outside of peace agreements defined in the initial data.

[43] The data are in the Online Appendix at https://dataverse.harvard.edu/dataverse/mata nock. The coding rules, and additional variables and analyses, are available from the author. Among all agreements, 18 cases are missing full text. In eight cases, detailed summaries provide confidence interpreting provisions, but in 10 cases, all from Chad, they do not. I drop these cases as robustness checks in subsequent chapters.

[44] Proposed, for example, by Barnett 2006; Brancati and Snyder 2013, for instance, find that longer transition periods contribute to peace. Other work explores transitional, or interim, governments in more depth; see Guttieri and Piombo 2007.

political parties in the early period, which often occurs in cases where groups seek autonomy or secession for part of the state ("territorial"), rather than power in the central government ("center-seeking"). These cases are included in the initial coding because each side seems to be bound into the electoral process. Regional transitional governments, however, may not provide all of the costs and benefits of participatory elections to combatants signing on as political parties, especially the international attention and assistance. In alternative specifications of the coding, I change these less clear cases, and the analyses in subsequent chapters are robust to these checks.[45]

My coding of these rebel group electoral participation provisions does not depend on implementation. Measuring actual electoral participation – an outcome measure indicating that these provisions have been put into practice – would wrap ex-post processes and pressures into the assessments of the causes and consequences of the decisions to hold these elections. Implementation depends on many more factors – and measuring implementation of other provisions may be more difficult than measuring participation provisions – so it is not the primary variation of interest. I do code it, however, and explore it (see Chapters 4 and 6). In this alternative coding, I take into account whether the government followed through on the agreement and actually held elections within 10 years, and whether the rebel group actually participated. The main analysis, however, focuses on electoral participation provisions.

These data indicate that 42 percent of all peace agreements between 1975 and 2005 include electoral participation provisions (see Figure 1.1 in Chapter 1 and a complete list of peace agreements in the Online Appendix at https://dataverse.harvard.edu/dataverse/matanock). The evidence on electoral participation provisions (previewed in Chapter 1 and further evaluated in Chapter 4) show that the end of the Cold War correlates even more strongly with electoral participation provisions than with peace agreements broadly. Such provisions were nonexistent before 1989 and then adopted in almost half of the agreements afterwards. The entire period presented in these figures is subsequent to the start of the third wave of democratization in 1974. But these electoral participation provisions only show an upward shift beginning in 1989; they do not correlate with the post-1974 period of increasing numbers of elections broadly.[46]

---

[45] That is, peace agreements that open the way for multi-party competition broadly and those where combatants participated in elections before the conflict are included, and those that integrate groups only in pre-election regional transitional governments are excluded, and the results in the analyses presented in subsequent chapters hold.

[46] Levitsky and Way 2010: 14, based on Huntington 1991.

The changing global context, then, produced a stark shift in the terms of peace agreements – dramatically increasing the inclusion of electoral participation provisions – that cannot be accounted for merely through the global spread of democratization. This shift demands a different explanation. I argue in Chapter 2 that a simultaneous change in how elections were conducted crucially allowed more external engagement. The next section of this chapter shows some evidence of these changes and then elaborates on the diffusion theory that explains them.

## Emerging Democracy Promotion Programs Help International Actors Coordinate around Elections

The coordination of enforcement of settlements to civil conflicts emerged from the consolidation of unipolar hegemony, but the U.S. position in that system also produced a rise of Western liberalism that increased involvement in promoting democracy.[47] Democracy promotion has sometimes been seen as a spark that starts conflict when it requires regime change,[48] but it has rarely been seen as a mechanism for ending conflict. Changes in the international system after the end of the Cold War, however, produced new ways for international actors to engage in electoral processes. These new mechanisms facilitated international intervention to monitor and offer incentives conditional on compliance with domestic arrangements. I argued in Chapter 2 that these institutions, with the information and leverage they supply, offer an efficient means of enforcing settlements when electoral participation provisions are included. Electoral participation provisions in fact enabled such low-cost engagement in part because of the coordination cycles they created and in part because of the institutions, and the conventions around them, that developed as democracy promotion programs emerged. This chapter describes the emergence of these programs.

After the Cold War, a new commitment to intervention to improve governance extended to different areas: peacekeeping, as just described, and democracy promotion.[49] During the Cold War, rather than push for democracy, Western democracies, especially the United States, "ignored human rights violations and sought clients wherever they could."[50] After the Cold War, however, clients were no longer so crucial, and liberal democracy became dominant, with the United States as its main exponent,

---

[47] Many changes occurred due to the power configuration, some specific to U.S. dominance (e.g. Ikenberry et al. 2011).

[48] Lo et al. 2008; Downes 2011; Peic and Reiter 2011; Downes and Monten 2013; Downes and O'Rourke 2016.

[49] McCoy 1993.      [50] Ake 1996: 63–64.

enabling serious efforts at democracy promotion.[51] The Clinton administration also came to view democracy as a component of global peace and so
had a strategic aim in such programs. For example, President Clinton
declared that "the best strategy to ensure our security and to build
a durable peace is to support the advance of democracy elsewhere."[52]
The concept of democratic peace was also supported by the research at the
time,[53] although later work pointed out some dangers associated with the
process of democratization.[54] Norms and incentives thus favored democracy promotion, and so these programs increased after the fall of the Berlin
Wall in 1989 and the collapse of the Soviet Union in 1991.[55]

The development of these democracy promotion programs, which
increased after the end of the Cold War but emerged at different rates
in each region, speaks to the cultural and normative coherence posited
in Chapter 2. U.N. resolutions in the late 1980s had endorsed both the
principle of "periodic and genuine elections" and the principle of
"sovereignty and non-interference."[56] However, when U.N. Secretary
General Perez de Cuellar in 1991 asked member states to comment on
the apparent conflict between these resolutions, they overwhelmingly
supported international election observation. Indeed, the E.U.
members that commented did not even mention issues of sovereignty or
noninterference.[57] The decision may have been based on the link
between international election observation and human rights: elections
were initially framed as important rights,[58] and then they were tied
more specifically to international involvement as concerns about violations produced the beginnings of humanitarian intervention, especially
around issues of apartheid.[59] Recent survey evidence suggests that
these conventions have become widespread. Polls across 17 countries
that differ on a variety of dimensions found 65 percent support for
international election observation.[60] The acceptance of election observation has not been accompanied by similar acceptance for monitoring
human rights more broadly, though, and so the mechanism remained
closely tied to elections.[61] For elections, however, the developing
norms were accompanied by changing behavior: in 1990 and 1991

---

[51] Dunning 2004: 412; McFaul 2010: 13–14.     [52] Clinton 1994.
[53] Russett and Oneal 1997; Carothers 1999: 5, 46; Russett and Oneal 2000; Mansfield et al.
2002.
[54] Mansfield and Snyder 1995, 2002, 2005.
[55] Levitsky and Way 2010: 14; Hyde 2011b.     [56] Kelley 2012: 23.     [57] Kelley 2012: 24.
[58] Kelley 2012: 21.     [59] Kelley 2012: 22, 24.
[60] Hyde 2011b: 87, citing data from "World Publics Strongly Favor International
Observers for Elections, Including their Own," Program on International Policy
Attitudes, University of Maryland, September 8, 2009.
[61] Kelley 2012: 19.

resolutions, the United Nations authorized its secretary general to develop election assistance.[62] Similar practices were adopted by Western regional bodies.[63]

While the U.S. win in the Cold War created broadly permissive conditions for democracy promotion, the promise of rewards for institution-building helped drive its diffusion. Recent work posits both a supply-side and a demand-side theory for the spread of a convention on election observation: international actors sought to foster peace by financing democratization, and democratizing governments sought to use that interest to reap rewards such as foreign aid from demonstrating "good" progress.[64] These theories extend diffusion mechanisms, focusing on the idea that international factors influence the information that domestic and international actors have about the available policy options, especially regarding their costs and benefits, through learning and emulation mechanisms.[65] Once some states adopt such technology for monitoring and incentivizing compliance, countries with which they are closely compared in the same regions adopt similar measures.[66] Some regions remained less affected by these mechanisms, especially in Asia and the Middle East, as this chapter and the next show.[67] The normative aspects of this type of engagement thus reinforce the instrumentalist aspects, creating conventions.

Democracy promotion programs are varied, but their use has increased substantially in the post-Cold War period. The next sections show the time trends, the regional diffusion, and the state characteristics that are associated with the availability of these tools.

*International Election Observation*

With the end of the Cold War, mechanisms increased through which international actors could monitor compliance by states with specific standards, including election observation and the presence of missions from non-governmental and intergovernmental organizations. This monitoring allowed international actors to assess whether all parties were meeting their obligations under the domestic arrangements.

International election observation ramped up, as did global attention to elections, regardless of regime type. As Figure 3.2 shows,[68] international election observation never rose above 20 percent of all national elections until 1989, but then increased dramatically. By 2004, about 80 percent were internationally observed.[69] International election observation spread

---

[62] Kelley 2012: 24.   [63] Kelley 2012: 22.   [64] Kelley 2012; Hyde 2011b.
[65] Simmons and Elkins 2004.   [66] Santa-Cruz 2005; Hyde 2011b; Kelley 2012.
[67] See, for example, Legro 2005: 174; Brownlee 2012.   [68] Hyde 2011a.
[69] Kelley 2008; Hyde 2011a.

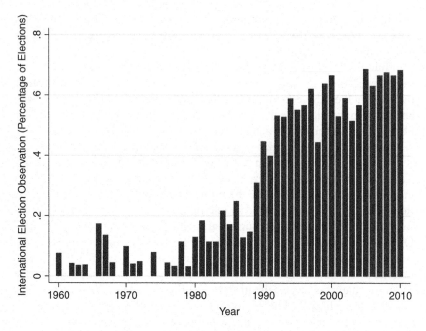

Figure 3.2 International Election Observation over Time
Note: Data are from Hyde and Marinov 2012, 1960–2010.

in discernible patterns after the end of the Cold War. International election observers are invited by governments because elections are a sovereign function, although governments are at times pressured into doing so. Much of the electoral observation process may have begun because democratizing governments were trying to prove their compliance with the standards of democracy and opposition figures were trying to disprove it.[70] Interestingly, however, the spread of international election observation became almost unstoppable: once international election observation was employed by states in a region, others in the same states began to employ it due to normative pressure to conform or due to functionalist pressure to avoid being seen as an obvious noncomplier, a concern that is well demonstrated across cases in regions with high adoption rates (where some still violate the standards of the international community).[71]

The most notable trend for the theory is the escalation of international electoral observation after the end of the Cold War (as just shown in Figure 3.2), but underpinning this pattern are regional trends that rise at

[70] Bjornlund 2004; Hyde 2011b.    [71] Kelley 2008; Hyde 2011a.

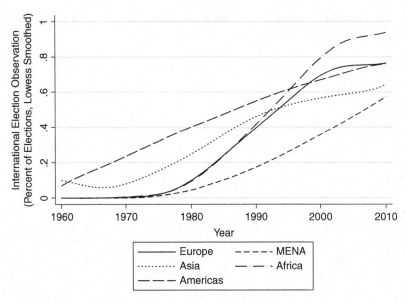

Figure 3.3 International Election Observation over Time by Region
Note: Data are from Hyde and Marinov 2012, 1960–2010.

different times and different rates (see Figure 3.3). Latin America was the
first region to receive international election observers, and it was the one in
which the United States was the most involved.[72] Eight out of nine transitional elections in the region between 1989 and 1993 were internationally
observed.[73] This trend was also observed in areas in which European
powers were particularly engaged, especially the Balkans and Eastern
Europe, but also the former Soviet Republics.[74] In these areas, the
United States and other Western powers had an interest in becoming
involved, especially as new institutions were needed with the collapse
of the Cold War regimes.[75] The evidence supports the theoretical
expectation described in that external engagement diffuses by region:
"a virtuous combination of member state will and institutional capacity
has resulted in entities like the Organization of American States (OAS),
European Union, Council of Europe, and Organization for Security and
Cooperation developing a strong track record of monitoring elections
and responding to electoral misconduct."[76] In sub-Saharan Africa,

[72] McCoy 1993; Carothers 1999; Santa-Cruz 2005; Kelley 2008; Hyde 2011b.
[73] McCoy 1993: 133.   [74] Carothers 1999: 40.   [75] Carothers 1999: 40.
[76] Donno 2013: 5.

which had been the site of many proxy wars during the Cold War, the United States and European states also became involved in monitoring.[77]

The trend lines in Figure 3.3 show the early use of international election observation in Latin America, followed by quick rises in Europe and Africa. Certain regions largely escaped this engagement until later. For example, with a few exceptions, such as the Philippines, Asian "values" or pressure from regional powers, especially China and India, to maintain norms of nonintervention meant that these regions did not receive this type of involvement until the 1997–1998 crises.[78] The Middle East was also largely excluded from this move toward monitoring, although it was also just less democratic throughout this period.[79] These different rates of regional adoption allow more specific measurement of variation in expectations of international election observation in the subsequent chapters. In background interviews, Carter Center and U.N. officials noted that, like interveners of other kinds, they strove to intervene in less stable states within regions; however, that selection decision does not seem to drive this regional diffusion. Empirical analyses show that these trends do not match stability or even the diffusion of democratization, rather that they reflect a shift in international attention specifically.[80]

International election observers assess much more than the quality of elections, a point which other chapters also address. International election observation also provides information about democratization and protection of rights in states broadly. Many of the reports from the United Nations, OAS, the Carter Center, and other organizations evaluate the electoral process itself and also the state's performance on democracy promotion and human rights protection policies.[81] This brings the focus of the international community to many of the major elements of negotiated settlements in post-conflict states. Democracy promotion programs specifically address the rule of law, for instance.[82] These observation reports, then, cover many of the provisions in peace agreements in post-conflict contexts.

Monitoring does not occur solely through international election observation. Non-governmental organizations, especially those focused on human rights, also spread during the post-Cold War era, although the data are harder to identify. In conjunction with increased media coverage around elections, as well as increasing access to Internet and social media, these organizations also help international actors monitor the implementation of

---

[77] Carothers 1999: 42.     [78] Carothers 1999: 43; Legro 2005: 174.     [79] McFaul 2010.
[80] Simpser and Donno 2012: 507.     [81] Hyde 2007; Kelley 2008.
[82] Carothers 1999; Bjornlund 2004.

peace agreements. The number of non-governmental organizations, in general, has increased since 1990, and even more substantially since 1995.[83] Organizations such as Amnesty International and Human Rights Watch are particularly active in releasing post-conflict reports on the implementation of peace agreements. It is harder to find data on these organizations in the Cold War period, but they have increased since 1989 at a rate that likely extended from the pre–Cold War period, according to those collecting these data. These organizations can spread information during the election cycles about implementation of peace agreements in post-conflict states. Increased media coverage during election periods raises the exposure of these assessments, so that they are particularly effective. U.S. media coverage of other states' elections is higher than for other events in those states, and it is highest in places where there has been conflict.[84]

### Democracy and Governance Aid

International pressure for democratization depends on leverage.[85] Mechanisms of leverage – alongside the mechanisms of monitoring just described – have become more available since the end of the Cold War. Democracy promotion, although important to the United States during the Cold War, was then overshadowed by other objectives for that state and was not important for many other states.[86] After 1989, many programs increased, including the aid (and sanctions) useful for leverage. In the 1950s, only five states were subjected to economic pressure aimed at changing some aspect of their regime, but by the 1990s, 47 were.[87] Elections, in particular, came to incorporate conditional benefits – especially democracy and governance aid – offered by international actors as part of the process. International observation became the key to "unlocking" these benefits, which thus became part of this democracy promotion process.[88]

Policymakers use economic, legal, political, and occasionally military tools to promote democracy in monitored contexts including around post-conflict elections (see Table 2.1 in Chapter 2).[89] These incentives, including democracy assistance, party funds, and election aid, for example, are available to apply to post-conflict cases, as well, especially when both sides participated as political parties. Intergovernmental organizations and other countries, especially the United States, led armed missions to install or reinstall democracies in some cases.[90] The framework

[83] Willetts 1996, as well as his updated data.    [84] Golan and Wanta 2003.
[85] Levitsky and Way 2010.    [86] Hyde 2011b: 143–144.    [87] Marinov 2005.
[88] McCoy 1993: 133.    [89] Carothers 1999: 6.    [90] Farer 2004; Dobbins et al. 2007.

for advancing democracy spread far beyond these cases of force. The United States and other Western powers, as well as intergovernmental and non-governmental organizations, provided diplomatic and economic pressure to democratize, offering rewards in cases of positive changes and punishment in cases of negative changes.[91]

Foreign aid is frequently conditioned on compliance with election standards.[92] The major Western powers all announced in the 1990s that they would tie development assistance to democratization.[93] Prior to that, even as late as the 1980s, development assistance was largely based on strategic interests.[94] While strategic interests remained important after the end of the Cold War, the European Union, the United States, and the United Nations, in particular, developed assistance programs and projects devoted to advancing democracy. The mission of USAID had initially been to counter communism through development, but after the Cold War, it increasingly began encouraging and assisting with elections.[95] For the United States, new regional programs, such as the Support for Eastern European Democracy (SEED) Act, emerged.[96] Global programs that had just been started in the 1980s – including the National Endowment for Democracy (NED), which also funded the International Republican Institute (IRI) and the National Democratic Institute for International Affairs (NDI)[97] – also expanded dramatically starting in the 1990s. Some European assistance shifted, as well.[98] Since the end of the Cold War democracy and governance aid as a percentage of total official development assistance has been increasing, as Figure 3.4 shows. Over the years for which data are available, this type of aid has risen from just under 2 percent to just under 20 percent.[99] While the data used in this book on democracy and governance aid are only reported after the end of the Cold War, experts say that the rate was near zero in the 1980s,[100] and it remained low until after 1989 (see Figure 3.4). By 1991, the U.N. secretary general also had resources and the backing of the member states to grant electoral assistance to any state requesting it.[101] In addition, international actors used other forms of diplomatic and economic pressure to encourage democratization, including trade benefits, balance-of-payments support, and economic sanctions.[102]

---

[91] Carothers 1999: 6.     [92] Carothers 1999.
[93] Levitsky and Way 2010: 17–18, 31–32.     [94] For example, see Schraeder et al. 1998.
[95] Knack 2004; Natsios 2006; Fukuyama and McFaul 2008.     [96] McFaul 2010: 20.
[97] McFaul 2010: 20.     [98] Azpuru et al. 2008; Youngs 2008.
[99] Finkel et al. 2007, including USAID and non-U.S. aid.
[100] Tierney et al. 2011; Bush 2015: 8.     [101] Farer 2004: 38.
[102] Carothers 1999; Marinov 2004; McFaul 2010.

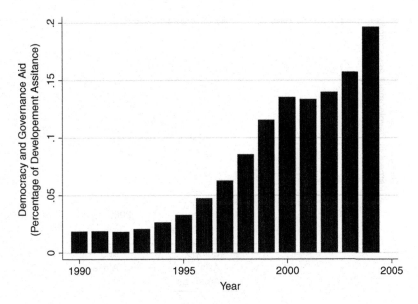

Figure 3.4 Democracy and Governance Aid over Time
Note: Data are from Finkel et al. 2007 (using USAID and non-U.S.
Official Development Aid).

Democracy assistance shows regional trends over time that are similar
to those for election observation (see Figure 3.5). U.S. aid flowedheavily
to Latin America initially and then gradually to other regions; European
aid began flowing within the region, and then, a little later, expanded,
primarily to Africa.[103] By 1999, this type of aid was directed to 100
states.[104] Democracy promotion developed in regional waves, although
they were not as differentiated as those for election observation. In each
region, the tools for promoting democracy thus allowed further engagement, especially through the electoral system, by international actors.

These benefits, especially programs for democracy and governance
assistance, were often conditional on compliance with specified standards. This aid provided a mechanism for external actors to intervene in
domestic politics with some legitimacy. Conditional democracy aid has
some standards that are case-specific, especially in post-conflict contexts,
and others that are applied across cases, such as those prohibiting
coups.[105] Democracy aid dovetailed with the aspects of post-conflict

---

[103] Azpuru et al. 2008; Youngs 2008.     [104] Carothers 1999.
[105] Azpuru et al. 2008; Carothers 1999: 6, 85; McFaul 2010: 20; Youngs 2008.

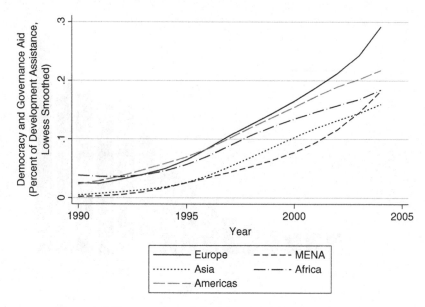

Figure 3.5 Democracy and Governance Aid over Time by Region
Note: Data are from Finkel et al. 2007 (using USAID and non-U.S.
Official Development Aid combined).

participatory electoral process produced by provisions allowing both sides'
former combatant parties to participate. A primary emphasis of such aid
was on elections, especially on seeking to strengthen capacity and encourage strong political party participation.[106] Some assistance could be
offered both to those inside and to those outside of the government:
many of these programs offered resources, including specific trust funds
in some cases, to develop political parties.[107] In the late 1980s, NED began
funding political party projects; beginning in the 1990s, even USAID,
which remains nonpartisan, expanded its party-related projects, which
were implemented by NDI and IRI.[108] By the mid-1990s, USAID devoted
more than $10 million annually to these projects, which was more than all
of NED's grants to NDI and IRI combined.[109] European assistance was
also largely this type of aid.[110] Trust funds for former rebel group parties,
such as the fund for Renamo in Mozambique, have been a specific
success.[111] The United Nations eventually established a peacebuilding

[106] Carothers 1999.    [107] Carothers 1999.    [108] Carothers 1999: 140–141.
[109] Carothers 1999: 141.    [110] Carothers 1999: 142.
[111] Bekoe 2008; Manning and Malbrough 2010.

fund to provide centralized support in post-conflict contexts. As of 2015, most of these funds existed in states with settlements based on electoral participation provisions.

*Conditioning Aid on Observation*   The theory requires that international actors are willing to criticize and sanction violations of the terms of the agreements put into place through the elections.[112] Threatening and imposing sanctions (freezing aid, for example) that have been tied to elections seem to have increased. The democracy and governance assistance seem to be conditional, at least in cases of clear violations, given the right characteristics of the state, including the region and time-period.[113] In the event of a coup, for instance, USAID funding for that state would automatically be suspended; it would not, however, be withheld from the political parties opposing the government.[114] After the Cold War, many organizations drew this line on coups. Beginning in 1991, for instance, the OAS General Assembly's Resolution 1080 required a ministerial meeting after any coup to decide on an appropriate collective response to "defend" the democratically elected government.[115] These international actors also sought to sanction other similar violations. For example, in 2000, a lapse in democracy in Latin America meant an 80 percent chance of receiving economic sanctions. In the following decade, in almost every instance in which democratic rights were suspended or human rights were grossly violated, the state was sanctioned. At any time in the past decade when almost any civil war has broken out in any region, the state has been sanctioned.[116] Peace agreements produce standards by which to judge "clear violations" in such cases. States that receive negative international election observation reports, whether post-conflict or not, face such sanctions.

Cutting off aid, and threats to cut off aid, due to noncompliance with the normal electoral process increased dramatically after the Cold War (see Figure 3.6).[117] Aid denials may be infrequent, although the data

---

[112] As discussed in Chapter 2, observers may avoid noting violations if, for example, they are concerned that their statements may cause more violence. However, elections that follow civil conflicts do *not* have significantly higher rates of observer endorsement, suggesting that observers may not act on such a concern in those cases; see Kelley 2009: 7, 15.

[113] Perhaps due to the inconsistent application of these tools, the findings on the effects of these programs on democracy have been mixed. See Carothers 1997, 1999; Bjornlund 2004; Dunning 2004; Knack 2004; Scott and Steele 2005; Hyde 2007; Kelley 2009; Hyde 2010; Levitsky and Way 2010; Hyde 2011b; Kelley 2012; Donno 2013.

[114] USAID 2009.    [115] McCoy 1993: 130.    [116] Marinov 2004, 2005; McFaul 2010.

[117] Data are drawn from Hyde and Marinov 2012 (Question 57), although these counts of violations and reactions are difficult to say with certainty, as discussed in this source and elsewhere.

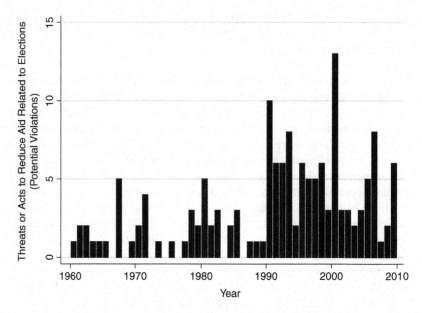

Figure 3.6 International Election-Related Aid Reactions
Note: Data are drawn from Hyde and Marinov 2012 (Question 57).

suggest that they, as well as IGO membership removals, are imposed after violations of existing rules.[118] The evidence is even starker given that aid sanctions can be difficult to definitively detect in the aggregate.[119] Many post-conflict cases show such sanctions.[120] Chapter 7 shows significant evidence of these and other responses, most often temporarily freezing funds or threatening to do so, in the main cases. In addition, Chapter 6 shows that conditionality and pressure – punishments or rewards, and "mediation, diplomatic missions, and shaming" conditioned on abiding by the rules of the game – are invoked in 77 percent of post-conflict elections after settlements with electoral participation (although data are only available from 1990 forward, so I cannot test whether the level changed as the Cold War ended).[121] Democracy and governance assistance is just one example of an incentive that can be conditioned on

[118] Boulding and Hyde 2005; von Borzyskowski and Vabulas 2014.
[119] Some states move more slowly in enacting violations; by contrast, Sweden and the European Union, among others, are more responsive to more violations.
[120] For example, see, Suhrke and Buckmaster 2005; Frerks 2006; Emmanuel and Rothchild 2007; Manning and Malbrough 2010.
[121] Donno 2013.

compliance; as with other forms of assistance, it can serve as both carrot and stick in these contexts.

### State Characteristics Alter the Effectiveness of Aid and Observation

The characteristics of a state may also affect international electoral observation and democracy and governance aid. Strong strategic or economic interests by outsiders, especially crucial alliances or trading partnerships providing valuable natural resources, leave this mechanism ineffective in some states.[122] A threat to sanction an important partner in the government may not be credible; thus the balanced engagement that could make electoral participation a useful component of peace agreements is lacking. Or, perhaps those in power in these states are less exposed to punishments from international actors; this argument is made about the lack of utility of aid conditionality in states that possess large reserves of natural resources (they are less concerned about losing aid because they have ample funds from this trade).[123] Governments with strategic or other special relationships with the West or other important actors may be more able to pursue whatever policies they prefer,[124] and so their credibility to commit to compliance with a deal is low. Natural-resource wealth and security ties to a hegemonic state may make "strategically, politically or economically important countries" difficult to punish.[125] Other studies similarly find that international enforcement in other contexts is reduced under these conditions.[126]

The availability of external engagement therefore varies, first, with the regional trends in monitoring and conditional incentives under democracy promotion programs, and, second, with state characteristics. Overall, states that have characteristics or are in regions that make them unlikely to receive nonpartisan engagement through the electoral process to enforce compliance simply may not hold post-conflict elections, or they may hold elections but without expectations of monitoring or conditional incentives, and therefore often also without provisions for rebel groups to participate as part of a settlement.

### The Availability of External Engagement Changes with the Global Context

The end of the Cold War represented an important change in the international community's involvement in civil conflict termination and

---

[122] Carothers 1999: 45.   [123] Girod 2011.   [124] Donno 2013: 21.
[125] Simmons 2009: 122; Donno 2013: 25.   [126] See, for example, Donno 2013: 29.

elections. With the fall of the Berlin Wall, international actors – especially the United States, other western powers, and related intergovernmental organizations – became more likely to coordinate to promote liberal values such as peace, human rights, good governance, and democracy. International actors could use the mechanisms they developed to monitor and sanction violations of these standards in any state – including post-conflict states. Much of this external engagement occurs through the electoral process. Democracy promotion has developed in regional waves, and, in each region, the tools for promoting democracy allowed further engagement, especially through the electoral system, by international actors. They diffused through learning and emulation across regions. This chapter has shown some initial historical evidence of these changes, which were implied by the theory in the previous chapter, and, in doing so, also provide the context in which the theory is situated. This context of emerging democracy promotion programs, in combination with the idea that violations can be observed more clearly under coordination cycles, help explain electoral participation provisions. The next chapters, using quantitative and qualitative evidence, present rigorous tests of particular implications of the theory, including comparisons across the end of the Cold War to study their causes.

# Causes of Electoral Participation Provisions

## Introduction to Part II

The previous chapter showed evidence – both historical and empirical – suggesting that external engagement has changed over time. Simultaneously, peace agreements, particularly those with electoral participation provisions, have increased. The theorized link between these patterns is that the end of the Cold War changed the global system in ways that enabled and encouraged international intervention, allowing combatants to settle civil conflicts by overcoming commitment problems through increased costs of noncompliance. Chapter 4 builds on the previous chapter to more rigorously test the relationships implied by the theory.

This section empirically investigates the puzzle of the causes of electoral participation provisions: when do combatants agree to transition to political parties to compete in post-conflict elections as the basis of a peace process? Terrorists and insurgents are agreeing to – and are being allowed to – become politicians. Many of the leaders of these groups must be removed from the U.S. Department of State's list of "foreign terrorist organizations" as part of the process, for instance, before they can campaign. Moreover, as described, combatants often only agree to engineered elections that may be intentionally designed to remove much of the uncertainty that holds democrats accountable to their populations, so that the elections do not produce a high degree of democracy.[1] The causes of the inclusion of electoral participation provisions are therefore intriguing.

Chapters 4 and 5, then, examine these transitions. The implications drawn from external engagement theory suggest that combatants agree to

---

[1] Schumpeter 1942; Lijphart 1968; Norris 2008; and, in post-conflict contexts, in particular, Walter 2002; Wantchekon 2004; Durant and Weintraub 2014; Hartzell and Hoddie 2015. See Chapter 2 for this discussion.

electoral participation provisions when their expectations of interested but nonpartisan international actors increase. As external actors became less tied to a particular side, and as they became increasingly interested in peace and engaged through elections, electoral participation provisions became useful for overcoming commitment problems that could otherwise prevent a deal. Chapter 4 finds correlations consistent with the implied patterns in cross-national evidence, and Chapter 5 identifies evidence of this causal mechanism through process-tracing in case studies. This chapter and the next also examine implications from other theories to see whether those better explain these perplexing transitions.

# 4    Trading Bullets for Ballots
## Examining the Inclusion of Electoral Participation Provisions

The campaign processes leading up to elections in Colombia in the early 1990s were tense. In 1985, the Revolutionary Armed Forces of Colombia (FARC) had formed the Patriotic Union (U.P.) to attempt electoral participation by running candidates during a ceasefire. The group sought to protect itself by not relinquishing its weapons or renouncing violence – indeed, not signing any peace agreement – because it remained concerned that the government would renege on the deal as it had in the past.[1] What followed was "politicide": party leaders, and even members, were assassinated by paramilitaries, at times backed by the military.[2] Despite having seen the politicide, however, in 1990 and 1991, the 19th of April Movement (M-19) and the other smaller groups signed peace agreements based on their electoral participation and formed political parties.[3]

Why were these rebel groups entering an electoral process – and potentially using it as a mechanism of enforcement? Many factors were similar in the 1980s and 1990s: the relative strength of the two sides on the battlefield was similar; the elections changed only slightly, allowing for more local and urban representation; and the government provided security to the opposition parties that was similar to what it had provided

---

[1] From my interview with the former negotiator Alberto Rojas Puyo in Bogotá, 2009. Jacobo Arenas, a FARC leader, pointed to past violations of peace agreements in making the decision to remain armed: "as soon as everyone laid down their arms ... the government failed to honor these promises" (quoted in Dudley 2004: 28).

[2] Bagley 1988; Ossa Escobar 1998: 9; Dudley 2004; and from my interview with the director of Reiniciar, a U.P. victim association, Jahel Quiroga in Bogotá, 2009.

[3] "Colombian Rebels Seek Status as Political Party" 1988; García Durán et al. 2008: 22–23. Informational and distributional concerns had likely been resolved by the mid-1980s: the government was locked in a stalemate with many of the guerrilla groups in Colombia, even as conflict was becoming more costly due to coca cultivation that created increasingly sophisticated challenges from each side (Riley 1993: 13; Chernick 1999: 173). In fact, a leader of M-19 at the time told me that they had "established beyond any doubt that the guerrilla movement could not win the war," and, if they could not establish the political gains that they wanted using guns, there was no point in continuing to attempt to do so (from my telephone interview with the former ADM-19 leader Antonio Navarro Wolff, 2012).

for the U.P.[4] The peace agreement and the involvement of international actors had changed, though. A deal with clear terms was signed, and international involvement was less tied to those opposing communism and more involved in ending the conflict in Colombia, allowing outsiders to help monitor and incentivize compliance with the settlement more easily. The United States had shifted from perpetual patron during the Cold War to skeptical participant in the war on drugs, as it conditioned aid on at least minimal protections of opponents and civilians after the U.S. administration changed.[5]

Election monitoring began in the 1990s. Observers had never been invited to the regularly held elections in the state in the past, but pressure mounted as more states in the region invited observers.[6] In this case, the Colombian government faced continued insurgency by other groups, and it only partially complied as a result of how it chose to fight the ongoing conflict. But the international community punished the Colombian government, and M-19 and the others accepted the partial compliance with continued peace.[7] The sanctions included restricted U.S. aid as well as investigations by intergovernmental organizations, including an Inter-American Commission on Human Rights visit after a decade of absence, in part to examine the assassinations of leftist leaders.[8] I return to these questions of sanction for partial compliance, including in this case, in Chapter 7, but, importantly, despite tensions in the 1990s, these electoral participants did not face the same politicide as in the 1980s.[9]

The Colombian case illustrates the possibility that a shifting role of external actors may be important for generating a peace agreement based on electoral participation provisions. Without that explanation, the case is puzzling. Not only had the M-19 and the smaller rebel groups recently experienced how badly politics could go, in the form of the FARC, but these smaller groups also had no chance of competing for significant power at the polls: the indigenous group was given a seat elected by the minority ethnicity, for example, and others were provided special combatant seats. What had changed to produce these electoral participation provisions in peace agreements in the 1990s?

---

[4] Pardo Rueda 1998: 19 Eaton 2006.
[5] National Security Council 1989b, 1989a; "Cocaine: A Supply Side Strategy" 1989; "En El 89, Washington Pensó En Enviar Tropas a Colombia" 2010.
[6] Santa-Cruz 2005.    [7] For example, see Ossa Escobar 1998; Pardo Rueda 1998.
[8] Organization of American States 1993; Cepeda Castro 2006.
[9] From my interview with the director of Reiniciar, a U.P. victim association, Jahel Quiroga in Bogotá, 2009; and from my interview with then president of the U.P., Mario Upegui, Bogotá 2009.

This chapter suggests that expectations of external engagement may explain some of the variation in the inclusion of electoral participation provisions.[10] Electoral participation provisions are likely to be included in peace agreements after the end of the Cold War and then typically when high regional rates of democracy promotion exist. These patterns proxy the availability of international actors, especially the United States and Western intergovernmental organizations, interested in peace and non-partisan in the conflict. When available, these actors can be engaged through electoral cycles in which the ex-combatant parties are set to participate in order to detect and sanction violations of deals. Increasing expectations of availability can be overridden by governments that have significant strategic or other special relationships with international actors, however, if the latter take sides in the conflict. Under the right conditions – expectations of nonpartisan external engagement – combatants should include electoral participation provisions to commit to a peace deal by easing detection and sanctioning of noncompliance. This chapter shows evidence that is consistent with these implications and less consistent with those of alternative explanations, which are also tested.

This chapter examines cross-national quantitative evidence to see if the correlates of electoral participation provisions are those implied by the theory. These tests can show whether associations hold across cases. Case studies in the next chapter identify the causal mechanisms. The two types of analysis, quantitative and qualitative, complement each other. To the extent possible with observational data about peace processes, this analysis focuses on plausibly exogenous variation in expectations in order to better identify relationships. I address questions about potential selection effects at each stage of the analysis.

The chapter first briefly discusses the variation of interest, building on the previous chapter. Next, using the hypotheses from external engagement theory and alternative explanations, it describes how each is tested in this context. The chapter then analyzes which peace agreements in civil conflicts include provisions for electoral participation. It addresses selection concerns related to signing and implementing agreements, including by testing which civil conflicts are most likely to terminate through this particular type of peace agreement as opposed to another outcome. Finally, this chapter turns to the alternative explanations. It concludes with a discussion that returns to the puzzle.

---

[10] This chapter draws on, and shares figures and tables with Matanock 2016a.

## Peace Agreements and Electoral Participation Provisions

This chapter uses the data described in Chapter 3 to examine the conditions under which peace agreements include electoral participation provisions. Analyzing variation across peace agreements is a nice test because the combatants may indicate by signing that the informational and distributional issues that might prevent a settlement at all have been solved in these cases.[11] The question is what type of provisions they include in the peace agreements to overcome commitment issues. Additional checks, however, consider questions of selection that could affect these results by moving in both directions in the set of choices that the combatants consider – back to whether to sign a settlement at all, and forward to whether to implement it.

The time period of the datasets, 1975 to 2005, allows examination of the third wave of democratization, which began in 1974, creating a comparison among cases that all experience normative pressure to hold elections.[12] Nonetheless, I am also careful to control for the end of the Cold War, and to drop the Cold War cases in alternative specifications, as well as other time periods (post-9/11, for example) in which other pressures to overlook noncompliance potentially may mount.

### Among Peace Agreements

The initial set of cases that are the focus of these cross-national analyses, then, is all peace agreements in civil conflicts, from 1975 to 2005, as described in the previous chapter. As discussed previously, the agreements are coded from the UCDP Peace Agreement Dataset, clustered by peace process, and separated by rebel group-government dyad. Coding by dyad becomes important in this analysis because different rebel groups in the same state can sign, and, more commonly, implement, different terms of an agreement. They also have different values on group-level controls, such as rebel force size, and dyad-level controls, such as the relative strength of the rebel forces vis-à-vis government forces, even though the main independent variables are at the state-year, region-year, and system-year levels. Dyadic data are thus preferable, although only 12 agreements have multiple dyadic signatories, so the results change little when data on the agreement level rather than the dyad level are used.[13] As also noted in

---

[11] Blainey 1988; and on civil conflict, see Powell 2006; Fearon 2007; although some do not believe that these issues are necessarily resolved, such as Mattes and Savun 2010.

[12] Huntington 1991; Levitsky and Way 2010: 14.

[13] The results in this chapter are similar when this analysis is performed as a robustness check. All analyses also always cluster the standard errors by state.

the previous chapter, these coding rules produce a set of peace agreements similar to other datasets, such as the Peace Accord Matrix.

### Among Civil Conflicts

As described, however, there could be a selection effect whereby some civil conflicts simply never reach a settlement, perhaps because they do not have international involvement available that would allow for enforcement through electoral participation provisions, and these conflicts could also be correlated with different variables than are peace agreements without electoral participation provisions. While considering only the decision within the set of peace agreements increases similarity among cases by conditioning on the ability of the two sides to negotiate a settlement, it may also produce different results than would considering all civil conflicts. In the secondary analysis I step back to the whole set of choices that the combatants consider, including not signing an agreement (see Figure 2.5 in Chapter 2).

The secondary set of cases, then, is all civil conflicts. This analysis identifies correlates of terminating through peace agreements with electoral participation provisions among all civil conflicts. I draw on data on civil conflicts reaching the 25-battle-death threshold from 1975–2005 using the UCDP Conflict Termination Dataset.[14] These data include each rebel group–government dyad from when it starts fighting until it definitively ends. I code definitively ending as the achievement of an alliance, a victory by either side, or a peace agreement of any sort.[15] If the conflict drops below the battle-death threshold due to a ceasefire or a petering out of fighting, I consider the dyad to continue to be a candidate for a peace agreement for eight years, which is the furthest out from active conflict that any peace agreements are seen in the dataset. Some cases have multiple entries over time because, for instance, a dyad returns to conflict after a settlement. The analysis parses which variables are associated with termination through a peace agreement that

---

[14] Kreutz 2010.

[15] This follows the coding categories in Kreutz 2010. His coding also includes some additions compared to the peace agreement data. For example, M-19 in Colombia is coded as signing a deal in 1989 in this dataset, which has electoral participation provisions, but is not in the peace agreement dataset. Each of these cases is listed in the Online Appendix at https://dataverse.harvard.edu/dataverse/matanock. This dataset seems to capture more cases that come close to terminating through a victory or some other outcome but where combatants still sign a peace agreement. Including these cases, through this secondary analysis, is also useful to overcome any selection effects that could result. Most of these cases are, however, if anything, more settled than other cases, so any expected bias would work against positive findings on peace. I appreciate an anonymous reviewer for suggesting this.

includes electoral participation provisions as opposed to another type of termination.[16] These data make an even clearer case than the peace agreements for conducting a dyad-level analysis because rebel groups differ on when, and how, their campaigns terminate.

Both tests seek to address the same question – what explains the inclusion of electoral participation provisions – but the comparison sets are different. Examining peace agreements may be the most effective test because the combatants may indicate by signing a settlement that the informational and distributional issues that may prevent an agreement have been resolved. Examining all civil conflicts, however, allows assessment of whether selection into an agreement drives the results.

*Electoral Participation Provisions*

The variation of interest is whether or not electoral participation provisions are included in a particular peace agreement. Electoral participation provisions consist of agreement on the two components described in the previous chapter: agreement to hold elections and agreement to allow participation by the rebel group as a political party. I analyzed the full text of each peace agreement to identify whether the deal includes clear expectations to hold elections and clear expectations that both sides will run candidates through the rules detailed in Chapter 3. As noted, electoral participation provisions are typically easy to identify, but less clear cases are recoded in robustness checks as discussed in Chapter 3.[17] The complete list, which notes the less clear cases, is in the Online Appendix.[18]

The resulting dataset contains 122 dyadic peace agreements between 81 different dyads in 49 civil conflicts in 43 states between 1975 and 2005. Of these, 51 peace agreements (42 percent) include electoral

[16] There are a few cases, such as Liberia, in which the terms of the agreement are renegotiated without a return to conflict. This analysis, as well as that in Chapter 6, examines the terms of the first deal because that terminates the conflict. The results are similar, though, if these cases are coded based on the terms of the last deal.
[17] The results in this chapter are similar under each robustness check reversing the coding decision on less clear cases. One coding decision that may be of particular interest for policymakers is the difference between electoral participation provisions created by implicitly legalizing the rebel group through its inclusion as a political party in a transitional government or by explicitly legalizing it in the peace agreement as a political party to run in elections, as described in Chapter 3. While separating these two categories decreases the sample size, of course, the signs on their coefficients are similar. There are more electoral participation provisions that fall into the first category and, not surprisingly, the estimated coefficients on that variable are larger and more consistently statistically significant. I also assess these two categories separately on conflict recurrence in Chapter 6.
[18] See https://dataverse.harvard.edu/dataverse/matanock.

participation provisions. Those without these provisions usually have alternative institutional arrangements written into their text, which are often regional autonomy arrangements.

*Implementation of Electoral Participation Provisions*    It is possible that electoral participation provisions may be included but never implemented. External engagement theory allows for this possibility, assuming the reneging side is sanctioned for noncompliance, as I discuss in later chapters. It is important that the measure of electoral participation provisions does not depend on implementation, however. Measuring participatory elections would mean assessing whether one aspect – electoral participation provisions – but not necessarily other aspects had been implemented. It would thus combine processes and pressures occurring after the inclusion decision into any assessment of what induces their plan to hold a participatory election.[19]

Failure to implement after including electoral participation provisions, however, could be due to a selection effect, as some actors may strategically choose to adopt such provisions in certain agreements without expectations of carrying them out. Thus, in additional analysis, I distinguish between those combatants that implement electoral participation provisions to which they agreed, and those that do not, which is taking a step forward in the set of choices that combatants face (as shown in Figure 2.5 in Chapter 2). I code whether the government followed through on the agreement to actually hold elections within 10 years and whether the rebel group actually participated. I show some summary statistics on when these provisions are implemented. The main analysis, however, removes these many potentially confounding factors by focusing on the inclusion of electoral participation provisions.

Implementation occurs in 81 percent of peace agreements that include electoral participation provisions,[20] meaning that the governments hold the elections and the rebel groups participate as political parties.

## When Are Electoral Participation Provisions Included?

This chapter examines when electoral participation provisions are included in peace agreements. Each of the hypotheses from external engagement theory, laid out in Chapter 2, is about changing expectations

---

[19] In examining the consequences of electoral participation provisions, performed in Chapter 6, measuring implementation would entail adding post-treatment variables into the analysis, which could result in bias, as I discuss in that chapter.

[20] Combining agreements that had peaceful renegotiations between them, as described regarding the conflict data, as well as the data in Chapter 6.

of international involvement through the electoral process. This is the mechanism hypothesized to allow both sides to commit to compliance through the threat of external enforcement.

Expectations of external engagement are difficult to measure *ex-ante*. These variables must capture beliefs from the combatants about external actors' willingness to engage through elections to seek information and provide conditional incentives based on compliance. Building on the theory, as well as the evidence shown in Chapter 3, the measures fall into three categories: systemic shocks, trends in conventions and institutions that shift across region and time, and characteristics of the state that may cause deviations from the expectations of external engagement otherwise associated with these shocks and trends. Most proxy variables for these expectations precede and are somewhat exogenous to decisions by combatants to include electoral participation provisions, thereby suggesting some support for a causal effect. This subsection briefly overviews each implication, and its measures, from external engagement theory before doing the same for alternative explanations.

### The End of the Cold War

The end of the Cold War increased international coordination on civil conflict termination, as described in depth in Chapter 3. The simultaneous emergence of new mechanisms for observing and incentivizing compliance through elections for both sides provided a potentially less costly method of international involvement, as also described in the previous chapter. Together, these developments increased expectations of nonpartisan international enforcement through the electoral process, which should increase the inclusion of electoral participation provisions in peace agreements. Chapter 3 initially explored these correlations, and this chapter more carefully examines whether electoral participation provisions are more prevalent in peace agreements after the Cold War (Hypothesis H1 from Table 2.2 in Chapter 2).

This chapter, as well as the case studies in Chapter 5, thus exploits the end of the Cold War, measured as a cut point in 1989, as a plausibly exogenous shock to these civil conflicts.[21] Measuring across it, I can examine whether the inclusion of electoral participation provisions increases (and also whether enforcement expectations increase, measured qualitatively, in the next chapter). The geopolitical shift, however, may also have

---

[21] Following existing intervention literature, including, for example, Fortna 2008.

had other effects on propensity for conflict. The other hypotheses examined in this chapter may therefore hold comparatively more weight.

### Trends in Democracy Promotion

Clear systematic variation in expectations of international engagement existed across cases after the end of the Cold War. Rates of democracy promotion increased by region, as shown in Chapter 3. As discussed in depth in Chapters 2 and 3, these rates should be positively correlated with expectations of external engagement through the electoral process, monitoring and providing incentives conditional on compliance with electoral rules; they should thus also be positively correlated with electoral participation provisions. The chapter therefore also examines whether provisions are more prevalent in peace agreements with higher regional rates of democracy promotion (Hypothesis H1a).

Variation in expectations of international engagement even after the end of the Cold War is thus best measured through proxy variables: (1) the percentage of legislative elections in the region that international missions observed in the year prior to the peace agreement, excluding the state under analysis;[22] and (2) the percentage of regional development assistance that is devoted to democracy and governance, averaged over the two prior years.[23] The expectation that these programs will be in place in post-conflict elections depends on the commitment of nonpartisan external enforcers.

These measures are closely tied to the theory about the institutions developed for democracy promotion. The regional election observation

---

[22] Hyde and Marinov 2012. Like studies of international election observation (Hyde 2011b; Kelley 2012), I drop "mature" democracies from regional calculations, which are 21 states from the analysis that have been steadily democratic since 1950 (Dahl 2003). Legislative elections are the most comparable measures across cases. Several cases had legislative elections that were technically unmonitored in the relevant years, but other elections in the same states are monitored in the same years (typically presidential elections taking place in another month). Because most of these cases worked against my hypotheses, I counted these as monitored. The results hold in either case. I also include all elections in an alternative specification, and the variables are similar in these data (correlated at 0.95). I also smooth over multiple years. The lagged variable is preferable because it captures when the combatants are likely assessing international actors' ability and willingness to engage without partisanship in elections. The estimated coefficients for these alternative methods of coding observation are positive and substantively similar. I also follow Hyde (2011b) in adopting five regions – Africa, the Americas, Asia, Europe, North Africa, and the Middle East – but I also code alternative specifications, such as continents, those sharing regional organizations, and UCDP's classification, which produce similar results but are slightly weaker (in the peace agreement data, for instance, they lose statistical significance at the standard levels with the controls added, except the UCDP classification).

[23] Finkel et al. 2007.

variable, in particular, represents expectations of international engagement through the electoral process; these expectations are likely higher in regions where international engagement spread more rapidly in relation to systemic characteristics, especially the level of international interest in the region, as Chapter 2 describes and Chapter 3 shows.[24] The evidence and the theories examined in the previous chapters identify diffusion mechanisms, suggesting that learning and emulation by domestic and international actors increase information about the available policy options, especially regarding their costs and benefits.[25] As some states adopt elections that democracy promoters support, other closely comparable states, often in the same regions, adopt similar measures.[26] Regions geographically closest to the Western major powers were affected first, while regions further away – especially Asia, as discussed – were affected last. As discussed in Chapter 2, this is not to suggest a fully functionalist argument, but combatants and the international actors who advise them seem to have learned from experience. The case studies in the next chapter show more evidence of the regional spread: for example, positive experiences enforcing a deal with electoral participation provisions in El Salvador and other democratic rules of the game in Central America seem to have influenced the design of Guatemala's peace agreement.

Regional democracy promotion variables are not likely to be determined by the future inclusion of electoral participation provisions in potential peace agreements in a particular state, and diverse studies show that these variables are also not likely determined by promising environments for peace due to a mechanism other than international interest. International election observation and other democracy promotion institutions spread geographically from the West at different rates, likely reflecting the amount of international interest in that part of the world, which then drove expectations about external engagement.[27] If selection occurs, background interviews with Carter Center and U.N. officials suggest it would be toward less stable states, like all intervention, across all regions. Broader testing in other work shows that these trends do not match stability or even the spread of democracy.[28]

These lagged regional variables are thus plausibly exogenous to the decision made by the rebel group and the government, which is crucial in seeking to identify causal relationships. The invitation of international election observers to the state being studied would not only be highly endogenous – if a rebel group and a government anticipate that their deal

---

[24] See Hyde 2011b; Kelley 2012.    [25] Elkins and Simmons 2005; Simmons et al. 2006.
[26] Santa-Cruz 2005; Hyde 2011b; Kelley 2012.    [27] Hyde 2011b; Kelley 2012.
[28] Simpser and Donno 2012: 507.

will stand due to some omitted factor, they may be more likely to include many provisions and invite many monitors, for example – but also an aspect of implementation of the agreement.[29] These lagged, regional variables – which also exclude the state in question in the regional election observation variable – are better able to identify a causal relationship because they would not be predicated on these endogenous factors. Regional variables are therefore good proxies, which others also use for similar purposes.[30]

These regional electoral observation and regional democracy and governance assistance variables correlate highly, as expected: 0.44 in the peace agreement sample. Each variable increases over time across regions, but the regional democracy and governance assistance variable fluctuates less and deviates less from a direct time trend, compared to the regional electoral observation variable, so the latter provides both greater explanatory leverage (see Chapter 3 for the trends over time by region); additionally, data on the former are currently only available after the Cold War.

### Strategic or Other Special Relationships with the West

States may still differ in the expectations of international engagement beyond the end of the Cold War and the regional trends in democracy promotion. As described in Chapter 2, special relationships with the state of interest weaken the leverage of potential interveners by reducing the likelihood that these international actors can, or will, impose serious sanctions for violations by the government side, in particular. Governments with valuable natural resources, or those of strategic importance may not need to adhere as strictly to the rules of any deal.[31] A strong relationship between potential enforcers and the government about to enter into a peace agreement may thus derail expectations of nonpartisan settlement enforcement. In these cases, the international actor is less likely to be trusted to enforce compliance by both sides. These correlations can be tested

---

[29] Most post-conflict elections that are held receive some international election observation, although the commitment to enforce compliance for both sides varies. Not all do, however: for instance, Mali after the 1991 agreement; Djibouti after the 1994 agreement; the Philippines after the 1995, 1996, and 2001 agreements; and the U.K. after the 1998 agreement did not. The majority of these agreements did not include electoral participation provisions, which is likely due to the expectation that they are in regions or have country characteristics (discussed below), that make them unlikely to receive this enforcement through the electoral process.

[30] See, for example, Simpser and Donno 2012.

[31] Shown in other cases of election observation and aid conditionality, including Girod 2011; Donno 2013.

quantitatively: this chapter examines whether electoral participation provisions are less prevalent in peace agreements in states with strategic or other special relationships with major powers (Hypothesis H1b).

The first measure of such relationships is a binary indicator of oil production, lagged one year.[32] As an alternative, I also consider a more exogenous variable, oil reserves,[33] although these reserves may not yet be under production and may be potentially costly to exploit, and the argument about overriding enforcement promises may be most relevant for states already supplying oil. The second set of measures of strategic partnership captures crucial relationships with specific major powers. One of these measures is a binary indicator of military aid from the United States, also lagged one year.[34] The United States provides more military aid worldwide than any other state and is the most likely to be involved in intervention after the Cold War. Moreover, given U.S. hegemony after 1990, other international actors are also unlikely to be able to serve as nonpartisan enforcers when the United States has a strong relationship with the state of interest. Certain colonial ties also remain important and may signal a strategic stake: France, as well as the United Kingdom, in particular, usually side with one domestic faction that receives their continued support. Thus engagement by these external actors carries lower expectations of sufficient nonpartisanship to credibly threaten to sanction either side. I therefore include indicators of former British and French colonies.[35] As alternatives, I consider other relationships, such as any previous colonial ties or alliances with the major powers, although they may not signal a sufficiently strong relationship to afford the government this trump card. I also consider relationships such as affinity with major powers in U.N. voting records that may indicate willingness for external actors to engage electorally in those states, rather than a relationship that would prevent states from doing so, as they may not signal a geostrategic stake that would bias these international actors.[36]

### Considering Other Explanations

Beyond external engagement theory, there are other possible explanations for variation in the inclusion of electoral participation provisions in

---

[32] Ross 2011.    [33] Lujala et al. 2007.

[34] USAID 2009. Alternatively, I use oil production, value, and per capita production, as well as U.S. military aid, both total and per capita; the estimated coefficients are usually negative and often statistically significant in the models presented in this chapter.

[35] Fearon and Laitin 2003.

[36] As expected, these relationships are more mixed, and the coefficients on any colony and on U.N. voting affinity are typically positive, perhaps indicating a signal of intention to engage to keep the peace rather than partisanship.

a peace agreement, mostly drawn from the alternatives described in more depth in Chapter 2; a few additional alternatives, however, are drawn from the broader democratization literature or the literature on holding nondemocratic elections. Other factors, aside from simply the considerations about external engagement, are likely to affect the decision to base a peace agreement on electoral participation provisions. Many of these alternatives complement external engagement theory, while a few compete with it.

The first set of alternative explanations relate to the international context, like external engagement theory: the escape explanation, in its more cynical version, argues that an international actor who has intervened will need at least the illusion of a partner government to exit that commitment. These actors must have a deployment from which they wish to escape, and larger engagements, especially in terms of troops, may produce more incentives to escape. Even in the less cynical version, in which international actors seek to establish a legitimate partner government before they exit, they must have intervened or be planning to intervene in order to have reason to establish an exit route.

The correlates of electoral participation provisions under this explanation are armed interveners – usually peacekeepers – in place or planned; moreover, more troops may imply a more urgent need to exit. The variables used to measure this alternative agreement are variables on armed intervention, and then troop size therein. The initial measure that I use is an indicator of intrastate U.N. peacekeeping mission presence when the deal is signed.[37] These missions are coded by country, but few have multiple conflicts, so coding at a lower level would change little. These data follow the convention of excluding interventions in interstate conflicts, such as the India-Pakistan conflict.[38] As alternatives, I consider indicators for provisions for U.N. peacekeeping in the settlement and U.N. peacekeeping missions that start by the end of the year in which the settlement is signed, because the international actor may have already been consulted prior to the mandate.[39] I also consider armed

---

[37] The data are drawn from Hegre et al. 2010, supplemented by data from the World Bank 2011, which extends the dates of the missions in Sierra Leone and Cambodia. The Kosovo mission also appears as occurring in Serbia until the independence of the new state. These match the cases included in the United Nations's list of peacekeeping operations, which does not include, for instance, the political mission in Guatemala before 1997. This coding should work in favor of the alternative escape theory as peacekeeping missions should be among those looking to exit. Alternative measures are considered as robustness checks, as described.

[38] Doyle and Sambanis 2006; Fortna 2008; World Bank 2011.

[39] In Sudan, for example, a U.N. representative visited the state just before the 2005 peace agreement was signed to make recommendations for how to design the mission (although

interventions by regional organizations or ad hoc state groupings,[40] and I consider past missions, of this type and of just the United Nations.[41] Finally, I also limit the analysis in an alternative specification to only "enforcement" missions because these robust force deployments may be the most costly.[42] In secondary tests, I also analyze the size of these missions by the number of troops in the year in which the agreement is signed, and, as an alternative, the maximum number of troops over the U.N. interventions.[43] The escape explanation implies that international interventions, perhaps especially large interventions, have cost concerns and are likely to push for elections to exit. A correlation between peacekeepers and electoral participation provisions, however, could also signal broader expectations of external engagement, so only the coerciveness and size distinguish between this alternative explanation and the book's theory.

The enjoinder explanation, the idea that external actors prefer to engage through elections over any other mechanism, will look almost the same in this set of implications as external engagement theory. However, the other implications, examined in subsequent chapters, will allow some tests between them.

Another alternative explanation that relates to the international context is an emulation explanation. It suggests that electoral participation provisions are chosen because of normative trends on how ruling *should* be done, implying that these provisions are more likely when certain characteristics are present. This emulation explanation produces similar implications to the broader literature on democratization, as well as the literature on holding elections in nondemocratic contexts, and together

this was in August 2004 after the political power-sharing agreement in May 2004); see Oswald et al. 2010: 494.

[40] Drawing on news sources, as well as Fortna 2008; Mullenbach and Dixon 2007.

[41] Each of these alternative specifications of armed intervention is similar in the results that they produce, compared to the preferred measure, and they are described in more depth in the Codebook in the Online Appendix at https://dataverse.harvard.edu/dataverse/matanock. These variables are somewhat correlated with regional election observation (0.20–0.30 in the peace agreement data), and provisions for peacekeeping in the settlement wash out the statistical significance of the latter, but usually only when the two are included without the strategic or other special relationship variables. Almost all of estimated coefficients for these peacekeeping measures are positive in the models presented in this chapter, and many of them are statistically significant when included without other variables but rarely with them.

[42] I use three different coding schemes for this measure: Chapter 7 missions coded based on Fortna 2008, also applying the Kosovo mission to Serbia until independence; Chapter 7 missions coded by Doyle and Sambanis 2000; and, finally, the Mattes and Savun's 2009 coding of "enforcement" missions, which incorporates Fortna 2008 and their own additional cases outside of the United Nations. These estimated coefficient variables are positive but generally not statistically significant when included with the other covariates in the models presented in this chapter.

[43] World Bank 2011.

they compose a potential selection effect. Electoral participation provisions may be more likely when systems, states, or groups have characteristics suggesting that they have a propensity to follow conventions on elections. I test whether these electoral participation provisions appear when anticipated by these explanations by examining whether their inclusion is correlated with such variables at the systemic, state, conflict, and actor levels, including whether the group has aims more consistent with elections and whether the government already holds elections in the state. In addition, economic development in the state may play a role in these contexts, as may some characteristics of the regime, not limited to its history with democracy.

The correlates of electoral participation provisions based on these explanations are these organizational characteristics at each level. At the actor and conflict levels, the measures are rebel group aims – including whether groups seek change in the central government as opposed to secession, and whether they are mobilized along ethnic lines or pursuing communism, which may both affect their propensity to participate in elections.[44] As alternatives, I also consider the ethnic and religious fractionalization and balance in the state, which, in the institutional design literatures, are frequently related to both democratization and conflict.[45] In addition, I add an indicator of whether the conflict is about total control of the structures of the state.[46] At the state level, the measures are both related to the development of the state[47] and its institutions, including its bureaucratic quality and regime type, including its experience with democracy.[48] In addition, I measure ties between the state and the international community that are thought to foster democracy more broadly, including aid dependence, trade openness, and membership in the GATT or WTO, plus, as an alternative, membership in densely democratic regional intergovernmental organizations.[49] At the systemic level, the measures include both region and time indicators, including those for the Cold War and for the period post-9/11, as well as the rate of democracy by region and, more specifically, within neighboring states.[50] This final element is most directly linked to the democratization arguments: as democracy increases around the world, electoral participation provisions should be increasingly included in peace agreements.

Another selection effect, the ease explanation, suggests that electoral participation provisions are included just for show in any cases that the

---

[44] Eck 2009; Kalyvas and Balcells 2010.
[45] See, for example, Fish and Kroenig 2006; Joshi and Mason 2011; Cederman et al. 2012.
[46] This concept is developed in Walter 2004; Kreutz 2010.     [47] Boix and Stokes 2003.
[48] These measures include those used by Brancati and Snyder 2013.
[49] Pevehouse 2002, 2005.     [50] Gleditsch and Ward 2006.

combatants expect to be easy to settle. Peace agreements may include these provisions not because of the exogenous context but because combatants expect the conflict to be settled easily for endogenous reasons. This explanation, then, suggests that the correlates of electoral participation provisions are conflicts that are more easily settled. Many of these variables are identified through a pre-1989 sample in which international involvement of any type should be minimal, so it should not affect the propensity of conflict recurrence, allowing identification of the influence of other variables.[51] It is also possible that if these provisions are included in peace agreements that are expected to be easy, they should correlate with many other provisions because any number of them could be added if the deal is already expected to stand anyway.[52]

The correlates of electoral participation provisions based on these explanations are indicators of these easier cases. Some strategic variables capture conflicts thought to be easier, including those without oil, for example. Beyond these, however, stronger states and smaller conflicts are also thought to be easier to settle, identified in pre-1989 data as just described. At the actor and conflict levels, the measures are the number of battle deaths and how many years the conflict is fought, as well as whether past agreements failed and the number of factions fighting.[53] Although less plausibly exogenous, I also consider the size of the rebel and government forces and the balance between the two sides, as well as how they fight and whether they are funded largely by contraband.[54] The variable capturing balance between the two sides should capture victories masquerading as settlements, which may be easier to settle, and which might also be tied to the decision to include electoral participation provisions. To assess whether certain peace agreements simply include all sorts of electoral participation provisions, I also use other provisions in the UCDP Peace Agreement Dataset and code a variable for whether further negotiations were called for but not

---

[51] Fortna 2008; I also employ this strategy, as discussed in Chapter 6.
[52] Hartzell and Hoddie 2015.     [53] Gleditsch et al. 2002; Lacina and Gleditsch 2005.
[54] Fearon and Laitin 2003; Cunningham et al. 2009. A component of this explanation, which also fits with the selection effect based on ease of emulation, is that rebel groups that are stronger and operate in weaker states may be better able to secure electoral participation provisions than weaker rebel groups operating in stronger states. The former may have more leverage in the negotiation of a settlement, and, crucially, they may also be more likely to win seats with such a settlement. (They may also, of course, be more likely to be able to earn any kind of concessions but perhaps also to win the conflict outright; see, for example, Gent 2011; Clayton 2013; Hultquist 2013.) As I will show, though, the correlations between strength and electoral participation provisions are not very robust (although more so in the conflict data than the peace agreement data). I appreciate this suggestion from an anonymous reviewer.

completed.[55] At the state level, the measures are about the strength of the state, including GDP per capita and, as alternatives, indexes of their capabilities and the difficulty of the terrain.[56] These, of course, relate to the development indicators discussed as tests of the emulation explanation. At the systemic level, I also control for whether any neighboring countries have conflicts. These controls go beyond a robustness check to allow characterizations of peace agreements based on different sets of provisions to be included together. (Tables A.4.1 and A.4.2 in the Online Appendix show summary statistics for the variables.)[57]

## When Do Peace Agreements Include Electoral Participation Provisions?

Among peace agreements, the variation of interest is the inclusion of provisions for electoral participation. As an alternative, the variation of interest is implementation of these provisions, as discussed. Inclusion and implementation of electoral participation provisions are not rare events; inclusion, for example, occurs in almost half of the cases. I therefore fit a logistic regression model using a binary indicator of electoral participation provisions as the dependent variable and, later, a binary indicator of their implementation.[58] The standard errors are clustered by state because there is some possibility for autocorrelation of the errors.[59]

### Inclusion across Peace Agreements

The end of the Cold War, as well as the regional indicators of international interest in democracy promotion, are positively associated with the

---

[55] Harbom et al. 2006; Högbladh 2012; and see Hartzell and Hoddie 2015, which characterizes these as important sets of provisions.

[56] See https://dataverse.harvard.edu/dataverse/matanock. Singer et al. 1972; Fearon and Laitin 2003; Heston et al. 2011.

[57] In addition to these variables, I include alternative variables: for conflict severity, logged battle deaths and conflict duration; for settlement difficulty, the main strategy used by the rebel group and others (see the Codebook for all of these variables in the Online Appendix at https://dataverse.harvard.edu/dataverse/matanock). The main results are similar across these specifications (unless, of course, controls with many missing values or multiple variables with strong correlations are included).

[58] Given the small size of the dataset, and the number of controls, I also run linear regression models (Angrist and Pischke 2009; Wooldridge 2002); the main results are similar. These models also enable tests of the outliers, and various tests suggest that there are only minimal influential outliers (for example, DFBETAs show no cases using the threshold of "1" although a number with a more sensitive threshold), but also that dropping these does not affect the direction or statistical significance of these models. I also re-ran the analysis, dropping each conflict as an additional robustness check.

[59] To address independence concerns, as mentioned, I also re-ran the analysis with the dependent variable as agreement instead of dyad; the results are similar.

Table 4.1 *Electoral Participation Provisions with Expectations of External Engagement*

| | Cold War (1975–1988) | Post (1989–2005) |
|---|---|---|
| Participation Provisions | **0% (0)** | **48% (51)** |
| None | 100% (15) | 52% (56) |
| | Fisher's exact=0.00 | |
| | Low Regional Election Observation | High Regional Election Observation |
| Participation Provisions | **25% (15)** | **59% (36)** |
| None | 75% (46) | 41% (25) |
| | Fisher's exact=0.00 | |
| | Low Regional Democracy Aid | High Regional Democracy Aid |
| Participation Provisions | **40% (21)** | **56% (30)** |
| None | 60% (32) | 44% (24) |
| | Fisher's exact=0.07 | |

inclusions of electoral participation provisions in peace agreements, as implied by external engagement theory. The correlation with the Cold War indicator is negative, and the relationship is statistically significant: none of the peace agreements negotiated during the Cold War include electoral participation provisions in these data, while 48 percent do afterwards (see Table 4.1). In the following models, I include an indicator for the Cold War, which perfectly correlates with no electoral participation provisions.[60] The democracy promotion variables, split at their medians, are also shown in these cross-tabs. The correlations with these – which vary by region and over time – are both positive, and these relationships are also statistically significant. They are also large: a 34 percent difference in the low versus high regional election observation categories, and a 16 percent difference in the low versus high regional democracy aid variable.

These simple comparisons show the expected relationships, and they remain consistent – in fact they increase in magnitude – with the inclusion of indicators of strategic and special relationships. The estimated coefficient for the regional election observation is the most consistently

---

[60] Adding this control in the logistic regression models, then, produces an identical result to running the analysis and dropping the 15 Cold War cases.

statistically significant across these models.[61] The regional election observation variable also varies most between the two democracy promotion variables, as mentioned, and deviates most from a simple time trend.[62] Thus, in the models with the controls, I use the regional election observation variable.

The estimated coefficients for the strategic and special relationship indicators also match the implications of external engagement theory, suggesting that international actors need to be nonpartisan. Estimated coefficients for indicators of lagged oil production, lagged U.S. military aid, and former British and French colonies are all negative and statistically significant at the standard levels in most specifications, except for those on oil and British colonies (particularly when controls for conflict intensity are included). The estimated coefficient for the alternative measure of oil – lagged reserves rather than production – is even larger, while that for the alternative measure of military aid – a logged lag rather than as a binary indicator lag – is not statistically significant with controls. The results of powerful colonial relationships are especially noteworthy, as the estimated coefficient for a binary indicator of *any* recent colonial relationship is never large or close to statistical significance at the standard levels. Those for other weaker variables, such as indicators of major power allies, are also not statistically significant, except for U.S. alliances, which is negative and statistically significant in some specifications.[63]

To interpret these results,[64] Table 4.2 also reports average marginal effects. They are large and statistically significant. For example, the

[61] The estimated coefficient for the regional democracy and governance assistance variable is always positive but often not statistically significant when additional control variables are included in the model.

[62] When included together, in the peace agreement data, for instance, the estimated coefficient for the regional democracy and governance assistance variable is no longer statistically significant at the standard levels, and, in some specifications, neither is that for the regional election observation variable; tests of the model, however, suggest that these variables included together improve the fit (compared to not being included). These variables are correlated and are used as measures for the same expectations, so it is not surprising that including them together should produce these results.

[63] These are, of course, weaker and more endogenous ties. Estimated coefficients for the colonial relationship indicators are usually negative in the analysis of the peace agreement but not the conflict dataset, but those for alliances are often positive (except usually U.S. allies), which may suggest that apart from these particularly invested Western powers, ties may actually indicate interest but not necessarily partisanship, increasing the inclusion of electoral participation provisions.

[64] The variation explained among peace agreements in these models is similar to that explained by other models of particular provisions. For example, efforts to analyze the number of power-dividing and power-sharing provisions in peace agreements are able to explain up to 20 percent of the variation (Hartzell and Hoddie 2007: 59). That is similar to what these models are able to explain. This, of course, suggests that there is other variation left unexplored, potentially due to idiosyncratic determinants or noisy measures.

Table 4.2 *Inclusion of Electoral Participation Provisions in Peace Agreements*

| | Model 1 | Model 2 | Model 3 | Model 4 | Model 5 | Average Marginal Effects[a] |
|---|---|---|---|---|---|---|
| Regional Election Observation (Percent, Lagged) | 2.24* (1.19) | | | 3.86*** (1.27) | | 0.71*** (0.20) |
| Regional Democracy/ Governance Assistance (Percent Development Aid, Lagged 2-year average) | | 7.06* (3.99) | | | 13.39** (5.46) | |
| Oil Production Indicator (Lagged) | | | −1.00** (0.42) | −1.11** (0.45) | −1.63*** (0.47) | −0.20** (0.08) |
| U.S. Military Aid Indicator (Lagged) | | | −1.24*** (0.41) | −1.34*** (0.45) | −1.11** (0.44) | −0.25*** (0.07) |
| Former British Colony | | | −1.04 (0.75) | −1.78** (0.79) | −1.31* (0.74) | −0.33** (0.15) |
| Former French Colony | | | −0.99*** (0.37) | −1.69*** (0.47) | −1.42*** (0.51) | −0.31*** (0.08) |
| Number of Observations | 107 | 107 | 107 | 107 | 107 | |
| Pseudo R-Squared | 0.04 | 0.03 | 0.13 | 0.21 | 0.20 | |
| Log Pseudo Likelihood | −70.73 | −72.00 | −64.13 | −58.15 | −59.60 | |

Note: Method is logistic regression analysis. DV is peace agreement with versus without electoral participation provisions. Numbers in parentheses are robust standard errors, clustered by state (maximum number of clusters is 41). Cold War indicator is always included and perfectly predicts failure (so 15 Cold War observations drop in all models).
* $p<0.10$, ** $p<0.05$, *** $p<0.01$.
[a] For Average Marginal Effects: These are based on Model 4. Table presents dx/dy, which, for factor level variables, is the discrete change from the base level. Numbers in parentheses are delta-method standard errors (robust).

predicted probability that a state in a region in which all elections in the past year were internationally observed will include electoral participation provisions is 71 percent higher than it is for a state in a region without election observation.

To further interpret these results, I also consider what the models would say about cases similar to those that I examine in the following chapter. The adjusted predictive margins on unlikely cases are very different from likely cases. Consider the example of Bangladesh in 1990, which does not sign a peace agreement with electoral participation provisions. The case features regional placement in Asia, no special or strategic relationships with likely external actors, no peacekeeping mission, no past peace agreements, and a conflict with territorial aims – thus, it is very unlikely to include electoral participation provisions because there is no expectation of the needed external engagement. Based on those values, the prediction is 0.03 (0.06). In contrast, consider the examples of El Salvador and Guatemala, which both obtained deals with these provisions. They scored differently from Bangladesh on most of these variables, and their predictions were 0.98 (0.03) and 0.90 (0.12), respectively. The analysis thus predicts a 3 percent chance of including electoral participation provisions in a case that looks like the Bangladeshi case, compared to a 90 to 98 percent chance in cases like those in Central America.

*Control Variables and Robustness Checks* When controls are added, the main results hold (see Table A.4.3 in the Online Appendix for the models).[65] In these specifications, all of the estimated coefficients on the variables described above are statistically significant, and that for the regional election observation variable is always positive, while those for the strategic and special relationship indicators are always negative. The size of these coefficients increases with the inclusion of many of these control variables, suggesting that the latter may moderate the relationship or reduce noise. The main results also hold when, as a robustness check, the analysis drops each conflict in turn.[66]

Including indicators of region, each decade in the data, and their interaction is a particularly difficult test of the regional democracy promotion variables, because, in the case of year indicators at the limit, these would be close to collinear. The estimated coefficients for these indicators are not individually statistically significant, but the estimated coefficient for the regional election observation variable remains large, positive, and statistically significant. This offers compelling evidence that the regional trend variable is not just identifying unexplained differences between regions or time periods in the data, but that its own changes are actually correlated with variation in the inclusion of electoral participation provisions.

---

[65] See https://dataverse.harvard.edu/dataverse/matanock.

[66] The only differences are: in ten cases with the time/region/interaction model, the estimated coefficient for the oil production indicator lost statistical significance, although it always remained negative. The same happened with that for the former British colony indicator in two cases. In seven cases the regional democracy and governance assistance variable lost statistical significance, although it remained positive, when it alone was included in the model; the same was true for the regional election observation variable with two cases (Burundi or Liberia).

These results, then, are consistent with the implications of external engagement theory. Before examining the alternative dataset of all conflicts, or considering the alternative explanations, I examine whether, among peace agreements, the correlates of implementation are the same as those of inclusion.

### Implementation across Peace Agreements

While inclusion is the most appropriate test of the theory, as discussed above, it is possible that combatants under particular circumstances sign peace agreements that include electoral participation provisions, but do not plan to implement them. External engagement theory anticipates some noncompliance, assuming the reneging side is sanctioned for violations, which I discuss in later chapters. But it is possible that the correlates of inclusion are not the same as those of implementation due to a selection effect. These provisions could be strategically included without an expectation of implementation in certain agreements. Therefore, I analyze when these provisions are implemented among the cases with peace agreements. This is one of the two selection explanations considered in this chapter.

In order to test the implementation of electoral participation provisions, I drew on the Militant Group Electoral Participation (MGEP) dataset, which examines when rebel groups participate as political parties in national legislative elections.[67] In those data, I assessed whether each rebel group participated in national legislative elections by running candidates under the banner of a political party, while fighting or in the 10 years after fighting ended.[68]

The analysis is thus now taking account of whether the government followed through on the agreement to actually hold elections, and whether the rebel group actually participated in those elections. Such implementation occurs in 34 cases among the peace agreements with electoral participation provisions, as noted.

Examining the implementation of, rather than provisions for, electoral participation produces similar results (see Table 4.3). The estimated coefficient for the regional democracy promotion variables are positive, while those for the indicators of special and strategic relationships are negative, and all are usually statistically significant at the standard levels, although those for the regional democracy and governance assistance

---

[67] Matanock 2016b.

[68] The data identify only three additional groups by using 10 rather than 5 years – the CNDD in Burundi, the MPA in the Comoros, the SPLM/A in Sudan – and the empirical patterns hold with or without their inclusion.

Table 4.3 *Implementation of Electoral Participation Provisions in Peace Agreements*

| | Model 1i | Model 2i | Model 3i | Model 4i | Model 5i | Average Marginal Effects[a] |
|---|---|---|---|---|---|---|
| Regional Election Observation (Percent, Lagged) | 2.32* (1.37) | | | 3.88** (1.51) | | 0.62*** (0.22) |
| Regional Democracy/ Governance Assistance (Percent Development Aid, Lagged 2-year average) | | 5.08 (5.41) | | | 11.16* (6.07) | |
| Oil Production Indicator (Lagged) | | | −0.84 (0.55) | −0.88 (0.55) | −1.27** (0.51) | −0.14 (0.09) |
| U.S. Military Aid Indicator (Lagged) | | | −0.91 (0.57) | −0.92 (0.59) | −0.80 (0.58) | −0.15 (0.09) |
| Former British Colony | | | −1.06 (0.84) | −1.73** (0.80) | −1.26* (0.74) | −0.28** (0.13) |
| Former French Colony | | | −1.55** (0.75) | −2.19*** (0.83) | −1.89** (0.81) | −0.35*** (0.10) |
| Number of Observations | 107 | 107 | 107 | 107 | 107 | |
| Pseudo R-Squared | 0.04 | 0.01 | 0.14 | 0.22 | 0.18 | |
| Log Pseudo Likelihood | −64.04 | −65.94 | −57.80 | −52.10 | −54.84 | |

Note: Method is logistic regression analysis. DV is peace agreement with versus without electoral participation (implemented). Numbers in parentheses are robust standard errors, clustered by state (maximum number of clusters is 41). Cold War indicator is always included and perfectly predicts failure (so 15 Cold War observations drop in all models). * $p<0.10$, ** $p<0.05$, *** $p<0.01$.
[a] For Average Marginal Effects: These are based on Model 4i. Table presents dx/dy, which, for factor level variables, is the discrete change from the base level. Numbers in parentheses are delta-method standard errors (robust).

variable, as well as the oil production and military aid indicators, drop below the standard levels. Measuring control variables after the peace agreement is signed, but others before it is signed, would be problematic because they could reflect aspects of implementation potentially affected by electoral participation provisions, so I use the same controls in examining implementation as in examining inclusions (captured by the time the treatment takes place). Most of the results for the controls are also similar, as I discuss below.

As discussed, measuring inclusion is more useful than implementation because it does not combine *ex-post* success into analysis of whether *ex-ante* expectations of external engagement affect the strategic calculus to use this mechanism in peace agreement design. Nonetheless, the fact that the same correlates of electoral participation provisions emerge in both analyses suggests that a selection effect is not driving certain agreements to be systematically included but not implemented.

### Which Conflicts End with Electoral Participation Provisions?

While the results from the analysis of the peace agreement data are consistent with external engagement theory, this secondary analysis broadens the comparison set. Comparing peace agreements to each other is useful because potential informational and distributional issues have likely been solved in all of those cases, but there could be a selection process by which only particular types of rebel groups and governments sign peace agreements with electoral participation provisions (the second selection effect considered in this chapter). That is, some dyads may keep fighting, for example, if they do not expect that their settlements can be designed around external actors monitoring and incentivizing compliance through an electoral process. The correlates of the inclusion of electoral participation provisions in the initial analysis, particularly the end of the Cold War and the democracy promotion variables, should also hold in examining termination through a peace agreement with electoral participation provisions across all active conflict years.

In the larger dataset of civil conflicts between 1975 and 2005, then, the variation of interest is an indicator of conflict termination by signing a peace agreement based on electoral participation provisions, compared to continued conflict and any other type of conflict termination. I therefore run a competing risks analysis using a multinomial logit, which is commonly used in such scenarios and essentially translates to asking in each year whether the combatants decide to stay in conflict rather than end conflict through different types of termination.[69] Finally,

---

[69] For example, see Fortna 2015; Leiras et al. 2015. There are multiple methods to estimate competing risks, including Fine and Gray's (1999) subdistribution hazard, which essentially asks what is the probability of the conflict ending through electoral participation provisions, given that it has not yet ended and could do so through different types of termination (directly related to the cumulative incidence). The method that I employ is recommended especially with conceivably discrete data and without a large dataset. Nonetheless, following Fortna 2015, I triangulate among methods, discussing the others in the Online Appendix at https://dataverse.harvard.edu/dataverse/matanock. The results are similar using these different methods.

in order to model time dependence, these models include transformations of the duration of conflict to the point of analysis.[70]

The main results in this analysis, too, are consistent with external engagement theory. First, the estimated coefficient for the Cold War indicator – a period of likely low expectations of enforcement – is negative and statistically significant, which indicates that this type of termination is more likely after the fall of the Berlin Wall. Across models with the same controls, as in the primary analysis, the estimated coefficients for the democracy promotion variables are always positive, and, for the regional election observation variable, in particular, it is also always statistically significant at the standard levels.[71] The estimated coefficients for special or strategic relationships also match the hypothesis: for the oil production, the U.S. military aid, and the British colony indicators, they are negative, although for the French colony indicator, it is not. These estimated coefficients are not statistically significant across all specifications, but most are. Overall, the results are consistent with external engagement theory.

Interpreting these models is more complicated, and so I also calculate the predicted effects. Across the continuous regional election observation variable, I calculate at each 10 percent increase, holding constant all of the other variables (see Figure 4.1). The figure displays a significant predicted increase in the probability of inclusion of electoral participation provisions over this range. For the discrete variables, I show the differences between the variable at zero and at one (also Figure 4.1). Again, the results on the Cold War, military aid, and former British colonies are especially large.

*Control Variables and Robustness Checks* These results hold in all of the other specifications of the models. Adding controls, including those for peacekeepers, do not remove these effects. Few variables that test the alternative hypotheses have statistically significant correlations with peace agreements with electoral participation provisions in these data, as I describe below. The persistence of these results with the controls suggests support for external engagement theory.

---

[70] Following Dafoe 2013, I present duration, duration$^2$, duration$^3$ but then also run models with no time and with a logarithmic transformation of duration of conflict (see the Online Appendix at https://dataverse.harvard.edu/dataverse/matanock). The results are similar across these specifications.

[71] The only specification in which the statistical significance falls below the 0.10 level is when the number of elections in the region in the past year, a component of this variable, is also included alongside the Cold War control. These variables are correlated at 0.42, so this result is not surprising. The estimated coefficient remains positive.

Table 4.4 *Conflict Termination through Electoral Participation Provisions (Multinomial Logistic – Relative to Ongoing Conflict and Accounting for Other Outcomes)*

| | Model 6 | Model 7 | Model 8 | Model 9 | Model 10 | Marginal Effects[a] |
|---|---|---|---|---|---|---|
| Regional Election Observation(Percent, Lagged) | 2.45*** | | | 2.20*** | | 9.02*** |
| | (0.75) | | | (0.66) | | (5.97) |
| Regional Democracy/Governance Assistance (Percent of Development Aid, Lagged 2-year Average) | | 0.05* | | | 0.07** | |
| | | (0.03) | | | (0.03) | |
| Oil Production Indicator (Lagged) | | | −0.48 | −0.44 | −0.73* | 0.64 |
| | | | (0.44) | (0.40) | (0.38) | (0.26) |
| U.S. Military Aid Indicator (Lagged) | | | −1.09*** | −1.12*** | −1.39*** | 0.33*** |
| | | | (0.40) | (0.39) | (0.39) | (0.13) |
| Former British Colony | | | −1.22* | −1.16* | −1.16** | 0.31* |
| | | | (0.64) | (0.59) | (0.58) | (0.19) |
| Former French Colony | | | 0.15 | 0.11 | 0.14 | 1.12 |
| | | | (0.59) | (0.59) | (0.66) | (0.66) |
| Cold War | −15.43*** | (No Obs.) | −16.62*** | −15.54*** | (No Obs.) | 1.79e−07*** |
| | (0.47) | | (0.31) | (0.46) | | (8.29e−08) |
| Number of Observations | 2,655 | 1,498 | 2,632 | 2,632 | 1,488 | |
| Pseudo R-Squared | 0.14 | 0.11 | 0.16 | 0.17 | 0.15 | |
| Log Pseudo Likelihood | −1221.41 | −769.76 | −1181.18 | −1173.41 | −722.07 | |

Note: Method used is multinomial logistic regressions analysis. DV is conflict termination through electoral participation provisions, accounting for all other types of conflict termination (full results shown in the Online Appendix at https://dataverse.harvard.edu/dataverse/matanock), compared to a baseline of continued civil conflict in each dyadic year. All baselines produce similar results (also shown in the Appendix). Cold War indicator is always included. Models also include duration specification described in the text; others are shown in the models in the Online Appendix. Numbers in parentheses are robust standard errors, clustered by state.

* $p<0.10$, ** $p<0.05$, *** $p<0.01$.

[a] For Marginal Effects: These are the odds ratios from Model 9.

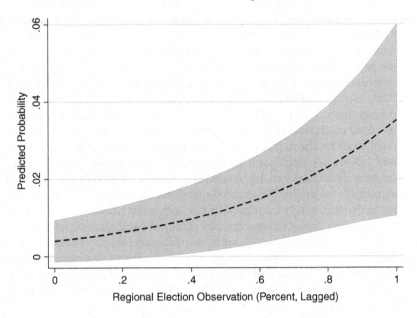

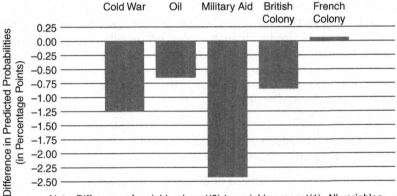

Note: Difference of variable absent(0) to variable present(1). All variables not varying are held at their median. Produced using prvalue.

Figure 4.1 Predicted Probability of Conflict Termination through Electoral Participation Provisions
Note: Predicted probabilities are based on Model 9 in Table 4.4 using the margins and marginsplot commands in Stata 13.1. All binary indicators are held at their medians and duration variables are held at their means.

As a placebo test, I compare termination through a peace agreement *without* electoral participation provisions, as opposed to *with* them, to continued conflict to see if they have the same correlates (see the second model in Table A.4.4c in the Online Appendix at https://dataverse.harvard .edu/dataverse/matanock). Aside from being more prevalent post-Cold War, as expected because peace agreements of all kinds are likely in that period, the correlates of termination through peace agreements without electoral participation provisions are not the same as above. The estimated coefficient for the indicator of a former French colony is actually positive, and statistically significant, and that for the regional democracy and governance assistance variable is actually negative, although not statistically significant. As implied by external engagement theory, then, these variables are only consistently correlated in the anticipated direction with termination through peace agreements *with* electoral participation provisions, not other types of termination, such as peace agreements *without* electoral participation provisions. Indeed, these correlates distinguish between types of peace agreements in the conflict data in other specifications (see Table A.4.4c in the Online Appendix at https://dataverse.harvard.edu/data verse/matanock).

Overall, expectations of external engagement through elections in post-conflict states – measured through the presence of strong regional democracy promotion and the absence of special or strategic relationships with the state – are associated with an increased probability of conflict termination through peace agreements with electoral participation provisions. The competing risks analysis in the conflict data, although potentially less clean than the comparison across peace agreements, thus shows correlations similar to the peace agreement data.

### Could Alternatives Explain Electoral Participation Provisions?

The control variables introduced in the models allow some assessment of alternative explanations, although none can be ruled out on these tests alone. The evidence is not as consistent with these alternative explanations as with external engagement theory. The evidence does not support the strong version of the escape explanation, in which such post-conflict contests are included only for the purpose of relieving interveners. U.N. peacekeeping missions are only present in 41 percent of cases that include electoral participation provisions in their peace agreements, and they are present in 10 percent of cases that do not include them, suggesting that troops to withdraw is not a prerequisite for the inclusion of these provisions. When included in the model, the estimated coefficient for the indicator of

U.N. peacekeeping mission is positive, although it is only statistically significant when included on its own or with just the Cold War indicator. This measure of U.N. peacekeepers is the least endogenous to the agreement – compared to mandates calling for these missions within the current year, for example – but the alternative measures produce similar results.

The tests on peacekeepers do not differentiate an escape explanation from external engagement theory as much as the qualitative tests do: peacekeeping missions may signal external engagement in a civil conflict, especially because all of the veto powers must sign on before a U.N. mission can be conducted. These variables are endogenous to the peace agreement, but they may also be measures of the independent variable of interest – expectations of international involvement – rather than a need for escape. To further test the escape explanation, I also include a model with the number of troops in place in the first year when a U.N. mission occurs in the peace agreement data (not shown). The correlation is negative, contrary to expectations, although it is small and not statistically significant in most specifications. While the test relies on few cases, the direction is the opposite of what the escape explanation implies.

The other alternative explanations likewise do not find significant support in these data (see Table 4.5 for the direction of the statistically significant estimated coefficients in the main control models; the models are shown in Tables A.4.3 and A.4.5 in the Online Appendix at https://dataverse.harvard.edu/dataverse/matanock). Estimated coefficients for variables capturing changes in the level of democracy in the state are negative, perhaps suggesting the opposite of what would be predicted by the broader democratization theories, but those for the share of the GDP that aid composes and for the indicator for post-9/11 are positive and statistically significant in the conflict data analyses, perhaps consistent with those theories. These variables also partially test the emulation explanation: with the exception of the aid variable, the variables capturing the characteristics of and contexts in which governments may feel pressure to democratize are often not correlated with electoral participation provisions, and some even point in the opposite direction; these include changes in the level of democracy, just described, and the level of democracy in the region (both estimated coefficients are negative).

Working against the implications of the ease explanation, the estimated coefficient for failed past peace agreements is positive and statistically significant, suggesting that these provisions may be tried in difficult cases. Many indicators of difficult conflicts and poor governance are also positively correlated with electoral participation provisions. Indeed, in both datasets, the estimated coefficients for the measures of conflict difficulty and state strength are not statistically significant in most specifications.

Table 4.5 *Other Correlates of Inclusion of Electoral Participation Provisions in Peace Agreements (Implemented)*

| | Peace Agreement Data | Both Datasets | Conflict Data |
|---|---|---|---|
| Positive Effects | Corruption | Past Agreement(s) | U.N. Peacekeeping Mission<br>Identity Conflict<br>[Marxist Goals]<br>Regime Type<br>Democracy Level<br>[Post-9/11]<br>Aid as a Share of GDP<br>Major Conflict Indicator<br>Rebel Group Fighters |
| Negative Effects | Identity Conflicts<br>Ever a Democracy<br>(since 1945) | [Change in<br>Democracy over<br>Past 5 Years] | Law and Order<br>Balance between Group and<br>    Government<br>Government Military<br>    Personnel |

Note: Full models and results are in the Online Appendix (at https://dataverse.harvard.edu/dataverse/matanock). The variables producing no effect in either model include Conflict Duration, Major Conflict Indicator (Based on Battle Deaths), Population, Real GDP per 1000 Inhabitants, Bureaucratic Quality, Rebel Groups with Total Goals, Factions Fighting, Regional Democracy Level, Post-9/11, Trade as Share of GDP, and Member of GATT or WTO. For the conflict data, results listed in "[ ]" only hold in the alternative specification of the competing risks models.

The direction is often opposite from that expected if these were easier conflicts (as shown in Table 4.5, and discussed further in Chapter 6).

On the flip side of the ease explanation, which is also a variant of the emulation explanation, rebel groups that are stronger and operate in weaker states may be better able to win seats, and so they may be more likely than weaker rebel groups operating in stronger states to seek electoral participation provisions. While measures on strength are hard to obtain – the variable rebel troops, for example, is coded for the entire conflict period prior to the peace agreement – none of these relationships are consistent across specifications. The estimated coefficient for the measure of rebel group fighters is generally positive, however, while that for the measure of government military personnel is generally negative. This perhaps suggests slight evidence against the ease explanation and for this variant of the emulation explanation. This is potentially a complement to external engagement theory.

To further assess a related implication, I examine data on ballot box strength, necessarily collected *after* the elections, to complement these

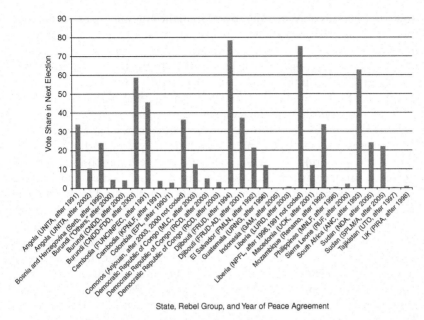

State, Rebel Group, and Year of Peace Agreement

Figure 4.2 Rebel Group Vote Share in the Election after Peace Agreements with Participation Provisions

assessments of battlefield strength. It is possible that the rebel groups that compete in elections are those that expect to do very well at the polls. Looking at the vote share for the first election after the peace agreement, however, there seems to be no indication that these are generally strong groups achieving a large share of the votes (Figure 4.2).[72] While it is hard to know exactly what group of cases to compare these to, the variation is so extensive that it hardly seems that it could be systematically differently from other contexts.

In these contexts, the elections should be designed to solidify each side's commitment to the settlement by dividing or sharing power similarly to the distribution expected from fighting. This variation from case to case is thus as expected by the basic bargaining model underpinning external engagement theory because these must match the expected payoffs from conflict. In the cases presented in the next chapter, I show that the electoral systems were systematically biased in certain ways (usually

[72] Ordering these groups by date suggests an overtime trend where the first rebel groups to make these transitions may have been stronger than those that did so later, which is an interesting pattern that should be explored further in future work.

toward the status quo) in order to maintain the amount of power that each side expected it could secure through continued conflict (which often requires favoring the government institutionally because it may be disproportionately stronger on the battlefield). In the main cases presented in Chapter 5, including both Guatemala with a relatively weak rebel group and El Salvador with a relatively strong rebel group, the electoral systems remained largely unchanged – and highly biased – in order to maintain the status quo for the incumbent government side. In the set of all ten cases assessed in Chapters 5 and 7, many even had more formal electoral engineering. In Sudan, for instance, there were quotas for how power would be distributed. Reforming regional bodies and limiting access to national legislatures was another formula, used for example in Northern Ireland in the United Kingdom and in Mindanao in the Philippines. Among the cases in the set, center-seeking conflicts, in addition to these secessionist conflicts, show similar dynamics: the seats reserved for the small parties in Colombia meant that the outcome of the vote had no effect on their share of electoral power. In South Africa, the settlement granted the minority's National Party some protections from being overmatched by the majority's African National Congress through a transition government that ruled for five years, and then through different voting rules that favored smaller parties, as well as deputy presidencies with consultation rights and proportionally-drawn cabinets. In just a couple of the cases examined, elections were designed as winner-take-all systems with powerful executive branches, and one of these failed, as Chapter 7 discusses, so advisors in other post-conflict contexts seemed to avoid these setups. While the cross-national data on quotas are not very well developed, post-conflict states, and particularly those with peace agreements that include participation provisions, seem to have higher rates of these arrangements than other elections between 1990 and 2010.[73] (They also have slightly higher rates of presidential systems, however, which is an institutional feature that could counter the idea of sharing power.)

While the ways in which these systems are designed may differ slightly from other new elections in order to allow for expected power distribution among the former combatant sides, differences in the combatant sides' relative strength does not seem to correlate consistently with the inclusion of electoral participation provisions across these cases. Given that this is *ex-post* evidence, however, it is hard to say definitively.

Other variables also are not consistent with the implications of the variant of the emulation explanation that suggests that certain cases

---

[73] Data from Butenschøn and Vollan 2011.

may be more inclined to include electoral participation provisions because the conflicts or rebel groups have characteristics that are more compatible with elections. The strength of the rebel group is the focus of the discussion above, but the type of conflict could also contribute to such an explanation. However, the measures of group aims or funding sources, in addition to strength, do not have the implied relationship with the inclusion of electoral participation provisions in these data. The estimated coefficients on the indicator of identity conflicts have the opposite signs in the peace agreement and in the civil conflict data, perhaps suggesting dynamics of international involvement in these conflicts are distinct, but this is beyond the scope of this study. Territorial conflicts, and many other conflict and rebel group characteristics, are not consistently correlated with the inclusion of electoral participation provisions, across the two different datasets.

The correlations between electoral participation provisions and other provisions may be able to provide some test of whether electoral participation provisions are simply included in easier settlements (additional tests of the ease explanation). In examining the correlation between electoral participation provisions and other provisions in settlements, the evidence also fails to support an ease theory, but it does bolster some of the theoretical dynamics of external engagement theory. Based on these correlations, electoral participation provisions are sometimes substitutes and sometimes complements of the provisions coded by the UCDP Peace Agreement Dataset. They positively correlate with disarmament, demobilization, and reintegration (DDR), and somewhat positively with force integration (see Table 4.6). External engagement theory implies such a correlation, as many DDR deadlines are linked to the electoral calendar, for example, and I posit that these ties help enforce these crucial provisions. However, electoral participation provisions negatively correlate with alternative mechanisms for overcoming the commitment problem, especially territorial division, as well as the implementation of partition.[74] They also negatively correlate with what may be an alternative mechanism for regulating center-seeking incompatibilities (rather than secessionist ones): a measure of calls for more negotiations beyond those that occur as part of a peace process (not shown in this table), as well as the UCDP-coded provisions to hold national talks as a mechanism for resolving the conflict. They are minimally correlated with provisions for integration of the rebel group into the government or the civil service. Overall, electoral participation provisions are correlated with certain other sets of provisions that reflect

---

[74] Sambanis 2000.

Table 4.6 *Correlation between Electoral Participation Provisions and Other Substantive Provisions in the Peace Agreement*

|  | Correlation |
|---|---|
| **Military Provisions** |  |
| Ceasefire | 0.08 |
| Withdrawal of Foreign Forces | 0.19 |
| Security Sector Reform | 0.27 |
| Disarmament, Demobilization, and Reintegration | 0.41 |
| **Political Provisions** |  |
| National Talks | −0.21 |
| Civil Service Integration | 0.03 |
| Government Integration | 0.10 |
| Power-Sharing | 0.21 |
| Interim Government | 0.26 |
| Political Party Formation | 0.42 |
| Electoral Reform | 0.46 |
| **Territorial Provisions** |  |
| Regional Development | −0.19 |
| Local Power-Sharing | −0.12 |
| Independence | −0.11 |
| Autonomy | −0.06 |
| Local Government | −0.04 |
| Federalism | 0.01 |
| Cultural Freedoms | 0.06 |
| Referendum | 0.24 |
| **Justice Provisions** |  |
| Amnesty | 0.09 |
| Release of Prisoners | 0.14 |
| National Reconciliation | 0.33 |

Note: Provisions are from the UCDP Peace Agreement Dataset.

aspects of them, such as accords to hold post-conflict elections, provisions solely for the right of rebel groups to transform into political parties,[75] and having had a political wing while fighting.[76] And they

---

[75] My variable, as described above, is more focused on which rebel groups are set to participate in elections: it includes those that are allowed in through a transitional government, for example, but then also requires that elections are set.

[76] Cunningham et al. 2009. In fact, offering further support for the argument in this chapter, in a concurrent study to this one, Söderberg Kovacs and Hatz (2016) find similar results for the end of the Cold War and international engagement among provisions solely for the right of rebel groups to transform into political parties, which is highly correlated with electoral participation provisions, although I also count transitional parties, as I decribe above, and require that elections are set which is not necessary in these cases.

are also often correlated with other provisions linked to the electoral calendar as the mechanism underpinning external engagement theory anticipates (see Chapter 2). But they are not simply included across all agreements that are expected to be stronger. And, the main results, consistent with external engagement theory, typically do not change when these other provisions are included in the specifications.[77]

Overall, then, these alternative explanations do not find substantial support in these data, and the controls that capture them do not alter the main results, which are implied by external engagement theory.

## Conclusions

This chapter examines a set of comparisons to test hypotheses from external engagement theory, as well as those of alternative explanations, about when rebel groups and governments are likely to include electoral participation provisions in peace agreements. The central finding in this chapter is that expectations of sufficient nonpartisan external engagement through elections in post-conflict states – captured mainly as regional variation in democracy promotion, which should indicate increases in these expectations, and special or strategic state relationships with the potential international interveners, which should reduce the expectations – are positively correlated with the inclusion of electoral participation provisions. The results are quite robust to the inclusion of controls, checks, and alternative measures. Among the controls themselves, few are consistently correlated with including electoral participation provisions, although the estimated coefficient on the indicator of U.N. peacekeeping missions is a notable exception. This result could support either the escape explanation or even external engagement theory, given that peacekeepers may either seek to escape or may signal that external engagement exists through their personnel. The escape explanation is less consistent with these data, however, in that having more troops in these missions is *negatively* correlated with these provisions (although the correlation is not statistically significant). Some explanations have similar implications for

---

[77] There are two "process" variables that are correlated with the dependent variable and that, when included, cause the estimated coefficient for the regional election observation variable to lose statistical significance: one is the UCDP-coded type of peace agreement, coded as process, partial, or full, and one is the UCDP-coding of the number of outstanding issues. Coding completeness on how the process is to be conducted and how issues are settled, or whether issues are excluded, may be directly driven by the inclusion of electoral participation provisions. As a robustness check, however, I drop the UCDP coding of "process" agreements from among these (often also "aborted") in which combatants only agree "to initiate a process" to resolve the conflict (i.e. limited to interim agreements), and the results hold.

the correlates of electoral participation provisions, so the later chapters present better tests between them. Similar results hold when the variation under analysis is the implementation of electoral participation provisions, rather than their inclusion in a peace agreement. Similar results also hold when examining termination through peace agreements with electoral participation provisions across all civil conflicts (as opposed to their inclusion among peace agreements only).

These results are consistent with external engagement theory, which suggests that electoral participation provisions should be included when both sides expect sufficiently nonpartisan external engagement through elections because the enforcement allows the combatants to commit to the deal. However, causal relationships, especially those involving beliefs or incentives, are difficult to establish through observational data. In Chapter 5, therefore, I use qualitative analysis to gain more insight into the mechanisms that result in inclusion of provisions for rebel group participation in some agreements but not others.

# 5  Shifting Expectations of Engagement
## Paving a Path for Peace Agreements Based on Electoral Participation Provisions

The previous chapters provided evidence consistent with external engagement theory. The inclusion and implementation of electoral participation provisions in peace agreements spread after the end of the Cold War. External engagement increased in this period as well, expanding regionally with waves of international democracy promotion, as Chapter 3 showed. These trends potentially serve as a proxy for expectations of international actors able and willing to enforce a settlement, suggesting that combatants engage these actors through participatory elections to monitor and punish noncompliance with their peace agreements as these trends change. The regional time trends are positively correlated with the inclusion and implementation of electoral participation provisions, as Chapter 4 showed. The analysis also suggested that if governments have significant strategic or other special relationships with these international actors (potentially decreasing expectations of nonpartisan external enforcement), then peace agreements are negatively correlated with electoral participation provisions. Chapters 3 and 4 thus began to evaluate external engagement theory and alternative explanations, and the results in cross-national data are consistent with external engagement theory.

This chapter builds on Chapter 4 in assessing empirical support for external engagement theory (and alternative explanations) of the causes of electoral participation provisions by exploring the underlying mechanisms through case studies. The method I employ is process-tracing within case studies. That is, I use narratives to examine causal mechanisms to probe the plausibility of external engagement theory and to probe the plausibility of alternatives proposed in Chapter 2.[1] I identify systemic shifts that change the independent variables of interest, and then I examine whether those changes also produce the expected change in the dependent variable of interest. This approach also allows me to test

---

[1] Buthe 2002: 482; Gerring 2007: 232; Collier 2011: 824, 826–827; also see Van Evera 1997; Mahoney 2010; Bennett and Checkel 2014.

some of the observable implications of the theory described in Chapter 2. Evidence of the expected causal chain would strengthen the plausibility of external engagement theory while weakening that of alternative explanations (which imply different causal chains).[2]

## Implications to Be Tested

Using this method, I examine whether an increase in expectations of external enforcement through the electoral process increases the propensity of combatants, driven by a demand from the rebel group, to include electoral participation provisions in order to overcome commitment problems that could otherwise prevent a peace agreement. This chapter thus tests two of the implications derived from the theory presented in Chapter 2 that focus on the causal mechanisms (see Table 5.1). First, the inclusion of electoral participation provisions increased with the end of the Cold War (as shown in Chapter 3), at least in particular states (as shown in Chapter 4), because combatants' expectations about international involvement should have shifted and allowed them to overcome commitment problems. Second, combatants – typically the rebel group – should request inclusion of electoral participation provisions to engage this external enforcement while political power is distributed (also shown cross-nationally in this chapter). As indicated, most of the correlations have already been tested in prior chapters, so this chapter focuses on testing the causal chain underpinning the theory.

There are, of course, alternative explanations that suggest different mechanisms behind inclusion and that also suggest different actors will request inclusion – the international actors, for example, should be expected to impose these provisions if the escape theory applies (see Table 5.1).

Beyond the obvious implications, the mechanisms underpinning two of the subtler alternative explanations, in particular, are tested through the case studies in this chapter. The first relates to emulation arguments in the diffusion literature, which implies that combatants will increasingly include electoral participation provisions simply because democratization's diffusion makes elections the obvious choice. Variation may continue, however, because conflicts differ in how straightforward it is to distribute political power through elections (also a dimension of a selection explanation). It may be particularly straightforward to distribute power through elections if the rebel group

---

[2] Collier 2011: 825, 828.

Table 5.1 *Mechanisms from the Main and Alternative Theories Tested through Case Studies*

| | Causes (Mainly tested in Chapter 5) | | Consequences (Mainly tested in Chapter 7) |
|---|---|---|---|
| | **Mechanisms behind Variation in Inclusion of Electoral Participation Provisions** | **Variation in Actor Requesting Inclusion** | **Mechanisms behind Variation in Peace after Inclusion** |
| **External Engagement Explanation** | Inclusion of electoral participation provisions increases with the end of the Cold War, at least in particular states (H1), *because combatants' expectations about international involvement shift and allow them to overcome commitment problems.* | Combatants – typically the rebel group(s) – request inclusion of electoral participation provisions (H2) *to engage external enforcement while political power is distributed.* | Electoral participation provisions decrease the risk of conflict recurrence (H3) *because external actors engage in election observation and provide conditional incentives, such as democracy aid, for compliance with the settlement.* |
| **Escape Explanation** | Inclusion increases *because peacekeepers, or other armed interveners, seek to escape.* | International interveners impose the provisions *to escape when they want to withdraw troops.* | No clear prediction. |
| **Enjoinder Explanation** | Inclusion increases *because international actors pressure governments for elections or democratization more broadly.* | International interveners impose the provisions as a condition *to their engagement in providing aid.* | No clear prediction on risk, but also *no conditionality on compliance for observation and aid.* |
| **Emulation Explanation** | Inclusion increases *as democratization diffuses, perhaps especially when distributing political power through elections is straightforward, because the rebel group(s) is strong and can compete easily for seats.* | Combatants – typically the government – request inclusion of electoral participation provisions *to participate in the democratization movement.* | No clear prediction. |
| **Ease Explanation** | Inclusion increases *as peace agreements take effect in easier cases to settle (longer, larger conflicts, etc.) with minimal commitment problems.* | No clear prediction. | Decrease in risk *but because few commitment problems need to be overcome (easy settlement).* |

is strong and can compete easily for seats against the government. I measured rebel group strength, including in comparison to the government, through rebel troops, government troops, and qualitative comparisons of their capabilities. The results in Chapter 4 did not suggest that rebel group strength had substantial effects on the inclusion of electoral participation provisions. These measures, however, are coded once for the entire conflict period prior to the peace agreement (not annually), and they do not necessarily capture strength at the ballot box, which may also differ from strength on the battlefield.

The second relates to a selection effect: selection in these contexts suggests that electoral participation provisions are included in peace agreements in conflicts with less intractable commitment problems that are easier to settle. Chapter 4 measures some dimensions of settlement ease identified in other studies, such as larger conflicts, and the results again do not show substantial effects, nor effects that change those of expectations of external engagement, on the inclusion of electoral participation provisions. Nonetheless, settlement ease may also be more subtle, and, specifically, it may depend on strength of the rebel group or civil society, which could then potentially enforce the agreement alone, overcoming commitment problems.

This chapter assesses the causal chain in the period leading up to the peace agreement, while Chapter 7 assesses it in the period following the peace agreement. Together these chapters test the mechanism of external engagement theory, as well as alternatives.

## Case Selection

To assess these implications, I thus sought to examine the peace process. For the "positive" case studies, I sought peace agreements that included electoral participation provisions, and, among the cases that met these criteria, I focused on conflicts that required clear shifts in credible external engagement (from partisan to nonpartisan). Such clear shifts allow assessment of the causal mechanism. Among these cases, in order to better assess those in comparison, I also sought those that differed on subtler dimensions relevant for alternative explanations. For a "negative" case, I sought a peace agreement in which electoral participation provisions were not adopted.

The main criterion for case selection was a clear shift in expectations of external enforcement around which to examine the causal chain. Such an event, at least in the regions neighboring Western powers, was the end of the Cold War.[3] The shift in major power relations, and the subsequent dominance of the United States, produced the two changes described in Chapter 3: coordination problems among the great powers were resolved, allowing them to help terminate civil conflict rather than using it to fight proxy wars, and democracy promotion programs emerged, offering low-cost, long-term mechanisms to enforce settlements.

Thus, as the Cold War ended – even in the late 1980s, as easing tensions between the United States and the Soviet Union produced new policy priorities and possibilities – the theory implies that expectations about external enforcement should increase. This change should drive the causal chain expected by external engagement theory (see "Implications" above).[4] I therefore chose civil conflicts featuring continuous fighting between rebel groups and governments that began before the Soviet Union started to collapse and that terminated after the end of the Cold War through inclusive peace agreements. Ten such cases base their settlements on electoral participation provisions (see Table 5.2).[5]

In these positive cases that cross the end of the Cold War, I can examine whether the mechanisms work as expected. Among these, I focus on cases in which the main international actors had to move from obviously partisan to nonpartisan, which make the causal test especially clear. Where rebel groups fought against U.S.-backed governments during the Cold War, international actors (particularly the United States and intergovernmental organizations to which it belongs) will need to change the most, and convince rebel groups of this change, before those combatants would seek to base their agreements on electoral participation provisions, if external engagement theory is correct. Rebel groups are likely to believe that these international actors will continue to back the same side as during the war – the government in these cases – until they are convinced otherwise. These are hard cases in the sense that a strong shift is needed to change their expectations. For leftist guerrilla groups in regions close to the United States, a shift from rejection to acceptance of enforcement by the United States and related intergovernmental organizations should thus be especially clear in these cases. We should then see rebel groups pushing to include electoral participation provisions in peace agreements that will engage the same international actors that they previously rejected

---

[3] In different terms, this could also be described as a "shock," before and after which I can compare the state to its best control, itself.

[4] Because these changes are driven by geostrategic factors across the system, exogenous to the civil conflict in any particular state, it's a particularly clean "shock" to examine.

[5] More detail on these cases is in Matanock 2012.

Table 5.2 *Evidence on Which Actor Requests Electoral Participation Provisions*

| State | Group | Year | Evidence that Could Be Identified on the Initial Decision to Include Participation Provisions |
|---|---|---|---|
| *Angola* | National Union for the Total Independence of Angola (UNITA) | 1991 | In 1989, Jonas Savimbi, the UNITA leader, called for multi-party elections after two years and rejected any other method of incorporating the rebel group into the state (McFaul 1989). The government accepted multi-party elections at the end of 1989, although it wanted to wait three years to be sure that consolidation and economic recovery happened first (Tvedten 1992). UNITA forced the September 1992 date for elections, stating "the Bicesse Peace Accords ends on 30 November and that, after that date, if the elections have not been held, then anything could happen" (Antsee 1996). UNITA had strong ties with the United States, and international actors were involved in the negotiations, but I could not locate any evidence that these international actors pushed this plan in the case studies that I read documenting this peace process. |
| *Cambodia* | National United Front for an Independent, Neutral, Peaceful, and Cooperative Cambodia (FUNCINPEC), Khmer People's National Liberation Front (KPNLF), Khmer Rouge (K.R.) | 1991 | In 1986, earlier than the other cases but when international engagement began to be a possibility in this case, a coalition of opposition forces advanced an eight point peace plan that included free elections under U.N. supervision after a coalition government consisting of the rebel groups and observed continuously by the United Nations (Acharya et al. 1989). The rebel groups worked closely with the United Nations, so it is possible that the idea originated with the international actor, although many studies of this conflict note that the settlement's terms were internally generated (e.g. Mayall 1996), and I could not locate any evidence that these international actors pushed this plan in the case studies that I read documenting this peace process. |
| *Colombia* | Popular Liberation Army (EPL), 19th of April | 1991 | In 1988, M-19 demanded to be allowed to participate in elections as part of a peace process (Grabe Loewenherz 2009). They had |

| | Movement (M-19), Quintin Lame Armed Movement (MAQL), etc. | | discussed participating in the early 1980s but had not due to commitment concerns that played out as the FARC had participated (Rojas Puyo 2009). The smaller groups then also asked for electoral participation provisions when they negotiated settlements with the governments (Andrade 2009; Flórez 2010; Peñaranda 1999; Van Cott 2005). The government agreed. I could not locate any evidence that any international actors pushed this plan in the case studies that I read documenting this peace process – and, notably, there is no intervention from which to escape in this case. |
|---|---|---|---|
| El Salvador | Farabundo Martí National Liberation Front (FMLN) | 1992 | The rebel group requested, as described in the case study in the text. |
| Guatemala | Guatemalan National Revolutionary Unity (URNG) | 1996 | The rebel group requested, as described in the case study in the text. |
| Mozambique | Mozambique National Resistance (Renamo) | 1992 | In 1989, the government renounced communism and adopted a constitution that allowed for multi-party elections in 1990 (Pascoe 1987; Simpson 1993), but it did not initially allow for Renamo to become a political party (Manning 2008). In negotiations in the same year, Renamo demanded to right to transform itself into a political party (Manning 2008). Renamo had strong ties with the United States, and international actors were involved in the negotiations, so, like Cambodia, it is possible that the idea originated with the international actor. But, again, I could not locate any evidence that these international actors pushed this plan in the case studies that I read documenting this peace process. |
| Philippines (Mindanao) | Moro National Liberation Front (MNLF) | 1996 | Elections were a strong institution in the Philippines: a domestic election observation organization, the National Citizens' Movement for Free Elections (NAMFREL) had established themselves as |

Table 5.2 (cont.)

| State | Group | Year | Evidence that Could Be Identified on the Initial Decision to Include Participation Provisions |
|---|---|---|---|
| | | | objective, credible monitors, and, indeed, their report in 1986 had led to massive pressure, first inside the country and then even outside the country, for the fraudulent victory of incumbent Ferdinand Marcos to be overturned (Bjornlund 2004). Once it was overturned, and the 1992 elections faced both internal and external observation, the MNLF immediately entered negotiations with the government (Hernandez 1996); it is not clear, however, who proposed the new Consultative Assembly that granted the region further autonomy and brought the MNLF in as a political party allowed to participate in both regional and national elections. Again, in this case, I could not locate any evidence that any international actors pushed this plan in the case studies that I read documenting this peace process – and, again, notably, there is no intervention from which to escape in this case. |
| *South Africa* | African National Congress (ANC) | 1993 | In the 1980s, during Nelson Mandela's earliest interview, he requested that the government, "legalize us, treat us like a political party and negotiate with us" (Zartman 1995). As the government and the rebel group did begin to negotiate, this remained a primary point (Horowitz 1991; Maharaj 2008; McGarry 1998; Wood 2000). While there was considerable international actor interest in the case, like the other cases, there is no evidence that these international actors pushed the plan in the case studies that I read documenting this peace process. This case, however, more than others is about these elections, and thus it is murkier than the others. |

| Sudan (*Southern Sudan*) | Sudan People's Liberation Movement/Army (SPLM/A) | 2005 | It was clear that SPLM/A demanded the referendum that ultimately split the countries, but it is less clear who proposed the other elections that were held in the interim (Ofuho 2006). The mediator for the two sides confirmed that the referendum demand was made by the rebel group, and that it was neither suggested nor imposed by any external actor, including the United States (Sumbeiywo 2006). Both he and the SPLM/A then later endorsed elections as the opportunity for all sides to compete for power (although power-sharing provisions, discussed in the next section, mostly determined how this competition would turn out) (Young 2007). The United Nations, which would eventually intervene, had not even mandated its advance political mission by the time that the two parties signed the political protocol in May 2004, so direct pressure on these parties by the international actor that would send troops is infeasible. Again, then, I could not locate any evidence that these international actors pushed this plan in the case studies that I read documenting this peace process – and, again, notably, there is no intervention from which to escape by the signing in this case. |
| --- | --- | --- | --- |
| United Kingdom (*Northern Ireland*) | Provisional Irish Republican Army (PIRA) | 1998 | Northern Ireland, like just a couple of other cases, already had election participation by all sides *during* the conflict. In 1982, Sinn Fein began running candidates in the Assembly election – it was important that the settlement continued to allow this type of contestation, but this, like South Africa, is a somewhat different case from many of those in the set because of the unique role elections were already playing (McAuley 2009; Morrison 2009). |

Note: This table shows the evidence that I could identify on which actor made the request for electoral participation provisions in the top secondary sources located (noted in the table) and in U.S. State Department documents released prior to the writing of this book.

This is not to claim that the coverage of each case is complete (and other actors may have pressured those making requests behind closed doors – the in-text description of this table and the in-depth cases discuss this possibility more comprehensively, although both note that governments rather than rebel groups in most of these cases should have been more susceptible to such pressure).

Excluded cases that otherwise meet these criteria are Afghanistan and Chad, because each had a power change in 1989 or 1990, which meant a change in the "government" actor during the period of analysis (although some rebel groups were constant during this period of analysis).

entirely. From among the 10 cases, Guatemala and El Salvador best fit these criteria.

I examine both of these cases, Guatemala and El Salvador, because, in addition to meeting the case selection criteria, they diverge on the crucial dimensions of these subtler alternative explanations (described above), which are difficult to test in cross-national data. Guatemala is a case in which the alternative explanations would not predict electoral participation provisions. The state had a weak civil society, and the conflict featured a much weaker rebel side than government side. It reached a stalemate by 1984. This allowed the combatants to identify a mutually beneficial deal well before the end of the Cold War, but severe commitment problems blocked it. Consequently, the case also allows assessment of whether geostrategic shifts increased the expectations of external engagement and enabled all sides to solve their commitment problem through a peace process with electoral participation provisions. Existing literature on conflict resolution stresses that confounding variables, especially shifts in the balance of power, may coincide with the end of the Cold War. While overcoming the commitment problem need not be the *only* obstacle to ending the civil war, the cleanest test of the mechanism is a case in which commitment is the main obstacle, so that the effect of external engagement can be best identified. Guatemala provides such a test, given the end of the Cold War. Moreover, it is *not* a case in which the rebel group would easily win seats, gain a substantial share of power, and then ensure the government's commitment on its own or where a strong civil society could enforce commitments (which the alternative explanations would anticipate would be present when including electoral participation provisions, as described above).

In contrast, El Salvador is a case in which the rebel group and the government were more evenly matched. In this case, the alternative explanations imply that the relatively strong rebel group would be more easily able to secure seats through elections to ensure the government's commitment through its own share of power. Indeed, during the conflict, each side had a chance at winning the war. Civil society was also much stronger. This case then seems like one in which the alternative explanations could explain the decision to distribute power through electoral participation provisions, and so it provides a case to compare these explanations. I can test whether there is evidence of commitment problems, as external engagement theory would imply, for example, or if any have already been easily solved, as the others would imply. It is, however, also a less clean test than Guatemala because the end of the Cold War may have also helped the conflict parties reach a stalemate.

Overall, examining both cases is useful because Guatemala provides an especially clean test in which external engagement theory, but not the subtler alternative explanations, predicts electoral participation provisions, and El Salvador provides a case in which they all do, but with different drivers so that I can distinguish among different mechanisms (and perhaps see if several may be operating). Moreover, if the emulation or selection explanations outlined above were driving variation in election participation provisions alone, then the provisions should not be included in Guatemala, only in El Salvador (and there they should be apparent in the causal chain). Instead, I show that both cases provide evidence consistent with external engagement theory, in terms of when and how these settlements emerged, as both were at least in part a means of overcoming commitment problems. These positive cases of electoral participation provisions in which expectations of credible external engagement were difficult to achieve thus also provide an ideal set in which to test subtler alternative explanations.

It is important to remember that, in these cases, I am examining whether a shift in external engagement encouraged the transition of the rebel group into a political party. While structural conditions certainly explain some of the institutional changes in these countries, they do not explain the decisions of the rebel groups – especially the weaker rebel group in Guatemala – to base their peace agreements on electoral participation provisions. They also do not explain the timing of these decisions. These cases are also useful because each had already begun slow processes toward more open elections and democratization, pressured by the United States even in the early 1980s and solidified by the Esquipulas II Agreement signed by five Central American countries in 1987, including both Guatemala and El Salvador. Elections, however, are "a necessary but not sufficient condition for ... transition from insurgent movement to political party."[6] This chapter, through these case studies, will explore whether the choice to base a peace agreement on electoral participation provisions, and when that choice occurred, may have depended on changes in expectations of external enforcement (and Chapter 7 will explore whether it, in fact, enabled that enforcement).

In addition to these positive cases, I also examine a negative case in this chapter: a civil conflict settlement from the same period that does not include electoral participation provisions. The negative case allows an even more robust test of the proposed causal mechanism. There are a handful of peace agreements from this period that adopt alternative provisions. Bangladesh is useful because it is in some ways similar to

---

[6] Wood 2000: 79.

Guatemala (a small state with a weak rebel group) but in a very different regional context. While the United States pursued its role as settlement enforcer in Latin America as soon as the Cold War came to a close, no international actor did so in such a way in Asia. Chapter 3 shows much slower rates of intervention, including initially lower rates of democracy promotion programs, in Asia compared to elsewhere, likely due to persistently stronger norms of nonintervention. Even after the end of the Cold War, these norms did not shift substantially due to the continued resistance by the major regional actors, China and India. Bangladesh, then, provides a case in which expectations of external engagement should not change. Subsequently, the settlement that the combatants signed did not include electoral participation provisions (and it was a weak settlement prone to peace failure).

While the main purpose of this chapter is not to establish generalizability, I assess one empirical implication in the set of cases that cross the end of the Cold War: I identify which actor requests the inclusion of electoral participation provisions. These requests are an implication that differs across explanations (H2, as shown in Table 5.1, as well as Table 2.2), but it is difficult to measure, so I assess it carefully for a small sample, given that evidence in the larger dataset is unavailable. I examine all 10 positive cases to see which actor makes the requests. This small-sample analysis tests an aspect beyond the mechanism. In the conclusion, I also examine evidence from across these 10 cases to point out that the mechanisms identified in Guatemala and El Salvador are not unique to leftist rebel groups, or small states, or center-seeking conflicts. Establishing generalizability, however, is more thoroughly accomplished through the statistical tests conducted in Chapters 3 and 4.

### Case Evidence

Analysis of the cases through process-tracing – aimed at assessing the causal chain posited by external engagement theory compared to alternative theories as described above – relies on observation of statements and actions, both current and historical, in order to triangulate among sources that may contain different biases. I conducted archival research on domestic and international decision documents, including from the George H.W. Bush Library (the administration in office during the initial Central American negotiations that began in 1989), the online resources of the William J. Clinton Library and the U.N. archives, digital access to the U.S. State Department and the National Security Archive collections on these countries, and from the archives of organizations devoted to documenting the rebel groups and peace processes in question (which are each described in this chapter). I also conducted interviews with decisionmakers in Guatemala, El Salvador, and the international community, on these and other cases. These primary sources are useful because they provide information about the motivations underlying decisions. Of course, the leaders of the rebel group and the government were attempting to negotiate for the best terms they could achieve in order to then sell those agreements to their electorates, so one cannot expect them to openly identify instrumental reasons for participating in elections; this, in any case, is not common among politicians or political parties in general. Many of those I interviewed from each side are now politicians, so their testimonies may be shaped by political motivations, in addition to reporting bias, given that nearly two decades have elapsed since the events under examination. Interviewees often emphasized normative motivations – that electoral participation would advance some greater good – which may be true, but they may have also received other benefits. Interviewing multiple individuals from different sides help reveal these additional benefits. Primary documents, especially contemporary notes from meetings and decisions, also help answer these questions. Secondary sources provide information on the actual behavior of these groups. Each source may have some bias, but, taken together, they help us understand the reasons for the inclusion of electoral participation provisions.

### Chapter Overview

In what follows, I first detour from testing the mechanisms to assess which actor requests electoral participation provisions, an implication of external engagement theory. To do so, I draw on evidence from the set of cases that cross the end of the Cold War. I then examine the cases of Guatemala and El Salvador by asking a series of questions: First, were commitment problems among the obstacles to achieving a settlement during the Cold War? Second, did combatants' expectations on international involvement shift as the Cold War ended? Third, did a peace agreement with electoral participation provisions then emerge? And, finally, did the design of the agreement engage external actors around electoral participation provisions?

At the end of each narrative, I assess how consistent it is with the causal chain implied by external engagement theory and alternatives. I then examine a negative case, Bangladesh. I conclude by discussing the mechanism driving the results of these case studies. (Chapter 7 focuses on settlement implementation, and whether noncompliance with the settlement – and external engagement around electoral participation provisions – continued in the implementation period.)

This chapter demonstrates that the end of the Cold War caused a shift in expectations in Central America regarding the availability of external engagement – specifically, nonpartisan enforcement through the electoral process became possible – which changed the solutions available to combatants for designing a peace agreement that could overcome the commitment problem. After this shift, the rebel groups in Guatemala and El Salvador requested, and all sides eventually signed, settlements with electoral participation provisions. These policy decisions are striking given the prior partisanship toward the government by the external actors involved. The same shift did not take place in Bangladesh. A small sample from across the end of the Cold War also lends some empirical support to the notion that rebel groups are more likely to request these electoral participation provisions.

## Evidence of Empirical Implication across Cases

The focus of this chapter is not to assess generalizability – which previous chapters have done – but rather to assess whether there is empirical evidence for the causal mechanisms posited by each explanation. Yet this chapter analyzes one empirical implication beyond the mechanism that I was unable to test in the cross-national data due to the difficulty of measuring it (H2): which actor requests electoral participation provisions. External engagement theory predicts that rebel groups should request these provisions, while alternative explanations suggest the request should come from the government or international actors (see Table 5.1). To examine this question, I turn to a slightly broader sample than the cases discussed in depth in this chapter: the 10 states that meet the "end of the Cold War" criterion, in that they had stable rebel groups fighting governments both before and after 1989, so they were susceptible to the systemic change that should produce increased expectations of external enforcement through elections according to external engagement theory (tested through process-tracing in subsequent sections).

The evidence suggests that combatants in each of these cases took the steps toward these transitions, and, further, that it was the rebel groups that typically made the initial request for electoral participation provisions. Table 5.2 provides the first identified request for electoral participation provisions in each case. The preponderance of the evidence across these cases suggests that rebel groups are the most likely to make these requests, regardless of their ideologies, and frequently without any overt pressure on them from an international actor. The rebel group is the weaker group in all of these cases – although the difference is slim in some cases, such as in Mozambique – and thus it may well have trusted state institutions less; this is consistent with external engagement theory's implication that these groups, as the most concerned about noncompliance by their opponents, would make these requests. While in some cases there may have been behind-closed-doors recommendations, or even pressure by the international community, on either the rebel groups to request these provisions or on the government to accept these provisions, I could not locate evidence of this even in these well-documented case studies. If the West were to exert pressure on one side to demand inclusive elections, the expectation would be that it would have the closest ties and the strongest influence with the anti-Communist (government) sides, but it was the rebel groups, leftists in many of these cases, that instead made these requests. In fact, the United States often initially opposed electoral participation provisions arising from rebels, as will be seen in the case studies of Guatemala and El Salvador.

None of this is to say that conditional benefits were not offered in conjunction with the contests: they often were, and they helped generate compliance (shown further in the cases in Chapter 7). But it does not appear that the international actors conditioned their involvement on combatants' signing a settlement with inclusive elections, nor did they appear to impose these provisions in these cases.

## Cases of Shifting Expectations of External Enforcement

Turning now to process-tracing to explore the causal chain in the selected cases, I summarize each case before analyzing the causal chain identified and hypotheses listed in the "Implications" section using the questions posed in the "Chapter Overview" section (both above).

### Guatemala

The Guatemalan Civil War (1960–1996) was a particularly brutal conflict. Between 1981 and 1983, a U.S.-backed government countered leftist guerrillas through tactics that included genocidal campaigns targeting their supporters, often indigenous communities. Tens of thousands were killed. By 1984, the war had reached a stalemate, but it was over a decade later before the fighting finally terminated through a settlement reached in 1996. The end of the Cold War gradually changed the perception that international actors would always side with the government, while thereby increasing the enforcement capabilities of electoral participation provisions, which allowed the rebel group and the government to overcome commitment problems and sign a peace agreement based on these provisions. One moment in particular was important in demonstrating those shifting expectations to the rebel group: in 1993, then president Jorge Serrano Elías perpetrated an "auto-coup" by suspending the constitution and dissolving other branches of government. The auto-coup occurred after peace talks, which had finally begun, faltered and failed. The international community reacted strongly to the auto-coup and demonstrated definitively that it would punish any side that violated the rules of the game. The expectations set by the policy changes during this period, including this response by the international community, demonstrated that noncompliance would be costly. This set the stage for a successful peace accord that provided for the rebel group's electoral participation, even though it was small and unlikely to win many seats. Leaders from the Guatemalan National Revolutionary Unity (URNG) and the Guatemalan government then signed the final piece of the settlement, the "Accord for a Firm and Lasting Peace," in 1996. The settlement centered on provisions for the URNG to transition from a rebel group to a political party set to compete against the government in post-conflict elections.

*Obstacles to a Settlement during the Cold War*    In part due to the devastating nature of the Guatemalan Civil War, a central obstacle to ending the fighting, at least by 1984, was commitment problems. The war was rooted in the 1954 overthrow of Jacobo Árbenz Gúzman by U.S.-backed forces who had been urged into action by multinational companies invested in the state that were concerned about nationalization. By 1961, resistance to the new regime emerged. Over the next decades, the Rebel Armed Forces (FAR), originally close with the Guatemalan Workers' Party (PGT), the Organization of the People in Arms (ORPA), and the Guerrilla Army of the Poor (EGP) joined the fight. In 1982, the rebel groups formed an umbrella organization, the Guatemalan National Revolutionary Unit (URNG), after the military's dominance forced closer collaboration. The U.S.-backed military conducted a campaign that included a large-scale "scorched earth" effort between 1980 and 1983, seeking to sever the support that the guerrillas drew from the indigenous community. The campaign destroyed hundreds of villages and left over 100,000 dead or "disappeared."[7] By 1984, the Guatemalan government had the upper hand.[8] The guerrillas could not win.[9] The URNG would not surrender, however, and the government

---

[7]  Allison 2009: 190–191; which also provides background on the case.
[8]  Azpuru 1999: 101; Jonas 2000a: 11; Allison 2006b: 147–148; Allison 2009.
[9]  See, for example, Allison 2006b.

could not overpower the guerrillas completely, so the conflict reached
a stalemate.

The weak and vulnerable URNG could not agree to a settlement
because, crucially, it could not count on nonpartisan external engagement to help overcome commitment problems. According to my interviews with leaders of the URNG, described in more depth below, the
concerns were that members of the group might simply be annihilated
once their weapons were laid down, and also that the government might
not comply with policy concessions in any accord.[10] The URNG was
weak, but it retained its fighting capabilities and forced the government
into a protracted counterinsurgency campaign,[11] so a deal would have to
be struck between "two semi-equal negotiating parties."[12]

Despite its weaker position, the rebel group appeared to recognize that
it would be in an even more vulnerable position if it disarmed – a likely
condition of any deal – and so it instead continued fighting.[13] In 1986,
according to news sources, the URNG hinted at creating "the conditions" for dialogue leading to negotiations, after it had lost hope of any
victory due to military operations in the early 1980s, yet it did not move
forward with a concrete proposal, as commitment problems continued.[14]
To reassure the URNG, the government would have had to draw down
its armed forces simultaneous to disarmament by the rebel group[15] or
would have to allow the URNG to remain armed, but these would have
been major concessions for a near victor. Instead, the government
insisted that the URNG demobilize before any other part of a peace
process could proceed.[16] Walter Félix – a leader of the rebel group
who would later serve as the member of Congress from Huehuetenango
as part of the ex-guerrilla party – noted in a 2013 interview that it
seemed like the government would "only negotiat[e] an honorable surrender of URNG."[17] Elections at that time offered little assurance for the

---

[10] For example, Carlos Mejía, from my interview in Guatemala City with URNG leaders,
2013.
[11] See Stewart 1995: A12; Stanley 2013: 9.
[12] Jonas 2000b: 104. Such situations produced negotiated settlements in other contexts
when, despite military dominance, neither side could claim a cost-effective victory (e.g.
Kecskemeti 1957), so why not settle in this case?
[13] Azpuru 1999: 104, Allison 2009: 197.
[14] "Guatemalan President Views Visit to Mexico" 1986; "Guatemalan Guerrillas Deny
Issuing Truce Communique" 1986; Jonas 2000a: 11; Jonas 2000b: 37.
[15] As was proposed by the group. See Stanley 2013: 17.
[16] Azpuru 1999: 104, Jonas 2000b: 37; Jonas 2000a: 11; indeed, the government resisted
any negotiations until "the guerrillas lay down their arms and reincorporate themselves
into the political system" ("Cerezo Nixes Dialogue with Guerrillas" 1986).
[17] Walter Félix, from my interview in Guatemala City with URNG leaders, 2013 (all
conducted in Spanish and transcribed/translated with help of Mike McDonald).

rebels. The government adopted somewhat open elections in the early 1980s, under pressure from the United States to improve Guatemala's international image, but the political opening did not extend to opponents on the Left. "Guatemalans did not feel protected by [elections] or behave as if their rights were protected."[18] The United States provided covert aid and even at times overtly supported the government during the Cold War, although it had not provided open military aid from 1977 to 1987 due to human rights abuses that "shocked" the international system.[19]

The URNG's statements in the 1980s clearly expressed concerns that the United States and allied organizations were highly biased toward the government. One document demanded "STOP THE GENOCIDE BY THE U.S.-BACKED MILITARY REGIME!"[20] As the URNG recognized these external actors' partisanship toward the government, the URNG also sought its own international ties with nonaligned countries, but no effective nonpartisan engagement emerged at this point.[21]

*Combatants' Increasing Expectations of External Enforcement through Elections*    As the Cold War ended, substantial shifts in perceptions of the nonpartisanship and credibility of international actors' engagement in the Guatemalan conflict provided a solution to combatants' commitment problems, which relied at least in part on the electoral process. With this shift, the rebel group began requesting electoral participation in a peace process with international involvement.

As early as the late 1980s, these international actors were exhibiting greater nonpartisanship and more support for peace. As the Democrats took control of both chambers of Congress in 1986 and President George H.W. Bush took office in 1989, leadership changes in the United States changed policy preferences. The change meant deemphasizing anti-

---

[18] Jonas 2000a: 19–20; also expressed in Azpuru 1999: 113.

[19] Jonas 1996: 148; Azpuru 1999: 101–103; Spence 2005: 482.

[20] URNG 1985: 2; URNG Undated [possibly 1982 based on the context], 1–2. These documents are part of an archive produced by the Guatemala News and Information Bureau (GNIB), an activist group, founded in 1978 in San Francisco, which systematically collected materials documenting the civil war and the peace process. The archive includes published and unpublished documents from the URNG and other organizations, including correspondence, communiqués, announcements, press releases, and other types of materials. In most cases, the URNG documents do not have individual authors, and it is possible that the leadership in country did not issue all of these documents (although I also have no evidence either way). Those used in this project happen to be in English: some are explicitly noted as having been translated (presumably by the GNIB) from Spanish to English; others, like international communiqués, may have been originally produced in English. Over 11,000 items from the archive have now been digitized by the Princeton University Library, which is how I accessed them.

[21] URNG 1986: 1.

communism policies in Central America.[22] For example, U.S. military aid to Guatemala was suspended in December 1990 due to a lack of progress on human rights, despite the ongoing civil war against the guerrillas.[23] In addition, the United Nations' reputation as a nonpartisan intervener improved: its deployment of a peacekeeping mission based on the Esquipulas II Accord to end all Central American conflicts assuaged some concerns about partisanship by international actors.[24] Other international organizations in the region also demonstrated their ability to monitor compliance, rather than being swayed by what had been the United States' strong anti-communist agenda: the Organization of American States (OAS) provided observers for the 1986 Nicaraguan elections that produced a victory for leftist leader Daniel Ortega, and shortly thereafter Nicaragua won a case against the United States in an international court.[25]

By 1990, the URNG's General Command had begun to incorporate U.N. and U.S. statements condemning the government's behavior into its calls for a peace process.[26] Dialogue between the URNG and civil society under the Commission on National Reconciliation began in 1990.[27] These talks did not yet involve the government or international interveners, according to internal U.S. State Department reports, but they did result in plans to "include the URNG in a National Constituent Assembly"[28] and "enable guerrillas to run for office."[29] These September 1990 reports are the first among these to mention such a demand.[30] Reports of a similar format in February and May 1990 does not mention the idea of electoral participation provisions. These demands were made during an independent process without government involvement or international mediation except for a U.N. mediator (although both the government and the United States had endorsed a settlement by this point).[31] Throughout the peace process, the rebel group focused on

---

[22] This is especially well documented through the El Salvador case, as in Karl 1992, 153, 156–157, 159; LeMoyne 1992; Munck 1993: 79; Wood 2000: 80; Álvarez 2010a: 24–25, 28.

[23] See, for example, "Guatemala Human Rights Report" 1991: 2; some pushed for this conditionality to go even further (see Romero 1991: 1).

[24] This mission is positively mentioned in an early call for considering negotiations, although Guatemala wanted its own process, see URNG 1987: 3. The Esquipulas accords were seen as particularly important in Guatemala; see Azpuru 1999: 104.

[25] International Court of Justice 1986.    [26] URNG 1990b: 1.

[27] Azpuru 1999: 104; Jonas 2000a: 11.

[28] Washington Office on Latin America 1990: 10.

[29] "1990 Country Report on Human Rights Practices" 1990: 18.

[30] The source of these documents is the U.S. State Department archive online (available at the time of writing), based on Freedom of Information Act (FOIA) requests.

[31] Alvarez 2002: 46–47; Stanley 2013: 4.

participation through elections, alongside some demobilization for the government.[32] In contrast to the escape theory's expectation, there is no evidence in these U.S. State Department documents that the United States or other international actors pressured the rebel group to call for (or agree to) electoral participation,[33] and Bush administration documents indicate support for preventing the guerrillas from winning as late as 1989 (thereafter the administration supports negotiations).[34] Instead, as external engagement theory implies, the URNG requested electoral participation as nonpartisan external engagement became more plausible, rather than after the 1984 stalemate or during the political openings presented during prior elections. The government and the URNG began peace talks, with the possibility of electoral participation provisions on the table, after the civilian-to-civilian transition in power took place in 1991.[35] The United Nations and others formally joined the negotiation process as witnesses.[36]

The URNG had initiated negotiations and considered electoral participation provisions, yet it remained wary until less partisan external engagement – especially through elections – became more credible after the international community's reactions to President Serrano's auto-coup attempt. The URNG's weak position, along with the brutality of the war in 1981–1983, made the group particularly concerned that the government might renege on a potential peace agreement.[37] Despite pockets of resistance,[38] the government and the military, especially after its failed annihilation offensive in 1988, supported the peace talks from 1990 onward,[39] also backed then by the United States.[40] The open question approaching these negotiations was how to arrange an agreement. The URNG still feared government noncompliance.[41] URNG leaders, including Carlos Mejía – a former guerrilla who later served as a member of Congress from San Marcos – noted in a 2013 interview that "there was a lot of skepticism as to whether or not [the government] would comply, which is what generated the most tension," especially in negotiating land reform; the violence that had occurred

---

[32] Azpuru 1999: 105–106.

[33] There is evidence that the United Nations and other international actors did push other issues later in the process, so any earlier pressure on these issues would likely also have been noted, as in Jonas 2000b: 57, 64.

[34] Quayle 1989: 5.     [35] Azpuru 1999: 106; Jonas 2000b: 38, 41.     [36] Azpuru 1999: 107.

[37] LeMoyne 1992; Munck 1993; Jonas 2000b; Allison 2006b, 2009.

[38] Jonas 2000b: 2–3.     [39] Azpuru 1999: 105.

[40] Romero 1990: 2, "Report in Spanish Re Michael Vernon Devine Case" 1990: 2; the U.S. ambassador was told about government plans for direct talks in November 1990 and then expressed a "willingness to help in any way behind the scenes" (McCulloch 1990: 1).

[41] Jonas 2000b: 2–3.

during the conflict also gave cause for concern.[42] The U.N.-hosted negotiations faltered after the 1991 accords. The process deadlocked and eventually failed over URNG-requested human rights protections, including a truth commission to investigate past crimes, but also over requested changes in the state's forces.[43] Each statement on a settlement in the Guatemala News and Information Bureau (GNIB) archive from this period raised concerns about government killings.[44] Into early 1993, the perception was that the international community had "eased off" its attention, at least in pressing for negotiations,[45] and so its credibility was in question.

Combatants' confidence in external actors increased, however, after the international community rejected President Serrano's attempt to seize power in excess of what constitution provided in 1993.[46] The United States and the OAS signaled their trustworthiness as enforcers by condemning the Serrano auto-coup and threatening to withhold assistance and limit trade, which the United States made credible when it froze aid immediately following the auto-coup.[47] U.S. State Department Spokesman Richard Boucher summed it up by saying, "There is no justification for resorting to non-democratic means to resolve Guatemala's problems,"[48] and the U.S. Secretary of State noted that this was "an opportunity to carry out one of President Clinton's highest priorities ... the promotion of democracy."[49] Democracy promotion played a central role. The response to the auto-coup reinforced the region-wide expectation that external actors, through economic means and even active armed intervention,[50] would punish noncompliance with standards of democracy, human rights protections, and good governance.[51] External condemnation complemented a domestic campaign to reverse the auto-coup, led by those concerned about losing access to international institutions, backed by the army whose leaders by then had even expressed a willingness to protect the URNG should it transition to a political party (and a hope of receiving more military assistance from the United States).[52] At the same time, the United Nations had successfully concluded the negotiations in 1992 in El

---

[42] Carlos Mejía, from my interview in Guatemala City with URNG leaders, 2013.
[43] See URNG 1987: 2–3; Reid 1992; URNG 1993a: 1–2; Azpuru 1999: 108; Jonas 2000a: 12; Allison 2006b; Allison 2009: 197; Stanley 2013: 21.
[44] For example, in a General Command statement, see URNG 1991: 2.
[45] National Network in Solidarity with the People of Guatemala 1993: 3.
[46] Jonas 2000b: 38; Santiso 2002: 567.
[47] Jonas 2000b: 51; Verstegen 2000: 48; Santiso 2002: 567.    [48] Wilkinson 1993a: 1.
[49] Boucher 1993: 3.    [50] Kelley 2012: 19, 255–258.    [51] Verstegen 2000: 48.
[52] "Ambassador Calls on MOD and Discusses Topics Surrounding Military-to-Military Relationships" 1993: 6–7; Azpuru 1999: 109–110; Verstegen 2000: 34, 38, 48.

Salvador, where the central role of international actors as security guarantors had been demonstrated.[53]

These developments changed URNG's perceptions regarding protection through international involvement alongside progress in democratic consolidation.[54] The URNG, initially skeptical that it could be protected by external involvement, had reluctantly made limited steps toward a settlement: for instance, an initial set of refugees who returned to Guatemala as part of the peace process "expressed fears" about the army.[55] These returnees told reporters that they were only willing to come because they believed that the international community would guarantee their safety. For all involved parties, this was seen as "sort of a test" to see if they could successfully return under protection by the United Nations High Commissioner for Refugees (UNHCR). The cost was $1.1 million for just a small group.[56] As the UNHCR representative said to the news media at the time, "There's no way money like that can be spent on subsequent returns."[57] Thus something like an electoral process that could tie domestic compliance to international observation and conditional incentives was needed. An internal memo from the General Command to the members of the URNG indicated that a political strategy would be the organization's primary approach to resolving the conflict, after observing international reactions to the autocoup.[58] While multiple factors made a settlement desirable for the URNG, including war-weariness and persistent hope that the organization could affect political change, the process succeeded when and how it did because of international pressure. In my interview, URNG member Carlos Mejía noted that "there were a lot of resources poured into letting people know about the peace accords and a lot of hope that the peace accords would be complied with."[59] The government, meanwhile, wanted to improve its image globally, because the provision of aid and other benefits had become clearly tied to compliance with international conventions such as electoral processes.[60] The United States and other international actors were aware of the importance of their nonpartisanship: a U.S. State Department memo noted during the talks that it had to

[53] Jonas 2000a: 10; Jonas 2000b: 51, 58–59, 66, 132; and Bentley and Southall 2005: 81; which also show that hardliner elites in El Salvador even warned their counterparts in Guatemala to block electoral participation provisions due to their effects in El Salvador (see below).

[54] McCleary 1997: 136; Stanley 2013: 24.    [55] Robberson 1993: A16.

[56] Robberson 1993: A16; "Returning Exiles Test Guatemala's New 'Democracy'" 1993: 15.

[57] "Returning Exiles Test Guatemala's New 'Democracy'" 1993: 15.

[58] Cited in Vinegrad 1998: 218.

[59] Carlos Mejía, from my interviews in Guatemala City with URNG leaders, 2013.

[60] Reid 1993: 8; Azpuru 1999: 107, 117.

be careful not to damage its "status as an honest broker in the peace process," especially after it had responded so well in the 1993 crisis.[61]

*A Peace Agreement with Electoral Participation Provisions Emerged*
With these more optimistic expectations of nonpartisan external engagement, the URNG General Command called for renewal of the negotiations in July 1993 in order to secure a settlement and transition to a political solution.[62] These expectations increased further with a monitoring mission sent by the United Nations. As negotiations resumed in 1994, the process changed – allowing a mediator appointed by the United Nations to lead the process, and establishing a "Group of Friends" that included the United States, external states that would support the process – and, in doing so, gained momentum.[63] An agenda and a timetable followed. A deal on human rights was finally struck once negotiations were backed by an unarmed mission, United Nations Verification in Guatemala (MINUGUA), which was a "down payment" on the promise to enforce the agreement (though not through military coercion, as discussed below).[64] The URNG even tried to have that mission deployed before continuing the talks.[65] The URNG General Command issued requests for the international community's "vigilance" at this "especially critical and dangerous moment" to ensure implementation of these aspects.[66] The role of international actors – beginning with MINUGUA – became essential in order to hold the stronger side, the Guatemalan government, to the terms of a deal. As the rebel group stated in 1994, "the moral weight of the United Nations and the guarantee that it will verify all of the accords, substantive as well as operational, is essential for a viable process."[67] U.N. involvement, including most obviously the monitoring mission that was MINUGUA, did not work by threatening military coercion. Instead, as the next section discusses (and Chapter 7 further demonstrates), the United Nations and other international actors worked through the nonmilitary coercive channels

---

[61] See, for example, "Background Information for Mr. Lake's November 21 Meeting with Jennifer Harbury" 1994: 2. Some of its pressure also helped push the government through difficult concessions during the peace process, which, if anything, made some suspect it was biased toward the URNG; for example, the U.S. Senate's "hold on the $10 million ESF for Guatemala helped [the government] focus on human rights" in "Guatemala Meeting with President Ramiro de Leon Carpio" 1994: 1.
[62] URNG 1993b; Azpuru 1999: 110; Jonas 2000b: 42.
[63] Willingham and Kusnitz 1994: 1; Azpuru 1999: 110.
[64] McCleary 1997: 137; Azpuru 1999: 117; Jonas 2000a: 12; Jonas 2000b: 48; Verstegen 2000: 48; Allison 2009.
[65] Hamilton 1994: 2; Stanley 2013: 33.    [66] URNG 1994b: 2; UNRG 1994a: 2.
[67] URNG 1990a: 2; InterPress Service 1994: 1.

described by external engagement theory, including threats to withdraw aid and other sanctions around the electoral process.

Once the United Nations was involved, the URNG made a "radical departure"[68] from past policy, issuing an "unprecedented"[69] call for its supporters to vote in the 1995 elections and for the international community to stay involved in the process. Ultimately a leftist party earned 8 percent of the presidential vote and six seats.[70] This was similar to the level of support for the URNG expressed in polls, around 10 percent at that time.[71] The election results reassured the URNG that the electoral process was secure and showed how much support its candidates could receive through the vote.[72] A settlement would not substantially change the expected vote share for the leftist parties, which gave them sustained participation but not significant policymaking power. This evidence is inconsistent with the subtler emulation explanation suggesting that only strong parties that expect to be successful in shaping policy will participate; indeed, the continued low returns for URNG in subsequent elections suggest that electoral success was not the crucial factor behind its decision to participate and push for elections. By participating in the electoral process, however, the URNG would be more protected from the government, draw party funds, and direct resources to its supporters.[73]

After the 1995 elections, the URNG's demand for participation – one of the most challenging aspects of the accords for the government – was solidified in the settlement.[74] The value of electoral participation provisions backed by external actors was clear to hardliner elites, who were "determined not to negotiate a settlement permitting a legal presence or political participation by the insurgent left or its allies"[75] and who, simultaneously, tried to reduce the role of the United Nations. They were warned by their counterparts in El Salvador that these aspects of an accord would increase the ability of these international actors to monitor and enforce compliance.[76] The hardliners did not have sufficient support, however, and failed to block these dimensions of the deal.

The accords were aggregated into the 1996 "Accord for a Firm and Lasting Peace." The settlement was based on these provisions for the

---

[68] "Guatemala Human Rights Practices, 1995" 1996: 14.    [69] Jonas 2000a: 21.
[70] URNG 1995: 2, 4; Sichar Moreno 1999: 80; Jonas 2000a: 21–22; Allison 2006a: 84.
[71] Jonas 2000b: 103.
[72] McCleary 1997: 133; Jonas 2000b: 103; Stanley and Holiday 2002: 435.
[73] Jonas 2000a; Stanley and Holiday 2002.
[74] "Agreement on the Basis for the Legal Integration of the Unidad Revolucionaria Nacional Guatemalteca on December 12, 1996".
[75] Jonas 2000a: 10.
[76] Jonas 2000b: 51, 58–59, 66, 132; Bentley and Southall 2005: 81; Stanley 2013: 32.

URNG to transition from a rebel group into a political party set to compete against the government in post-conflict elections. The URNG had survived fighting at a severe disadvantage for over a decade to secure an agreement: the peace deal redistributed a small share of what had been the government's political power to the URNG – commensurate with its strength at the time – while requiring disarmament of the rebel group and reform of government forces. Political power was distributed through a participatory electoral process with external engagement, to which the force revisions were also pegged, helping to encourage compliance with these aspects of the agreement.[77]

*The Agreement Design Engaged External Actors around Electoral Participation*    Evidence on the post-settlement period is presented in Chapter 7, but the form that the settlement in Guatemala took (participation by all sides as political parties) clearly engaged external actors to monitor and incentivize compliance with the peace process. The U.N. observer mission remained small. In January 1997, fewer than 200 military observers were dispatched for just a few months, despite the fact that many major deadlines were not scheduled until 1999.[78] The longer-term mission consisted of several hundred nonmilitary personnel. This evidence is inconsistent with the escape explanation, as the exit of military observers was planned well before the 1999 elections. The mission had a challenging task, however, given its limited mandate.[79] MINUGUA was to monitor the peace and verify some of the agreement's provisions, but its size and scope were limited.[80] Armed peacekeepers were not even scheduled to be in-country for much of the implementation period, and they were never authorized to threaten or use force as punishment for noncompliance. Indeed, MINUGUA could basically only report on and influence international behavior; it could not use force even to defend its own monitors.[81] Guatemalan consent depended on this dimension to avoid breaching the state's sovereignty.[82] Even as MINUGUA was enacted, a Western diplomat speaking to a reporter warned that "we have much more important crises to pay attention to"; thus relatively limited resources were devoted to the mission.[83] Yet the URNG still acknowledged the importance of the mission: in an interview with me, for example, URNG Congressman Mejía said that, "the international

---

[77] Jonas 2000b: 104, 236; Azpuru et al. 2004: 9–10, 19; Allison 2009: 189, 99.
[78] Santiso 2002: 563, 566–567; Stanley 2013: 124.     [79] See Scott 1995: 2.
[80] As is often the case with peacekeeping missions; see Fortna 2008.
[81] Stanley 2013: 71.     [82] Stanley 2013: 124.     [83] Collier 1995: 2.

community has given great support, especially the United Nations who supported us through MINUGUA."[84]

The settlement thus needed a mechanism, other than military coercion, to increase the costs of noncompliance. That mechanism was to involve international actors in monitoring and incentivizing compliance around electoral participation provisions. The argument is not that MINUGUA did not contribute to overcoming commitment problems, but rather that its personnel, augmented by other international actors, worked through non-military coercion based on the participation provisions and the electoral process. Guatemala had a prior history of election monitoring, which is highly predictive of continued election monitoring.[85] In order to convince the U.S. government that it was democratizing – which was necessary to regain international aid – the Guatemalan government had invited OAS observers for the 1980 municipal elections and, beginning in 1984, national elections.[86] In 1995, the last elections before the final settlement was signed, approximately 650 international observers were present.[87] International election observation had also grown dramatically in the region. During the Guatemalan negotiations, about 50 percent of elections in Latin America were observed by international organizations.[88] International verification of the Guatemalan accords and protection of human rights, at first through MINUGUA and later through these other forms of involvement, improved the situation.[89] For the URNG leadership, the support was crucial: Mejía stated that "almost all the electoral processes that we have participated in, we have had the support of brother countries that have come as international observers. That has helped us, in some cases, defend some electoral processes."[90]

The settlement also used the electoral process to generate incentives conditioned on compliance, as expected by external engagement theory (Chapter 7 discusses this in much more depth). In addition to allowing the URNG to participate in elections, the settlement tightly tied the reforms of state forces to the electoral timeline, including disbanding paramilitaries and replacing repressive troops with civilian police, which would protect the party beyond specific promises to ensure safety during the peace process.[91] Some factions within the government initially resisted the electoral demands by the rebel group, but once the agreement

---

[84] Carlos Mejía, from my interview in Guatemala City with URNG leaders, 2013.
[85] Hyde 2011b.    [86] Santa-Cruz 2005: 679–681.    [87] Inter-Parliamentary Union 1995.
[88] Hyde and Marinov 2012.    [89] Azpuru 1999: 118; Santiso 2002: 567.
[90] Carlos Mejía, from my interview in Guatemala City with URNG leaders, 2013.
[91] Allison 2006b; 2009. The URNG linked these force reforms to the electoral process rather than its own demobilization (Jonas 2000: 238); this may have been due to the relative weakness of the rebel group, which agreed to a much shorter demobilization than that of the government, or it may have been due to advice from FMLN leaders to URNG

was signed, compliance with detailed demobilization and reinsertion plans was monitored by a special commission composed of members of each side, which had international donors as consultants.[92] The November 1999 elections were the deadline for certain aspects of the agreement: "by late 1999, a new National Civil Police force, comprised of at least 20,000 members, shall be functioning throughout the national territory."[93] The U.N. mission was initially scheduled to last through implementation, which was to be just after the first post-conflict elections (1999, so mandated through 2000), but then extended to ensure the terms were enacted through the second post-conflict elections (2003, so extended through 2004), which was supported by the parties; the elections and administration changes were explicitly noted by the U.N. leadership as crucial moments to be present and visible.[94] Given the URNG's weak position entering negotiations, it is unsurprising that the police and military were able to propose relatively weak reforms, and that many political and economic reforms failed when a referendum on these aspects submitted to the population failed to pass.[95] The government negotiator, during the negotiations, told U.S. officials that "there is no major public pressure in the country to grant major concessions to end the war."[96] Nevertheless, political participation and the force integration tied to it were largely achieved.[97] Guerrilla demands had long been "(1) democratic participation in Guatemalan politics, including legal protection for the URNG; (2) guarantees of free speech ... (3) physical protection for the URNG and those who agree with it."[98] The electoral process and international attention were the only leverage that the URNG had over the government.[99] They insisted on international involvement throughout the peace process, including by the U.S. once its nonpartisanship was established, and pushed for conditionality and some funds not channeled through the government.[100] The URNG leadership credits "allied countries

leaders about the difficulties of the demobilization process (based on an interview with a senior member of the rebel group in Jonas 2000: 249).

[92] In addition to the agreement, see Jonas 2000b: 89–92.

[93] "Agreement on the Strengthening of Civilian Power and the Role of the Armed Forces in Democratic Society" 1996.

[94] United Nations General Assembly 2003: 1, 3; Annan 2003: 2. The United Nations also was careful to seek funding very publicly until the end of 1999, even as it was just beginning; see Prendergast 1997: 1.

[95] See, for example, Stanley 2013: 45; also the current URNG leadership estimates compliance at only 10 percent overall, according to Carlos Mejía, from my interview in Guatemala City with URNG leaders, 2013.

[96] "Review of Key Issues" 1992: 3.     [97] Azpuru et al. 2004: 10; Allison 2009.

[98] "Guatemala: Negotiating Peace" 1994: 8.     [99] Jonas 2000b: 241.

[100] "Guatemala: Negotiating Peace" 1994: 11–12.

[including the United States, but also many European nations and several neighboring states] that have always kept their eyes on Guatemala and on the government, trying to enforce the peace accords" as crucial for ensuring the compliance that did accompany the agreement.[101]

*Concluding Thoughts on the Guatemala Case Compared to the Implications*  While structured primarily to test the mechanisms underpinning external engagement theory, the evidence presented in this narrative also addresses some of the alternative explanations. The escape explanation does not find support in this case because, although electoral engagement was used in combination with a very small peacekeeping mission, all armed peacekeepers' exit was timed well before the elections. Beyond that, international actors had not intervened when the electoral participation provisions were requested, nor did they seem to have had any role in requesting them. Working against both the enjoinder and emulation theories is the fact that although elections had been held in Guatemala since the early 1980s, consistent with theories of a third wave of democracy, there was no apparent pressure from the international community to explicitly include the rebel group as a political party in the 1990s.[102] Moreover, the side that should have been the target of more of this pressure, the U.S.-backed government, was not the side that proposed electoral participation provisions. Another dimension of the emulation explanation – that rebel groups that are able to successfully compete for a substantial share of seats under the elections will be those that request these provisions – also does not find support. Guatemala had a very weak rebel group that did not become – and had not been expected to become – a strong political party. Finally, despite a conflict that was already costly and stalemated by 1984, as all sides acknowledged, this was not an easy case to settle: the evidence shows that this conflict was plagued by severe commitment problems that persisted until credible international involvement, not partisan to a particular side, could provide a solution.

This case therefore suggests that the mechanism underpinning external engagement theory plausibly explains the inclusion of electoral participation provisions in the 1996 peace agreement. The weaker side pushed for

---

[101] Carlos Mejía, from my interview in Guatemala City with URNG leaders, 2013.

[102] I asked about this in each of my interviews with members of the international community, and I examined many sources, including the U.S. Department of State documents that have been released. These documents often report later contact between U.S. officials and the guerrilla groups, suggesting that if the pressure had existed, it would have been noted.

these provisions as expectations of credible, nonpartisan external engagement through elections increased. This is not intended to suggest that other factors were not also influential. An electoral solution worked particularly well because of its normative appeal as political openings occurred, but democratization had begun well before the deal was completed, as discussed. Particular politician and party attitudes helped the process along, and all sides, particularly the far right, faced a somewhat more costly fight during this period, which perhaps made the bargain more attractive by comparison.[103] It is clear, however, that the increase in credible international involvement that was not partisan to either side was crucial in enforcing a deal to which all sides would and could commit. Prior to the end of the Cold War, there had been no way to credibly assure the URNG and its supporters protection, with power commensurate with the combatants' relative strength. After U.N. involvement in the region in 1989 and a unified international response to the government's auto-coup in 1993, internationalized elections provided a mechanism by which the international community could monitor and incentivize the government's compliance with the settlement, while providing the rebel group with the small share of power commensurate with its relative strength.

This argument explains the peace agreement's electoral participation provisions, and especially their timing, in Guatemala; more evidence of the international community's role in the post-conflict context is presented in Chapter 7. Next, we turn to El Salvador.

### El Salvador

The conflict in El Salvador had a strong rebel group, the Farabundo Martí National Liberation Front (FMLN), which fought the government for over a decade before signing a peace agreement in 1992. The settlement finalized in January 1992 featured participation provisions for the FMLN in a minimally altered electoral system. The deal was therefore quite similar to the agreement produced in the more asymmetric Guatemalan conflict. In El Salvador, the settlement required identifying a mutually beneficial deal distributing power between the two sides, but commitment problems also had to be solved in order to strike that deal. In this case, then, both factors changed as the geopolitical system shifted. The end of the Cold War helped bring the two sides to the negotiation table and, as in the Guatemalan case, resolved the commitment problems by bringing less partisan and more credible external enforcers engaged through the participatory electoral process.

---

[103] See Kierkegaard 1994: 2; Stewart 1995: A12; Stanley 2013.

*Obstacles to a Settlement during the Cold War*    The robust insurgency in El Salvador (1980–1992) that broke out in 1980 with the FMLN had its roots in the widespread inequality generated by issues over land rights and labor policies.[104] The right-wing government of El Salvador, led by the Nationalist Republican Alliance (ARENA), which had U.S. backing during the Cold War, fought the leftist guerillas, which had foreign support from the Soviet Union. A settlement to the civil conflict faced two main problems in reaching a peace agreement during the Cold War. First, the two sides did not agree on any bargain through the mid-1980s. Second, even once mutually beneficial bargains could be identified – as the conflict was becoming increasingly costly and the fight was reaching a stalemate – each side faced problems in committing credibly not to renege on an agreement.

The first major obstacle to a settlement was that there was thus no convergence on any settlement. Neither side faced substantial costs in fighting – especially because both were bankrolled by their respective state sponsors – and each believed it might win during the 1980s.[105] Negotiations as early as 1984 – which were not fully supported by the government due to opposition from the military and, importantly, from the United States – were doomed from the start and no agreement was signed. The military's opposition stemmed from its belief that it could simply defeat the FMLN on the battlefield at a cost that it found acceptable.[106] In fact, the military received significant U.S. aid, which made the fight less costly for this actor.[107] Meanwhile, the FMLN's demands at the negotiating table were extensive, as it had looked like it had the potential to win the war in 1983, for example.[108] The rebel group wanted power-sharing in a transitional government that would then set up a new order including a reformed constitution, which would potentially set the stage for a reorganized military and eventual elections (although they were not the basis for power-sharing in this proposed settlement).[109] The negotiations failed, and, indeed, had only occurred because the French and Mexican governments had demanded in 1983 that the ruling regime in El Salvador negotiate with the "representative" political force in the form of the FMLN.[110]

Throughout the 1980s, however, the two sides became more open to a settlement, as the cost of what became a stalemated conflict increased. Over the decade, external assistance gradually diminished for all sides.[111] In addition, constitutional changes made in 1983 reduced the incentives

---

[104] Baloyra 1998: 15, 17, 31.    [105] Karl 1985: 328–329.    [106] Munck 1993: 78.
[107] Munck 1993: 78.    [108] Karl 1992: 149.    [109] Karl 1992: 150.    [110] Karl 1992: 149.
[111] Karl 1985: 328–329; Karl 1992: 149; Munck 1993; Call 2002: 547; Santiso 2002: 564.

of El Salvador's business class to protect the agricultural sector.[112] A 1986 earthquake initiated broader economic decline (later compounded by a shock to coffee prices in 1989), which was another catalyst for declining popular support for combatants on each side.[113] The situation reached a stalemate by 1987, if not earlier.[114] The FMLN acknowledged that the "strategic equilibrium" required a settlement as a solution; "a military solution demanding another six years of national bloodletting is not acceptable."[115] Polls overwhelmingly supported a negotiated settlement to end the conflict.[116] The FMLN did manage a final offensive in 1989, which drove home the need to find a deal, but also cemented a stalemate that neither side could win. The stalemate likely increased the range of potential deals acceptable to each side, as it clarified that neither could win, alongside the increased costs to each of fighting. In this case, the end of the Cold War precipitated multiple changes in El Salvador, allowing for both identifying a bargain (just described) and credibly committing to it (described next).[117]

Commitment problems plagued any possibility of a settlement in El Salvador. From its earliest communications, any end to the conflict for the FMLN would have required "power-sharing arrangements that would guarantee [FMLN] security and political leverage."[118] The government had been pressured by the United States to hold elections in 1981 to improve its image, but leftists had been excluded.[119] The FMLN began to explore participating as early as 1983, but it wanted to do so only after establishment of substantial power-sharing in a transitional government that would transform the state, along with other security guarantees based on arms controlled by each side.[120] Negotiations in 1984 therefore failed.[121] The FMLN "refused to recognize a system that would not guarantee its safe participation."[122] Even the government admitted that "the rebels could not safely lay down their arms,"[123] yet it demanded disarmament as it feared that the FMLN would gain power through a peace process and then renege.[124] Each side incorporated further democratization into its proposals for peace, but each articulated fundamentally different ideas for power distribution and protection.

---

[112] Wood 2000: 76–77.    [113] De Soto and del Castillo 1994: 70.
[114] Karl 1985: 313; Karl 1992: 148–149.    [115] Quoted in Karl 1992: 151.
[116] Karl 1992: 151.    [117] Karl 1992: 148; Wood 2000: 76–77.    [118] Sharpe 1986: 482.
[119] Karl 1992: 149–150; Munck 1993: 78.    [120] Álvarez 2010a: 31.
[121] Sharpe 1986: 482; Karl 1992: 148; Álvarez 2010a: 30–31.    [122] Karl 1992: 150.
[123] Karl and Herman 1985: 588.
[124] Karl 1985: 326; President of El Salvador José Napoleón Duarte, from Duarte and Page 1986: 215–226; Colonel Carlos Reynaldo López Nuila, Vice-Minister of Public Security for El Salvador, from Prisk and Manwaring 1988: 373–375.

By 1987, the conflict had become more costly and more convincingly stalemated, yet efforts to reach a settlement still failed. Democratization was gradually taking place during this period, perhaps also driven by changes in the structural conditions that produced U.S. pressure for elections and also produced economic interests in El Salvador that were more aligned with democracy.[125] But the commitment problems for the rebel group still had to be overcome. Even if the rebel group had used force to effectively produce some of these changes, once they disarmed they would need another mechanism to enforce a settlement, implementing and protecting the changes over time.[126] Initial demands at the 1986 and 1987 talks were similar to those in 1984, although the talks progressed further – as far as terms for a ceasefire – suggesting that there might have been room to maneuver toward a deal.[127] But, before any accords were signed, the assassination of the president of the country's Human Rights Commission caused the FMLN to terminate further negotiations.[128] The FMLN remained concerned about protection during the process, while the government continued to worry that the guerrillas would grab more power by returning to fighting.[129]

At this point, neither side expected nonpartisan international involvement to help enforce a deal. Even in 1985, activists seeking peace had asked the United States to make aid conditional so that "any faction that chooses not to play the democratic game will be isolated from domestic and international support."[130] The United States, however, continued to back the government and oppose negotiations.[131] Despite threats by the U.S. Congress, the government in El Salvador had not been sanctioned strongly enough to generate compliance with human rights standards sufficient to protect a peaceful opposition.[132] The government was confident that the United States would not "[turn] against a U.S. ally and [encourage] Soviet intervention."[133] The rebel group shared this view: for example, according to then member of the FMLN General Command, Comandante Shafick Jorge Handel, the United States was then firmly backing the government, and so it certainly would not have been a credible external enforcer of a deal.[134] The United Nations had been

---

[125] See, for example, Wood 2000.    [126] Wood 2000: 79.    [127] Hopmann 1988: 377.
[128] Hopmann 1988: 377.
[129] Karl 1985: 326; Karl 1992: 150; Karl and Herman 1985: 588; Hopmann 1988: 377.
[130] Karl 1985: 328–329.    [131] Karl 1985: 321; Karl 1992: 152.
[132] Schwarz 1991: 23–24.    [133] Quoted in Didion 1983: 95, cited in Schwarz 1991: 62.
[134] Handel 1984: 15. This document and others cited in this case study are part of an extensive collection of published and unpublished documents from the FMLN and the government that is housed at the Hoover Institution Archives.

viewed as impotent and the United States as biased well into the late 1980s.[135]

I argue that overcoming these persistent commitment problems depended on external engagement through elections alongside the transition of the rebel group into a political party. The slow process toward more open elections in El Salvador was "a necessary but not sufficient condition for its own transition from insurgent movement to political party."[136] Most of the existing work has focused on explaining the transition to more open elections, not the transition of insurgents to political parties as part of a peace agreement, but, as the subsequent sections theorize, the latter transition is crucial to securing a settlement.

*Combatants' Increasing Expectations of External Enforcement through Elections*   In El Salvador, the change in expectations about external enforcement was a reaction to a systemic shift and to a new U.S. administration, rather than due to the international reaction to a particular domestic political crisis, which had helped in the especially severe Guatemalan case. After the Democrats gained a majority in the 1986 U.S. Congressional elections, and even more so when George H.W. Bush came to power in 1989, more conditions were applied to U.S. foreign aid policy, especially involving human rights protections for peaceful opponents within foreign states. These general constraints were communicated to states like El Salvador.[137] As the Cold War waned, U.S. support for a peace agreement to end the conflict increased. Among the documents in the George H.W. Bush Archives, early letters from the Bush administration express support for negotiations, as long as no preconditions were set by the FMLN, and commit to sending aid in such a way that would be consistent with terms of a settlement: "U.S. assistance to El Salvador is explicitly conditioned on continued advances in democratization, respect for human rights, and adherence to the rule of law."[138] The 1989 murder of Jesuit priests in El Salvador, allegedly by members of the military, allowed U.S. Democrats to press even harder for additional involvement supporting all sides in securing peace in this particular case.[139] The administration, however, did continue apportioning existing military aid, stating that once the FMLN stopped its offensive whatever remained could be used for peacebuilding.[140] But even Republican pressure increased on the Bush administration to more actively help move toward peace: for

---

[135] LeMoyne 1992; Munck 1993.    [136] Wood 2000: 79.
[137] Karl 1992: 151–159; LeMoyne 1992; Munck 1993; Wood 2000: 80; Call 2002; Álvarez 2010a: 24–25, 28.
[138] Romero 1989: 2.    [139] Karl 1992: 153.    [140] Mullins 1991: 1–2.

example, a letter from Republican Senator John Chafee urged the president to "endeavor to create a climate which will be conducive to the achievement of a peaceful settlement of the civil war in El Salvador."[141] At the same time, international interventions in the region brought the FMLN back to the negotiating table. The 1989 U.S. invasion of Panama and more evenhanded U.N. monitoring of the conflicts in Central America – actions that only became possible as the Cold War wound down – revealed that no regime would receive unconditional support. This substantially changed perceptions about potential international involvement.[142]

In January 1989, the FMLN took an "unprecedented" step by asking to participate in the March elections, if the government would postpone them by six months and adopt minor modifications to make them more transparent.[143] The government initially rejected the proposal, but an FMLN ally, the leftist Democratic Revolutionary Front (FDR), participated in the elections anyway.[144] The FDR was much better protected in these elections than leftists had been in previous years; according to one researcher who has studied the FMLN in depth, with many interviews, "the decrease in repression since the mid-1980s, *added to some of the guarantees that were awarded to the electoral processes because of the effect of the pressure from the international context*, and in particular, the process of Esquipulas II on the Salvadoran government, made it possible to start a legal political struggle with the allies of the guerrilla organizations" (emphasis added).[145]

The behavior and attitudes of FMLN members shifted based on these expectations of less partisan external engagement. After the initial electoral contest, peace negotiations began that featured the FMLN's proposal to participate.[146] This peace process was conducted under the auspices of the United Nations following a November 1989 request by the FMLN that the government agreed to by January 1990.[147] U.S. and U.N. records do not suggest that these international actors pushed for electoral participation, and, indeed, they did not join the process and could not put forward proposals until after the FMLN had made its demand.[148] Considering that the group was viewed as a threat to the United States, and that even supporting a settlement represented a departure from prior U.S. policy, there would be little reason to expect

---

[141] Chafee 1991: 1.    [142] Whitehead 1991: 158; Santiso 2002: 564.
[143] Roca et al. 1989; Wood 2000: 80; Álvarez 2010a: 32.
[144] Karl 1992: 153, 156–159; LeMoyne 1992; Munck 1993: 79; Wood 2000: 80; Álvarez 2010a: 24–25, 28.
[145] Álvarez 2010b: 23.    [146] Wood 2000: 80.    [147] Karl 1992: 154.
[148] Karl 1992: 156.

that the FMLN would be encouraged to become a political party by external actors.[149] Additionally, despite FMLN contact with U.S. Democrats during the 1980s, there is no evidence that the U.S. Democrats, let alone the Bush administration (which opposed the peace process up until the Cold War ended), urged the rebels to pursue this action.[150] The FMLN approached the Bush administration just after the latter was elected about holding conversations, but U.S. administration sources in the same records call the contact in 1991 the first contact with the FMLN.[151] In either event, the FMLN pushed electoral participation throughout the negotiations, and the process linked other provisions, such as disarmament, to the electoral calendar. Demobilization and disarmament – issues at the core of the commitment problems – were the most difficult items on the agenda.[152] The engagement of external actors through the electoral process became crucial.

The FMLN responded favorably as international actors provided further assurances that they would enforce compliance with the peace agreement. U.S. officials and officers began meeting with guerrilla commanders in 1991 to assure them that the United States would "back demilitarization, democratization and economic development" to "encourage lasting stability in the region," with elections at the center of the strategy.[153] Such meetings were, by this point, seen as important so that the United States could "inform the FMLN that it [was] ready to 'act as a guarantor' or whatever [would be] agreed to in the peace accord."[154] At key points in the negotiations, the U.S. secretary of state joined the Soviet foreign minister in expressing strong support for the U.N.-led peace process.[155] Presidents Bush and Gorbachev issued a joint statement backing the negotiations and suggesting an increased role for the United Nations.[156] These shifts at the systemic level produced changes in attitudes on the part of the rebel group and the government regarding the credibility of international actors as backers of a peace agreement. The United States could help enforce the commitments of the government of El Salvador, especially to refrain from attacking those disarming and to reform the military.[157] An FMLN leader Ana Guadalupe Martinez remarked: "Our attitude has changed. We think the U.S. military group [U.S. military advisors and the U.S. Embassy,

---

[149] Karl 1992: 153.
[150] Villalobos 1989; Karl 1992: 153; Eduardo Sancho, cited in Álvarez 2010b: 27.
[151] Handel 1988: 1; "Re: GOES/FMLN Talks" 1991: 2.
[152] Karl 1992: 155; Wood 2000: 80, 106.
[153] Interview quoted in LeMoyne 1992, which also reports on other interviews; the same is also evident from U.S. Department of State documents from 1991.
[154] Walker 1991: 2.    [155] Karl 1992: 157.    [156] Karl 1992: 159.
[157] LeMoyne 1992; Munck 1993.

according to the report] can help in the transition to peace."[158] At the same time, international actors sought to reassure the government that the FMLN, too, would lose its support if it failed to comply.[159] Indeed, U.S. government discussion on an observation mission to the 1991 elections (pre-settlement but with participation from leftist parties with ties to the FMLN) focused on supporting the legitimacy of all parties and also on checking any allegations of fraud from each side.[160]

*A Peace Agreement with Electoral Participation Provisions Emerged*
The United Nations and OAS, as well as religious groups, observed the negotiating process beginning in 1989. The United Nations and the "Group of Friends" – states that initially were involved as an alternative to the United States, including Colombia, Mexico, Venezuela, and Spain[161] – facilitated further negotiations in 1990–1992. In these negotiations, the two sides signed a series of agreements between April 1990 and January 1992. The final 1992 settlement was based on provisions for the FMLN to participate in the electoral system, and the international community strongly backed the agreement. It even sent a small U.N. peacekeeping mission.

Once the international environment shifted beginning in the late 1980s, the demands of the rebel group had come to emphasize its electoral participation as a political party, rather than through power-sharing in a provisional government. I suggest that this is linked to the enforcement mechanism for the settlement that the electoral process now provided, given lessened external actor partisanship.[162] The FMLN shifted its position abruptly beginning in 1989 and began to call for its right to participate in a pluralist democracy.[163] The electoral participation provisions in the peace agreement are often referred to as a concession to the FMLN.[164] Yet while the elections redistributed power between the two sides to some extent, they did not give the rebel group substantial power within the system. Instead they protected the status quo to the extent needed to negotiate the deal with the government, while also serving to ensure compliance by all sides.

What the rebel group ended up accepting, and what it negotiated hardest for, were actually not objectively "fair" conditions for the elections, but

---

[158] Interview quoted in LeMoyne 1992.
[159] LeMoyne 1992; Stanley and Holiday 1997: 32; Howard 2008: 94.    [160] Roy 1991: 1.
[161] Prantl 2006: 180.
[162] A small segment of the guerrillas had advocated political participation beginning in 1983 (especially through Secretary General Eduardo Sancho's "Democratic Revolution," which advocated a pluralist and representative political system), but it was not until after 1987 that such a plan was adopted by the group (Álvarez 2010b).
[163] Karl 1992: 151.    [164] See, for example, Vickers 1992: 5.

instead conditions under which the status quo shifted only slightly. Election reform was to be managed by the Supreme Electoral Tribunal, which was widely known to be biased toward the incumbent.[165] The counter-majoritarian aspects of the electoral system affected the candidates who were elected and the policy changes that resulted.[166] But it was part of the deal in order to balance power between the two sides, and so the FMLN, as well as El Salvador's new human rights monitors and most of the election monitors, did not challenge the outcome of the tribunal's later decisions, nor did the rebel group return to fighting over them.[167] The FMLN's major demands were actually that reforms of the state forces be completed before the elections and that the FMLN be able to become a legal political party (although it would not be likely to win elections, at least not initially); implementation had to come from continual backing by international actors.[168] The guarantees on force reform and power distribution through electoral participation came not so much from internal power-sharing mechanisms as from these international actors, something recognized even by studies focused on the importance of internal mechanisms.[169]

*The Agreement Design Engaged External Actors around Electoral Participation*    The post-settlement period is discussed in more depth in Chapter 7, but the design around international involvement through these electoral participation provisions is clear even in the immediate aftermath. Looking toward the elections, the FMLN would continue to depend "more on international pressures than on legislative clout or popular mobilization to achieve its goals."[170] The commitment problems were ultimately overcome when the FMLN "accepted COPAZ [the National Commission for the Consolidation of Peace] and the United Nations as guarantors of its security."[171] The final deal was signed in 1992. Complementary mechanisms were employed as well: for instance, the United Nations established a small peacekeeping mission during the negotiations in 1991 to enhance the credibility of its guarantee. U.N. Secretary General Boutros Boutros-Ghali called it "the first in a new generation of United Nations operations whose purpose is post-conflict peacebuilding." Fewer

---

[165] Wood 2000: 87.
[166] United Nations 1993, cited in Baloyra 1998: 23–24; Wood 2000.
[167] Baloyra 1998: 30.    [168] Wood 1995: 256; Wood 2000: 79, 83–84, 86–87.
[169] For example, on El Salvador, see Wood 2000, above, and more broadly, Wantchekon 2004: 17, 27. Indeed, some suggest that, even in the more successful cases, democracy has not been consolidated because, for example, reforming these domestic institutions to be more open is not the focus of these international interventions; see De Zeeuw 2005.
[170] Rosa and Foley 2000: 151.    [171] Karl 1992: 160.

than 300 military observers were deployed to verify disarmament, however; moreover, as U.N. resources were constrained, it was clear that more troops would not be dispatched.[172] The size and scope of the mission – as observers and buffers, not enforcers[173] – meant that the enforcement mechanism was not military coercion.

Instead, material and political incentives from the international community were tied closely to compliance, especially through the electoral process. The argument is not that the U.N. mission failed, or that it was not crucial in overcoming commitment problems, but rather that it worked through nonmilitary coercion based on the participatory elections established by the peace agreement. The international election observation was seen as being crucial to unlocking conditional aid: the OAS had monitored the 1991 legislative assembly and local elections, which increased the confidence of the left that the international community could credibly monitor the situation.[174] Aid was linked to this process. The United States continued to contribute 70 percent of official assistance to the government, and it assured each side of "substantial funding," combined with $800 million in national reconstruction funds pledged by foreign states. Aid was unofficially but clearly conditioned on all sides abiding by the terms of the peace accord,[175] thus providing compelling reasons to comply with the peace deal.[176] All sides "needed financial resources to implement institutional reforms, land transfers and reconstruction projects," and the United Nations "was in a position to certify or decertify the good faith and democratic vocation ... and thereby to influence the prospects for major international funding."[177] (Chapter 7 shows how, when any side failed to comply fully, the United Nations and other international actors threatened to block participation and remove aid that could have lost either party essential support in the elections; this created the necessary incentives to ensure compliance by all sides.)

*Concluding Thoughts on the El Salvador Case Compared to the Implications* The evidence in this narrative, like in Guatemala, tests the mechanism underpinning external engagement theory; it also speaks to some of the alternative explanations. The escape explanation still does

---

[172] From the "Report of the Secretary-General Concerning the Formal End of the Arms Conflict in El Salvador," U.N. Doc. S/25006, December 23 1992, quoted in Katayanagi 2002; Call 2002: 555–556.

[173] Fortna 2008.    [174] Sullivan 1994: 86–87.    [175] Rosa and Foley 2000: 137.

[176] Sullivan 1994: 86–87; Rosa and Foley 2000; Wood 2000: 94.

[177] Stanley and Holiday 1997: 23.

not find compelling support, despite the larger U.N. mission in this case: the mission was not mandated for military coercion, but instead relied on election observers and other monitoring mechanisms around that process to allow lower-cost enforcement (described further in Chapter 7). Some of the forces were scheduled to withdraw after the 1994 elections, but the mission continued until 1996, and even afterwards through the next electoral cycles. In addition, in the El Salvador case, international actors seemed to have no role in requesting electoral participation provisions. This evidence is the opposite of what is implied by the enjoinder explanation. The emulation explanation also does not find much support in El Salvador. As in Guatemala, the United States and other international actors pressured the governments to democratize in the mid-1980s, but they rejected the FMLN's inclusion as a political party as late as 1989, in part because of its recent attacks in the capital.[178] In this case, a selection or emulation explanation in which the rebel group seeks to participate because it expects success in elections is more plausible than in Guatemala. But, as noted, the FMLN still did not expect immediate success in the early elections and did not secure many seats until much later (see Chapter 7 for more details).[179] Finally, the ease explanation is also not supported by this evidence. It is clear in this case that the end of the Cold War both increased the cost of fighting – making the conflict easier to settle – and provided external engagement through electoral participation provisions as a solution to commitment problems. The crucial obstacle posed by commitment problems are easier to demonstrate in Guatemala because the timing is so far apart, but even in the El Salvador case, the conflict became more costly before commitment problems were resolved and a settlement was reached. A related institutional explanation often told about this case is that economic shifts and democratic institutions somehow overcame the commitment problem. However, even those who stress the importance of, for example, internal mechanisms in advancing democracy also recognize the importance of international actors on this particular dimension.[180] (And, as Chapter 7 shows, significant noncompliance later in El Salvador required threats and incentives from these international actors to overcome.)

El Salvador, like Guatemala, offers evidence that commitment problems were an obstacle to peace, and that, after the Cold War, increasing expectations that external actors would enforce a peace agreement through the electoral process helped overcome these concerns. The case also provides specific evidence that the rebel group's expectations of this

[178] Karl 1992: 153.    [179] Allison 2006a: 58.
[180] Wood 1995: 256; Wood 2000: 79, 83–84, 86–87.

engagement changed, producing its request for electoral participation, as predicted. Both cases also show that other changes resulting from the end of the Cold War – in particular, the increase in costs of fighting as foreign funding decreased, as well as a shifting economic system – contributed to terminating the conflict. Alternative explanations – such as the fact that the FMLN was politically stronger and better organized compared to the government than were rebel groups in other states – may have also contributed to its willingness to participate in elections. But they do not explain the URNG's decision in Guatemala. Indeed, even the FMLN relied on external actors for its protection as a new political party and to help implement policy, especially initially. None of these potential alternative explanations accounts for the timing of the peace agreements in these cases. The internationalized electoral process was a crucial component to achieving stability. Buoyed by the end of the Cold War, the expected engagement in elections of increasingly nonpartisan international actors – especially the United States, the United Nations, and regional intergovernmental organizations – allowed for the external enforcement of peace agreements through the ability to monitor and incentivize compliance. Over time, these electoral contests set deadlines, required all sides to campaign at regular intervals, and established them as accountable to their domestic populations as well as to these international actors. (Chapter 7 discusses this post-settlement period in more depth.)

### A Case without Shifting Expectations of External Engagement

To further test whether shifting expectations of international involvement allowed combatants to overcome commitment problems through elections, it is useful to examine the mechanism in a negative case in which the peace agreement does not provide for electoral participation, Bangladesh. (Chapter 7 further examines these three cases – Bangladesh, Guatemala, and El Salvador – as well as positive cases with failed peace, to fully explore the mechanism post-settlement.) In Bangladesh, the same commitment problems plagued a settlement, even after the conflict stalemated and allowed the two sides to identify the balance of power between them. But, in contrast to the Central American cases, the end of the Cold War did not produce the same change in expectations of external engagement, due to the state's regional placement. Rather than being involved in a partisan way in the fighting, international actors had not been involved in any substantial way in this case during the Cold War, and that did not change as it ended. In the absence of strong expectations of external enforcement – whether due to partisanship or lack of international interest – my theory implies that electoral participation provisions will not be adopted in this case (which, as Chapter 7 shows, means that the best mechanism for overcoming commitment problems will be a weaker alternative).

The conflict began just five years after Bangladesh gained independence from Pakistan in 1971, when the tribal people in the Chittagong Hill Tracts (CHT) rebelled. They had been denied autonomy in the new constitution, and they faced revenge attacks after having been drafted by the Pakistani government to fight against Bengali secession in the war for Bangladesh's independence. In this case, a weak rebel group faced a small but comparatively well-armed state, similar to Guatemala.

The main rebel group, the military arm of the Jana Samhati Samiti/ Shanti Bahini (JSS/SB),[181] was constantly concerned about government commitment to any proposed bargain. In 1984, the group kidnapped employees of a multinational oil company in an effort to gain a share of regional resources directly from the multinational corporation, rather than relying on governmental redistribution.[182] International lack of interest rather than partisanship was the major problem in attracting external engagement during this period. During six rounds of negotiations between 1985 and 1989,[183] the JSS/SB unsuccessfully demanded U.N. mediation in April 1987 and requested U.N. peacekeepers to guarantee the terms and protect the rebels and their supporters in the event of a deal.[184] But external actors did not engage in the conflict,[185] so the rebel group rejected an agreement.[186]

After the Cold War, there is evidence that the shifting expectations about international engagement that permeated other regions did not spread to Asia. Mechanisms ranging from the presence of peacekeepers to assistance that could be conditioned on compliance remained scarce in the region, likely due to the preferences of the major regional powers. India in particular, but also China, opposed intervention of any type in the region.[187] Regional rates of this type of international involvement – peacekeeping, electoral monitoring that could unlock conditional incentives, and conditional assistance[188] – remained very low. Even though conflicts and post-conflict elections may attract attention – the elections in Bangladesh in 1991 and 1996 were monitored[189] – incentives

---

[181] Referred to as the JSS/SB from here for convenience.    [182] Ghosh 1989: 75.
[183] Mohsin 2003: 40, 90.    [184] Ghosh 1989: 76.    [185] Fortna 2008: 61.
[186] Mohsin 2003: 90.
[187] Discussed broadly in, for example, Carothers 1999: 43; Legro 2005: 174.
[188] Santa-Cruz 2005; Azpuru et al. 2008; Fortna 2008; Youngs 2008; Hyde 2011b; Kelley 2012.
[189] Hyde and Marinov 2012.

did not exist to enforce deals through these mechanisms; these elections in Bangladesh and elsewhere in the region were seen as "not particularly susceptible to influence by international monitors."[190]

The rebel group still tried to solicit international enforcement for a settlement, but it failed. The leader of JSS/SB, Shantu Larma, said later that "we appealed to the international community, but the response was not enough to get a third-party role. We didn't get very positive responses – [just] some encouragement from human rights organizations, such as Amnesty International and the Anti-Slavery Society. We appealed to government, in both the Western and Eastern blocs, but no one came forward."[191] The regional refugee problem between Bangladesh and India drew most international interest, and so there was a possibility that the group could have petitioned UNHCR. But India would have likely resisted, due to its reluctance to have the United Nations potentially involve itself elsewhere, in Kashmir and other regional conflicts. The secretary of international relations for the political group that emerged from JSS/SB, Rupayan Dewan, believed that "they could have come unofficially."[192] The rebel group "struggled to get the outside world to pay attention to their plight, knowing that international pressure is one of the few levers they have with the government."[193] The conflict experienced relatively low levels of violence, which may have made it less pressing relative to other conflicts for the international community, yet the case was similar to Guatemala by the time external engagement occurred there. The rebel group's attempts to gain international attention for any terms of any settlement in Bangladesh appear to have been foiled by its regional location.

In Bangladesh, the JSS/SB eventually settled for an agreement using a different mechanism to overcome commitment problems, because the rebel group's preferred strategy of international involvement was unavailable. In 1991, the JSS/SB declared a temporary ceasefire and initiated new political talks. Fighting continued, although at a lower level, until a settlement was finally signed in 1997. The cost of fighting continued to increase, making a deal appear more attractive: in 1996, for instance, India signed a new water deal with Bangladesh and then withdrew its backing of the JSS/SB.[194] Like the URNG in Guatemala, the rebel group was still in a very weak position, but it continued fighting because the government could not commit to a settlement. The alternative that finally emerged granted some regional autonomy to the group to protect

---

[190] Kelley 2012: 218.    [191] From an interview quoted in Fortna 2008: 62.
[192] From an interview quoted in Fortna 2008: 62.
[193] Mohsin 2003; Fortna 2008: 135–136.    [194] Mohsin 2003; Fortna 2008: 53.

itself and allowed it to wield some small share of power through a Regional Council that would have more authority than previous bodies.[195] Many aspects of the agreement were ambiguous, including a timetable for military withdrawal and the scope of the Regional Council's power. This ambiguity was necessary, according to an anonymous interview, for the deal to happen.[196] (As Chapter 7 will show, the enforcement of the settlement was weak. This is consistent with external engagement theory, given that this case lacks electoral participation provisions.)

This negative case, Bangladesh, experienced commitment problems similar to the Central American cases. The end of the Cold War did not, however, produce the same expectations about international involvement through the electoral process, due to low expectations of any intervention in the region. Therefore, electoral participation provisions could not be secured by the rebel group (or any other actor) to help overcome their commitment problems. This is consistent with external engagement theory.

## Discussion and Conclusions

The process through which electoral participation provisions were adopted in these cases offers evidence that commitment problems were a primary obstacle to a peace agreement. After the Cold War ended, in regions experiencing international involvement, shifting expectations of external enforcement through electoral processes overcame these concerns. The cases also show that other changes occurred. For example, the cost of fighting generally increased as foreign funding decreased and as economic changes made peace, even with concessions, more profitable. These factors along with external enforcement through electoral participation provisions helped overcome commitment problems. But overcoming commitment problems through this mechanism was a crucial component of securing a settlement in each of these cases.

### Considering Alternative Explanations

The evidence from Guatemala and El Salvador, but also examples from the larger set of all 10 positive conflicts that cross the end of the Cold War and then settle with electoral participation provisions, allow for an assessment of alternative explanations. As discussed in the narratives presented in this chapter, the evidence is more consistent with the mechanism underpinning external engagement theory than it is with alternative

[195] Mohsin 2003; Fortna 2008: 53.     [196] Fortna 2008: 54.

explanations. The escape explanation does not find much support in the cases because, although electoral engagement was sometimes used in combination with small peacekeeping missions, troop exits and reductions were timed to coincide with elections in only a few of these cases, such as El Salvador, Angola, and Mozambique. Even then, there is no evidence that the peacekeeping missions made their involvement conditional on holding elections.[197] In other cases with missions, there was no coincidence, such as in Guatemala, where armed peacekeepers were mandated for just six months after the peace agreement, while the participatory elections were not to be implemented until two years from that date. Two other cases in this set, Colombia and the Philippines, both had no armed peacekeeping missions seeking to exit.

In contrast to the expectations of the escape explanation, as well as the enjoinder explanation, the evidence presented in the previous section suggests no international imposition, at least not overtly, of the inclusion of electoral participation provisions in peace agreements. This evidence, of course, cannot rule out the possibility that rebel groups or governments were told behind the scenes, in still classified documents or unrecorded meetings, that assistance would follow only if they held elections. The crucial question for distinguishing between the external engagement explanation and the enjoinder explanation, besides who requested the mechanism to be enacted, is whether the assistance is conditional on compliance with the accords, which is only predicted by external engagement theory (discussed in Chapter 7). The evidence so far works against the escape and enjoinder explanation.

The emulation explanation also does not find much support in these cases. Guatemala and El Salvador both show evidence of U.S. pressure on the governments to democratize in the early 1980s, as part of the third wave of democracy that was solidified in the terms of the Esquipulas II agreement's broad provisions. However, this pressure did not extend to enabling rebel groups to participate in elections as political parties in the next decade. Even if the governments were to adopt norms of increasingly open elections, there is no reason to require these transitions for the rebel groups be written into the peace agreements. In fact, these provisions faced initial resistance from the United States. A more compelling explanation for these particular clauses is the protection of the rebel groups when they settle for a share of power, overcoming commitment problems, as external engagement theory argues. In contrast to the emulation explanation, none of the evidence suggests that actors whose views most resembled a democratic ideology were most likely to adopt these

---

[197] For example, on Mozambique, see Wurst 1994: 82; Lyons 2005: 84; Nuvunga 2007.

provisions: indeed, among the set of rebel groups requesting electoral participation provisions, there were more hardcore pro-communist groups (three) than anti-communists (two). The evidence for the emulation theory is thus not compelling. None of the cases, however, rules out a normative component, which is indeed important across explanations, including to external engagement theory, in that it enables elections to attract so much external engagement.

There is an aspect of the selection and emulation explanations that suggests that perhaps rebel groups more able to compete for a substantial share of seats under the elections will be those that adopt these norms and seek these provisions. Guatemala, in contrast to El Salvador, featured a very weak rebel group that did not experience a smooth transition, yet both included electoral participation provisions. These cases and the data presented in Chapter 4 do not suggest that well-organized groups are any more likely to compete. Even in El Salvador, however, it was clear that the rebel group needed external enforcement, despite being more able to compete as a successful political party, especially over time.

Finally, I turn to the ease explanation: all of these conflicts appear to have been plagued by severe commitment problems that were not resolved until external engagement was available at the end of the Cold War, so these do not appear to be easy cases for settlements that then select electoral participation provisions. I showed evidence of concerns about commitment in this chapter, and provide further evidence in Chapter 7. It is possible that the end of the Cold War, or other changes that coincided with it, increased the cost of fighting, which in turn eased identification of mutually beneficial settlements. But I have shown evidence in the case studies that the end of the Cold War provided a solution to commitment problems through external engagement around electoral participation provisions, either alone or in addition to allowing the identification of a mutually beneficial settlement; this is especially demonstrated by the timing. In El Salvador, the Cold War winding down indeed did make a settlement easier to identify by increasing the cost of fighting, but that the conflict was still hard to settle due to commitment problems. The Guatemala case provides clearer evidence, because even though the conflict was relatively costly for each side early on, commitment concerns drove the rebel group to keep fighting until the end of the Cold War could provide this enforcement solution through these provisions. Further evidence that is also inconsistent with the overall ease explanation follows in the subsequent chapters.

*Findings*

Post-conflict elections that include provisions for electoral participation by combatants have become common since the end of the Cold War. The current literature tends to portray post-conflict elections cynically, as external impositions intended to allow international actors to escape armed interventions in insecure environments. In contrast, this chapter reexamines and recasts those ties by examining cases in which rebel groups and governments sign on to participate in elections as part of a peace process. The end of the Cold War, at least in regions that had received the diffusion of democracy promotion institutions, brought about the possibility of external enforcement, especially through elections, allowing international actors to monitor and incentivize compliance. These provisions were not imposed by outsiders and could potentially produce peace.

The evidence in this chapter thus bolsters Chapter 4: the tests are most consistent with the theory that electoral participation provisions are obtained when combatants expect that such provisions will enable external enforcement. This engagement seems to allow international actors to monitor and incentivize compliance with peace agreements, securing those deals, and potentially making them more likely to endure. In Chapter 6 and 7, I turn from the causes to the consequences of electoral participation provisions.

*Part III*

# Consequences of Electoral Participation Provisions

## Introduction to Part III

The previous chapters examined quantitative and qualitative evidence to understand when peace agreements include electoral participation provisions. Chapters 4 and 5 tested the components of external engagement theory that imply that combatants are more likely to agree to electoral participation provisions when their expectations of involved – although not overly invested or partisan – international actors increase. Chapter 4 showed quantitative evidence demonstrating that electoral participation provisions in peace agreements correlate with proxies for these expectations of external engagement, while Chapter 5 showed qualitative evidence that, with the end of the Cold War, these expectations changed and then that these provisions were included as the centerpiece of subsequent settlements.

Chapters 6 and 7 empirically investigate the most essential question in this book: what are the effects of electoral participation provisions, especially in terms of enduring peace? Understanding how to secure a durable end to conflict, particularly through a settlement, is of crucial importance to international security. Existing work suggests that some post-conflict elections may be inconsequential for enduring peace, or even dangerous to it, but this book identifies certain conditions that can change those effects.

Chapters 6 and 7 analyze the consequences of electoral participation provisions. The implications drawn from external engagement theory center on the argument that electoral participation provisions allow combatants to commit more credibly to the settlements they negotiate, by engaging an external actor through the electoral process to observe and incentivize compliance with the deal. The theory thus implies that electoral participation provisions can stabilize peace agreements, producing a more enduring peace in those settlements that include them compared to those that do not (Hypothesis 3). More specifically, the theory implies that the pacifying effect of electoral participation provisions increases with expectations of international engagement (Hypothesis 3a). An additional implication is that cases with electoral participation provisions have higher rates of monitoring and conditional incentives in these cases, although the correct comparison to test this implication is more difficult to identify. These implications distinguish the theory from alternative explanations, including the claim that post-conflict elections are imposed externally to enable armed international interveners to "escape" especially insecure contexts. Chapter 6 initiates the tests of these implications with quantitative analysis of the chance of returning to conflict after a settlement. It also provides some evidence about monitoring and conditional aid in the elections produced through these provisions.

# 6   Participating for Peace
## Examining the Effect of Electoral Participation Provisions on Peace

The settlement that ended the 2001 civil conflict in Macedonia allowed the Albanian National Liberation Army (NLA) to compete in the 2002 elections as a political party, after it had become allied with other Albanian political parties during the peace process. The electoral process that followed provided an opportunity for external actors to engage in monitoring and incentivizing compliance with the peace agreement over time. In fact, European states organized the largest electoral observation mission to date for the September 2002 elections, including 800 Organization for Security and Cooperation in Europe (OSCE) observers to be deployed to a state of just two million people.[1] These monitors supplemented the 180 OSCE ceasefire monitors and other personnel who were on the ground.[2] The objectives of the election observation effort, as well as the more general monitoring efforts, were broader than ensuring a fair election, however. In a press release, U.S. Department of State Deputy Spokesman Philip T. Reeker warned that international involvement in Macedonia's economic renewal depended on parties meeting standards, not just of fair competition, but also of peace promotion.[3] The electoral deadlines were tied to other aspects of the agreement, including demobilizing and disarming, granting amnesty, and passing legislation to protect minority rights, so it would be clear by the time of the elections whether all sides were complying with these aspects of the peace agreement. Incentives offered throughout the campaign period would be conditioned on compliance. The electoral observation and conditional incentives had been on the minds of the negotiators during the process. James Pardew, U.S. negotiator, recalled in an interview with me that each side knew they had to comply because "we would all be, first of all, monitoring and, secondly, they knew that anybody who got caught failing to hold up their end of the bargain would

---

[1] Bjornlund 2004: 285.
[2] Phillips 2004: 184, 186; and from my telephone interview with U.S. negotiator in the case, James Pardew, 2011.
[3] Reeker's press release, quoted in Liotta and Jebb 2004: 181.

184    Participating for Peace

be held accountable," including by international actors who could delay or deny the state membership in popular European intergovernmental organizations and treaties.[4]

Conditional incentives from the international community seem crucial in this case, and they seem to have had an even more concentrated effect due to the electoral campaign and timeline to which the terms of the peace agreement were linked. Western powers had plenty of incentives that they could condition on compliance. For example, Macedonia had hopes of E.U. and NATO membership, supported by these organizations, which were very popular with voters in the state.[5] Either would provide a "'good housekeeping' seal of approval that assures security guarantees and makes a region more attractive for outside investment."[6] In addition, Macedonia was highly dependent on foreign aid – the government was "wholly dependent on external funds from these countries [in the European Union] for survival" – which provided powerful leverage for these international actors.[7] In December 2001, the U.N. agencies in Macedonia appealed for $41 million for conflict relief operations for the following year.[8] International actors used this aid as leverage, especially against the government, during the electoral campaign in order to ensure that it complied with its commitments. As parliament delayed the Ohrid Framework Agreement ratification process, for example, the E.U. postponed its donor conference until March 2002, after the ratification vote. And in March 2002, donors then rewarded ratification, exceeding the government's expectation by pledging $515 million.[9] This aid, devoted to reconstruction, development, and state budget, provided a new campaign platform for the ethnically Macedonian politicians who had supported an agreement that included more minority rights, which were not popular with the majority. Just a few months later, however, these politicians again delayed passing the actual legislation for these minority rights "because of the election campaign."[10] The international actors made it clear that the hundreds of millions of dollars earmarked by the E.U. was conditional on this legislation ("implementing Ohrid") and that the state also risked forfeiting assistance from the International Monetary Fund (IMF) and the World Bank.[11] Again, although this legislation was unpopular, such losses in assistance would have been even more unpopular. So, by June 2002, the parliament approved the laws. An analyst of the decision said that "the president's office expected that only pressure from NATO, the E.U. and the OSCE would lead to laws being passed."[12]

[4] From my telephone interview with Pardew, 2011.    [5] Liotta and Jebb 2004: 41.
[6] Liotta and Jebb 2004: 85.    [7] James Pettifer, quoted in Phillips 2004: 118.
[8] Phillips 2004: 185.    [9] Phillips 2004: 186.    [10] Phillips 2004: 197.
[11] Phillips 2004: 197.    [12] Phillips 2004: 197.

It was not just the government that would face these costs for noncompliance but also the rebel group. On the rebel side, the new party led by Ali Ahmeti received protection from opposition arrest and harassment by the government.[13] In addition, the party appears to have received internationally backed training and expected to share in government funding after the elections, which made its compliance possible to incentivize as well.[14] Ultimately, compliance on both sides has been reward as the state became a candidate for the E.U. accession in 2005 and NATO in 2008 (pending resolution of a naming dispute with Greece), in addition to receiving substantial aid. While these particularly strong intergovernmental organizations are somewhat unique to Europe, similar monitoring and conditional incentives can be provided in other states. This case suggests that such external engagement around elections played the expected role in helping to stabilize the peace agreement. Specifically, it seems to have increased the cost of noncompliance for each side preparing to participate in elections through the provisions in the peace agreement. The case illustrates how credible external involvement through elections, consistent with external engagement theory, may operate.

The chapter shows broader evidence that matches the implications of external engagement theory.[15] I examine cross-national quantitative evidence in this chapter, as in Chapter 4. I examine whether peace agreements with electoral participation provisions fail less frequently than agreements without these provisions.

Consistent with the implications of external engagement theory, and inconsistent with alternative explanations, I find that peace agreements with electoral participation provisions are correlated with lower rates of conflict recurrence than agreements without these provisions. Other factors could produce these correlations. This is a particular concern when considering the endurance of peace. In particular, decisions to include these provisions might reflect private, potentially unobservable, information that combatants have about the stability of the deal. Evidence presented in Chapter 4, however, suggests that conflicts that are easier to settle are *less* likely to include electoral participation provisions – and, indeed, that harder cases for peace may be more likely to do so – using measures of settlement ease in pre-1989 data that should not be influenced by international involvement. These results may lessen selection concerns because they should bias the estimates in the opposite direction than implied by the theory. However, to increase confidence

---

[13] National Democratic Institute 2002.
[14] Ash 2001; National Democratic Institute 2002; Pickering 2004.
[15] This chapter draws on, and shares figures and tables with Matanock 2017.

in the association, I control for possible confounding factors drawing on work on conflict recurrence, in particular, and I show that electoral participation provisions have distinct relationships with peace, compared to other provisions that often accompany peace agreements and that might also be similarly chosen strategically. In addition, I identify plausibly exogenous sources of variation in electoral participation provisions – expectations of external engagement – and use these variables interacted with electoral participation provisions to estimate the effect. This is also the test of the more specific moderating hypothesis that emerges from external engagement theory.

This chapter also assesses implementation, rather than inclusion of electoral participation provisions, as the independent variable of interest. There are problems with doing so, because the analysis compounds success in the peace agreement with its provisions, so the results should be stronger – and they are stronger, as anticipated. Examination of these settlements in which electoral participation provisions are included but not implemented, while rare, also sheds light on the mechanism (see Chapter 7).

Finally, the chapter shows some initial evidence that elections produced by these participation provisions are associated with higher rates of monitoring and more conditional aid. The findings provide support for external engagement theory, and they provide reason for optimism for the successful use of elections to resolve conflict, under certain circumstances. The results linking these electoral participation provisions to enduring peace run counter to most empirical studies of post-conflict elections, which are discussed at the end of the chapter. (Chapter 7 turns to qualitative evidence to examine the mechanism.)

This chapter first discusses the variation of interest, which is conflict recurrence, while electoral participation provisions and external engagement – discussed at length in Chapters 3 and 4 – are now the explanatory variables of interest. Using the hypotheses from external engagement theory, and alternative explanations, the chapter describes the expected relationships, as well as how they are tested. Next, the chapter presents results on the relationship between peace and electoral participation provisions, and then assesses how the relationship is moderated by expectations of nonpartisan external engagement. This section also discusses selection concerns. The chapter then presents analysis on implementation, which leads to a discussion of the mechanism. It also assesses evidence on monitoring and conditional aid in post-conflict elections. Finally, I contrast this analysis with other more pessimistic analyses on post-conflict elections.

## Peace Agreements and Conflict Recurrence

This chapter uses the data on electoral participation provisions across peace agreements, described in Chapter 3, to examine their relationship with conflict recurrence. External engagement theory implies that having these provisions, and potentially implementing them, stabilizes settlements and produces more durable peace. External engagement theory also more specifically implies that the pacifying effect of electoral participation occurs when expectations of enforcement by external actors are high. I test these implications in a focused comparison in which all cases have signed a peace agreement. The question is whether settlements with provisions for electoral participation, moderated by expectations of external engagement, correlate with lower rates of conflict recurrence, compared to settlements based on other provisions. Later sections also examine implementation of the provisions and external engagement and, in doing so, begin to explore the mechanism.

### Peace Agreements

The set of cases in this cross-national analysis comprises all peace agreements signed between 1975 and 2005 that solve, regulate, or outline a process to resolve the "incompatibility" between at least two sides fighting conflicts that reached at least 25 battle deaths per year.[16] This is the main dataset used in Chapter 4, as well. The comparison across cases that have signed peace agreements reduces some of the heterogeneity between cases – victories, for example, produce less conflict recurrence than do other outcomes[17] – and generate a counterfactual that makes sense. Again, the time period includes the entire third wave of democratization, limiting the comparison to cases that experience normative pressure to hold elections,[18] but the results are not significantly different when an indicator of the Cold War is included to divide the data. Chapter 3 provides summary statistics on these settlements and describes how they were coded in more depth. As noted in Chapter 4, I cluster continuous peace processes to treat sets of negotiations that end with a single solution together, which matches the coding in other datasets like the Peace Agreement Matrix, and I convert these data to dyadic agreements between each signing rebel group and the government. This is important for several reasons: the

---

[16] Harbom et al. 2006; Högbladh 2012.    [17] Licklider 1995; Toft 2009, 2010.
[18] Huntington 1991; Levitsky and Way 2010: 14.

crucial factor is that conflict recurs on a dyadic level, as rebel groups can implement different terms of a settlement – or the settlement at all. For example, in Cambodia, three rebel groups signed the Paris Agreement in 1991, but the Khmer Rouge rejected the settlement within a year, returning to fighting, while the National United Front for an Independent, Neutral, Peaceful, and Cooperative Cambodia (FUNCINPEC) and the Khmer People's National Liberation Front (KPNLF) participated peacefully in the first elections. More broadly, the theory only implies that dyads that agree to participate in elections expose themselves to international observation and incentives for compliance, reducing the value of reneging on a deal, which makes each side less likely to renege and return to conflict. Again, most of the comparison in the analysis occurs across agreements – only 12 have multiple dyadic signatories – but I analyze the results on the dyadic level to test the theory accurately.[19]

### Conflict Recurrence

I am interested in whether peace endures better among peace agreements with particular provisions. I thus examine conflict recurrence in each case while controlling for the conditions as the conflict ends. I code conflict recurrence within each dyad using the Uppsala Conflict Data Program/Peace Research Institute Oslo (UCDP/PRIO) Armed Conflict Dataset; I identify whether the rebel group reenters the dataset, under the same name or UCDP-coded alliance or merger.[20] As alternatives, however, I also consider the UCDP Peace Agreement Dataset coding of two variables: first, whether the implementation failed, which it defines as one or more of the signatories contesting the agreement's validity or withdrawing from the agreement; second, whether the conflict recurred at all, which it defines as any signatory restarting fighting within five years, rather than just recurrence within the dyad. These variables are further from the precise theoretical implication, that the dyad signing the agreement will see an increased cost for noncompliance and therefore

[19] The results in this chapter are similar when analyzed only at an agreement level, but they are sometimes weaker, which is not surprising because the number of observations is smaller. In addition to re-running the analyses on the agreement level as a robustness check, I also always cluster the standard errors by state.
[20] Gleditsch et al. 2002; Themnér and Wallensteen 2012.
   In rare cases, initial agreements are later renegotiated without intervening conflict, so, given the recurrence coding, I include only the initial agreements because including the renegotiations would inflate the success after the fact. I do, however, re-run the data with the renegotiations, and, as expected, the results are stronger. The duration models in the Online Appendix at https://dataverse.harvard.edu/dataverse/matanock take these cases into account (as technically censored when a renegotiation occurs). The conflict data in Chapter 4 discusses the same cases.

remain committed enough to it that neither side reverts to conflict, but both add to our understanding of the effects of electoral participation provisions. In some cases, lower-level conflicts reignite, splinters restart conflicts, or new rebel groups start conflicts, but these do not seem to be systematically linked to electoral participation provisions based on the reports in the UCDP Peace Agreement Dataset.[21]

Of the 110 dyadic peace agreements over time (with 12 emerging from settlements with multiple signatories),[22] 47 returned to civil conflict within five years (43 percent of these agreements). (The list of agreements is shown in the Online Appendix.)[23]

## When Is Enduring Peace Expected?

This chapter draws on the cross-national data on electoral participation provisions to examine whether peace agreements that include electoral participation provisions fail less frequently than agreements without these provisions.

### Electoral Participation Provisions

Among the implications of external engagement theory is that electoral participation provisions should be stabilizing, making peace more likely to endure between the signatories to settlements that include these provisions. If agreeing to participate generates mechanisms for monitoring and incentivizing compliance, each side should expect marginally greater costs for noncompliance, making each less likely to return to conflict, either preemptively or to punish the other side. Thus, the first hypothesis to test is whether peace agreements with electoral participation provisions are associated with a lower likelihood of conflict recurrence than peace agreements without these provisions (H3). (The theory is discussed in more depth in Chapter 2.)

Using the inclusion of electoral participation provisions – again, measured as agreement on holding elections in which each side is set to participate as political parties – I analyze the relationship with conflict recurrence. As described in Chapter 3 and 4, based on the text of the agreements, each is coded for whether it sets clear expectations that

---

[21] Future work should study these effects, however, as it is possible that these elite deals will produce lower levels of democracy, potentially provoking mass movements over time (also discussed in Chapters 1, 2, and 8).

[22] This is less than the number of agreements in Chapter 4 because this excludes peaceful renegotiations (see the note on peaceful renegotiations above).

[23] See https://dataverse.harvard.edu/dataverse/matanock.

elections will be held and that each side will run candidates, usually by legalizing the rebel group as a political party for the government-run elections.[24] As discussed in Chapter 3, most cases are clear as to whether they contain electoral participation provisions.[25]

Following the coding in Chapter 4, this definition of electoral participation provisions does not depend on implementation. Comparing settlements with electoral participation provisions to settlements with other provisions where implementation may be harder to observe could bias the results. Because implementation is ultimately important, I present results on it later in the chapter, and the positive correlation with peace durability are even stronger with it, as expected. But the provisions are the primary independent variable, to avoid bias in the observability of implementation across different peace agreements. Variation in implementation can be produced by either side violating the peace agreement. In a few cases, governments did not hold elections, or held them late; in a few cases, rebel groups did not participate, despite the provisions. As external engagement theory implies, and as I will discuss when considering implementation, the uncooperative side was generally punished and subsequent conflict recurrence was mixed.

Of the 110 dyadic peace agreements, 42 include electoral participation provisions (38 percent). Those without these provisions typically outline other institutional arrangements for sharing power, such as through regional autonomy arrangements. Full implementation occurred after 34 of the 42 agreements with electoral participation provisions, including six that were renegotiated, producing peaceful electoral participation by the ex-combatant parties within 10 years.

---

[24] The legalization of the rebel group in the settlement can occur by implicitly legalizing the rebel group through its inclusion as a political party in a transitional government, or by explicitly legalizing it as a political party to run in elections, as described in Chapter 3. It is possible that the inclusion of transitional governments, rather than electoral participation provisions, is driving any reduction in conflict recurrence (Brancati and Snyder 2013, for instance, find that longer transition periods contribute to peace). To test this, I replace electoral participation provisions with two separate categories for explicit and implicit legalization in the models, and I find that both coefficients are statistically significant and negative, as the theory predicts. Explicitly legalized parties have a larger coefficient. A likelihood ratio test, however, suggests that including these two components separately does not significantly improve the fit of the model compared to including them together (p-value is 0.25). Thus, there is justification for coding these types of electoral participation provisions together. For the skeptic, though, this test suggests that participation in a transitional government alone is not driving the results.

[25] The less clear cases are recoded in robustness checks as discussed in Chapter 3. The results in this chapter hold. The complete list, which notes the less clear cases, is in the Online Appendix at https://dataverse.harvard.edu/dataverse/matanock.

*Expectations of External Engagement*

External engagement theory also implies that the pacifying effect of electoral participation provisions increases with expectations of external engagement through elections to monitor and incentivize compliance. The first hypothesis tested in this chapter may hold because enforcement by external actors is expected in many cases where settlements include electoral participation provisions (H3), but this second hypothesis is a truer test of the theory (H3a); it suggests that these provisions act as commitment mechanisms when external actors are expected to enforce the deal for each side.

In advance of a peace agreement, certain proxies of these expectations exist, as discussed in much more depth in Chapter 4. One such measure is the end of the Cold War, which coincided with both increased international coordination on civil conflict termination and the spread of democracy promotion institutions allowing electoral processes to be more easily observed and conditionally incentivized by international actors. The end of the Cold War thus plausibly produced an exogenous increase in expectations of sufficiently nonpartisan involvement. However, it is also a treatment that is correlated with many changes beyond just these expectations. I therefore also use other proxies to examine variation in these expectations: (1) the percentage of legislative elections in the region that international missions observed in the year prior to the agreement, excluding the state under analysis,[26] and (2) the percentage of regional development assistance devoted to democracy and governance, averaged over the two prior years.[27]

These measures are closely tied to diffusion theories about the spread of democracy promotion, which underpins the mechanism allowing

[26] Hyde and Marinov 2012. The measure, and alternative specifications also used in this analysis, is described in more depth in Chapter 4. I also re-ran this analysis with the observation measure estimated as multiple-year averages, different regional groupings, and including all elections (not just legislative, the most comparable), as described there, and the results hold.

An alternative would be to measure election observation in post-conflict elections held in the state, rather than expectations in the region, but that is problematic. The effect of *actually receiving* observers during the elections, like *actually holding* the elections, is quite strong, but, aside from being highly endogenous, this effect is based on an *ex-post* measure of implementation of provisions. Successful implementation should, of course, be correlated with peace. Refer to the discussion on provisions versus implementation in the section on electoral participation provisions, above, for more on why *ex-ante* measures are needed. I explore summary statistics on this external engagement in post-conflict elections, but these are the most appropriate measures.

[27] Finkel et al. 2007. Again, the measure is described in more depth in Chapter 4.

The democracy promotion variables take values that are well distributed from 0–1.00 for observation and 0–0.20 for aid, so I only report probabilities within these ranges, in the interaction models.

international actors to detect and sanction noncompliance. The election observation variable represents expectations of sufficiently nonpartisan external engagement, as it emerges more or less rapidly due to systemic characteristics, especially the level of international interest in the region.[28] International election observation also unlocked conditional incentives, including democracy and governance aid, which similarly spread at different regional rates.[29] The diffusion of democracy promotion, as discussed in much more depth in Chapter 4, allows the use of these regional trends as a proxy for increased expectations of external engagement in the relevant states.[30]

These lagged regional variables are plausibly exogenous. Measuring whether international election observers were invited to or actually observed the particular post-conflict state would be both highly endogenous and an aspect of implementation, but these regional variables, lagged and even excluding the state in question, do not suffer from these problems.[31] They are unlikely to indicate promising environments for peace due to a mechanism other than international interest. Background interviews that I conducted with Carter Center and U.N. officials indicate that they select less stable states and regions which are, if anything, *less* promising contexts for peace. Broader testing suggests that trends do not simply reflect the spread of democracy or another dimension of governance.[32] Regional variables thus represent plausible proxies – and are the best identified – for combatants' expectations of international engagement (as discussed in more depth in Chapter 4).[33] In the analyses, these variables are interacted with electoral participation provisions, which vary at the dyadic level.

### Considering Alternative Explanations and Implications

Some alternative explanations about why peace agreements include electoral participation provisions differ from external engagement

---

[28] Hyde 2011b; Kelley 2012.    [29] Azpuru et al. 2008; Youngs 2008.

[30] Hyde 2011b and Simpser and Donno 2012 use the regional election observation trend, for example, in similar ways in other studies.

[31] See the problems with measuring implementation discussed in a prior footnote. As discussed in previous chapters, there is regional variation over time in whether post-conflict elections receive international election observation; some do not, such as in Mali after 1991, Djibouti after 1994, Philippines after 1995, and so on. These agreements also typically did not include participation provisions, as expected, likely due to low expectations of engagement.

[32] Simpser and Donno 2012: 507.

[33] Other scholars have used external trends excluding the unit under analysis as proxies, even as instruments, including Simpser and Donno 2012.

theory in that they do not imply more enduring peace with these provisions – other explanations, in contrast, imply the same pacifying effect but suggest that different factors produce it. A particular concern when considering the endurance of peace is that decisions to include these provisions might reflect private, potentially unobservable, information that combatants have about the stability of a settlement. In this section, I discuss how evidence drawn from Chapter 4 points *against* such an "ease" explanation. However, at the end of the section, I also describe additional analyses conducted in this chapter to increase confidence in causal relationship implied by external engagement theory.

The alternative explanations of electoral participation provisions do not all imply less conflict recurrence between the signatories. Most institutional explanations suggest that including provisions for participatory post-conflict elections should have no relationship with peace beyond whatever other power-sharing provisions and guarantees are in the agreement. However, if the elections are arranged to the detriment of other power-sharing provisions, these could prove a danger to peace. The other explanations of these provisions based on international involvement have no clear implications about peace. To the extent that the escape explanation has any implication about peace, interveners may be especially concerned about the costs of remaining in unstable contexts, so they may be more likely to impose faulty elections to withdraw under a façade of governance in these cases, where conflict is also more likely to recur. The enjoinder and emulation explanations are even less clear on any particular relationship between electoral participation provisions and enduring peace. To summarize, external engagement theory implies a positive relationship between electoral participation provisions and enduring peace, specifically when expectations of external engagement exist, while most of the other explanations of electoral participation do not – and they even perhaps imply the opposite in some cases. These empirical tests therefore can separate these alternative explanations from external engagement theory.

As mentioned, however, studying the consequences for peace raises concerns about what is driving any correlation, bringing selection effects to the fore. The provisions do not occur at random, so it is possible that the decision to include them might reflect combatants' private information – which is potentially unobservable – about the accord's stability or about other pressures that they face to do a deal. These possibilities suggest that electoral participation provisions may simply indicate, rather than causally contribute to, a greater propensity for peace.[34]

Yet electoral participation provisions are not systematically included in easier cases, as Chapter 4 initially indicates. What are easier cases? A previous study identified certain types of conflicts that were easier to settle in the pre-1989 period, before any international involvement of any type was common and could have changed propensity for peace failure.[35] The study finds that conflicts with more deaths and displacement, those with contraband funding, and those mobilized on identity cleavages were more likely to recur, while secessionist conflicts were less likely to recur. Using a similar strategy in the 15 peace agreements that occur pre-1989 in my data, I also find that conflict intensity is positively correlated with failure, although not the other variables (noting, however, the very small number of observations for this period in my data).

Using these variables identified in the pre-1989 period, especially on conflict intensity, then, the evidence works against the standard selection effect: electoral participation provisions are more likely in cases that are seemingly *harder*, not easier, to settle.[36] Electoral participation provisions are more likely in cases with more conflict deaths, lower state capacity, and more contraband financing, though not statistically significantly so on all measures.[37] These results are similar to peacekeeping, which is perhaps not surprising, because any type of external engagement may be directed toward the conflicts with the most need. Likewise, we know from the analysis in Chapter 4 that electoral participation provisions are also less likely with indicators and predictors of democratization, including regional rates of democracy. I show the comparison of means on the "ease" variables, reflecting the analysis in Chapter 4, in Table 6.1.

These results are reassuring, but there could still be unobservable information indicating the opposite. I therefore adopt a multi-prong strategy to increase confidence in a causal relationship as implied by external engagement theory, although the possibility of selection bias remains, as with all observational data. Under this strategy, first, like

[34] A correlation between electoral participation provisions and peace could still suggest that these provisions have effects, even if it is due to their strategic selection (a point made more broadly about selection in Schultz 2010).
[35] Fortna 2008: 187–189.    [36] Building especially on Fortna 2008.
[37] The evidence is also somewhat consistent on conflict type: peace agreements in both territorial and identity conflicts are less likely to receive electoral participation provisions, and my pre-1989 correlations with recurrence are also negative for both conflict types, although Fortna (2008) finds the opposite effect on identity (and the same effect on territorial) in her larger number of pre-1989 observations.

Table 6.1 *Cases with Electoral Participation Provisions May Be Harder to Settle*

|  | Mean with Electoral Participation Provisions | Mean without Electoral Participation Provisions | p-value on test that these are the same |
|---|---|---|---|
| **Conflict Recurrence Predictors (Expected Direction Predicting Increase)**[a] |  |  |  |
| Conflict Intensity Measured as Battle Deaths, Logged, Lagged (+) | 10.63 | 9.50 | 0.01 |
| State Strength Measured by Real GDP per capita, 1,000s, Lagged (−) | 2.16 | 2.73 | 0.51 |
| State Strength Measured by Mountainous Terrain, Percent, Logged (+) | 2.36 | 1.92 | 0.08 |
| Rebel Reversion Measured by Contraband Financing (+) | 0.45 | 0.33 | 0.20 |

[a] Contraband financing is the consistent predictor of failure beyond termination type prior to international intervention, according to Fortna 2008; the other variables are standard measures of conflict difficulty and state strength. Models including these, and the controls listed below (on conflict size, duration, failed past agreements, etc.), generally show in even stronger correlations between electoral participation provisions and peace.

other studies, I control for possible confounding factors, including the predictors of conflict recurrence. This analysis is conditional on how conflicts ended – through peace agreements,[38] comparing those with and without electoral participation provisions – so there is less heterogeneity in these data. As discussed and shown in Chapter 4, electoral participation provisions tend to be included in "hard" peace agreements in which conflict recurrence is likely. Nonetheless, I include controls for *conflict severity* (including conflict size and duration, state strength measured using GDP per capita, and the military balance between the rebel group and the government), *settlement difficulty* (including the number of past failed agreements, the number of factions signing and not signing, and whether further negotiations were stipulated in the agreement), *group goals* (including territorial aims, ethnic and religious conflicts, and Marxist organizations, as well as groups with goals of total control over the state), *international relationships* (including peacekeeping missions, but also indicators of significant breaks in time for the system such as the Cold War and 9/11), and *measures of democracy and development*

[38] Asymmetric bargaining situations may also produce agreements, so I control for whether either side dominated during fighting (based on Cunningham et al. 2009).

(including democracy levels at the state and region level, as well as population size).[39] In the interest of space, many additional controls are also included but, as just noted, in alternative models. One important set of such additional controls are those on good governance. Good governance could drive an effect of electoral participation provisions on enduring peace.[40] I control for "corruption," "bureaucratic quality," and "law and order" (which is sometimes called rule of law), but none are statistically significant (see Table A.6.2 in the Online Appendix at https://dataverse.harvard.edu/dataverse/matanock). These variables are also not highly correlated with electoral participation provisions. In addition, I consider the institutions and level of development when the peace agreement is signed, which may contribute to conflict recurrence, with less divided and better designed systems potentially producing more enduring peace.[41] The controls are all measured during the conflict, or as the settlement is signed, in order to avoid post-treatment bias by adding those measured after the provisions are decided. I also control for region indicators, time-period indicators, and the interaction of these variables,[42] as well as regional variables that may work separately from the external engagement mechanisms proxied through observation and conditional aid, including conflict and level of democracy in neighboring countries.[43]

Second, I introduce another important set of variables for this analysis: other provisions in peace agreements, including those for other types

---

[39] Hartzell and Hoddie 2003, 2007; Walter 2004; Doyle and Sambanis 2006; Mukherjee 2006; Fortna 2008; Gilligan and Sergenti 2008; Nilsson 2008; Mattes and Savun 2009; Toft 2009; Mason et al. 2011. In addition to these variables, I include alternative variables: for conflict severity, battle deaths, conflict duration, strength of the rebel group and the government, size of each of these sides' forces, government capabilities, amount of mountainous terrain, and level of infant mortality; for settlement difficulty, measures of ethnic and religious divisions, the main strategy used by the rebel group, and institutional controls such as whether the state had been partitioned, but also more on regime type and democracy level; for international relationships, presence of any peace-keeping mission, past U.N. peacekeeping missions, and those with an enforcement mandate, aid and trade dependence, U.S. military aid, alliances, and colonial relationships with major powers. The results hold (unless, of course, controls with many missing values or multiple variables with strong correlations inducing multicollinearity are included).

[40] See, for example, Fearon 2011; Walter 2015.

[41] Sambanis and Schulhofer-Wohl 2007; Flores and Nooruddin 2012; Brancati and Snyder 2013.

[42] I show the 10-year period variable, but I also ran the five-year period variable and the results hold. Approaching year indicators interacted with region indicators approaches collinearity with the regional democracy promotion variables, so those models naturally will not converge.

[43] Gleditsch and Ward 2000, 2006; Gleditsch and Beardsley 2004; Hegre et al. 2011.

of power-sharing. It is plausible that the rebel group and the government have private information to indicate whether peace will be durable, and, when they believe that it will be, they include other precise and demanding provisions, alongside electoral participation provisions, in the peace agreements. Thus, these agreements would be stronger along a variety of dimensions and also be associated with a longer duration of peace, but due to an unobserved variable. These settlement provisions, aside from electoral participation provisions, would then be associated with a longer duration of peace and be codetermined with electoral participation provisions. If these variables are all highly correlated with peace and with each other, this could suggest that an omitted variable makes each side expect to uphold the deal, generating both stronger agreements and a longer duration of peace. By including controls for other provisions in the agreement, I can assess whether each of these makes the agreements more likely to hold, as well as whether all types of strong provisions are simply grouped together in agreements that are likely to stand for other reasons. I can also see if the main results hold with these as controls.

I thus examine provisions to disarm, demobilize, and reintegrate combatants, reform the security sector, and integrate government or civil service, each of which may reduce conflict recurrence.[44] A set of studies discusses the importance of requirements for revisions to the national army and police, especially through integration of the two sides' forces into one new entity that both can trust to protect their interests.[45] Security sector reform (SSR) – that is, reconstituting and restructuring armed forces – is associated with more durable peace.[46] Disarmament, demobilization, and reintegration (DDR) provisions may also help disband illegal forces more quickly.[47] Additionally political power-sharing agreements may have a similar ameliorating effect on fear, which may help keep the agreement in place, although other conditions may be needed to enact these.[48] This type of power-sharing may be accomplished through electoral participation provisions, as discussed in Chapter 2, but alternatively could be accomplished by integrating government or the civil service.[49] I use the UCDP variables, which broadly define any provisions that could fit these categories, and avoid any bias in coding.[50] If combatants have private information about prospects for peace and thus include more provisions in more stable agreements, then these provisions should be negatively correlated with conflict

[44] See, for example, Hoddie and Hartzell 2003.
[45] Hoddie and Hartzell 2003; Toft 2009.      [46] See, for example, Toft 2009.
[47] For one example among many, see Werner 1999.
[48] Walter 1999, 2002; Derouen et al. 2009.      [49] Mukherjee 2006.
[50] Harbom et al. 2006; Högbladh 2012.

recurrence and positively correlated with electoral participation provisions.

The measures used in the analysis are all summarized in Table A.6.1 of the Online Appendix at https://dataverse.harvard.edu/dataverse/matanock.

Finally, and perhaps most importantly, I test the specific moderating hypothesis – that electoral participation provisions may only have a pacifying effect only when external actors are expected to engage – captured through an international shock and regional trends that are plausibly exogenous sources of variation (discussed in the section above). This test, too, provides a mechanism to parse between external engagement theory and alternative explanations, including selection effects, as only the former implies that the pacifying effect of electoral participation provisions increases with these expectations of external engagement.

## Does Peace Endure with Electoral Participation Provisions?

External engagement theory implies that electoral participation provisions are associated with a lower likelihood of conflict recurrence, but the alternative explanations do not imply the same. This analysis therefore examines settlements to determine whether electoral participation provisions are associated with enduring peace among combatants.

When peace agreements fail, they typically do so early. Examining whether the conflict ever recurred for the dyad through 2010 (see Figure 6.1), states seem to be at the greatest risk in the first few years after the peace agreement. Early failure is consistent with commitment problems, because these initial periods of implementation may be those during which each side is most concerned about noncompliance and thus trying to preempt or punish any perception of the other side reneging by returning to fighting.

In terms of modeling conflict recurrence, the interesting variation is in whether they fail, not their specific duration, as just discussed. Moreover, I seek to assess whether electoral participation provisions affect peace failure, so the treatment occurs at the time of the settlement. This chapter therefore examines whether or not the conflict recurred between the signatories within five years, using simple bivariate tests, survival estimates and cross-tabulations, and then fitting a logistic regression model.[51] This is a common way of modeling termination type's

---

[51] Given the small size of the dataset and number of controls, I re-ran these as generalized linear models; the results are substantively similar.

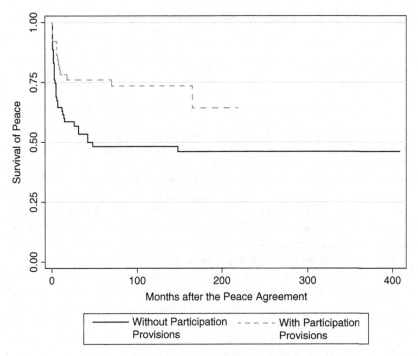

Figure 6.1  Kaplan-Meier Survival Estimates of Peace
Note: This figure is also shown in Matanock 2017.

association with peace failure.[52] Another appropriate way to conceptualize conflict recurrence is through duration models,[53] which explicitly model the time to recurrence based on the conflict characteristics. I discuss these models further and show their results as an alternative in the Online Appendix.[54] Finally, because observations may be related, I cluster the standard errors by state in both specifications.[55]

The results suggest that peace agreements with electoral participation provisions are positively associated with peace in simple

---

[52] For example, see Toft 2010.
[53] "Fails within five years," is a hazard rate similar to those estimated in some duration models (Box-Steffensmeier and Jones 2004).
[54] The duration models, including a Cox proportional hazard model, confirm the findings of these logit models, as shown with extensive discussion in the Online Appendix at https://dataverse.harvard.edu/dataverse/matanock (especially Table A.6.3–4).
[55] The results also hold clustering by conflict. As noted, to address independence concerns, I also re-ran the analysis with the dependent variable as agreement instead of dyad; the results hold, just losing statistical significance with the time period and region indicators and their interaction (which is not surprising given the smaller set).

Table 6.2 *Conflict Recurrence after Peace Agreements*

|  | Participation Provisions | None |
| --- | --- | --- |
| Conflict Recurrence | **21% (9)** | **56% (38)** |
| None | 79% (33) | 44% (30) |
|  | Fisher's Exact=0.00 |  |

comparisons, as external engagement theory implies. The initial Kaplan-Meier estimates indicate a positive relationship between the survival of peace and settlements that include electoral participation provisions (Figure 6.1). A log-rank test for equality of survivor functions shows a statistically significant difference between the curves (at a 0.01 level). The relatively flat shape of the survival estimates, after the initial drop, also indicates that conflicts that recur usually do so within five years, as just discussed.

Peace agreements with electoral participation provisions are associated with a lower likelihood of conflict recurrence than other peace agreements in these survival estimates, and also in simple cross-tabulations. Conflict recurs within five years in just 21 percent of agreements with these provisions, but in 56 percent of those without.[56] This relationship is statistically significant (Table 6.2).

Switching from cross-tabulation to logistic regression models, the results hold (see Model 1 in Table 6.3). The estimated coefficient for electoral participation provisions is negative and statistically significant. The interpretation of this marginal effect is identical, as it should be because the comparisons are the same, and electoral participation provisions are associated with a 35 percentage point decrease in the risk of conflict recurrence.[57] Another way of saying this is, in these data, peace holds 80 percent more frequently when these provisions are included than when they are not (79 percent compared to 44 percent).

### Other Factors

Even controlling for other provisions and possible confounding factors, the pattern in the data remains consistent with external engagement

---

[56] This variable captures all but three failures identified in the data in Figure 6.1. The three excluded happen much later, potentially driven by new leaders, perhaps even splinters. For example, the failure of the peace agreement between the Colombian government and Ejército Popular de Liberación (EPL) which failed after thirteen years.

[57] All analysis in this chapter was run in Stata 13, and the interpretations were produced with the new margins and marginsplot commands, which can be applied to interactions (Williams 2012).

Table 6.3 *Electoral Participation Provisions and Conflict Recurrence*

| | Model 1 | Model 2 | Model 3 | Model 4 | Model 5 | Model 6 | Model 7 | Model 8 | Model 9 |
|---|---|---|---|---|---|---|---|---|---|
| Participation Provisions | -1.54*** | -1.34** | -1.99*** | -1.62*** | -2.04*** | -1.50*** | -1.55*** | -1.61** | -3.77** |
| | (0.56) | (0.54) | (0.56) | (0.59) | (0.58) | (0.55) | (0.56) | (0.63) | (1.56) |
| DDR Provisions | | -0.89** | | | | | | | -1.93** |
| | | (0.45) | | | | | | | (0.74) |
| SSR Provisions | | -0.00 | | | | | | | -2.04 |
| | | (0.48) | | | | | | | (1.27) |
| Government Power-Sharing Provisions | | 0.50 | | | | | | | |
| | | (0.58) | | | | | | | |
| Civil Service Power-Sharing Provisions | | 0.13 | | | | | | | |
| | | (0.49) | | | | | | | |
| Major War | | | 0.94 | | | | | | 2.17* |
| | | | (0.71) | | | | | | (1.21) |
| Duration of the Dyad's Conflict | | | 0.03 | | | | | | 0.06 |
| | | | (0.03) | | | | | | (0.06) |
| Real GDP per capita (1,000's, Lagged) | | | 0.02 | | | | 0.04 | | 1.07*** |
| | | | (0.06) | | | | (0.06) | | (0.40) |
| Balance between Group and Government | | | -0.45 | | | | | | |
| | | | (0.41) | | | | | | |
| Past Agreement(s) | | | | 0.15 | | | | | |
| | | | | (0.31) | | | | | |
| Number of Active Factions Not Signing | | | | 0.10 | | | | | |
| | | | | (0.08) | | | | | |
| Number of Factions Signing | | | | 0.49** | | | | | 0.33 |
| | | | | (0.22) | | | | | (0.35) |
| More Negotiations Stipulated in Agreement | | | | 0.92 | | | | | 0.60 |
| | | | | (0.57) | | | | | (0.94) |
| Territorial Conflict | | | | | 0.13 | | | | -2.27 |
| | | | | | (0.80) | | | | (1.47) |

Table 6.3 (cont.)

| | Model 1 | Model 2 | Model 3 | Model 4 | Model 5 | Model 6 | Model 7 | Model 8 | Model 9 |
|---|---|---|---|---|---|---|---|---|---|
| Identity Conflict | | | | | -0.38 (0.64) | | | | |
| Marxist Conflict | | | | | -0.62 (0.54) | | | | |
| Rebel Groups with Total Goals | | | | | 1.56* (0.86) | | | | 0.11 (1.20) |
| Cold War | | | | | | -0.70 (1.17) | | | |
| Post-9/11 | | | | | | 0.15 (0.69) | | | |
| U.N. Peacekeeping Mission (Present) | | | | | | 0.31 (0.64) | | | 2.65 (2.10) |
| Regional Election Observation (Percent, Lagged) | | | | | | -1.19 (1.15) | | | |
| Regional Democracy Level (Lagged) | | | | | | -2.26* (1.37) | | | -0.45 (5.53) |
| Level of Democracy (Lagged) | | | | | | | -0.04 (0.06) | | |
| Population (1000's, Lagged) | | | | | | | -0.00 (0.00) | | -0.00 (0.00) |
| Region, Decade, Interaction | | | | | | | | IN | IN |
| Number of Observations | 110 | 110 | 108 | 110 | 108 | 110 | 110 | 97 | 96 |
| Pseudo R–Squared | 0.09 | 0.12 | 0.15 | 0.14 | 0.16 | 0.15 | 0.10 | 0.11 | 0.38 |
| Log Pseudo Likelihood | -68.48 | -66.10 | -63.25 | -64.63 | -61.66 | -65.00 | -67.81 | -59.02 | -40.73 |

Note: Method is logistic regression analysis. DV is conflict recurrence by government-rebel group dyad within 5 years (binary). Numbers in parentheses are robust standard errors, clustered by state (maximum=43). Number of observations varies, aside from control missingness, because region/time-period/interaction perfectly predicts success/failure (five regions and three time-periods).
*** p<0.01, ** p<0.05, * p<0.1

theory's implication on electoral participation provisions and enduring peace. Considering other provisions in the peace agreement first: including these indicators of alternative forms of power-sharing leaves the estimate coefficient for electoral participation provisions negative, similarly sized, and statistically significant (Model 2 in Table 6.3). Not all provisions are associated with a lower likelihood of conflict recurrence, however. Estimated coefficients for provisions to integrate the civil service and government are positive and, for the former, statistically significant in some specifications. The estimated coefficient for DDR provisions is negative, however, and statistically significant. This suggests that other aspects of settlement design are also important, although only certain other provisions may have beneficial effects on enduring peace. The main result, however, holds even with these other provisions included.

Peace agreements with electoral participation provisions also are not highly correlated with other provisions, as shown in Chapter 4, which otherwise could suggest an omitted variable about propensity for peace. Aside from DDR provisions (36 percent), none of these are similarly included together with electoral participation provisions. These variables represent plausible economic, military, and other political provisions – three of the four main categories identified as important in the literature.[58] Variables representing the fourth category, territorial power-sharing, are negatively correlated with participation provisions. Overall, electoral participation provisions are not merely included in agreements alongside other provisions that all reduce the likelihood of conflict recurrence, suggesting that an omitted variable for "propensity for peace" is not driving the results.

The relationship between electoral participation provisions and peace in these data also holds when controlling for other possible confounding factors (Table 6.3, Models 3–9). The estimated coefficient for electoral participation provisions remains negative and statistically significant.[59] In these models, I include controls for other provisions, conflict difficulty, rebel group aims, and systemic and state characteristics; Model 9 includes all those that are statistically significant in any specification from among these. (I include other controls in Table A.6.2 in the Online Appendix at https://dataverse.harvard.edu/dataverse/matanock.) Aside from the other provisions, few controls are either positively or negatively associated with conflict recurrence across specifications. The estimated coefficients for the size and length of the conflict are positive and

---

[58] See, for example, Hartzell and Hoddie 2007.
[59] Robustness checks include dropping each conflict and using alternative control variables (described above); the results are similar.

sometimes statistically significant, suggesting that larger and longer con-flicts are more likely to recur. The estimated coefficients for indicators of rebel groups with territorial goals and without aims of total control of the state are negative, while those for indicators of conflicts with more factions are positive, and each correlation is sometimes statistically significant. The estimated coefficient for peacekeeping is not statisti-cally significant, controlling for all of these other variables, although it is in some of the alternative specifications. These results suggest that the main result is not driven by peacekeepers who employ elections but are only having a causal effect themselves, through a security guarantee enforced by military coercion, for example. They also suggest that correlation with enduring peace is not driven by easier cases to settle in which electoral participation provisions are simply included without consequence, which works against a selection explanation based on factors measured directly and indirectly. The results do not support a good-governance explanation either: the estimated coefficients for the governance controls are not significantly significant, and they do not change the relationship between peace and electoral participation pro-visions in these models, suggesting that they are not driving that main result (shown in Table A.6.2 in the Online Appendix at https://data verse.harvard.edu/dataverse/matanock). In Model 8 and 9, I add the region and time-period indicators and their interaction. The estimated coefficient for electoral participation provisions remains negative and statistically significant, and it is substantively similar across models.

### Expectations of External Engagement

External engagement theory also implies that pacifying effect of electoral participation provisions increases with expectations of external engage-ment for enforcement (H3a). I use the same specifications as above, but include proxy variables interacted with electoral participation provisions to assess this relationship.[60]

The data indicate that *all* peace agreements with electoral participa-tion provisions occur after the Cold War (as discussed in Chapter 4).[61]

---

[60] Regional democracy promotion variables are most plausible as proxies for expectations of sufficiently nonpartisan external engagement (as discussed above), providing traction for the analysis by offering some plausible exogeneity, but they *could* instead be thought of as instruments for electoral participation provisions. As a robustness check, I used both variables as instruments, separately and together. The latter is weak, but the results generally hold.

[61] Coding electoral participation provisions is less clear in a couple of early cases, so they are included in the re-coding robustness check noted in the data section; the results are similar.

Table 6.4 *Electoral Participation Provisions, Expectations of External Engagement, and Conflict Recurrence*

|  | Model 10 | Model 11 | Model 12 | Model 13 |
|---|---|---|---|---|
| Electoral Participation Provisions | 1.24 | 1.95* | 0.76 | 0.58 |
|  | (0.92) | (1.17) | (0.73) | (0.86) |
| Regional Election Observation (Percent, Lagged) | −0.30 | 0.43 |  |  |
|  | (0.84) | (1.00) |  |  |
| **Elect. Part. Provisions\* Reg. Election Observation** | **−4.03\*\*\*** | **−5.20\*\*\*** |  |  |
|  | **(1.50)** | **(1.83)** |  |  |
| Regional Democracy and Governance Assistance/ Development Aid (Lagged Two Year Average) |  |  | 9.71 | 8.59 |
|  |  |  | (6.97) | (10.27) |
| **Elect. Part. Provisions\*Reg. Dem. and Gov. Assistance** |  |  | **−32.30\*\*\*** | **−31.12\*\*\*** |
|  |  |  | **(10.19)** | **(10.59)** |
| Region, Decade, Interaction |  | IN |  | IN |
| Number of Observations | 110 | 97 | 96 | 84 |
| Pseudo R-Squared | 0.13 | 0.16 | 0.17 | 0.21 |
| Log pseudolikelihood | −65.13 | −55.77 | −53.24 | −45.23 |

*Note:* Method is logistic regression analysis. DV is conflict recurrence by government-rebel group dyad within 5 years (binary). Numbers in parentheses are robust standard errors, clustered by state (maximum=43). Number of observations varies because region/time-period/interaction perfectly predicts success/failure.
* $p<0.10$, ** $p<0.05$, *** $p<0.01$

The coefficient on these provisions, when including an indicator for the pre-1989 period, therefore can be considered a moderated relationship. After the exogenous shock of the Cold War ending, the reduction in the risk of conflict recurrence thus still negative and statistically significant.

I also specify models with electoral participation provisions, regional election observation, and their interaction (Model 10 in Table 6.4), as well as each of the other models (showing the specification that adds regional and time-period controls, as in Model 11). I do the same for democracy and governance assistance as a percentage of development aid (Models 12 and 13).

The estimated coefficient for the interaction term is negative and statistically significant, but their interpretation is more complicated.[62] Using these models, I calculate the adjusted predicted probabilities across the values of each regional proxy. Figure 6.2 shows the

[62] Brambor et al. 2006.

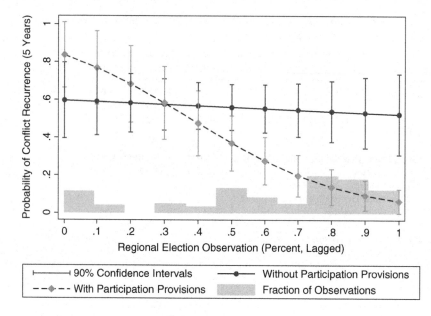

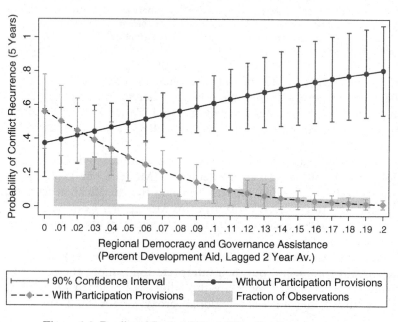

Figure 6.2  Predicted Probabilities of Conflict Recurrence
Note: From Model 10 and Model 12 with 90 percent confidence
intervals. These figures are also shown in Matanock 2017.

relationship with peace (main y-axis), in agreements with electoral participation provisions compared to those without these provisions (two lines), across the values of the mediating variables (x-axis). When at least 40 percent of elections held in the region during the previous year were internationally observed, electoral participation provisions are associated with a decreased risk of conflict recurrence (the association is statistically significant when at least 60 percent of elections were observed). When democracy and governance assistance constitutes at least 3 percent of aid distributed to the region over the previous two years, electoral participation provisions are associated with a lower likelihood of conflict recurrence (and at 7 percent, the association is statistically significant). The interpretation of the other models is similar. This relationship is striking given that the inclusion of region and time-period controls indicates that identification is based on variation in the prevalence of programs for democracy promotion, rather than a simple time or regional trend.

The theory's implications on peace hold. Electoral participation provisions are negatively related to conflict recurrence in these data. This result is especially striking considering these provisions may be more prevalent in cases in which conflict recurrence is otherwise *more* likely. The findings hold when controlling for factors that previous studies find predict peace, including power-sharing and peacekeeping. In addition, some of the other provisions for power-sharing arrangements have the opposite correlation with conflict recurrence. This suggests that private information is not producing the main result by leading both to the incorporation of multiple provisions and enduring peace, for example. The data do not support alternatives, especially the escape explanation, and imply the absence of a correlation or a negative correlation between electoral participation provisions and peace. The specific moderating relationship implied by external engagement theory also holds in this analysis.

### Considering Other Outcomes

I also analyze slightly different measures of the failure of peace. First, considering whether the peace agreement failed, including rejecting the deal but not returning to conflict, I find an even stronger correlation with electoral participation provisions. A simple cross-tabulation of electoral participation provisions and their failure shows that peace agreements fail in 17 percent of agreements with these provisions, but in 57 percent of those without (Table 6.5). Second, considering a slightly

Table 6.5 *Different Measures of Conflict Recurrence after Peace Agreements*

|  | Participation Provisions | None |
|---|---|---|
| Failed According to Signatories | 17% (7) | 57% (39) |
| Not | 83% (35) | 43% (29) |
|  | Fisher's Exact = 0.00 | |
| Any Signatory Returns to Fighting | 26% (11) | 56% (38) |
| None | 74% (31) | 44% (30) |
|  | Fisher's Exact = 0.00 | |
| Any Revived Conflict | 67% (28) | 75% (51) |
| None | 33% (14) | 25% (17) |
|  | Fisher's Exact = 0.39 | |

broader measure of conflict recurrence that includes reversion to fighting by *any* of the combatants who signed the settlement, I find very similar results to the main tests. Conflict recurs within five years in 26 percent of agreements with these provisions, in contrast to 56 percent of those without. These results hold with the same model specifications presented for the main measure.

Interestingly, and not unexpectedly, the reduction in conflict recurrence is no longer statistically significant when including any existing or new group that was not a signatory to the agreement. These existing groups that did not sign, and new groups that emerged after an agreement was signed, should not experience the same dynamic as those who struck the deals composing these settlements.

### Analyzing Implemented Electoral Participation and the Persistence of Peace

I now consider actual electoral participation after the inclusion of provisions in peace agreements. The implementation of electoral participation provisions *may be easier to observe* than the implementation of peace agreements with other provisions (for example, due to the benchmarks and milestones that they provide, as discussed in Chapter 2). Analyzing the endurance of peace following implementation rather than inclusion also drops the cases in which conflict recurs before the elections. Both of these problems in the analysis may bias an association with peace – potentially increasing a positive association. Most of the analysis, therefore, treats provisions as the primary independent variable to avoid that bias. In 28 cases, not including six

Table 6.6  *Conflict Recurrence after Peace Agreements (Implemented)*

|  | Implemented Participation | None |
|---|---|---|
| Conflict Recurrence | 7% (2) | 55% (45) |
| None | 93% (26) | 45% (37) |
|  | Fisher's Exact = 0.00 | |

peaceful renegotiations, the electoral participation provisions are fully implemented within 10 years of the agreement, as described in Chapter 4. In the other cases, however, one side or the other failed to implement them by 2015.

Specifying the independent variable of interest as the *implementation* of participatory post-conflict elections within 10 years of the agreement, rather than the inclusion of electoral participation provisions, indicates that conflict recurs in 7 percent of cases, compared to 55 percent otherwise (Table 6.6). This relationship is also statistically significant. Most elections are monitored, including all with rebel group electoral participation, as the next section describes. Both holding and monitoring elections depends on successful implementation of agreements; the association is thus expectedly larger using this measure (a 48 percentage point difference when these provisions are in, compared to when they are not, in this specification, as opposed to 35). Thus, peace is even more persistent when only considering cases of implemented electoral participation provisions. This correlation, however, conflates implementation with the independent variable and adds bias, as discussed.

Implementation can fail in one of two ways in these cases: first, the government might fail to hold elections or hold them only irregularly. These cases include Rwanda, where the 1993 agreement was entirely broken by the genocide, and Afghanistan, where the 1993 and the 1996 deals had not produced any elections before the Taliban overthrow upset both signatories to the agreement in 1996. In each case, fighting began again.

Second, the rebel group might fail to participate even when provisions are in place and the government holds the elections. These cases include the Khmer Rouge in Cambodia, which abandoned the Paris Accords soon after signing in 1991, and the Movement for Democracy in Liberia (MODEL), which, unlike the Liberians United for

Reconciliation and Democracy (LURD), did not participate in the elections after the 2003 deal.[63] The Khmer Rouge returned to fighting, while MODEL did not; LURD's electoral engagement, alongside international actors, seems to have enforced sufficient compliance from the Liberian government. Most of these cases fit into the latter category in which groups were generally allied with the other rebel groups that participated as political parties in the elections.

Further examination of cases of failure can be useful in identifying whether the expected mechanisms are operating: specifically, noncompliance should be followed by punishment for the offending side if external engagement theory is operating. Indeed, I find that the uncooperative side was generally punished and subsequent conflict recurrence was mixed. I consider this evidence in Chapter 7.

### Exploring the Mechanism behind the Persistence of Peace

Before turning to these cases, however, I examine additional data that can begin to test the mechanism underlying these correlations. External engagement theory implies that this correlation should hold *because external actors engage in election observation and provide conditional incentives, such as democracy aid, for compliance with the settlement.* In particular, the electoral cycles should provide opportunities for external actors to detect and sanction noncompliance. An implication from this theory, then, is that the mechanisms should be in place for external enforcement. I examine international election observation and democracy aid, as well as conditionality on these incentives through comparisons of post-conflict elections in this section, as an initial test of the mechanism (in addition to examining case studies shown in Chapter 7). However, many dimensions of implementation success will certainly affect any correlations run, and the correct comparison group is also a challenge. I analyze post-conflict legislative elections that follow electoral participation provisions compared to post-conflict legislative elections that follow any other type of termination.[64] An additional challenge is that the data on

---

[63] In Burundi, Frolina, at least, and perhaps Palipehutu, participated in communal elections alongside the National Council for the Defense of Democracy (CNDD) and the CNDD-FDD in 2005, and they seem to have participated in the national elections, but data coders could not find a full listing of the small "other" parties for that contest (Matanock 2016b).

[64] Post-conflict legislative elections are the most clearly comparable (because, for example, presidential elections are more often monitored, as discussed in Chapter 3), but the

conditionality with peace processes are difficult to obtain, in part because policymakers have not standardized use of particular types of funds for these purposes. For instance, trust funds for political parties in these post-conflict contexts exist in Mozambique, Nepal, and several other cases, but they are not consistently deployed. Instead, in many cases, states work through democracy aid or even development aid, alongside election observation, to clearly but unofficially condition assistance on compliance. I discuss the need for more consistent means of providing conditionality further in the conclusion. In the meantime, while cross-national comparisons in the data can take a cut at analyzing the mechanism, and can speak to generalizability, the case studies in Chapter 7 are able to provide a more careful accounting of these mechanisms and their use in enforcement.

To test whether these mechanisms are in place, comparing across post-conflict elections, I use data on election observation and democracy aid by state, as well as conditionality and pressure in the lead-up to elections. The theory implies that external actors will engage through electoral processes once these peace agreements are signed. Table 6.8 shows that post-conflict elections that follow peace agreements with electoral participation provisions are positively correlated with international election observation and democracy and governance assistance. The first relationship is statistically significant at the standard levels. In addition to these data, which underpin the regional variables used throughout this project, I also examine new data on conditionality just before elections. That data codes conditionality as "threatened or imposed punishments (political, economic, legal)" and "promised or granted rewards (political, economic, legal)" conditional on "democratic electoral change," which is deemed to be essentially abiding by the rules of the game.[65] It also codes mediation, diplomatic missions, and shaming conditional on the same. These measures capture some of the conditionality and pressure that external engagement theory implies in response to any potential noncompliance in the lead up to the elections. Table 6.7 shows that post-conflict elections that follow peace agreements with electoral participation provisions are also positively correlated with conditionality and pressure. The relationships are often statistically significant at the standard levels despite the small number of observations. Together, these results suggest that participation provisions increase external engagement through

results are similar using all post-conflict elections, as well as considering even elections in which the entire conflict is not ended but at least one dyadic conflict has terminated.

[65] Donno 2013: 204.

Table 6.7 *External Engagement in First Post-Conflict Elections*

| | Post-Conflict Elections after Settlements with Electoral Participation Provisions | Post-Conflict Elections after Other Types of Termination |
|---|---|---|
| International Election Observers | **94% (15)** | **53% (56)** |
| None | 6% (1) | 47% (41) |
| Fisher's Exact = 0.01 | | |
| U.S. Democracy and Governance Aid as a Percentage of Development Aid (Logged, 2-Yr Avg.) | **2.51** | 1.01 |
| Fisher's Exact = 0.19 | | |
| Non-U.S. Democracy and Governance Aid as a Percentage of Development Aid (Logged, 2-Yr Avg.) | **2.85** | 2.18 |
| Fisher's Exact = 0.15 | | |
| Conditionality or Pressure before Elections | **77% (10)** | **44% (26)** |
| None | 23% (3) | 56% (33) |
| Fisher's Exact = 0.06 | | |
| Conditionality before Elections | **38% (5)** | **17% (10)** |
| None | 62% (8) | 83% (49) |
| Fisher's Exact = 0.13 | | |
| Pressure before Elections | **77% (10)** | **41% (24)** |
| None | 23% (3) | 59% (35) |
| Fisher's Exact = 0.03 | | |

the electoral process as implied by the theory. The case studies further examine the mechanism.

Finally, the theory also implies that international engagement through elections can make noncompliance more costly by providing a mechanism through which external actors can monitor and sanction deviations from the deal *over time*. A piece of data to assess, then, is whether the *second* elections were held as they were supposed to be held. Of the electoral participation provisions that were put into place, over 90 percent have held a second election without major delays. The mechanism of participation thus continues over time.

These data provide an initial test of the mechanism of external engagement theory, and they are strongly consistent with it. The mechanism is examined in more depth through the case studies in Chapter 7.

## Examining All Post-Conflict Elections or Periods

Finally, examination of all elections that follow peace agreements, or even all post-conflict elections, and all periods following conflicts demonstrates the importance of electoral participation provisions. Not just any elections will work according to the theory: what is needed for stability is provisions in peace agreements for participatory elections with external engagement.

First, I assess the coefficient of *all* electoral settlement provisions on peace. I test electoral provisions with *and* without participation provisions.[66] Some elections do not require including all sides as political parties. Instead, combatants may receive non-elected positions in the cabinet, military, or other government bodies. The estimated coefficient for an indicator of all elections is negative, but very small and not statistically significant, consistent with previous studies.[67] Only by narrowing the focus to electoral *participation* provisions does the estimated coefficient become large and statistically significant (and, of course, still negative), compared to electoral provisions without participation and to no electoral provisions, even separately (see Table 6.8 below).[68] Both of these alternative provisions in peace agreements structure payoffs through fixed formulas, rather than through each side's planned participation in elections. This suggests that provisions for participation by each side in post-conflict elections – crucial for external engagement theory – may have a different relationship with peace from other post-conflict elections. This also shows why my results differ from the more pessimistic literature on post-conflict elections.[69]

---

[66] To provide a closer comparison to the literature on post-conflict elections, considering data on all post-conflict elections (Flores and Nooruddin 2012), I examine a variable for the post-conflict elections produced by electoral participation provisions. Compared to all other post-conflict elections, such as those held unilaterally by the government side, elections produced by participation provisions had a 177 percent larger effect on sustained peace in those data. This additional analysis could suffer the same bias as discussed above, because it requires successful implementation to be included, which the provisions variables do not require. See Matanock 2016b for more detail on this comparison.

[67] See, for example, Collier et al. 2008.

[68] Other studies examine *all* post-conflict elections whether or not they follow peace agreements, but this theory does not have an implication as to whether these provisions *should* stabilize peace with respect, for example, to victory (such as Brancati and Snyder 2011, 2013).

[69] Similarly, in a concurrent study to this one, Marshall and Ishiyama 2016 find that elections that include rebel groups as political parties, compared to all other peace spells that follow settlements and that have an election, are associated with more durable peace.

Table 6.8 *All Electoral Provisions and Conflict Recurrence*

|  | Model 13 | Model 14 |
|---|---|---|
| All Electoral Provisions | −0.31 (0.51) | – |
| Electoral Participation Provisions | – | (omitted as baseline) |
| Electoral But No Participation Provisions | – | 1.70*** (0.63) |
| No Provisions on Elections | – | 1.21* (0.64) |
| Number of Observations | 105 | 105 |
| Pseudo R-Squared | 0.00 | 0.09 |
| Log pseudo-likelihood | −71.19 | 64.66 |

Note: Method is logistic regression analysis. DV is conflict recurrence by government-rebel group dyad within 5 years (binary). Numbers in parentheses are robust standard errors, clustered by state (maximum=43).Also note: Chadian cases with missing text were difficult to interpret as to whether they had *any* electoral provisions (although not electoral participation provisions), so they are dropped in this analysis.
* $p<0.10$, ** $p<0.05$, *** $p<0.01$

Second, to provide a closer comparison to the existing literature on conflict recurrence,[70] I have modeled all peace periods of at least one year following a civil conflict, and the results suggest that peace agreements with electoral participation provisions are the second best option, after an outright military victory by one side, in terms of establishing enduring peace.[71] Compared to low-level conflict – a period during which international actors may be able to intervene to push one side or the other to victory, or to help negotiate a settlement – a victory reduces the hazard rate of renewed conflict by 90 percent, while an agreement with electoral participation provisions reduces it by 74 percent. These reductions are both substantively and statistically significant. By comparison, an agreement without these provisions reduces risk of renewed conflict by 65 percent, and ceasefires with conflict regulation by 46 percent (and without by 26 percent).

## Conclusions

Are post-conflict elections effective tools for securing and sustaining peace? This chapter has argued that electoral participation provisions –

---

[70] I appreciate an anonymous reviewer's suggestion to examine this comparison. Much of the other work on conflict recurrence indicates an important effect of victories; see Toft 2009, 2010.

[71] Data are from Kreutz 2010. Again, however, this additional analysis could also suffer the bias discussed above, because it requires that the conflict successfully end for a year to be included.

alongside expectations of external engagement – contribute to durable peace by allowing combatants to overcome the challenge of credibly committing to a settlement. Consistent with the patterns implied by external engagement theory, electoral participation provisions, and their interaction with expectations of external engagement (which are more exogenous to the peace process), are associated with a lessened risk of conflict recurrence in these data.

Counteracting growing concern that post-conflict elections are ineffective or even conflict-inducing, these findings suggest that under certain conditions, elections can contribute to peace. In doing so, it highlights the importance of disaggregating electoral participation provisions and exploring the effects of different types of electoral arrangements in post-conflict settings to seek approaches that could save lives. Post-conflict elections that are participatory and internationalized, which are demanding conditions, have discernibly different associations with peace in these data than do other elections. Future research should consider other disaggregation of these elections.

The primary conclusion from this chapter is that electoral participation provisions can be stabilizing when accompanied by expectations of sufficiently nonpartisan external engagement, although the limitations of the data prevent full identification of the underlying causal mechanism producing the correlations shown. Chapter 7, then, turns to process-tracing in order to examine that mechanism.

# 7   Engaging through Elections
## External Observation and Incentives around Elections during Implementation

---

Chapter 6 provided striking evidence that electoral participation provisions are correlated with more enduring peace. Peace between signatories succeeds 80 percent more often frequently when settlements are based on electoral participation provisions, compared to when they are based on alternative provisions. Even more crucially, cases where combatants had reason to expect external engagement around these electoral participation provisions drive this relationship. The empirical pattern held through a variety of statistical tests, suggesting that a selection effect was not causing the settlement stability. This evidence is consistent with external engagement theory, and it is not consistent with most alternatives, or with existing pessimistic impressions of post-conflict elections. Yet the analysis in the previous chapter could not rigorously test the causal mechanism connecting electoral participation provisions with more durable peace.

This chapter examines empirical evidence to understand *why* conflict recurrence is less likely when electoral participation provisions are included in peace agreements, using case studies to complement the cross-national analysis in Chapter 6. I employ process-tracing within case studies to identify the causal mechanisms at work, further probing the plausibility of external engagement theory and distinguishing it from other explanations. These case studies examine the implementation period *after* the settlement is signed, and so should be considered in conjunction with Chapter 5, which examines why electoral participation provisions are adopted. The causal chain in this period, then, begins with the peace agreement. This chapter's main purpose is not to assess generalizability – which Chapter 6 has demonstrated through cross-national comparison – but rather to understand why these correlations hold.

### Implications to Be Tested

My theory implies that electoral participation provisions decrease the risk of conflict recurrence *because external actors engage in election observation and provide conditional incentives, such as democracy aid, for compliance with the settlement* (see Table 5.1 in Chapter 5). In particular, the coordination cycles established by electoral participation provisions should provide periodic opportunities for international actors to coordinate the detection and the sanctioning of noncompliance. The culmination of these cycles in elections should provide points of maximal information and impact for increasing accountability by means of these actors' leverage over the candidates and their parties. Chapter 6 demonstrated evidence consistent with some of the mechanisms necessary for external enforcement – international election observation and democracy aid, as well as conditionality and pressure using these incentives in the pre-election period – through comparisons of post-conflict elections. While these comparisons are consistent with external engagement theory, they are not well identified. Case studies can thus provide much more careful accounting of these mechanisms. The cases can also examine particular instances of noncompliance and show whether enforcement action follows. We may observe relatively few acts of enforcement should ex-combatant parties be deterred from noncompliance by the threat of significant costs should they fail to comply,[1] but we should see some threats of enforcement, at a minimum. Ex-combatant political parties may fail to comply initially – perhaps to test the international actor's commitment to impose a cost, or perhaps due to something more innocuous, such as a lack of capacity – and external actors should then detect and sanction that noncompliance. This pressure should typically be sufficient to produce ex-combatant capitulation and compliance before noncompliance proceeds very far, although partial compliance may sometimes be tolerated under some circumstances (modeled in the Appendix and discussed in these cases).

The causal chain implied by the theory would, of course, be detectable when settlements include electoral participation provisions and combatants expect external engagement. Settlements in which compliance and, potentially, peace fail, however, are also informative. These failed cases, in contrast to successful cases, may include electoral participation provisions but not appropriate expectations of external engagement. Across "positive" cases – agreements that have electoral participation provisions, including those that succeed and those that fail – I assess whether the mechanisms predicted by my theory are available for international actors, and I evaluate whether this expected causal chain occurs in instances in which ex-combatant parties fail to comply. While failed cases are rare – outliers in the statistical analysis – they can help clarify why conflict actors do not comply and thus further elucidate the mechanism underpinning

---

[1] Off-the-equilibrium-path behavior, conceptualized by Weingast 1996.

these outcomes. I also briefly examine a "negative" case, a settlement without electoral participation provisions, to assess whether it lacks mechanisms to similarly sanction noncompliance and thus stabilize peace. In each of these cases, I can observe the process of implementation, including sequencing, and assess multiple measures of compliance and enforcement.

Alternative explanations imply different causal chains in the post-conflict period. The ease explanation, in particular, implies that the conflict is decisively settled due to exogenous factors, so combatants should not have serious concerns about noncompliance or conflict recurrence. None of these explanations imply that external actors should engage through the electoral process to monitor and incentivize compliance. Indeed, the alternative explanations beyond selection considerations do not anticipate any correlation between electoral participation provisions and peace at all, so naturally they struggle to explain why it occurs (again, see Table 5.1). Beyond the alternative explanations outlined in Chapter 2, broader theories of peace agreements and governance also have implications for peace. Some theories of peace agreements attribute stabilization to an armed security guarantee by peacekeepers.[2] Evidence of substantial troop presence using military coercion would therefore strengthen these theories. External engagement theory can also function through peacekeepers – but, in contrast to these alternative explanations, it implies that international actors, U.N. missions and others, will use monitoring and nonmilitary coercion around participatory elections. These different mechanisms can be discerned in the case studies. Theories of governance would attribute successful peace processes to strong institutions (power-sharing) or civil society (democratization) that allow domestic actors to threaten to sanction noncompliance. They may also more directly attribute peace to good governance because the dividends that it pays inspire all actors to stick with peace.[3] These alternatives are discussed and tested in Chapter 6, but I also test these additional alternatives through the case studies.

### Case Selection

For process-tracing, I need "positive" cases that include electoral participation provisions so that I can analyze the implementation period in depth. Among the positive cases identified as facing a clear change in combatant expectations of external enforcement at the end of the Cold War, I focus initially on the same two Central American cases again for

---

[2] See Walter 2002; Fortna 2008.   [3] Fearon 2011; Walter 2015.

this chapter. Guatemala and El Salvador were especially clear tests of the theory in Chapter 5 because the rebel groups had to be persuaded of the external actors' shift toward nonpartisanship and thus their credibility as enforcers because those actors had backed the government during the Cold War, before they would sign onto a settlement based on electoral participation provisions. Now we can examine whether these changed expectations of credible enforcement are borne out. Strikingly, if the evidence is consistent with the theory, these cases should feature a former foreign backer threatening to sanction its previous government partner over noncompliance. Examining both cases also provides a nice comparison on subtle dimensions related to rebel group strength that assessed the plausibility of those alternative mechanisms, as in Chapter 5. (Again, this chapter also does not seek to establish generalizability, which was done through the cross-national analysis in Chapter 6, so convincingness rather than some difficulty criterion can be used in deciding which cases to test.)

This chapter also discusses failed cases from the larger set of 10 positive settlements to conflicts that were fought across the end of the Cold War. Two of these cases, where peace failed, are outliers based on the statistical correlations in Chapter 6. These cases are Cambodia and Angola. The other two cases that I examine, Northern Ireland and Colombia, had compliance failures, although peace succeeded for the signatories. Examining these cases allows further understanding of the mechanism and comparison with alternatives. Each of these cases shows evidence that is consistent with external engagement theory.

Finally, I return to the same negative case (an agreement without electoral participation provisions) as in Chapter 5. Bangladesh offers insight on whether the mechanisms to ensure compliance are absent when these provisions are not included.

### Case Evidence

I use the same process-tracing on these cases as described in Chapter 5 and the same mix of primary and secondary sources, this time for the implementation period.

### Chapter Overview

The first two sections, which examine the positive cases of El Salvador and Guatemala, focus on the mechanisms driving post-settlement peace and whether external engagement around electoral participation provisions is employed as a means of enforcement in instances of initial noncompliance. These sections also examine alternative explanations. I then turn to cases of substantial noncompliance, including Colombia and Northern Ireland, and cases in which peace fails – the outliers of Angola and Cambodia – after settlements with electoral participation provisions. Finally, I evaluate the mechanism in a case without electoral participation provisions, Bangladesh. I conclude by discussing the overall findings from these cases.

To preview the findings, in the positive cases, expectations of external engagement are borne out. Electoral participation provisions establish mechanisms for enforcement, which are then employed in instances of initial noncompliance. The electoral participation provisions assist in the process by providing fixed cycles that culminate in power distribution and that enable international actors to coordinate on detecting and sanctioning noncompliance at times of maximal effect. The failed cases, particularly the outliers, provide evidence of insufficient sanctions for noncompliance due to inadequate or partisan external enforcement. The negative case also shows evidence of no such sanctions for noncompliance. The evidence is thus consistent with external engagement theory and not the alternative explanations.

## Cases of Successful Enforcement around Electoral Participation Provisions

Turning first to process-tracing in the selected positive success cases, as described above, I analyze the causal chain identified and hypotheses listed in the "Implications" section using the sequencing posited in the "Chapter Overview" section (both above).

### El Salvador

In El Salvador, the Farabundo Martí National Liberation Front (FMLN) and the government signed a peace agreement with electoral participation provisions in 1992, after expectations of appropriate external engagement increased. Reaching that settlement required identifying a solution to commitment problems that, among other issues, had prevented any success in a peace process during the Cold War. Even once a bargaining range emerged as continued conflict became more costly and eventually stalemated, no settlement was reached because, prior to 1989, despite elections and negotiations, each side recognized that the rebel group "could not safely lay down [its] arms."[4] However, the United States, in particular,

---

[4] Karl and Herman 1985: 588.

began to take a less partisan role in the state to secure peace as the Cold War wound down and the more conciliatory George H.W. Bush administration came into office.[5] At the same time, U.N. involvement in the region cut off military support and simultaneously bolstered beliefs in less partisan intervention.[6] In 1989, the FMLN took an "unprecedented" step by seeking to participate in elections.[7] The contests provided reassurance to the rebels due to "the guarantees that were awarded to the electoral processes because of the effect of the pressure from the international context."[8] After that election, peace negotiations under U.N. auspices featured the FMLN's proposal to participate in elections. During the talks, U.S. officials met with guerrilla commanders to assure them of U.S. support for a strategy based on peace building elections that would be tied to economic development to help promote stability. The FMLN then declared that, "our attitude has changed"; the leadership began to believe that the United States could "help in the transition to peace."[9] The deal, based on a request from the rebel group at the beginning of the negotiations, legalized the FMLN explicitly to participate in the next election. The FMLN's acceptance of the United Nations and other actors as guarantors of its security, especially though elections, helped the group overcome its commitment problems, as shown in Chapter 5.

This chapter focuses on what happened once the peace agreement was signed. I show that the electoral participation provisions in El Salvador allowed extensive external engagement to monitor and incentivize combatants' compliance with the peace process. Much of the international engagement emerged around elections, which offered a particularly effective coordination cycle during which to monitor and incentivize compliance. The preponderance of evidence suggests that these mechanisms, rather than power-sharing through the elections or open elections backed by voters, were influential in ensuring enforcement. Moreover, the evidence demonstrates that commitment problems arose during the implementation, suggesting that compliance would not necessarily have been the preferred strategy for each combatant side during this entire period, potentially endangering the settlement. As I show, external actors intervened to enforce compliance by the incumbent government and by the rebel group when each stalled on implementing particular terms of the deal. The participatory electoral process alongside this type of international involvement appears to be responsible for the compliance of each side in these cases, which helped peace persist.

[5] Karl 1992: 151–159.   [6] See Santiso 2002: 564.   [7] Wood 2000: 80.
[8] Álvarez 2010b: 23.   [9] LeMoyne 1992: 2.

*Mechanisms for External Enforcement*   Throughout the peace process, the role of external actors in enforcing the peace agreement was undeniable. The political party formed by the rebel group, the FMLN, acknowledged the important role of international involvement in bolstering its influence – as long as it complied with the peace agreement.[10] External engagement helped guarantee the FMLN's security,[11] and pressure from international actors – more than the FMLN's political clout or popular mobilization – assisted the rebels by ensuring compliance with the accords by the government.[12] Indeed, according to U.S. State Department officials documenting the FMLN disarmament, one of the organization's leaders, Chief Leonel Gonzalez, emphasized "that the 'important rules of the game' had been established during the peace process, and the FMLN planned to insist on respect for these rules."[13] At first the group could enforce respect through its own arms, but it later needed pressure that came through monitoring and conditional incentives provided by the international community. Part of the enforcement was done directly by the United Nations Observer Mission in El Salvador (ONUSAL), but not through military coercion commonly envisioned for peacekeeping operations. ONUSAL was small – under 300 military observers in the year following the settlement, 300 police observers from 1992 to 1994, and then less than 200 total observers following the elections – "a relatively low number of military observers" compared to other peacekeeping operations.[14] The mission had to work through observation in combination with incentives from donors, rather than punishing noncompliance with force, because its mandate – and its capabilities – did not allow military coercion.

Much international engagement by the United Nations and by other external actors focused on elections, which offered particularly effective moments to monitor compliance. The U.N. mission dramatically increased in 1993 when it formed an electoral division. Its 900 additional observers more than doubled the size of the mission.[15] The role of the United Nations in election observation was seen as reinforcing its other observation functions.[16] The day-to-day director was Rafael López-Pintor, who had designed and conducted the quick count in the Nicaraguan elections, which provided additional legitimacy to the operation.[17] Beyond the expansion of U.N. personnel, the electoral process attracted an influx of international attention to El Salvador: other states and

---

[10] Wood 2000: 79, 86–87.   [11] Karl 1992: 160.   [12] Rosa and Foley 2000: 151.
[13] "FMLN Begins Destruction of Arms" 1992: 3.   [14] Call 2002: 555–556.
[15] United Nations 1996: 737, cited in Howard 2008: 100. Also see Call 2002: 582.
[16] Stanley and Holiday 1997: 24–25; Call 2002: 590.
[17] Montgomery 1998: 124; Howard 2008: 122.

organizations also sent election observers totaling approximately 4,000.[18] Elections continued to attract international attention throughout the decade, in part through large election observation missions. After successfully monitoring the 1991 elections, the Organization of American States (OAS) was seen by each side as a credible arbiter of compliance with the rules of the process.[19]

The international attention generated at these moments increased the ability of external actors to enforce compliance with various dimensions of the peace deal in El Salvador. Because the electoral cycle was "non-negotiable" and fixed by the 1983 constitution, it presented a "constraint on the timelines and deadlines of the peace process."[20] Not only could the United Nations exploit specific moments in the electoral cycle to threaten the ability of various actors to participate in the process – which would have affected the power distribution – but donors could use the monitoring leading up to these moments to condition their aid for maximal effect. The instances of noncompliance, described below, show that international actors not only *could*, but they in fact *did* use these mechanisms. U.N. election observation allowed the organization to "certify or decertify the good faith and democratic vocation [of various actors] ... and thereby to influence the prospects for major international funding."[21] Providing these assessments of the implementation of the accords helped increase the donors' pressure for compliance.[22]

The international election observation was thus crucially tied to the provision of foreign aid,[23] popular with voters in this context and crucial to both parties at the time.[24] This provided considerable leverage to sanction any noncompliance. The government was a direct beneficiary throughout the electoral process, but so was the FMLN, because some of the aid was specifically funneled through the FMLN's political party in order to provide funds for its "affiliated" non-governmental organizations and former combatants.[25] USAID, which donated directly, also pledged to make its allocations "consistent with decisions resulting from consultations with the FMLN" in addition to government decisions, so that each side benefited.[26] The elections were among the last steps in the peace process, although the legalization of each side as political parties had allowed them to sit on the verification commission long before voting.[27] According to El Salvador's Central Bank's records, the United States continued to contribute over 70 percent of the economic aid that the government received at least through 1995, and so U.S. openness to involving each side and to

---

[18] Montgomery 1998: 131.    [19] Sullivan 1994: 86–87.    [20] Call 2002: 581.
[21] Stanley and Holiday 1997: 23.    [22] Call 2002: 558–559.    [23] Sullivan 1994: 86–87.
[24] For example, see Wilkinson 1993b: 2.    [25] For example, see Johnson 1993: 7–8.
[26] USAID, quoted in Karl 1992: 162.    [27] Wood 2000: 91.

substantial conditioning on compliance was crucial.[28] Through the World Bank's Consultative Group, donors from the broader international community were also able to assure each side that they would receive "substantial funding." Foreign states pledged an initial $800 million in national reconstruction, and the sum later increased.[29] Much of the aid was unofficially but clearly conditioned on each side abiding by the terms of the peace accord, especially the aid controlled by the United Nations but also that of the United States.[30] This provided a strong impetus for compliance.[31] Each side "needed financial resources to implement institutional reforms, land transfers and reconstruction projects"; the United Nations was the judge of whether each side demonstrated the "good faith and democratic vocation" required to gain access to these funds.[32] Besides the direct punishment of losing material resources, the conditionality of foreign aid had a potential indirect impact as well: by losing aid, each side could lose votes, due to the value that voters placed on aid resources, so at these culminating moments, loss of aid might indirectly change the power distribution. These conditional incentives, while costly to the international community, were not nearly as expensive as maintaining troops; moreover, much of this assistance was already part of standard development and democracy aid, "negligible compared to the global demand for assistance from the international community."[33]

Coordination to enforce compliance was a difficult proposition given the many actors involved, according to the U.N. officials,[34] but the focus around electoral participation provisions helped facilitate it. The United Nations was directly working with the group of "Four Plus One" friends – the United States, Colombia, Mexico, Spain, and Venezuela – which had also been involved with the negotiations.[35] In addition, it worked with the World Bank and other individual donor states, many of which had their own conditions.[36] The United States was the major donor, and it funneled some but not all of its aid through the United Nations. Outside of the organization, for example, USAID spent $319 million on El Salvador in support of the peace process.[37] Examining USAID funds in particular,

---

[28] Rosa and Foley 2000: 115–116, 150.    [29] Rosa and Foley 2000: 123.

[30] Rosa and Foley 2000: 137, 141, 150.

[31] Sullivan 1994: 86–87; Rosa and Foley 2000; Wood 2000: 94.

[32] Stanley and Holiday 1997: 24; the IMF and World Bank, in particular, were less transparent and flexible than other donors in post-conflict contexts, which continued to make coordinating with them more difficult, even in a relatively successful case like El Salvador; see de Soto and del Castillo 1994: 75, 77.

[33] De Soto and del Castillo 1994: 73; Rosa and Foley 2000: 115–118, 145.

[34] De Soto and del Castillo 1994.    [35] Call 2002: 557–558.

[36] De Soto and del Castillo 1994.

[37] Tully Cornick, USAID official, from my telephone interview with him, 2014.

one set of analysts said that the United States "played a significant role in conditioning aid disbursements on compliance with specific require-ments," and described this as a "clear case" of political conditionality: the United States threatened to withhold military aid if the recommenda-tions of a Truth Commission, established as part of the settlement, were not met.[38] In this instance and others, "the United States was the U.N.'s ultimate stick, and it was content to act within that framework."[39] The United Nations and the United States used the electoral process to incentivize compliance especially with requirements for demobilization prior to the election, making this a condition of aid for reconstruction.[40] A central role of the elections, therefore, was to provide assurance from international actors that the rebel group would be protected and receive aid if it complied with the terms of the peace process.[41] The electoral cycles emerging from the participation provisions offered specific points at which all international donors, and domestic actors to the extent that they could be drawn in, could coordinate on enforcement.

*Alternative Mechanisms for Enforcement?* This case raises the possibility that alternative mechanisms might be at work, even perhaps a more nuanced explanation than the enjoinder and ease alternatives discussed in the next section. In particular, it is possible that domestic actors in El Salvador overcame the commitment problems on their own, either through strong power-sharing or through enforcement from strong domestic democratic institutions. El Salvador is a useful test case for these alternative explanations because it features a strong rebel group, which almost won the conflict in the early 1980s and would eventually win the elections. Even with this relatively strong rebel group – stronger than the URNG in Guatemala, certainly, and also other rebel groups – an argu-ment that domestic actors are sufficient to overcome the commitment problems is not convincing. At least for the initial implementation period, international actors were needed to enforce the settlement, although over the next decade both the FMLN as a political party and domestic demo-cratic institutions developed to some extent and emerged as potential additional means of enforcement.

A mechanism involving strong domestic democratic institutions seems unlikely in this case because El Salvador's civil society and the institutions through which it could have acted were both weak. In fact, civil society was not only weak but also polarized, as predicted by

[38] Rosa and Foley 2000: 137.
[39] LeVine 1997: 252; and it had served as a strong ally from MINUGUA's creation (e.g. "Harbury/Bamaca Case: Supporting MINUGUA" 1994: 1).
[40] Wood 2000: 90–91.    [41] LeMoyne 1992.

external engagement theory in Chapter 2. Those working on the Central American conflicts, including U.N. officials, found the population to be "politically passive and therefore unavailable for mobilization,"[42] and also highly influenced by the elites from one side or the other.[43] The threat of losing support at the polls occasionally came into play in combination with international pressure, as the examples show. Yet the state's domestic electoral institutions were not highly democratic. While electoral participation was seen as a concession to the FMLN,[44] the elections protected the balance of power by continuing to favor the government.[45] Electoral decisions were delegated to the Supreme Electoral Tribunal, a body biased toward the incumbent, although part of its mandate was to increase voter registration (which would generally favor the challenger).[46] The elections, therefore, were not "fair," as they only marginally changed a domestic political system that had already been acknowledged as weak and biased.[47] Suggestions on reform of the electoral process did not have much effect until 2004.[48] Other domestic institutions designed to enforce the peace process were no more helpful; one such body, the Peace Consolidation Commission (COPAZ), which was set to work with ONUSAL, for example, "was never a well-functioning mechanism."[49] Reliance on domestic democratic institutions, potentially in combination with a strong civil society, to detect and sanction compliance therefore seems unlikely to have been effective even in this case.

Another alternative explanation is that the FMLN secured a sufficient share of power so that each side could simply sanction the other for violations. Yet even the relatively strong FMLN was never expected to secure enough seats in the early elections to be able to produce such a reciprocal threat. The expectation was that the FMLN would fare better than lesser-known leftist parties that had won 12 percent of the vote in 1991. The FMLN would ultimately receive almost 25 percent of the presidential vote and earn 21 out of 84 seats in the legislative elections in 1994.[50] In El Salvador's unitary presidential system with a centralized legislative assembly, however, such a vote share would not yield enough power to provide the FMLN a veto. The FMLN did fare better over time after moderating its policy platform substantially from the far left.[51] However, during the first 15 years after the peace deal was reached, the electoral process looked more like an attempt by the opposition to hold the government to a peace agreement than an effort to achieve more

---

[42] Arnault 2001: 11.    [43] Stanley 2013: 289.    [44] Vickers 1992: 5.
[45] Discussed in more detail in Chapter 5, but see especially Wood 2000.
[46] Wood 2000: 87.    [47] Wood 2000: 87.    [48] Kelley 2012: 225–227.
[49] Howard 2008: 102.    [50] Lehoucq 1995: 179–180.
[51] See, for example, Manning 2008.

political power. During this period, the FMLN accepted the decisions made by the biased Supreme Electoral Tribunal, a system that was part of the deal to preserve the balance of power; it neither challenged the tribunal's decisions nor resumed fighting because of them.[52] Instead, the FMLN focused on making sure that the government reformed its forces, as it was supposed to do, before the elections.[53] Disarmament and demobilization for each side was tied to the electoral process, and the international community used these links to enforce compliance, as the next section shows.

It is clear, even from those who emphasize the importance of domestic mechanisms, that external enforcement was needed to stabilize peace in El Salvador, at least initially.[54] Over time, the elections offered the possibility of incremental change to improve domestic institutions, while also gradually allowing more input from civil society as it developed and become more effective.[55] The central role of external enforcement, however, especially through the electoral process, is repeatedly credited by those involved in the process in El Salvador as to why peace held.[56]

*Instances of External Enforcement*   Entering the implementation period, each side failed to comply initially on particular provisions of the peace accord, either deliberately or due to logistical challenges. Examples of noncompliance are consistent with external engagement theory – which suggests that external engagement is needed precisely because each side will not always have incentives to implement the terms of a deal fully – and are inconsistent with the ease explanation that implies the opposite. In response to noncompliance in El Salvador, international actors threatened to block participation or to remove aid, which could have cost the noncompliant parties essential support from the voting population. This created the necessary incentives to obtain sufficient compliance and secure peace.[57] These examples of enforcement are, of course, also consistent with external engagement theory, but they are inconsistent with the enjoinder explanation, which predicts that assistance will be provided unconditionally as long as elections are held, regardless of compliance with each provision.

---

[52] Baloyra 1998: 30.    [53] For example, see Karl 1992: 154.

[54] On El Salvador, see Wood 2000: 79, 83–84, 86–87; and more broadly, Wantchekon 2004: 17, 27.

[55] A point made by Wantchekon 2004, and mentioned elsewhere, including Beaulieu 2014: 132. But, again, others are skeptical about whether post-conflict democracy promotion truly advances democratization. See De Zeeuw 2005, for example. I discuss this further in Chapter 8.

[56] For example, see LeMoyne 1992; Howard 2008, 103.

[57] Fortna 2008: 90–94, 162; Howard 2008: 94, 103.

The first examples of noncompliance are from the government side. The government failed to comply with major reforms mandated by the peace agreement, including combining and demobilizing existing forces, while deploying new forces.[58] The United Nations and the United States therefore leveraged the incentives that they could offer as the elections approached to enforce sufficient implementation to maintain the peace. Early on, there were clear moments during which other instances of noncompliance could be detected across security sectors, and, when crises arose as initial deadlines were not met, U.N. mediators were called to intervene and help resolve them.[59] As implementation proceeded, compliance with the deadlines for the drawdown was sometimes less than clear – for instance the purge of military leaders was mostly carried out in secret[60] – and international actors paid less attention to noncompliance. But the elections in particular still served as a fixed moment around which to attract external attention, an especially important moment given the consequences of the results for the distribution of domestic political power.[61] An instance of later noncompliance was the assassination of FMLN leaders in 1993, which were either a failure of the new security services, or perhaps perpetrated by them.[62] These events received significant attention because of their proximity to (and implications for) the elections. The mechanisms by which the international community enforced compliance in these cases included public statements by the United Nations to embarrass the government into implementing the terms of the agreement, especially reforming the military, accompanied by threats from the United States and others international actors to withdraw aid.[63] In the case of the assassinations, once the United Nations took these steps to hold the government accountable, including the establishment of a joint investigative commission, these incentives altered the government's behavior, and there were fewer assassinations in the first months of 1994, just before the elections.[64] Aside from experiencing international embarrassment, the government risked losing crucial foreign aid, on which it had become increasingly dependent, according to the U.N. Development Programme (UNDP). Thus, even though some aid (for example from the United States) was not formally conditioned on the peace agreement (in contrast to some other donors such as the Scandinavian governments), it informally served

---

[58] Call 2002: 568.    [59] Call 2002: 565; Howard 2008: 115–116.
[60] Wilkinson 1993b: 1–3; McCormick 1996: 296–297.
[61] On an instance just before elections, for example, see Stanley and Holiday 1997: 36.
[62] Call 2002: 576.    [63] Generally, see Fortna 2008: 90; Howard 2008: 94, 115–116.
[64] Call 2002: 577.

the crucial purpose of incentivizing compliance with the terms of the peace process.[65]

Analysts emphasized that the timing of these external threats was crucial: they came just before the elections.[66] The incumbent candidate for the presidency faced stiff competition; the loss of foreign aid funds, crucial as they were to state development, could have been very unpopular with voters, particularly those leaning toward the left.[67] Domestic pressure therefore complemented international pressure. For example, after the government failed to fully fund its own reinsertion programs (facilitating re-entry of former combatants into civilian life), former combatants stormed the legislature repeatedly beginning in 1993 in efforts to gain recognition and, perhaps, influence in the electoral process.[68] These efforts added to the pressure exerted by external actors, and both were, critically, coordinated around the elections, maximizing the costs of noncompliance for the government.

The FMLN also engaged in noncompliant behavior, and here, too, U.N. officials were able to use the elections as a mechanism to enforce compliance. The United Nations was sometimes seen as lenient on the rebel group, especially in its certification of the rebel group's disarmament in 1992. Such perceptions changed after the U.N. response to a 1993 explosion in an arms cache in Managua, Nicaragua, that was attributed to the FMLN. The U.N. Secretary General criticized the FMLN in the most forceful terms, while the government suggested that the rebel group be banned from elections.[69] The United Nations did not explicitly back a ban on the FMLN participating in elections unless it disarmed, but it did not deny the threat; others also did not.[70] The strong reaction against the rebel group and the potential threat of keeping its political party from participating in elections appeared to work: the FMLN immediately revealed and destroyed more than 100 other weapons caches, and it even deemed some of its candidates who had been involved "too damaged to run" in the elections.[71] In addition to enhancing the accountability of each side in the period prior to the elections, the electoral process fixed firm deadlines for the most crucial components of the peace agreement, that is, power distribution, to take place on election day. As one observer noted, "when serious delays occurred, the

[65] Rosa and Foley 2000: 150.    [66] Rosa and Foley 2000: 142.    [67] Wilkinson 1993b: 2.
[68] Stanley and Holiday 1997: 33.
[69] Evidence comes from U.N. Doc S/26005, June 29, 1993, as well as interviews with members of ONUSAL staff, cited in Call 2002: 560.
[70] U.S. State Department documents discuss this possibility; see "FMLN Legalization – Contingent on Demobilization" 1992: 1–2
[71] Call 2002: 560; also on this point, see Stanley and Holiday 1997: 27, 32; Howard 2008: 117–118.

possibility of the FMLN's competing in the March 1994 elections ... was jeopardized."[72] Others note that these deadlines allowed international actors to pressure the government, as well, for timely compliance.[73]

Many instances of attempted noncompliance occurred during the implementation process; international engagement through the elections in which each side was to participate continued to be crucial moments around which to enforce compliance. For instance, the government failed at timely issuance of voter registration cards for more than a quarter of the eligible population, a delay that could have lost the FMLN votes, because fewer leftist voters would have been registered for previous elections. In response, Congress froze $70 million in U.S. Economic Support Funds in August 1993; this aid freeze produced an increase in the pace of registration, leading the United Nations to declare by October that 90 percent of potential voters would likely be registered by the November deadline.[74] Another noteworthy instance was an attempt by the government to move the polling stations in FMLN strongholds to the capitals of those departments; this would effectively have disenfranchised many voters, who would have had to travel much further to reach polling places, which would have reduced votes for FMLN candidates.[75] The government claimed a security risk, but that claim was disputed by the U.N. electoral observation mission on the ground; eventually the government capitulated, allowing these polling stations to stay if the United Nations provided security, something that the large mission tied to the elections was able to do easily.[76] Thus, even beyond disarmament, there was noncompliance with the accords relating to power distribution, but external engagement around the electoral process continued to enforce the agreement.

These accountability mechanisms were employed even after the 1994 election. In 1997, for example, the government had not initially invited international election observers to the upcoming legislative election – which are typically monitored less frequently than presidential elections (as described in Chapter 4) – because the government believed that the 1994 elections had adequately demonstrated the general fairness and freedom of the process. (Indeed, reports from organizations such as the Carter Center, were "good" on those elections, and the parties accepted the reports.)[77] That decision not to then invite observers to the 1997

---

[72] Call 2002: 581.    [73] Rosa and Foley 2000.

[74] Human Rights Watch 1994: 4; LeoGrande 1998: 108. The United Nations on the ground also worked nonstop as the elections approached to ensure registration was as extensive as possible; see Howard 2008: 123.

[75] Montgomery 1998: 131.

[76] ONUSAL document and other evidence, cited in Montgomery 1998: 131.

[77] See, for example, Hartlyn and McCoy 2001: 24.

election was reversed, however, in the weeks before the election.[78] The FMLN was gaining strength in the mayoral election in San Salvador and wanted to be sure it would not be defrauded out of a win. Approximately 1,000 international election observers were sent, including a substantial number by the United States.[79]

The presence of the election monitors allowed for an investigation of repeated accusations by each side that the other was subverting the peace agreement in order to gain more power. For example, Congresswoman Ana Guadalupe Martinez, a former FMLN leader who left the party, accused it of selling weapons to finance electoral campaigns.[80] The provision of conditional aid also continued, which could have been used to punish violations discovered by the observers. In early 1996, U.S. Secretary of State Warren Christopher signed an agreement providing $10 million in additional U.S. aid for a land distribution program to support the 1992 peace accords. Other donors continued to provide high levels of funding throughout the 1990s that could easily be made conditional on these processes.[81] Considerable engagement remained, including from the United Nations, even after ONUSAL officially ended in 1995.

Peace persisted in El Salvador, then, following the implementation of a peace agreement that included provisions for electoral participation by each party to the conflict. The FMLN eventually evolved politically, moving from a far left position to a more moderate one.[82] The FMLN gained 33 percent of the vote in 1997, compared to 21 percent in 1994.[83] In 2006, it even took the presidency, earning a rare win (compared to other rebel groups among the sample of those that participated as political parties in post-conflict elections; see Figure 4.2 in Chapter 4). Compliance in the interim by each side was sometimes slow and imperfect. Also troubling was that the peace deal was structured to leave in place a relatively closed electoral system, which persisted as part of this elite pact.[84] The concluding chapter of this book returns to these less desirable aspects of the post-conflict peace. Overall, however, the deal was kept on track throughout its implementation and into its execution, in part through the careful monitoring and incentivizing of compliance by international actors who kept each side in check. This positive case is thus consistent with the mechanism underpinning external engagement theory, but not with the enjoinder or ease explanations, due to the patterns of noncompliance and subsequent enforcement through the electoral

---

[78] Kelley 2012: 225.
[79] "El Salvador Elections" 1997; Manning 2008; Montgomery 1998: 137.
[80] Farah 1997: 1.    [81] Rosa and Foley 2000.    [82] For example, see Manning 2008.
[83] Allison 2006a: 70.    [84] See Wood 2000.

process that occurred in the case. Additional mechanisms, such as military coercion through armed peacekeeping troops, or domestic enforcement, were not apparent in the case.

## Guatemala

The Guatemalan National Revolutionary Unity (URNG) and the government of Guatemala signed a final peace deal in 1996; it included electoral participation provisions after expectations of appropriate external engagement increased. The guerrillas in Guatemala were much weaker, relative to the government, than in El Salvador, and they faced a greater obstacle to a settlement: even after the conflict clearly became costly for each side and the combatants had reached an asymmetric but persistent stalemate by 1984, acute commitment problems prevented a peace agreement until 1996. The end of the Cold War gradually changed combatants' expectations about whether external actors could enforce a deal for each side, rather than always siding with the government (as the United States, in particular, had done during most of the conflict). Despite the rebels' weakness on the battlefield, they faced a high risk of extermination if they disarmed, so they continued fighting.[85] After the Cold War, as the credibility and means of the United States and other international actors to enforce peace agreements increased – discussed in depth in Chapter 3 generally and in Chapter 5 for this case – the URNG gradually began to consider pushing for a peace agreement that would feature electoral participation provisions. The deal was sealed when, after the president attempted a coup against the rest of the government, external actors demonstrated their willingness and ability to sanction noncompliance with the rules of the game.[86] Changes in these expectations allowed the rebel group and the government to commit to a settlement that entailed each side participating as political parties in post-conflict elections, so that each could be monitored and incentivized to comply with the agreement, as Chapter 5 shows.

This section examines what happened after the settlement was signed in Guatemala. Electoral participation provisions in this period provided an important mechanism through which combatants could be assured of a certain level of compliance, through external enforcement, that each preferred over a return to civil conflict. As in El Salvador, the electoral system accepted under the settlement in Guatemala was not particularly

---

[85] Azpuru 1999: 104; Allison 2009: 197.
[86] Jonas 2000b: 51; Verstegen 2000: 48; Santiso 2002: 567.

democratic,[87] and aspects of a URNG-supported referendum to reform the system were rejected by voters. Given the weak rebel group, Guatemala is an even cleaner test case than El Salvador, because the sources of enforcement would need to be international rather than domestic. Commitment problems arose during implementation in this case as well, again demonstrating that the possibility for noncompliance existed, which could have destabilized the settlement. But as I show, the electoral process established by the participation provisions, in combination with external enforcement – rather than something like military coercion from armed peacekeepers – produced some compliance. This is not a case of perfect (or near-perfect) implementation, and certainly the failure of the referendum proposing policy changes requested by the URNG was disappointing to the rebel group and its supporters, but it succeeded in exacting a level of compliance from the government and peace held between the parties, a "significant achievement."[88]

*Mechanisms for External Enforcement*  The URNG had little leverage with the government, but it gained the compliance that accompanied the peace agreement through external enforcement alongside a participatory electoral process.[89] According to URNG leaders whom I interviewed, international pressure was a pivotal source of the governmental compliance with the peace agreement that was achieved.[90] Through the electoral participation provisions, the URNG could be protected from government aggression, could draw party funds, and could direct resources to its supporters.[91] The settlement also tied the electoral process to other provisions, as anticipated by external engagement theory, especially those for reforming government forces, such as disbanding paramilitaries, reducing the size of the military, and creating a new civilian police force.[92] These demobilization campaigns, as well as the reinsertion plans for the rebel group, were to be overseen by a special integration commission that had members from each side, and, in a consultative capacity, international actors including donors.[93] The election dates were set as the completion dates for many provisions, including the formation of a new National Civil Police force.

External enforcement in the Guatemalan case certainly did not come from a coercive U.N. peacekeeping mission. The peacekeepers' presence

---

[87] For example, see Azpuru et al. 2004: 39.       [88] See, for example, Salvesen 2002: 9.
[89] Jonas 2000b: 241.
[90] Walter Félix, Carlos Mejía, and others from my interview in Guatemala City with URNG leaders, 2013.
[91] Jonas 2000a; Stanley and Holiday 2002.       [92] Allison 2006b, 2009.
[93] In addition to the agreement, see Jonas 2000b: 89.

was small and brief. In January 1997, 188 military observers arrived, and they were operational until May 1997, even though many of the major implementation deadlines set in the peace process were not until 1999.[94] Military coercion to enforce compliance by these troops was not an option, given their mandate, number, and, especially apparent, the timing of the mission.[95] This did not change as the peace process unfolded. MINUGUA was always intended to be a limited-resource mission, and international actors did not want to commit substantial resources to it,[96] so a mechanism aside from military coercion was needed to engage external actors to help combatants overcome their commitment problems. This is not to argue that MINUGUA failed, or was not crucial to enforcing the settlement, just that it did not apply military coercion, and that other external actors also assisted in the mechanism that was employed.

That mechanism consisted of monitoring and nonmilitary coercion, which often occurred through the participatory elections established through the provisions in the peace agreement. The international actors providing this external engagement were the United Nations and many allies, which included other observers and, perhaps most importantly, international donors. The U.N. mission was small but crucial throughout this period: its unarmed personnel were initially scheduled to be in Guatemala through the 1999 elections (mandated through 2000), but their stay was extended to ensure the terms were enacted, just after the 2003 elections (extended through 2004), with party support; the elections and administration changes were explicitly noted in requesting the extension as important moments to observe and enforce.[97] International election observers also bolstered these capabilities. Invitations were issued for 650 in the 1995 elections, while almost 1,000 international election observers were certified for the 1999 election.[98] The United Nations, meanwhile, regularly had fewer than 600 personnel of all kinds as part of the peace process from 1997, numbers that diminished over time.[99] Election missions thus greatly increased monitoring on the ground. Many of the election reports indicated that the elections were "good" and, notably, free from violence, despite isolated events in the

---

[94] Santiso 2002: 563, 566–567; Azpuru 2004: 54; Stanley 2013: 124.

[95] For example, news sources indicated that there were still transgressions, see Scott 1995: 2, which could at best be documented, but not punished, by U.N. force. Fortna (2008) points out that punishing perpetrators with force more broadly is rare.

[96] Collier 1995: 2.

[97] United Nations General Assembly 2003: 1, 3; Annan 2003: 2. The United Nations also was careful to seek funding very publicly until the end of 1999, even as it was just beginning; see Prendergast 1997: 1.

[98] Inter-Parliamentary Union 1995; Stanley 2013: 188.     [99] Salvesen 2002: 27.

major cities.[100] In fact, the initial conclusion by the international community was that voters went to the polls in "a completely peaceful climate."[101] These reactions held despite significant complaints from the opposition about government misuse of state property for electoral purposes and, more significantly, about a shutdown of public transit in Guatemala City on Election Day, which was allegedly "engineered" to prevent some segments of the population from voting.[102] The standards for evaluation seem to have been more closely tied to the settlement, hence the emphasis on peaceful conduct, rather than standards of freedom and fairness in the electoral process. The United Nations, in particular, detailed how closely it was watching the government for violations, and noted its disappointment that more major reforms had not been adopted before the elections.[103] This is not unusual for post-conflict elections.[104] The URNG leadership in particular found that the involvement of external actors helped them ensure compliance with the rules agreed on for these elections.[105]

International actors not only helped monitor compliance, they also provided incentives that could be conditioned on that compliance, including those tied to the electoral processes. This provided an enforcement mechanism. The amount of international donor assistance in Guatemala rose substantially from an annual average of $200 million between 1990 and 1995 to $600 million annually between 1996 and 2002.[106] Those tied to the Consultative Group coordinated by the Inter-American Development Bank, which was composed of the central financial contributors, including donor countries and also the World Bank, had pledged $2.5 billion by January 1997.[107] They had formal conditions, particularly focused on growth, and pressured the implementation of the peace agreement, as described below.[108] Among these donors, the United States had also earmarked aid that it had withheld from the government in the late 1980s to use as a "peace fund," according to State Department documents.[109] The state, rather than civil society actors, receive 89 percent of the aid in this context.[110] Much of this funding was tied to benchmarks and milestones related to the electoral process. More than $66 million received by Guatemala from international sources between 1996 and 2001 was designated specifically for democratization, and

[100] Stanley 2013: 188.      [101] For example, see the 1999 OAS report.
[102] For example, see the 1999 OAS report.
[103] For example, see United Nations General Assembly 1999: 5–6.
[104] See Chapter 2, especially citations of Kelley 2012.
[105] Carlos Mejía from my interview in Guatemala City with URNG leaders, 2013.
[106] Figures from Fuentes and Carothers 1998, initially found in Azpuru et al. 2004: 6.
[107] Azpuru et al. 2004: 7.      [108] Salvesen 2002: 29
[109] "US Policy toward Guatemala" 1994: 1.      [110] Azpuru et al. 2004: 10.

international donors focused on strengthening the electoral process, which meant funding all parties involved in the process, including both the government and the rebel group.[111] In fact, electoral assistance was specifically directed to political parties; for example, an OAS program devoted to strengthening and building consensus among political parties was established with Soros Foundation funding in 1998.[112] The URNG specifically has been supported by foundations linked to the Spanish Socialist Party and the Popular Party also in Spain.[113] Moreover, during the transitional period, the newly legitimate URNG gained access to committees, in equal representation with government representatives (although perhaps not equal resources), which were to shape how demobilization and reintegration would proceed.[114]

Particularly in the lead-up to the elections, international actors were able to help enforce compliance with at least the operative accords to demobilize, disarm, and reform the forces that had previously waged war against each another. Coordination was easier to achieve in Guatemala than elsewhere, although certainly not easy,[115] because there were several strong actors involved. The UNDP, among other institutions, was able to coordinate many of the donors, especially around electoral-cycle benchmarks and milestones. The UNDP intended to use "peace aid" conditionally for compliance; this worked to produce some of the compliance discussed below.[116] The accord that legalized the URNG in December 1996 also called for funding to "facilitate the flexible and effective implementation of the integration." USAID funding, for example, was to be used, "in consultation with donors, to facilitate agile and effective compliance."[117] By early 1997, a trust fund had been established by the UNDP for the benefit of forcibly displaced populations with $8 million from donors.[118] The URNG also received direct support from Spanish party foundations, including training, which was conditional on its peaceful political participation.[119] International actors had leverage over each side, especially through the electoral process, and they used the timing of future elections to threaten the government if it failed to comply, as the instances discussed below show.[120] Willingness of

---

[111] Azpuru et al. 2004: 14. Not all donors classify all human rights, media, and even certain election assistance as "democratization" aid, so this category may be underestimated (and, indeed, data collection on democratization aid in Guatemala is difficult for similar reasons); see Azpuru et al. 2004: 16.

[112] Azpuru et al. 2004: 24, 28.    [113] Azpuru et al. 2004: 30.

[114] Jonas 2000b: 89; Stanley and Holiday 2002: 440-441; Azpuru et al. 2004: 6.

[115] Salvesen 2002: 30.    [116] Verstegen 2000: 62.    [117] Heard 1999: 25.

[118] Stanley and Holiday 2002: 446.

[119] Based on interviews with a URNG member cited in Azpuru et al. 2004: 30.

[120] While international actors had the tools to achieve at least an acceptable level of compliance to maintain the peace agreement, especially through the participatory electoral process as external engagement theory implies, conditionality remained

external actors to criticize noncompliance was sometimes seen as inconsistent, however, perhaps in part because some failures of implementation were not seen as direct government violations.[121]

Overall, the widespread international attention surrounding the participatory electoral process – including formal monitoring and the availability of conditional incentives for each side – provided a mechanism for enforcing significant compliance with the provisions of the peace process in Guatemala.

*Alternative Mechanisms for Enforcement?*   The political environment in Guatemala was even less conducive than in El Salvador to enforcing combatant compliance with the peace process through domestic mechanisms. In terms of power-sharing, the URNG could not have secured enough of the vote to give it power to punish or deter governmental noncompliance by itself. Indeed, even decades after the settlement, the URNG leadership sees the party as a watchdog that can alert others to government malfeasance, but that lacks sufficient leverage to respond on its own.[122]

It was apparent by the mid-1990s how much political power leftist parties could earn under Guatemala's electoral system, well before each side even agreed to electoral participation provisions. The URNG likely knew that its vote share would be around 10 percent (and, in 1999, the leftist coalition including the URNG gained 12 percent of the vote). When, in 1995, a leftist coalition not including the URNG, although the URNG for the first time had called on the electorate to vote,[123] had entered the electoral arena the result was similar: the vote share for the New Guatemala Democratic Front (FDNG) was actually seen as surprisingly high, given the institutional setting, earning 8 percent of the presidential vote and gaining 6 congressional seats.[124] The elections in 1995/1996 provided an opportunity for the government and the

---

imperfect due to structural weaknesses in the case. Guatemala is highly underdeveloped, and so much of the formal "peace conditionality" by the international community focused on development goals, which were difficult to achieve, regardless of the government's political will (Azpru et al. 2004: 29). There was disagreement among international actors regarding whether to punish the government when it failed to enact some of the development reforms. Scandinavian states took a harder line, while the United States was more forgiving on some of these socio-economic issues (Azpuru et al. 2004: 30). Ultimately, even the most skeptical interpretations of implementation note that international actors did apply external leverage at some points (e.g. Stanley and Holiday 2002: 438–443), but that it could not overcome all of the structural barriers in Guatemala (Stanley and Holiday 2002: 423–424, 437–443, 457–458).

[121] For example, see Salvesen 2002: 28.
[122] Carlos Mejía from my interview in Guatemala City with URNG leaders, 2013.
[123] Jonas 2000a: 21.    [124] Jonas 2000a: 22.

United Nations to show the URNG its potential as a political party and for all actors to determine how much popular support it could expect to receive. Indeed, according to one assessment, the 1995 elections "created the conditions for the completion of the negotiations" because, first and foremost, "the presence of MINUGUA opened political space for the left."[125] A *Prensa Libre* poll in 1999 reported that 25.9 percent of Guatemalans claimed to have leftist leanings.[126] However, a figure of 10 percent was a much more realistic assessment of the level of popular support that could actually be mobilized in elections.

Because the URNG was so weak, the government could easily maintain the status quo on many dimensions. The Guatemalan government began to develop a record of staging elections free from fraud, even though it systematically excluded those on the left.[127] Even the constitutional reforms from the peace accords that were presented as questions on a referendum – which ultimately all failed the popular vote although with low turnout[128] – did not stipulate substantial changes to the presidential system. Thus, power distribution mechanisms were not substantially altered immediately after the peace agreement (nor were they agreed to be).[129] However, the forecast of a small percentage of the popular vote for the URNG encouraged the rebel group to seek allies, including external influencers, to help it accomplish its goals, which continues to this day.

This case thus also clearly demonstrates that external enforcement is needed to stabilize peace.[130] It was not just the initial weakness of the rebel group that placed it in an insecure position. Guatemala did not experience the incremental shift toward stronger democratic institutions and power-sharing domestically that was seen in El Salvador.[131]

This evidence, and evidence shown in the next section, is also inconsistent with the argument that these Central American peace processes succeeded due simply to the promotion of liberal democratic norms by peacekeepers. This constructivist argument suggests that the governments in these states signaled credible commitments to these norms, once various international actors promoted them, and that this gave rebel groups confidence in their safety and security, even in weaker states.[132] This case, as well as El Salvador, however, show minimal changes to the biased status-

---

[125] Stanley and Holiday 2002: 435.    [126] Jonas 2000b: 250.    [127] Jonas 2000b: 102.
[128] Stanley and Holiday 2000: 437.    [129] See, for example, Azpuru et al. 2004: 25.
[130] Wantchekon 2004: 17, 27.
[131] Guatemala's lack of change was due, in part, to what are often described as "parallel" powers that have power in the government; see, for example, Stanley and Holiday 2000: 437–438, as well as the structural factors described in the next section.
[132] Peceny and Stanley 2001.

quo institutions – and then sustained noncompliance with the new electoral process, requiring external enforcement – that do not fit this liberal democratic norms theory.

*Instances of External Enforcement*   During the implementation process, the Guatemalan government, in particular, failed to comply initially with some provisions of the peace process. External enforcement followed these instances of noncompliance. This evidence is consistent with the mechanism underpinning external engagement theory, which anticipates noncompliance but also international enforcement that should detect and sanction, and thereby reduce, that noncompliance. In contrast, this case does not yield evidence for the ease explanation, which does not anticipate deviation, nor the enjoinder explanation, which does not anticipate sanction.

Implementing these provisions of the peace agreement – the "operative" accords that would help protect the URNG and its supporters from government forces on which MINUGUA reported satisfactory compliance in 1999[133] – was quite difficult in an underdeveloped, deeply conflicted state, especially because many of them required substantial development and institution-building. A U.N. report just before the elections indicates there had been satisfactory compliance with the operative accords, which included the ceasefire, demobilization, and reintegration of the rebel group, and the return of refugees;[134] there was also partial implementation of the accords dealing with security sector reforms and human rights protections.[135] The implementation that occurred was viewed positively. Political pariticipation, and the military force reform that was tied to it, had largely been enacted, at least by observable measures. For instance, the new National Civil Police force had been created, the military reduced by 33 percent, and the paramilitaries formally disbanded,[136] even if the "new" police force was not entirely new and did not entirely live up to expectations.[137]

Not all of the failure to implement the accords in Guatemala was due to intentional governmental noncompliance – but some was. The URNG's weak position in a relatively closed electoral system, the lack of state capacity, and deep corruption of state institutions contribute to an explanation of why many of the political and economic reforms proposed in the peace deal did not become official policy;[138] part of this failure occurred

---

[133] Salvesen 2002: 9–10.
[134] MINUGUA 1999: 21–22, 39–44, cited in Salvesen 2002: 9.
[135] Salvesen 2002: 10–13.   [136] Salvesen 2002: 10–11; Allison 2009: 189.
[137] Azpuru 1999: 61–62; Stanley 2013: 167.
[138] See, for example, Azpuru 2004: 64–65.

with the rejection by voters of the popular referendum on reforms, although with low turnout.[139] Some of the changes that the rebel group requested were not implemented due to a lack of power within Guatemalan society and its governing institutions, rather than deliberate noncompliance by the government.[140] By July 1999, the government had complied with only three of the 12 commitments in the accord on strengthening civilian power over the military, however, according to the URNG-tied think tank IPES. And some of the main constitutional reforms that would have enacted these provisions were abandoned when the popular referendum on related aspects failed to pass.[141] These were, however, "radical" changes ("more substantial change than what would be indicated from the balance of power") to ask of the Guatemalan context.[142] It was difficult to significantly sanction the government for the failure of the referendum, for example, as it had followed the rules established in the peace deal, at least to the letter if not the spirit. Nonetheless, the government was supposed to have done more to promote the referendum, as discussed below.

U.N. monitoring, including through the elections, and conditional donor engagement were seen as crucial, although not always perfectly coordinated nor sufficient to overcome the structural challenges, to the compliance that was obtained.[143] MINUGUA conducted the monitoring needed to identify compliance, with the highest reported rates of political rights violations investigated in election years, and then also coordinated its partners to punish those instances (described in theory in Chapter 2).[144] One U.N. official, David Stephen, had initially tried to have the international community formally "make its financial support for the peace process in part conditional on the process itself," giving the U.N. "a role to play in some form of certification process," but what resulted, instead, was informal conditionality, due to resistance from both domestic Guatemalan political circles and organizational politics within the United Nations.[145] Informally, however, "MINUGUA could affect the attitudes and priorities of donors by escalating politico-diplomatic pressure on specific issues."[146]

---

[139] Salvesen (2002) describes implementation over the five years after the peace agreement is signed; see also, for example, Stanley and Holiday 2002: 437–438; Stanley 2013: 289, 292.

[140] Jonas 2000b: 236.    [141] Jonas 2000b: 236.    [142] Salvesen 2002: 19.

[143] Salvesen 2002: 9, 19; Stanley 2013: 291; the United Nations, however, was criticized for not doing more about government noncompliance, although this may have been difficult, given that some implementation failure was not directly due to this factor (e.g. Salvesen 2002: 28).

[144] For example, see Azpuru et al. 2004: 66–68.    [145] Stanley 2013: 103–104.

[146] Stanley 2013: 299.

Electoral participation provisions, alongside nonpartisan external engagement, helped enable the level of compliance that was achieved – and international actors, together with domestic civil society partners, continued to try to strengthen implementation in the lead-up to the 1999 elections, even by encouraging the passage of the referendum linked to the peace process. International donors, for example, funded substantial publicity to turn out the vote prior to the referendum, which was rejected by voters although with very low turnout.[147] The Consultative Group, composed of international donors and Guatemalan partners, postponed its meeting in 1998 and threatened to cut foreign assistance until the government increased support for certain constitutional reforms. According to one observer, the threat to cut aid "may have constituted sufficient pressure upon the Guatemalan government" to ensure compliance with at least some of the provisions.[148] Compounding this pressure was the fact that voters in upcoming elections might punish the government's party for any losses of foreign aid. The Consultative Group also required the government to explain the failure of the referendum, and its failure to implement certain recommendations by the transitional committees, just before the 1999 elections.[149] The Comisión de Acompañamiento, composed of members from each combatant side and civil society leaders,[150] pushed to support candidates that backed implementation and lobbied for long-term reforms suggested by the transitional committees.[151] Domestic actors in these contexts, including in Guatemala, however, are not always able to drive change through mobilization.[152] The URNG had pushed for conditionality for international aid sent to the government, and some funds not channeled through the government, during the process.[153]

The continued importance of the international community conditioning on compliance was acknowledged by Jean Arnault, Special Representative of the Secretary General for Guatemala and Head of MINUGUA during implementation.[154] He and others worried that donors might not be willing to actually sanction noncompliance, or that the Guatemalan government might not be responsive to sanctions, given that it had lost aid previously.[155] Some funds were directly administered by U.N. agencies, such as a trust fund established to strengthen government institutions provided by the United States, Denmark, Netherlands, Norway, and

---

[147] Stanley and Holiday 2002: 437–438.    [148] Salvesen 2002: 29.
[149] Jonas 2000b: 243–244.    [150] Azpuru et al. 2004: 6.
[151] Jonas 2000b: 243, 250–251.    [152] For example, see Arnault 2001: 11.
[153] "Guatemala: Negotiating Peace to Foster Democracy" 1994: 11–12.
[154] Arnault 2001: 10–11; Stanley 2013: 134.
[155] Based on an interview with Arnault, cited in Stanley 2013: 134, 290.

Sweden.[156] Other donors, such as the IMF, were also viewed by U.N. actors as credible participants in this process.[157] These international actors from across the spectrum collaborated, as aspects of the deal were not enacted due both to the failure of the referendum and also to other impediments. For example, inducing compliance depended on donor willingness "to allow MINUGUA to set criteria for projects and aid conditionality, which did not develop until donors fully grasped the scope of failures under the Portillo administration [then president]."[158] There were, of course, also concerns about conditioning certain aspects of aid that may not have hurt others besides those failing to comply.[159] Later, the mission had greater success when, "in close collaboration with UNDP and the IFIs ... the most important international donors were unified and imposed 'constructive conditionality' on the government to follow through with the peace process."[160]

As external engagement theory anticipates, the processes and procedures aimed at ensuring former combatants' compliance with the peace accord in Guatemala continued long after the 1999 elections. Even in 2003, the Netherlands Institute for Multiparty Democracy, together with UNDP, funded and organized a project that aided parties and promoted an agreement ("Shared National Agenda") in which many political parties signed on to work on particular issues, including fulfilling the broader pledges from the 1996 settlement that had not been implemented, just a month prior to the second post-conflict elections.[161] The United Nations stayed through this second set of post-conflict elections specifically to help ensure the terms of the peace agreement were enacted, and its leadership encouraged donors to continue to do so after its mandate ended.[162]

In general, international pressure has been crucial in the post-conflict period, as "interest in receiving financial and technical aid has prompted various parties to take important measures that they would not have taken otherwise."[163] The international community's pressure was also seen as crucial to ensure protection of former rebels.[164] The government had anticipated these pressures: by 1996, when it was just about to secure a deal with the URNG, the government tried to reduce the role of the United Nations. Members of the government in El Salvador had warned members of the government in Guatemala that these external actors could effectively monitor and enforce compliance, according to interviews with those involved.[165]

---

[156] Stanley 2013: 94.     [157] Arnault 2001: 19.     [158] Stanley 2013: 198.
[159] For example, see Salvesen 2002: 30.     [160] Stanley 2013: 240.
[161] Azpuru et al. 2004: 38; UNDP Undated: 12.     [162] Annan 2003: 2, 16.
[163] Azpuru et al. 2004: 99.     [164] Salvesen 2002: 9, 19.
[165] Guatemalan government documents cited in Jonas 2000b: 51.

The URNG's political agenda has not succeeded, compared, for example, to that of the FMLN, nor has Guatemala's government undergone substantial reform. But "operative" aspects of the accords, especially force reform to protect former combatants and to allow their participation in politics, were implemented to some extent as discussed above.[166] These changes led to the removal of Guatemala from the list of countries under the supervision of the U.N. Commission for Human Rights (UNHCR) in April 1998.[167] While the post-accord period included moments of satisfaction for the URNG leadership,[168] and implementation continued as another timetable was established just after the 1999 elections in order to extend efforts on aspects of partial compliance,[169] many political reforms did not take place. Corruption and organized systems of coercive control remain rampant in Guatemala. Yet the URNG, although lacking sufficient popular support in the 1990s to challenge the status quo effectively on many dimensions of governance, continues to participate in elections. In 1999, as part of an alliance, it won nine seats in Guatemala's Congress and came in third in the presidential elections with 12 percent of the vote. It participated in 2003, 2007, and 2011, winning two seats each time (although the number of seats has expanded, so it has won a slightly smaller share of power each time). The URNG leadership considers itself to be a watchdog of the system through its continued participation in politics.[170] The URNG has continued to use the mechanisms of international pressure to obtain further compliance by the government with both the letter and the spirit of the agreement. The international community has responded by reducing aid when the government strays too far from the rules established in this case; the former guerrillas credit their own activism through the political party.[171] The group also credits external engagement in the form of observers for helping to resolve legal challenges in some of the later contests.[172]

The deal has thus stood in Guatemala, and neither side has returned to the conflict. The URNG has not made much political progress in the elections, nor was it able to accomplish much systemic change. This is not surprising, given the URNG's weak position by 1984. The party's

---

[166] MINUGUA 1999: 21–22, 39–44, cited in Salvesen 2002: 9.
[167] Azpuru 1999: 118.
[168] Carlos Mejía from my interview in Guatemala City with URNG leaders, 2013.
[169] For example, see Salvesen 2002: 9.
[170] Carlos Mejía from my interview in Guatemala City with URNG leaders, 2013.
[171] Carlos Mejía and Walter Félix from my interview in Guatemala City with URNG leaders, 2013.
[172] Carlos Mejía and Walter Félix from my interview in Guatemala City with URNG leaders, 2013.

continued success in participating to serve as a watchdog, while achieving compliance at least with the "operative" aspects of the peace agreement, which were tied to the electoral process, are notable. Given early concern that the rebel group would simply be annihilated should it ever disarm, even this outcome is remarkable. In this case, even more than in El Salvador, the peace process did not create an open electoral process, and, indeed, parallel powers have persisted in the state. Overall, however, at least enough compliance needed to keep ex-combatants committed to the peace agreement was accomplished through the inclusion of these provisions for electoral participation accompanied by external engagement. In this case, it is also even clearer that other mechanisms, such as a coercive threat by peacekeeping troops, were not at work. Moreover, it is apparent that this was not an easy settlement and that continued conditionality, often around electoral participation provisions, was needed. The evidence is therefore consistent with external engagement theory, rather than the alternative explanations.

\* \* \*

El Salvador and Guatemala, taken together, are positive cases that show evidence of the mechanism linking electoral participation provisions, external engagement, and post-conflict peace, as implied by my theory. Extending beyond the simple correlations made in Chapter 6, each case study provides consistent evidence that conflict parties considered noncompliance on occasion in order to gain more power than the deal provided, and that such attempts to evade the terms of the peace deal were rendered more costly by the nonpartisan engagement of external actors that monitored and incentivized compliance by each side. Although these cases are quite different in terms of the level of power provided to the rebel group under the deal, in both instances international actors were able to help secure some level of compliance and stabilize the settlements. Each also has lessons for how to coordinate external enforcement even more effectively around electoral participation in future missions. In addition, the cases show evidence of a trade-off between stability and democracy. Neither case produced the free and fair system that promises real democracy,[173] yet both established stability between the former combatants.

---

[173] De Zeeuw (2005) directly discusses the lack of democratization following international assistance in these cases. Zürcher (2011) and Arnson (2012: 15) provide an overview of the literature suggesting a sometimes conflicting relationship between democratization and peace building, as well as cases that demonstrate the tension. Chapter 8 returns to this point.

## Cases in Which Compliance, and Sometimes Peace, Fails

The two cases explored so far have initial instances of noncompliance during the settlement's implementation, but additional cases of more serious and sustained noncompliance can help evaluate the underlying causal mechanism. The cases analyzed in this section include electoral participation provisions, although not always accompanied by appropriate external engagement, either because it is inadequate or partisan. It should generally be rare to observe substantial noncompliance because, as long as combatants believe that noncompliance will be detected and sanctioned to the extent that it is more costly than compliance, external actors will deter that behavior.[174] But it occasionally occurs, and when the conflict recurs, these are then outliers in the analysis in Chapter 6. I analyze positive cases that suffered from serious and sustained noncompliance from among the 10 explored in Chapter 5 (which are cases in which the conflict was fought before and after the end of the Cold War, such that combatants experienced a shift toward expectations of less partisan and thus more credible external engagement in most regions, and they then included electoral participation provisions in their settlements). The first two cases in this section, Colombia and Northern Ireland, further explore noncompliance that did not produce conflict recurrence, like El Salvador and Guatemala. These cases had more serious violations, which allows examination of more substantial enforcement. The second two cases in this section, Angola and Cambodia, also had severe violations, but these eventually produced conflict recurrence. These two outliers allow analysis of whether external engagement failed to make compliance more costly than noncompliance, and if so, *why*.

### Noncompliance, Substantial Enforcement, and Sustained Peace

Two of the 10 cases that settle with electoral participation provisions after 1989, following fighting during the Cold War, feature more serious noncompliance than El Salvador and Guatemala. Peace holds, however. The cases of Colombia and Northern Ireland therefore demonstrate sanctions meted out to parties that do not comply in substantial ways, which is consistent with external engagement theory. They also emphasize an interesting corollary from the theory (see the model in the Appendix): sometimes each side accepts some noncompliance by one

[174] For a conceptual discussion of off-the-equilibrium-path behavior, see, for example, Weingast 1996.

side, and the subsequent cost imposed on it by the international community, as the best option. The conditions under which this seems to happen, based on these cases, is when substantial rebel groups remain outside the settlement and pressure one of the parties to violate the deal, notwithstanding the provisions in the deal and the punishment that party then receives.

To illustrate this, I turn first to the Colombian case (described at the beginning of Chapter 4). By 1991, the government enacted peace deals that included electoral participation provisions for M-19 and a number of smaller rebel groups. The government did not meet all of its obligations, however: significant violations were attributed to the military that, by many accounts, continued to treat all of the rebel groups as enemies, even those that signed peace agreements, and allowed the paramilitaries to attack them.[175] But the government needed the military to continue fighting the ongoing conflict on many fronts, so it could not completely marginalize those responsible, as it might have sought to do otherwise.[176] The military thus lacked constraints, and the paramilitaries were not dealt with quickly. One result was the April 1990 assassination of Carlos Pizarro, the presidential candidate for the political party formed by M-19.

International scrutiny and sanctions followed these incidents. M-19 and the other demobilized rebel groups stuck to the settlement and continued to participate electorally. International news media and non-governmental organizations stepped up their coverage of these events as the Cold War drew to a close. The government faced particularly strong criticism after the Pizarro assassination. As one report suggested, "the Barco administration [then president] has been criticized far more over the Pizarro assassination than over the previous deaths," even by the president's own party, "a damaging occurrence during an electoral season."[177] In 1990, Pizarro's assassination generated 45 articles in international news sources (identified through a LexisNexis search), far more than the 16 articles on the 1987 assassination of the U.P.'s Pardo Leal. In 1990, both presidential candidates received much more international news coverage than any demobilized leader who was without a political party. In 1993, a new non-governmental organization called Reiniciar was established to disseminate information about the assassinations and mass murders of those on the left.[178] With this increased attention came punishment by the international community. In 1993, the U.S. government diverted funds from the

---

[175] For example, see Ossa Escobar 1998; Pardo Rueda 1998.     [176] Pardo Rueda 1998.
[177] Dermota 1990: A8.
[178] Jahel Quiroga, from my interview with Reiniciar in Bogotá, 2009.

military to the police, due to human rights abuses by the former.[179] In 1996 and 1997, it went one step further and even decertified the Colombian government, so it could not receive military assistance for counter-narcotics purposes, because the state could not meet the requisite human rights standards. Other organizations also criticized this governmental noncompliance. UNHCR condemned Colombia's human rights abuses every subsequent year through an advisory panel or chair statement. These condemnations appeared to carry consequences in diminishing the amount of aid the government could receive from the World Bank and other sources.[180] With the international pressure and punishment, the Colombian Administrative Department of Security (DAS) and the other government agencies responded to these assassinations. Partially due to international scrutiny, M-19 and the other groups that entered Colombia's electoral politics as parties in the 1990s did not meet the same fate as the politicide suffered by U.P. members in the mid-1980s.[181] A former leader of M-19's political party emphasized in an interview the role of public support in Colombia in getting the government to comply to the extent that it did. Some of these monitoring and enforcement roles were played by Colombia's relatively strong institutions and civil society, but "the international community, in our case, was instrumental as a second-line."[182]

Northern Ireland offers another example of international punishment for noncompliance with the terms of a peace deal, but the noncompliant party in this case was the rebel group. The Progressive Unionist Party (PUP), the political wing of a Northern Ireland rebel group called the Ulster Volunteer Force (UVF), also was exposed to observation and punishment through the increased responsibility that comes with electoral participation. The UVF was a Protestant group that fought in the sectarian civil war against the Catholics. As part of the peace process around the 1998 Good Friday Agreement, the UVF's political wing, the PUP, participated in elections. The PUP increasingly served to link the government and non-governmental organizations with poor Protestants, a segment of the population not previously represented in traditional Northern Ireland politics. International organizations and the government of the United Kingdom came to view the PUP as a legitimate partner to work with when sending funds to Northern

---

[179] Evans 2002 citing Public Law 103–306, August 23, 1994: 108 STAT. 1621.
[180] See Lebovic and Voeten 2009.
[181] Jahel Quiroga, from my interview with Reiniciar, a U.P. victim association, in Bogotá, 2009; Upegui 2009.
[182] Antonio Navarro Wolff, from my telephone interview with former M-19 rebel and then party leader, 2012.

Ireland.[183] It would also be held accountable in the event that its rebel constituency – the UVF leadership – violated the terms of the agreement. In 2004, for example, paramilitary violence escalated, and, although responsibility for most of the fighting could not be attributed to a particular group, the UVF leadership was aware of it and permitted it to continue. In response, the U.K.'s secretary for Northern Ireland, Paul Murphy, suspended the PUP's annual fund for community work and considered cutting its leader's salary.[184] This sanction hurt the party's chances in a political environment in which party leaders are required to provide for their constituencies, and, according to my interview with the PUP, it was eventually able to work with the UVF to halt the violence.[185]

These cases are not outliers but still show serious noncompliance that allows observation of international sanction for noncompliance.

### Noncompliance, Some Enforcement, But Conflict Recurrence

In another two of the 10 conflicts that cross the end of the Cold War and then terminate through settlements that include electoral participation provisions, substantial noncompliance produced conflict recurrence. In Cambodia, peace failed in the period between the peace agreement, which included electoral participation provisions, and implementation of the provisions. In Angola, peace failed just after the first election. In these outliers, external engagement appears to have been insufficient, given the design of the peace agreement (Angola) or the partisanship – or interest – of the international actors (Cambodia – and the negative case, Bangladesh). These cases thus reaffirm that an international actor must be involved, but not excessively invested, consistent with external engagement theory. Angola, in particular, also underscores a key condition: political power distribution in the peace agreement must be designed to approximate power on the battlefield before an appropriately involved international actor can sanction noncompliance effectively. (This point is also made theoretically in Chapter 2.)

The 1991 Angola settlement, where peace failed just after the elections, is not unexpected under external engagement theory, and it demonstrates an additional condition that is important to the design of any settlement. If agreements allow for anything other than incremental shifts toward political power redistribution that matches what combatants could expect

---

[183] Dawn Purvis from my interview with the PUP leader in Belfast, 2009.
[184] Happold 2004: 1.
[185] Edwards and Bloomer 2004: 23; Dawn Purvis from my interview with the PUP leader in Belfast, 2009.

to secure on the battlefield, then even external enforcement may lack sufficient leverage to ensure compliance. The 1991 Bicesse Accords called for the rebel group, UNITA, to participate as a political party in elections in 1992 and established a new U.N. mission to oversee the peace process. The 1992 elections were designed to provide substantial power to the office of the president. Both the ruling party, the People's Movement for the Liberation of Angola (MPLA), and UNITA "were centralized, hierarchical organizations, led by strong men convinced that they were going to win the elections, and thus interested in making that presidency powerful."[186] The president would have almost full control over the budget and economic development; little would interfere with "governmental and administrative unity of action."[187] It was not initially clear who would win, however. The Ovimbundu, potential UNITA backers, made up 37 percent of the population, while the Mbundu, potential government backers, made up 23 percent of the population; other ethnic groups did not lean entirely one way or the other.[188] Western intelligence assessments continued to forecast a win for UNITA's Jonas Savimbi through the summer,[189] while a poll at the same time suggested a government lead.[190] International actors revised their estimates by September 1992, however, and requested a power-sharing deal in a renegotiation before the election, but the MPLA refused.[191] UNITA did not seem to change course despite its backers' loss of confidence in its electoral prospects. Most analysis suggests that "each side assumed it would win," even as late as the eve of the elections, which led to "grim, zero-sum perceptions."[192]

Thus the elections in Angola delivered substantial power in a single step to the winning side. Participating was a gamble on winning, not an elite pact that could placate each side with something close to what it expected from conflict. Thus even external enforcement would not be enough to keep the losing side from seeking a better outcome by returning to the battlefield. Predictably, after UNITA lost the first round of presidential elections, it had little incentive to remain at peace. The international community tried to punish the rebel group, but it did not have sufficient leverage to do so, because the group would basically hold no political power in either event, while on the battlefield it was relatively strong. Margaret Anstee, U.N. Special Representative to Angola at the time, said later that "control of the government [was] the prize [and] there [wasn't] anything else."[193] UNITA refused to accept the results of the elections in September 1992.

---

[186] Ottaway 1998: 140.
[187] Article 54e, quoted in Ottaway 1998: 139; also see Amundsen et al. 2005.
[188] Ottaway 1998: 136.      [189] Vines 1993: 6.      [190] Pereira 1994: 19.
[191] Vines 1993: 6.      [192] Rothchild and Hartzell 1995: 196.      [193] O'Toole 1997: 2.

External actors, focused on this cumulative moment of power distribution, brought their resources to bear on the noncompliant party – but they simply were not sufficient given the settlement's design. The United Nations first threatened and then imposed sanctions to keep UNITA from access to arms, military equipment, and fuel.[194] UNITA thus became the first non-state actor subjected to such U.N.-endorsed punishment. The Clinton administration had been holding off on recognizing the MPLA, in the hopes that this would provide "extra leverage over UNITA," but did so after the election in May 1993.[195] But UNITA had little to gain by laying down its arms, unless the MPLA would agree to fundamentally reform the government. After the agreement and its electoral victory, however, the MPLA was in compliance while UNITA was not, so the status quo had changed. UNITA was now weaker either way, and it could not demand a renegotiation for anything more than its weakened troops could expect to extract by force. In this case, electoral participation provisions were included, but they were not designed to share power through a process of incremental integration, so only a single participatory election was held before conflict recurred (rare in such conflicts, as Chapter 6 shows).

In future elections, the international actors, especially the United Nations, thereafter sought to design different institutions and to promise continuing support for those institutions.[196] The U.N. Peace-Building Commission, established in 2005, later formalized this learning process.[197] While international actors had sanctioned UNITA, it was not sufficient to deter the politically defeated party from exerting its strength on the battlefield, due to the design of the peace agreement. International actors applied what they had learned in this case to Mozambique. The design of the peace process in Mozambique was similar to that of Angola, although power was not quite as concentrated within the executive, and a substantial amount of power-sharing was part of the transition process.[198] Indeed, when it became clear that the rebel group (Renamo) would lose, South Africa as an outside observer also requested that the government renegotiate the terms for more power-sharing after the elections for Renamo, but the ruling party refused.[199] The difference in comparison to Angola, however, was explicit recognition of incentivizing continued peace for Renamo: the demobilization process was more carefully linked to the elections, and thus it was more costly for Renamo to return to conflict; moreover, the international community was

---

[194] Fowler 2000; le Billon 2001.     [195] Vines 1993: 4, 15, 16.     [196] Ottaway 2003.
[197] Collier and Hoeffler 2004.
[198] See, for example, Turner et al. 1998: 158; Lyons 2005: 109.
[199] Turner et al. 1998: 163–164, Lyons 2005: 84.

paying attention to the lead up to the elections, and when the renegotiation was refused, the international community added more money to a trust fund established for Renamo to avoid its electoral boycott.[200] Ultimately, this provided Renamo significant benefits, and the rebel group was persuaded to participate in the elections peacefully, and the settlement produced peace.[201] International actors were particularly committed to the peace process in Mozambique, which came soon after the failure in Angola, and the cost of paying off the rebel group was relatively low. Better institutional design could have avoided these problems in both cases by establishing greater power-sharing in the design of the electoral participation provisions, so that external enforcement would have been sufficient to make compliance less costly than noncompliance in Angola (and, presumably, a smaller trust fund would have sufficed in Mozambique).

Cambodia, which experienced peace failure before implementation of its agreement when the Khmer Rouge opted to return to violence rather than participate in the 1993 elections, demonstrates a core insight from the external enforcement theory: international actors must be engaged but not overly invested or partisan, in order to solve the commitment problem for the combatants. This case shows what happens when international actors hold strong preferences among the combatant sides. The Cambodian conflict had been highly internationalized, in contrast to many other conflicts in Asia. In 1978, Vietnamese forces invaded Cambodia and overwhelmed the Khmer Rouge army. When the conflict finally ended, international actors were intensely involved. The first peace plan in 1986 was initiated by FUNCINPEC, an organization led by Prince Norodom Sihanouk, one of many factions in the conflict. It called for U.N. observation of the initial coalition government and U.N. supervision of the electoral process.[202] The ruling Cambodian People's Party (CPP) also invited the United Nations in this capacity.[203] The United Nations established an extensive transitional operation, the United Nations Transitional Authority in Cambodia (UNTAC), backed by tens of thousands of military and civilian personnel. The United Nations had final authority in the state, through UNTAC, until the elections. The mission was under a great deal of pressure to succeed, especially given the cost, as well as regional resistance to intervention.[204] The United Nations thus had the strongest ties to FUNCINPEC, although it applied substantial pressure to gain cooperation through post-hoc arrangements between FUNCINPEC and

[200] Turner et al. 1998: 161.   [201] Turner et al. 1998: 162, 172; Nuvunga 2007.
[202] Acharya et al. 1989.   [203] Mayall 1996.   [204] Peou 2004.

the incumbent CPP.[205] It alienated the Khmer Rouge with its ties and concessions for the other combatants. The Khmer Rouge perceived the mission as biased even before the election, and accused the United Nations of using its policing capabilities to advantage the other political parties.[206] Even the CPP, which received beneficial treatment after the elections just to keep it in the agreement, saw the United Nations as partisan: its leader would later say that "international standards exist only in sports."[207] Meanwhile, the Khmer Rouge boycotted the 1993 election, rejected peace, and returned to fighting.[208] This shows that while international actors must be involved in the post-conflict settlement process, they must not be partisan to such an extent that it compromises expectations that they will enforce the rules for all combatants.[209] Such a balance became easier after the end of the Cold War, although not everywhere at all times.

The negative case of the Chittagong Hill Tracts (CHT) in Bangladesh, as well as later cases of failure,[210] demonstrate the importance of sufficient international involvement. As discussed in Chapter 5, Bangladesh did not attract much international attention around the settlement of its civil conflict. Consistent with external engagement theory, then, enforcement of the settlement was weak, and many other aspects of the peace agreement were not implemented.[211] The agreement also suffered from ambiguities on rules and deadlines, which would have made such conditionality difficult to implement, even if it had been credible. The agreement might have been further implemented if somebody had pressured each side, but "'there is nobody to put pressure on either side to comply,'" according to a source in Dhaka.[212] In Bangladesh, there were limited attempts by international actors to enforce the agreement through foreign assistance: the E.U. declared in 1999 that it would not give aid projects to the CHT unless the accord was implemented, but its threat and follow-through were weak and were targeted only at the region, not at the central government, which was failing to comply.[213] Such an instance of an attempt at this kind of conditionality is rare in the secondary literature on this case. This conflict may have been somewhat easier to settle; indeed,

---

[205] Doyle 1997; Jarstad 2006.     [206] Mayall 1996.
[207] Bjornlund 2004: 191; Howard 2008.     [208] Mayall 1996.
[209] Cambodia was, however, a difficult operation for other reasons, as well; see Doyle 1997.
[210] In Rwanda, for example, a settlement was signed that included electoral participation provisions in August 1993. It was then followed by the costly loss of U.S. troops intervening in Somalia. Criteria including requiring a national interest at stake in its aftermath for intervention likely produced some of the reluctance to act in Rwanda in April 1994 (e.g. Howard 2008).
[211] Fortna 2008: 54.     [212] Interview quoted in Fortna 2008: 135–136.
[213] SAHRDC 1999, cited in Fortna 2008: 136.

it may have had this alternative mechanism for overcoming the commitment problem because it was a territorial conflict.[214] But the rebel group would have preferred an international enforcer of some kind; there was not one, however, and the government failed to fully implement the bargain.[215] While ambiguity made the agreement work to some extent, because each side was satisfied with something close to the status quo, it was not the most stable mechanism. A leader of the JSS/SB said, "we signed the agreement in the presence of the whole world," but the world knew nothing of the agreement by the JSS/SB, nor about compliance with it.[216] After its armed wing disbanded and 1,500 of its rebels turned in weapons, the government ruled this to be disarmament; however, the group most likely maintained almost all of its weapons caches and surrendered only old weapons. Eventually, another rebel group, the United People's Democratic Front (UPDF), formed in protest and refused to accept the peace agreement that the government had signed with the JSS/SB, producing additional fighting.

While it is rare that settlements with electoral participation provisions fail, these cases of failure provide evidence consistent with external engagement theory; this case of a settlement without electoral participation provisions also does. Stabilization of peace processes does not occur without an appropriate level of involvement by external actors who have sufficient information and credible leverage to make noncompliance with the settlement more costly than compliance. The failure in Angola reinforces the notion, derived from the bargaining literature, that the further a deal deviates in its distribution of power from combatants' expectations, the more leverage the international community will need to enforce the agreement (and even so, it may not be successful). Finally, cases where punishment is actually inflicted and peace is then sustained, also rare, provide even more evidence of the same mechanisms as the initial cases in which only limited instances of enforcement occur. Each supports external engagement theory's causal logic, rather than that of any alternatives.

## Discussion and Conclusions

This examination of the mechanisms through which peace is maintained after a settlement is signed provides evidence consistent with the mechanism underpinning external engagement theory. The electoral process, according to these cases, provides a vehicle for international actors to engage with combatants to detect and sanction instances of noncompliance with a settlement. The instances of noncompliance in

---

[214] Fortna 2008: 133.    [215] Mohsin 2003: 115.    [216] Fortna 2008: 135–136.

the cases in this chapter show evidence of just such enforcement: ex-combatant parties sought more power than the peace agreement gave them. But, as also expected by external engagement theory, the electoral participation provisions established coordination cycles around which external actors checked and incentivized compliance at crucial moments of power distribution. This coordination yielded maximal effect in making noncompliance more costly than compliance. Reconstruction, development, and political party aid, which were frequently provided, were subject to withdrawal where compliance was slow, especially with the core aspects of the peace agreements. In some cases, the rebel groups, in particular, were threatened with not being allowed to participate as political parties if they did not correct their noncompliance. The core aspects for each side were the revision of forces and political power distribution through the electoral process, which are both linked to the electoral participation provisions. The threats to revoke conditional benefits over failure to comply or, more frequently, delay in compliance, were often made in public forums, which could change the level of domestic support for these actors if their noncompliance continued; this produced an additional cost.

The mechanism is also revealed by examination of the failure of settlements with electoral participation provisions. In two cases, when substantial conflict continued by actors who were outside of the peace agreement, a government and a rebel group responded to multiple cost and benefit calculations by choosing strategically to violate the agreement while accepting the costs, at least for a time. In many cases, all of the major rebel groups enter the peace process along with the government – in most cases, there is only one major rebel group – and so this dynamic is not observed often. Nonetheless, it is an interesting source of deviation from compliance by each side, which, as expected in the model, results in external punishment through the electoral process. In two cases, international interest, or leverage due to the settlement's design, was not sufficient to make noncompliance costly enough to compel compliance by both actors. These cases provide further support for the mechanism, while also underscoring the limitations of external engagement.

Peacekeeping missions were deployed to some of the states analyzed, but external engagement through the electoral process to monitor and punish noncompliance, rather than military coercion, was used by U.N. missions and other international actors. The threats made and the sanctions enacted to gain compliance did not entail military coercion. As discussed in Chapter 5, the exit dates for these missions did not coincide with the elections, nor were the missions authorized or equipped to do anything beyond monitor and influence conditional incentives, often alongside the electoral process. In terms of other alternative mechanisms, even the FMLN, a strong rebel group, was not able to rely on its own coercive power, nor on civil society, to enforce compliance by the other side. Instead, international actors working through the electoral process were needed to enforce the peace agreement by altering incentives.

*Part IV*

# Conclusion

# 8　Securing Peace
## Conclusions about Electoral Participation
## and External Engagement in Post-Conflict States

This book argues that a sea change in the dominant approach to designing peace agreements has contributed to a global decline in civil conflict. Peace agreements began to include electoral participation provisions only after the end of the Cold War, and, even then, only in cases with a credible expectation of external monitoring and enforcement, which is consistent with combatants seeking to use this nonmilitary mechanism to overcome commitment problems. Most importantly, peace agreements with these electoral participation provisions endure better than those using other types of provisions for power distribution, suggesting that these provisions thus establish elections that help secure settlements and sustain peace. These results not only counter existing pessimism on post-conflict elections, but the book also explicates important mechanisms of international intervention to help solve domestic political problems.

Returning to the case of Nepal with which the book opened, the argument suggests that the 2006 settlement designed around subsequent elections in which the Maoist rebel group would participate as a political party against the incumbent government may have *helped*, rather than hurt, a durable peace. All sides benefited from participating in the process, as they would have from any acceptable power-sharing deal. But the design of the deal – based on electoral participation provisions – also allowed the international community to check periodically on all sides' compliance. Implementation of elections in the wake of the settlement has been somewhat bumpy, but, a decade later, the process has remained largely peaceful and has mostly proceeded as agreed. When implementation faced a major challenge in the second post-conflict election in 2013 – when the Maoists did not fare as well as they had in the first election – external donors used the U.N. Trust Fund and the Nepal Peace Trust Fund (NPTF) to offer continued incentives for the rebel group and its supporters (in the form of party funds and community resources for affected populations) to stick with the process through the implementation phases rather than returning to conflict. The United Nations, non-governmental organizations, and donors to the trust fund came together before the 2008 and 2013 elections to monitor whether all sides were complying with the peace agreement, and to be able to threaten sanctions at moments of maximal impact for any noncompliance. Nepal has not been alone in using electoral participation provisions to allow external engagement for enforcement assistance; the same mechanisms apply in many other cases examined in this book. External engagement that accompanies electoral participation provisions in numerous settlements helps combatants to overcome commitment problems and achieve enduring peace.

In the remainder of this chapter, I briefly summarize my theory and alternative explanations, as well as the results from empirical tests. I then discuss implications of external engagement theory for post-conflict elections and for international intervention, considering the effects on both peace and democratization. Finally, I offer some discussion of the specific policy recommendations that emerge from this theory to suggest how international actors can effectively enforce settlements and produce peace.

## Theory in Brief

This book explores two puzzles: why electoral participation provisions are included in peace agreements and whether they are associated with more enduring peace. While elections may be normatively appealing as a form of governance, they may be dangerous, and, to work around that, they are often designed to favor stability in ways that inhibit electoral legitimacy. Uncertainty otherwise in elections produces a possibility that the losing side may have incentives to return to conflict rather than complying with a peace agreement, in addition to potentially even using violence during the campaign period to avoid losing. Any peace agreement must offer payoffs to all sides that match what they expect to receive from fighting in order to remove these incentives, and so such provisions frequently require elite pacts that minimize uncertainty in the power distribution. This design, however, reduces the legitimacy that emerges from allowing citizens complete choice among potential leaders. Moreover, even if some uncertainty is removed for the combatants, under certain conditions elections may still incite communal violence, and potentially produce protest or further rebellion. So, if elections may lead to further conflict, why base peace agreements on provisions for combatants to participate in them?

These concerns are real, but I argue electoral participation provisions can increase the probability of external engagement, which stabilizes peace between combatants. By easing the effort and reducing the costs to the international community of involvement, these provisions make external actors more likely to engage and, thereby, to help combatants commit to settlements. Settlements often fail because one side becomes temporarily stronger during the implementation of a peace agreement, which gives it an incentive to try to grab more power than it was initially allocated. The power grab may push all sides back to conflict. Or, if one side becomes concerned that the other is making, or will make, a power grab, that side may return to fighting preemptively or as punishment. The risk can be ameliorated by providing better detection and potential sanctions for violations so that the payoff for noncompliance becomes lower than the payoff for continued compliance. International actors can enforce agreements by monitoring for compliance and promising punishment that increases the cost of noncompliance. But they are rarely able to do so credibly by threatening to monitor with troops on the ground and to punish violations with force throughout the implementation period.

I posit that external actors do not always need to intervene militarily to enforce compliance. Instead, they can engage through other mechanisms to detect and threaten sanctions for noncompliance. The theory of external engagement set forth in this book highlights the utility of electoral participation provisions, which create coordination cycles easing the collection of information and provision of conditional incentives, and thus pave the way for enforcement of compliance around them. Electoral processes set public benchmarks and regular milestones that culminate in the distribution of political power, which make these processes able to focus attention and accountability, providing information and leverage to sanction any noncompliance by ex-combatant parties. The spread of democracy promotion programs facilitated efficient *external* engagement around these processes. Normative conventions about how to distribute power legitimately underpin the mechanism. Electoral participation provisions thus reduce the cost of detecting and sanctioning noncompliance by use of international election observation and conditional incentives, particularly foreign aid, which often includes funds for party development. International involvement through electoral processes can thus incentivize all sides to remain committed to a deal, even as conditions shift over time as the combatants implement the settlement.

But a set of conditions must be met in order for the type of post-conflict elections discussed in this book to succeed in producing enduring peace. First, with respect to the combatants, the conflict must be costly enough that all sides are willing to negotiate a settlement, and the settlement must be designed to produce a division of power that will benefit each side at least as much as it could expect continued conflict to do. With respect to international actors, the most fundamental condition is that they must be able to detect and have the leverage to sanction noncompliance by either side – at a low enough cost throughout implementation that their enforcement is credible to combatants. Such low-cost, long-term enforcement became far more feasible after the Cold War ended, with the rise of international election observation and other democracy promotion programs (although their spread varied from region to region). These programs reduced international actors' enforcement costs by providing the infrastructure to engage and by coordinating external engagement that was not viewed by domestic actors as violating state sovereignty. External engagement may still be unavailable in cases when international actors are either not committed to providing any observation or resources, or so committed to one side that the other would not expect international actors to follow-through on sanctions against the favored side – but often it is available.

This book tests two sets of empirical implications derived from external engagement theory: the first relates to when electoral participation provisions are included in peace agreements, and the second relates to relationship between electoral participation provisions and enduring peace. I summarize the main findings of the book before turning to the implications of the theory for elections, democracy, external engagement, and peace.

### Findings on the Causes of Electoral Participation Provisions

To assess the main causes of the inclusion of electoral participation provisions in peace settlements, I collected new cross-national data to evaluate which peace agreements signed from 1975 to 2005 included electoral participation provisions. The summary statistics in Chapter 3 and the analyses in Chapter 4 show that settlements with these provisions – compared to all settlements, as well as to all types of civil conflict termination – are more likely when combatant have reason to expect that external actors will engage in the electoral process. Democracy promotion programs, a mechanism of international intervention, vary by region over time. These programs – and with them increasing expectations of engagement – emerged in waves after the end of the Cold War, beginning in Latin America, sub-Saharan Africa, and Eastern Europe in the early 1990s, eventually expanding to Asia, and more recently to North Africa and the Middle East. The evidence on electoral participation provisions show that they also emerged only after the end of the Cold War and that their uneven spread thereafter correlates with these waves. There are limits to these expectations of external engagement, however: states with valuable natural resource production or strong strategic importance to the United States, for example, are markedly less likely to include these provisions in their settlements, perhaps because expectations are lower that international actors will be willing and able to sanction governmental noncompliance in these cases.

While this set of findings is consistent with external engagement theory, aspects of it are also consistent with alternative explanations driven by international involvement, including the escape explanation (the idea that international actors are often more involved in these cases and thus may need a convenient means to end their troop deployment) or the enjoinder explanation (the idea that international actors may prefer to provide assistance to the states that hold elections for domestic strategic or normative reasons). The latter is similar to, but slightly different from, external engagement theory: both rely on Western preferences for democracy, but only external engagement theory implies that the demand for elections is more likely to arise from the rebel group(s), and only it assigns a functional role to the electoral process in engaging external actors to detect and sanction noncompliance with conditions of the peace deal. In contrast, the alternative explanations anticipate that the external actors are more likely to demand these provisions and that the elections will not serve any purpose in maintaining peace. The implications from external engagement theory better match the empirical results from Chapters 3 and 4.

Chapter 5 began to assess the mechanism at work with case study evidence, and further tested external engagement theory against the alternative theories. It examined the causal chain leading to settlements in cases where conflict began during the Cold War and ended after the Cold War. The shift at the systemic level – from partisan international involvement in conflict to nonpartisan democracy promotion and efforts to build peace – that took place with the end of the Cold War, especially in regions proximate to the western powers, allows evaluation of a central claim: whether commitment problems in the first period were resolved in the second period by external enforcement, enabled by electoral participation provisions that the combatants – especially rebel groups – requested to be included in the peace agreements. I examined a set of

10 cases, including close process-tracing in Guatemala and El Salvador – both of which experienced this shift and signed peace agreements with electoral participation provisions but differed on dimensions important under alternative explanations – and a comparison case, Bangladesh, which did not experience such a shift or include these provisions. I found that international actors had to establish their credibility in detecting and sanctioning noncompliance by each side before a settlement was signed. The cost of conflict was also crucial in these cases for generating initial negotiations – in Guatemala and El Salvador, for example, both the government and the rebel group lost foreign backing and faced growing war-weariness from their domestic supporters – but, even after each side in the cases would consider a peace agreement, they still had to tackle commitment problems. Overcoming these concerns was central to the form that the peace agreement took: before the combatants would agree to settlements based on electoral participation provisions, they had to be convinced of the credibility of the international actors. Once they were convinced, they signed settlements based on electoral participation provisions. In these cases, it was the rebel groups – the side that was more suspicious of the existing structures of the state – that demanded electoral participation provisions (rather than the international actors themselves, or the government side, which had more links to the international actors involved in these cases).

The evidence presented in these chapters also suggests an extension to the theory that should be tested further in future work: international actors are the principal enforcers of peace agreements, but, in states in which civil society remains strong, can domestic actors also help combatants commit to peace deals through elections? In cases in which much of the state was less affected by conflict, civil society's polarization may also be less. While most settlements will likely need the approach seen in most of the other illustrations and cases in this book (and described in the theory), a bottom-up approach may occasionally help secure a settlement from the start. The Philippines provides an example. A conflict began in 1972 between the national government and the Moro National Liberation Front (MNLF), which fought for the independence of the island of Mindanao. In 1996, after 24 years of fighting, the MNLF and the government signed a peace agreement that, among other provisions, created a new Consultative Assembly that granted Mindanao further autonomy and allowed the MNLF to become a political party to participate in both regional and national elections. The United States was not entirely nonpartisan during this process; it had provided substantial strategic assistance to the government both during and after the Cold War. The MNLF, therefore, would have had little reason to have faith that the United States would impartially enforce peace settlement provisions. But a domestic election observation organization, the National Citizens' Movement for Free Elections (NAMFREL), worked hard in the 1980s to establish itself as an objective and credible monitor. NAMFREL's report on the 1986 presidential election had led to massive pressure, first inside and then outside the country, to overturn the fraudulently achieved victory of incumbent Ferdinand Marcos.[1] Having thus established its credibility, NAMFREL, accompanied by international observers, monitored the 1992 elections and successfully challenged fraud in the 1995 elections. Meanwhile, the MNLF was engaged in peace negotiations with the government, and finally signed a peace agreement in 1996 with elections as a component of the settlement.[2] Libya and the Organization of the Islamic Conference, supported by the Islamic Conference of Foreign Ministers, supplied external engagement at this time at the request of the MNLF.[3] A variety of domestic and international actors pressured all sides to commit to the deal that emerged from the peace process. Although the deal was not fully implemented,[4] each has remained involved, and NAMFREL appears to have helped pressure the government to play by the rules.[5] In most cases, international actors have been central to ensuring compliance with peace settlements, but the Philippines, which has an electoral past and a vibrant civil society, shows how domestic actors, too, may be able to help serve this function.[6]

### Findings on the Consequences of Electoral Participation Provisions

While Chapters 3 through 5 examined the factors that lead peace negotiators to include electoral participation provisions in settlements, Chapter 6 and 7 turned to the consequences of these provisions for enduring peace. Using my original cross-national data on electoral participation provisions in peace agreements from 1975 to 2005, I analyzed whether the presence of electoral participation provisions was correlated with enduring peace after a settlement had been signed. I found that combatants signing settlements with these provisions have a much lower likelihood of returning to conflict compared to their counterparts signing without such provisions. This pattern, shown in Chapter 6, is consistent with external engagement theory. It is not directly implied by any of the alternative explanations. An even better test, however, involves

---

[1] Bjornlund 2004: 214–217.     [2] Hernandez 1996: 143, 145.
[3] Hernandez 1996: 145; 1997: 205; Eder and McKenna 2008: 74.
[4] Niksch 2002: 16; Eder and McKenna 2008: 75.     [5] Bjornlund 2004: 217.
[6] Bjornlund 2004: 234.

examining the relationship between peace and electoral participation provisions interacted with the regional waves of international involvement in democracy promotion. These waves are an apt proxy for combatants' expectations of external engagement through elections; external engagement theory strongly implies that peace can be expected to endure only when electoral participation provisions engage external actors. The analysis presented in Chapter 6 showed that the relationship between electoral participation provisions and peace is indeed conditional on expectations of that external engagement.

Chapter 7 returned to the case studies and examined the causal mechanism that maintains peace in these cases. After a peace agreement, the cases showed, international actors provided monitoring and conditional incentives to enforce compliance with the terms of the settlement, and leveraged the electoral cycle in doing so. In Guatemala and El Salvador, for example, the United Nations and other intergovernmental organizations monitored the elections, based not on compliance with universal standards of freedom or fairness, but on compliance under the agreed-on standards in the settlements. Further, international donors coordinated with these organizations to condition the assistance that they offered on the reported compliance. Threats to revoke conditional incentives in response to noncompliance, especially just before elections, contributed to maintaining compliance in these cases. This evidence matches the mechanism hypothesized by external engagement theory and not the alternative explanations.

The post-settlement findings in the case studies are also supported by cross-tabulations on post-conflict elections (presented in Chapter 6): those produced by electoral participation provisions tended to receive more monitoring, democracy and governance assistance, and see more pre-election conditionality, than other post-conflict elections. While the comparisons can be muddied by many post-conflict processes and pressures, these results are consistent with external engagement theory. However, the collection of these indicators is still underdeveloped, and, perhaps even more importantly, policy is also underdeveloped. The proxies that I use to measure expectations of external engagement are only useful through 2005 because then they then became so widespread, but diluted, that they can no longer reveal useful variation.[7] These variables, when used to indicate external engagement in these post-conflict elections, only scratch the surface of what often is, or could be, conditioned on compliance. International actors seem to be developing

---

[7] Hyde 2011b.

more sophistication in how they enforce these deals. One example that demonstrates this is Nepal: the explicit use of the trust fund during the electoral process represents the state of the art in settlement design. Trust funds have only been used sporadically since 1989, however. If more policymakers were to adopt these explicit mechanisms more consistently – a recommendation that I discuss below – I posit that we would see more peace, and we would also be better able to measure the impact on enduring peace.

### Peaceful Post-Conflict Elections and a Potential Democracy Tradeoff

This book is devoted to the study and practice of post-conflict elections. It shows evidence that international involvement through electoral participation provisions has a positive relationship with peace, and so scholars and policymakers must rethink current views on post-conflict elections that tend to discourage their use. However, while the evidence presented in this book shows that external engagement through electoral participation provisions raises the probability of enduring peace in post-conflict contexts, it also shows that such engagement may have detrimental effects on democracy. The evident tradeoff between peace and democracy in post-conflict elections merits further study.

In contrast to much extant scholarship, the evidence in this book suggests that certain post-conflict elections help terminate conflict and build peace, and that they can operate more as a coordination cycle that eases detection and sanction of noncompliance for external actors, rather than as a mechanism for determining the final distribution of power and resources. Findings on the association between post-conflict elections and peace have been mixed. Some research has found that post-conflict elections are stabilizing, while other research has shown them to be useless or even destabilizing under certain conditions. The elections examined in this book, produced by participation provisions included in settlements, have not received much systematic attention. This book shows that they have a positive relationship with peace between signatories when compared to alternative power distribution strategies, suggesting that this particular type of post-conflict election can contribute to peace.

These post-conflict elections are not, of course, representative of all elections (or even all post-conflict elections). Underlying the argument for the expanded use of electoral participation provisions, the importance of distinguishing different types of contests in post-conflict contexts becomes clear in this book. Participatory and internationalized elections, designed as provisions in peace agreements, have a discernibly different effect on peace than other arrangements. Just any election is not enough: electoral participation provisions only benefit peace when combatants expect external actors to monitor and enforce the terms of settlements for all sides. When combatants do not have such expectations, electoral participation provisions are unlikely to be included in final peace settlements, and, if they are included, they are unlikely to produce more enduring peace.

Elections derived from peace agreements with electoral participation provisions are seen in many, but not all, of the crucial post-conflict cases from the past decades. Post-conflict elections that are hastily organized and implemented by the government without rebel group participation – such as the election in Afghanistan in 2009 – are not likely to bring peace.[8] Elections generated through settlements that include appropriate external engagement may not be as easy to arrange, but they are essential to ensure enduring peace. In the next section, I return to the questions of how policymakers can recognize when electoral participation provisions are likely to work, and what they can do to encourage them.

The post-conflict elections that I examine in this book are relatively certain mechanisms for power-sharing, relying either on status-quo bias or outright electoral engineering, rather than open lotteries or substitute mechanisms for distributing power.[9] There are examples of post-conflict elections that deviate from the ideal type described by external engagement theory (e.g. Angola's election in 1992). However, most of the elections in which both rebel groups and governments participate do fit this characterization and, by ensuring a relatively certain outcome and thus reducing domestic actors' incentives to return to conflict, demonstrate the effectiveness of this type of post-conflict election in securing peace.

The mechanism underpinning the theory posited in this book contributes to the idea that elections and other institutions, such as constitutions, may serve as focal points for external engagement in post-conflict settings.[10] This theory also contributes to a broader debate over why elections are held even in different contexts in which they are not

---

[8] Those cases in which rebel groups win and then organize elections without government parties, however, may do so, although they may be prone toward strong single-party systems; see Lyons, 2016.

[9] Walter 2002; Wantchekon 2004; Durant and Weintraub 2014; Hartzell and Hoddie 2015.

[10] Weingast 1997; Fearon 2011.

particularly open,[11] and how elections can be designed to be useful in these contexts.[12]

Despite the successes that this books shows in securing peace in post-conflict contexts, these elections often do not lead to democratization. The data presented in Chapters 6 and 7 are consistent with the expectation that these post-conflict elections, in conjunction with international engagement, build peace. Other studies have found that they do not necessarily build democracy in later years,[13] however, and that pushing too hard for democracy may even be dangerous and counterproductive to development.[14]

In a study of cases of post-conflict elections, Lyons notes that "'success' with relation to one goal, say war termination, does not necessarily mark 'success' relative to another, such as democratization."[15] But the theory presented in this book goes further, suggesting a possible inverse relationship between democracy and stability. This returns to the questions about the role of norms that surround these contests. My external engagement theory posits that electoral participation deals are effective *because* they are somewhat undemocratic elite pacts. This may also account for the low levels of liberalism, the sustained cleavages, and the focus of election observation on peace rather than democracy that are associated with these elections. Prior studies have demonstrated poor democracy in these contexts, but have not attributed it to the trade-off with stability. This book argues that successful post-conflict elections arising from electoral participation provisions in post-conflict settlements are designed differently, and they are monitored and incentivized using distinct criteria that favor stability over democracy. The norms surrounding elections in democratic or democratizing contexts rest on the idea that elections will produce a more representative, and thus legitimate, government than other power distribution mechanisms

---

[11] There is a large literature emerging on various purposes of such elections, which range from arguments that they contribute to a move toward liberalization (if slowly) to arguments that they help entrench dictators by providing information and pathways for patronage to them; see, among many others, excellent reviews by Gandhi and Lust-Okar (2009) and Brancati (2014), as well as studies featuring some cross-national analyses (e.g. Schedler 2002; Geddes 2003; Howard and Roessler 2006; Lindberg 2006; Gandhi 2008; Wright 2008; Levitsky and Way 2010; Svolik 2012; Simpser 2013; Beaulieu 2014, Pop-Eleches and Robertson 2015), and studies of particular cases (e.g. Lust-Okar 2005, 2008; Brownlee 2007; Greene 2007; Magaloni 2008; Wedeen 2009; Blaydes 2011).

[12] For example, on this, see Schumpeter 1942; Lijphart 1968, 1984, 1989.

[13] See, for example, Ottaway 1997; Irvin 1999; Zahar 1999; Manning 2004, 2008; Lyons 2005; De Zeeuw 2008; Söderberg Kovacs 2008. De Zeeuw and Kumar 2006 examine a number of dimensions of democracy, including elections, human rights, and media.

[14] See, for example, Paris 2004, especially if done too quickly; see Flores and Nooruddin 2009a, 2012; Brancati and Snyder 2013.

[15] Lyons 2004: 272.

would produce. But the post-conflict elections discussed in this book often deviate from the democratic ideals that underpin electoral institutions in democratic societies. Understanding the normative dimension of elections is thus crucial to external engagement theory. It could also contribute to the development of broader theories about how conflict affects democratization directly.[16]

Future research should more thoroughly integrate the study of security and democracy in these post-conflict contexts, and consider how peace arising from post-conflict elections may be reconciled with democracy in the medium and long run. Indeed, not many elections are truly uncertain in practice.[17] As a state develops a post-conflict electoral history, it also may be possible to move away from some of the rigid guarantees of representation that are potentially in tension with democracy.

Loosening these guarantees over time may, paradoxically, reduce the risk of later types of conflict that could otherwise follow in these contexts. These electoral participation provisions are also not guarantees of complete peace. While post-conflict elections reduce the risk of return to conflict in combatant dyads that sign peace agreements, the conflict may not terminate entirely: some rebel groups may refuse to sign the peace agreements, or new groups may emerge reigniting it.[18] The theory makes no claims about whether these post-conflict electoral contests will address the grievances of all rebel groups or the population that once supported these rebel groups. The beneficial effect on peace identified in the book is based solely on conflict between parties that signed settlements. The very same elections might polarize or alienate other populations or leaders. This is a risk when rebel group leaders who embrace radical nationalist platforms seek and win election to powerful offices.[19] It is also a risk as power changes over time, and leaders or populations become frustrated with the system agreed on in the settlement. In Burundi and Mozambique, for example, the stronger combatant side in each case sought to consolidate its power decades after reaching the peace agreement. These power grabs produced flares of low-level violence long after the demobilization of the combatants. In each context, assistance had been conditioned on

---

[16] See Fortna and Huang 2012; see the following for how democratization potentially affects conflict of various types in coming cycles: Gleditsch and Ward 2000; Snyder 2000; Davenport 2004; Paris 2004; Mansfield and Snyder 2005; Birnir 2006; Licklider 2006; Daxecker 2007; Cederman et al. 2010; Chenoweth 2010.

[17] Not just post-conflict elections (e.g. Horowitz 1991), but contentious elections and elections more broadly (e.g. Norris 2004; Alberts et al. 2012).

[18] Spoilers, from either inside or outside of existing rebel groups, often have to be dealt with in negotiating a settlement, including sometimes through international inducements; see Stedman 1997; Kydd and Walter 2002.

[19] Snyder 2000; Jarstad 2008.

complying with the terms of the peace agreement, although it was reduced and became less effective in Mozambique as natural resource extraction provided alternative sources of funds.[20] In Burundi, however, aid suspensions helped create some incentives to end the fighting, as the theory predicts, although whether these measures will be sufficient leverage to overcome the incentives to fight remains to be seen.[21] In Bosnia and Herzegovina, it was the population that eventually protested against a system that, although it had produced peace, was also corrupt because leaders were so secure in their positions.[22] Such potential effects of post-conflict elections lie outside of the scope of this project, but they should be explored. Examining the combatants that do not sign onto settlements in states with elections produced by post-conflict contexts, and examining these longer and lower-level effects after the existing combatant groups that sign have settled into peace, would be instructive. Loosening rigid guarantees of representation might help democracy succeed in these contexts, while also reducing the factors that might make these states more prone to longer-term and lower-level violence, although such institution design would need to be weighed against the risk of conflict continuance or recurrence among signatories of settlements.

This potential tradeoff with democracy also importantly demonstrates a limit to these elections. The evidence in this book suggests that electoral participation provisions can create and sustain peace between signatories to a settlement, but, of course, they cannot solve every economic, social, and political problem in the state.

## Implications for External Engagement

This book hypothesizes and shows evidence that peace agreements with electoral participation provisions can reduce the chance of conflict recurrence. But its most important implications are about the role of external engagement that occurs through those elections. Those who study international involvement in sovereign states, in response to civil conflict, have long been focused on intervention by armed peacekeepers, whose troops are ready to threaten punishment by force.[23] But even armed peacekeepers employ an array of mechanisms to enforce compliance, including information gathering and using conditional incentives to reward compliance or punish noncompliance.[24]

---

[20] Guilengue 2013.    [21] Sanders 2016.    [22] Smale 2014.
[23] See, for example, Walter 2002.
[24] For examples on this, see Fortna 2008. And there may be domestic political politics that may push certain foreign actors to continue to use the mechanism of the military, even if it is not primarily leveraging force (e.g. Milner and Tingley 2016).

Despite that other forms of external engagement are more common than armed interventions, scholars have only begun to consider these other forms. Some recent studies examine international involvement in governance both inside and outside of civil conflicts.[25] This book contributes to the growing body of work on how international actors might usefully involve themselves in civil conflict termination and peace-building, either in combination with or in place of troops on the ground, a compelling component of global governance.[26] This book presents a comprehensive theory of external engagement based on enforcement that detects and sanctions noncompliance, and it identifies a particular form – electoral participation provisions – through which such external engagement occurs. There are a variety of other forms, apart from force, that such external engagement takes. Many of the dimensions that contribute to the success of electoral participation provisions, and that could be applied on their own if elections are unavailable, should be further studied. For instance, initial case-based studies suggest that aid conditionality in post-conflict contexts is prevalent and may be beneficial for peace, even though it may not help development, but little rigorous cross-case analysis has been conducted.[27]

The uneven spread of electoral participation provisions across regions and time suggests that we should not expect the conditions for successful external engagement to be met everywhere. Although this book identifies certain conditions that international actors must meet in order to enforce agreements credibly, there are other strategies that these actors might use to broaden the number of cases in which they are seen by combatants as credible.

International actors need to be seen as willing and able to identify and sanction noncompliance with the peace agreement. Their credibility can be enhanced, first, by being explicit about the goals of post-conflict elections. If the explicit goal is external enforcement of compliance with a settlement (rather than a goal split between peace and democracy promotion), policymakers may be more able to effectively monitor compliance. They might send missions out to former combatant strong-holds in the lead-up to elections, for instance, rather than only to compe-titive regions, and they might be able to condition aid more effectively on compliance by, for example, providing trust funds in more cases for

---

[25] For example, see Krasner and Risse 2014; Matanock 2014.

[26] Much of the existing work so far focuses on forced global governance in these post-conflict contexts, which then operate with huge missions but less success, such as U.N. neo-trusteeships; see, Fearon and Laitin 2004; Krasner 2004; Lake and Fariss 2014.

[27] See Suhrke and Buckmaster 2005; Frerks 2006; Emmanuel and Rothchild 2007; Manning and Malbrough 2010; Girod 2011; Matanock and Lichtenheld 2016.

ex-combatant parties. Even if they cannot identify or measure the full impact of their role in these processes, some policymakers have already implemented aspects of this monitoring and conditionality in post-conflict contexts. For example, the work by those designing the Central American interventions, as well as the recent Nepal trust fund, discussed in this book, were often explicit about these ends. Recognizing the mechanisms at work in maintaining peace may encourage more such customization. Further work should explore whether and how well policymakers understand their actions in these contexts.

Second, to enhance credibility, robust international organizations are crucial in implementing election-oriented external engagement to end civil conflict. International actors must be interested but nonpartisan in the conflict if they are to be trusted by all sides to detect and sanction noncompliance (the "Goldilocks" dimension identified in Chapter 2). In some cases, strong external states that have strategic or other special relationships with conflicted states may be unable to raise expectations that they will enforce settlements with sufficient nonpartisanship; they may particularly be seen as unlikely to punish the incumbent government that has been their partner. Intergovernmental bodies that design policy through coordination among many of their members, however – particularly those that may be on different sides of geostrategic debates – could work around concerns that one side will receive special treatment. Experimental studies on how international election observers were perceived suggest that there are differences in the credibility assigned to each.[28] This type of study should be conducted in conflict contexts, to understand which external actors are most credible. The involvement of strong international organizations, such as the U.N.'s Security Council, would take careful crafting, but the possibility that they could decrease conflict recurrence in a wider set of cases may make this approach worthwhile.

The utility of external engagement in post-conflict contexts under examination in this book, focusing on electoral processes, also suggests that recent attempts to integrate normative and instrumental views in international relations should be expanded.[29] The motivation for international actors to intervene through electoral processes is a combination of normative and instrumental reasoning: the normative changes with respect to democracy after the end of the Cold War reduced the costs of coordination among international actors, and reduced domestic actors' sovereignty concerns. As I argue in Chapter 2, normative and instrumental aspects converge to foster electoral participation provisions at a cost

[28] Bush and Prather 2016.    [29] Hyde 2011b.

that makes them credible for those demanding enforcement. Somewhat surprisingly, I did not find that the sides that were more closely allied with the United States or the West during the Cold War – presumably the side more likely to be influenced by the norms of the West during peace negotiations – were more likely to demand electoral participation provisions. Instead, the side that advocated for these provisions in these cases was the side that would be relatively disadvantaged in the status-quo state institutions, the rebel group. Normative and instrumental logics, then, may fit alongside each other to explain electoral participation provisions. The combination also implies path dependency, and potential constraints, on the argument developed in this book: for instance, if the Soviet Union had won the Cold War, coordinating points for sovereignty intrusion in states emerging from civil conflict might be entirely different (as outlined in Chapter 2). Other focal points might not be as effective in enabling enforcement as electoral participation because, for instance, they might not provide the same properties as electoral processes' coordination cycles that culminate in power distribution among combatants. Still, other studies should examine potential alternative focal points, such as truth and reconciliation commissions, to assess whether their attention and accountability could make them good substitutes if elections were unavailable.

Future research should also address the combination of normative and instrumental dimensions of the argument made here. Experimental work may be particularly valuable. This book draws on interviews with former rebel group and government leaders to develop an inductive theory of the benefits of electoral participation provisions compared to alternative power distribution arrangements. Systematic experiments could further assess how instrumentalist leaders are in their decisions, as well as whether there are any cases in which the normative dimension might prevent the use of elections to distribute power (for instance, if a criminal group attempted to transition to a political party, which other actors might reject as illegitimate).[30]

Tying this book into larger ideas about compliance and enforcement broadly conceived suggests a much expanded role for global governance under which international actors can help solve domestic political problems, perhaps at the request of competing factions within the county. If this book is correct about the mechanism, external engagement to monitor and incentivize compliance, using aid and other nonmilitary mechanisms, can help solve domestic political problems beyond combatant commitment problems in settling civil conflict. Situations in which

---

[30] For example, see Matanock and Garbiras-Díaz 2016.

both sides would like to cooperate to avoid costs, but face shifting power, are most likely scenarios for this type of external engagement. The problems are likely to be those in which the global community is interested, including reducing violent repression and fraud during leader transitions, or even tackling corruption in divided governments. In some contexts, self-enforcement or enforcement by domestic civil society may be insufficient, as the book details. The external engagement mechanism could be used to exact compliance in all of these cases, given the right conditions, in a credible way given its relatively low cost. These conditions include coordination cycles that focus actors' attention and leverage on moments of power distribution, produced in this context by elections, and international interest in resolving these problems over any partisan interests in the state. While not available in all contexts, these domestic political problems occur often, and there is some possibility that they can be solved in similar ways.[31]

In short, this book identifies a mechanism for engaging external actors to enforce peace agreements that, when available, can stabilize settlements. The empirical findings demonstrate that electoral participation provisions help overcome one of the most persistent obstacles to peace – conflict recurrence after a settlement – and in so doing, contribute to existing literature on civil conflict resolution. Future research on similar mechanisms to engage external actors in such global governance in other contexts would be a natural extension to this book.

## Fostering Successful Settlements in Practice

This section makes the abstract principles more concrete by turning to the lessons that could be applied to peace agreements to help them stick. First and foremost, this book suggests, policymakers need not shy away from promoting post-conflict elections, as long as combatants buy into the process by signing peace agreements that provide for their transition into political parties, as outlined in Chapters 1 and 2. The United Nations and other international peacemakers should propose the inclusion of electoral participation provisions to combatants considering a settlement in each peace agreement. There are scope conditions for peace agreements that may not be met in some cases (see Chapter 2 on this point), but, once they are, these proposals should be made. Not just any elections will do: the distinctions among types, which have been overlooked in other work on post-conflict elections, are critical.

---

[31] The mechanisms could be characterized as similar in some existing studies, including, for example, Simmons 2009; Hafner-Burton 2005, 2013; Donno 2013.

The election produced by electoral participation provisions in a peace agreement may need to be engineered so the outcome is somewhat certain. Linking D.D.R. efforts, and other provisions common to settlements, to the electoral process may also help stabilize peace in these contexts.

External engagement theory has implications for the direct role that international actors can play in peace processes, too, beyond proposing electoral participation provisions in settlements to governments and rebel groups. First, this book suggests that nonpartisan international involvement is crucial, and, for international actors to be able to punish settlement violations by any combatants, they must have sufficient information and credible leverage against all sides. The external actor must engage in monitoring the process, must apply the standards of the peace process (rather than universal norms of freedom or fairness) to judge compliance, and must condition benefits, such as democracy aid and party funds, for all sides on that compliance. External actors therefore need to be monitors. Peacekeepers – small observer missions that do not need to threaten force – and international election observers are therefore crucial in these contexts. In addition, external actors need resources to leverage. Aid, especially democracy and governance assistance, is important. Party trust funds may provide particularly useful leverage. As I have shown, in post-conflict environments, political parties and their supporters may receive substantial assistance, sometimes in the form of a trust fund. Trust fund conditionality on combatant compliance with the conditions of the agreement is useful for securing targeted leverage for international actors. Aid of all kinds is needed and typically provided in these contexts; supplying funds for party development but conditioning it on compliance with the peace agreement, in particular, can help convince combatants of credible enforcement and produce peace.

In the case of Afghanistan, where the elections that have been held do not meet the participatory standards to be included in this study, the problem of an overly invested external actor became quite clear. After the 2001 invasion, the Afghan government became a strategic ally of the United States and NATO in a fight against global terrorism, including Al Qaeda, which had links to Mullah Mohammed Omar's faction of the Afghan Taliban. The systemic concerns that led the United States and NATO into a strategic alliance in Afghanistan had not changed by 2006, when both international actors sought to bring the Afghan Taliban to the negotiation table. As a consequence, the Taliban had no reason to believe that these actors would punish governmental noncompliance with a peace agreement as harshly as they would noncompliance by the Taliban, whether the United States and NATO engaged through an electoral process or otherwise. Indeed, in the 2009 elections – in which some rebel candidates who had disarmed were able to run against the government candidates – external actors allowed very high levels of manipulation and fraud.[32] This led to election results that were widely considered illegitimate. The Taliban would have had no reason to perceive these international actors as credible and therefore little incentive to accept an electoral arrangement – or any other deal – backed by them.

There are thus cases in which credible external engagement through elections is likely to be unavailable, perhaps because relevant international organizations are strongly committed to one side in the conflict, as in the Afghanistan example, or because combatants perceive them to be apathetic about the state. Apathy is less likely with this type of international involvement because, as the world is increasingly connected, and this intervention has low costs, even diffuse threats should be enough to urge this type of action.

It is more difficult for international actors to be nonpartisan in countries in which they have vital security or economic interests. But what else can they do? One option, discussed above, would be to strengthen intergovernmental organizations so that no single state is entrusted with determining noncompliance or imposing sanctions unilaterally. In the absence of sufficiently strong intergovernmental organizations, in extremely partisan settings such as Afghanistan, the only option might be for the partisan international actor to act in partnership with another international actor who is either nonpartisan or partisan but toward the opposite combatant side. In the Philippines, the U.S.-linked government had a hard time achieving credibility in the peace process, even with the necessary structures in place. The MNLF distrusted the United States and related intergovernmental organizations as enforcers, through the electoral process or beyond it. Therefore Libya and the Organization of the Islamic Conference, supported by the Islamic Conference of Foreign Ministers and other civil society organizations were asked to broker the deal and to monitor its implementation.[33] Philippine civil society was sufficiently developed to undertake some of the functions that might otherwise have been delegated to an international actor. Such nonpartisan or differently partisan international actors, or domestic actors, however, may not be available in all cases.

---

[32] For more on this case, see Lafraie 2011.
[33] Hernandez 1996: 145; Hernandez 1997: 205; Eder and McKenna 2008: 74.

## Looking Forward

All around the world, states with civil conflicts need solutions. This book offers some solutions that derive from external engagement. I show that certain post-conflict elections – those in which rebel groups and government both participate, in order to engage international actors to monitor and deter violations of their peace deals – can be more effective tools for ending civil conflict with stable peace. These conclusions contrast with pessimistic work on post-conflict elections that fails to differentiate between types of elections, and that focuses on democracy over peace. Certain conditions that must be met in order for post-conflict elections to help produce peace: conflict must be costly for all sides, and an international actor must be sufficiently interested in terminating the conflict to become a nonpartisan enforcer, and to provide the resources necessary to detect and sanction noncompliance by either side. Electoral participation provisions make it easier for external actors to engage in these contexts. Stabilizing post-conflict states through elections, however, often involves considerable electoral engineering, which may reduce the potential for future democratization. Despite the risk that post-conflict states that include electoral participation provisions will slow democratization, the evidence presented in this book suggests that electoral participation provisions with credible external engagement have become the dominant approach to peace agreement design and that they can help secure enduring peace.

# Appendix: Formalizing the Model

## Basic Model

The basic theoretical framework builds on the existing literature. I formalize the strategic nub of the interaction based on earlier models that capture the commitment problem (Fearon 1995; Walter 2002), and the later iterations of the model in Chapter 2 and this appendix focus on variation in international actor engagement. Initially, the model has two strategic actors, the government (G) and the rebel group (R). In the model, the government and the rebel group have an expected payoff in terms of power or policy change that each can gain through fighting or through establishing a peace agreement that shares power between them.

I make simplifying assumptions to focus on an important aspect of the strategic interaction between the government and the rebel group. The first assumption is that there is a single rebel group fighting a government. In reality, multiple rebel groups may fight a government simultaneously. The basic logic of the interaction between each dyad applies to all of the dyads in the state, although having multiple rebel groups may have some effect on the interaction (for more, see Cunningham 2006, 2007). Next, I assume that the government and the rebel group both want to control as large of a share of power as possible. I also assume that either actor will renege on the promises that it has made if it expects that such a move will increase its share of power. In most cases, these dyads have been fighting for years, and so there is no inherent trust or norm of reciprocity between them. In addition, I assume that the government and the rebel group each have a single set of preferences. In reality, each side may contain divisions, but, given that the leaders of both the government and the rebel group are sitting down at a negotiating table, they represent the interests of some population of that side. Finally, a last assumption is that there is a cost to fighting, which is captured by $z \in (0,1)$. The model, then, allows the cost of fighting to enter into the strategic calculus of both actors. As this value approaches

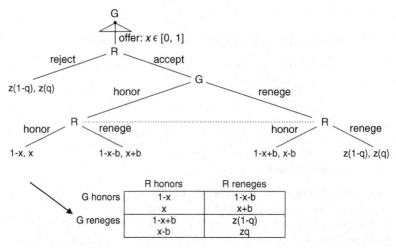

Figure A.1 Civil Conflict Termination without International Involvement

one, it destroys more resources, so fighting is more costly. And as the value approaches zero, it destroys fewer resources, so fighting is less costly. I assume that this parameter never reaches zero or one, so that fighting is always destroying some resources, but never all resources. Within these parameters, though, the cost may vary, and, indeed, may become close to costless for the actors involved with funds from foreign sponsors, or loot- or rent-seeking domestically (Abrahms 2008; Collier and Hoeffler 1999, 2004; Zahar 1999).

In the model, the government and the rebel group are engaged in fighting when they come to the negotiating table. In the first stage of the game, the government offers the rebel group some share of power or policy influence over time, $x \in [0,1]$. In the second stage of the game, the rebel group decides whether to accept the peace agreement. If the rebel group does not accept the peace agreement, both sides return to fighting, which eventually yields $z(1 - q)$ to the government and $zq$ to the rebel group. In the third stage, the government and the rebel group then simultaneously decide whether or not to honor the deal. If both the government and the rebel group renege on the deal, both sides again return to fighting, yielding $z(1 - q)$ and $zq$, respectively. If both actors honor the deal, the government gets $1 - x$ and the rebel group gets $x$. If the government reneges, though, while the rebel group honors, the government then gets $1 - x + b$, while the rebel group gets $x - b$, where $b$ is $\in (0,1)$. There is thus a payoff for taking advantage of the "sucker" that honors the deal while getting reneged on. The opposite is then true, as well: if the rebel group reneges and the government honors, then the government gets $1 - x - b$, and the rebel group gets $x + b$.

I solve the game using the concept of subgame perfect Nash equilibrium – an equilibrium such that each actor's strategy is a Nash equilibrium in each subgame – and having both the government and the rebel group honor the agreement is never an equilibrium. This equilibrium concept allows me to eliminate incredible threats because no actor is allowed to act contrary to their own interests in any stage of the game.

### Proposition

If $b + zq < 1$ and $b \geq zq$, then there exists an equilibrium in which the government offers $x^\star = b + zq$, the rebel group accepts and honors, and the government reneges. This is an equilibrium because (1) the rebel group's payoff of $zq$ is at least as good as it can get by either refusing the deal or reneging and (2) the government's payoff of $1 - zq$ is superior to what it can get by making an offer that the rebel group would reject or renege on, $z(1 - q)$.

### Proof

In the proof, I adopt the convention that if actors are indifferent between two options, they will choose the more cooperative one: offering, accepting, and honoring instead of not offering, rejecting, and reneging. Examining the normal form game that is the final stage of the extensive form game, I identify when the rebel group would choose to honor. If the rebel group chooses to honor, the government will choose to renege in the final stage since it can get a better payoff from doing so. Comparing the rebel group's honor and renege payoffs, then, given that the government will renege, that the rebel group will only honor if $zq \leq x - b$. Thus, if $x \geq zq + b$, the rebel group will honor in the final stage, even though the government reneges. If $x < zq + b$, the rebel group will also renege. Moving up the game tree, the decision for the rebel group is the same in its first decision: it is comparing $zq$ to $x - b$, so, again, it will accept if $x \geq zq + b$, and it will reject otherwise.

In order to examine the government's initial offers and the payoffs that would result, we need to know its actions in the normal form that is the final stage of the extensive form game, and then how these relate to those of the rebel group: in the final stage, the government will consider whether how $1 - x - b$ relates to $z(1 - q)$. If $1 - x - b \geq z(1 - q)$, then the government will choose to honor in this subgame even if the rebel group will renege. This rearranges to $x \leq 1 - b - z + zq$. I can now identify two cases: one in which $zq + b > 1 - b - z + zq$ (which simplifies to $2b > 1 - z$), and one in which $2b < 1 - z$. In the first case (Case 1), the strategies in the final subgame are G honors, R reneges at $x = 0$ through up $x = 1 - b - z + zq$, both renege from there until $x = zq + b$, and then G reneges, R honors up through $x = 1$. In Case 2, the strategies in the final subgame are G honors, R reneges at $x = 0$ up through $x = zq + b$, either G honors, R reneges or G reneges, R honors from there until $x = 1 - b - z + zq$, and then G reneges, R honors up through $x = 1$. In each case, then, the government can decide its best strategy in terms of the initial offer $(x)$ that it makes.

In Case 1, the government will compare its payoff from offering 0, which the rebel group will renege on $(1 - b)$ to its payoff for offering $b + zq$, which is the lowest possible amount that the rebel group is expected to honor $(1 - (b + zq) + \rightarrow 1 - zq)$: if $1 - b > 1 - zq$ (which simplifies to $b < zq$), the government will offer $x^\star = 0$, the rebel group will reject it (unless $b + zq = 0$, but given that b must be greater than zero, this cannot be the case), and then, off the equilibrium path, G will honor and R will renege. If, on the other hand, $b \geq zq$, the government will offer $x^\star = b + zq$, the rebel group will accept it, and then G will renege and R will honor. The government cannot offer more than 1, according to the game since this would be a case in which it would be offering to give more than the power and resources that the two sides are to divide between them. So, if $b + zq < 1$, $b \geq zq$, and, since this is Case 1, $2b > 1 - z$, G will offer $x^\star = b + zq$, R will accept, G will renege, and R will honor.

In Case 2, the government will also compare its payoff from offering 0, which the rebel group will renege on $(1 - b)$ to its payoff for offering $b + zq$, which is the lowest possible amount that the rebel group is expected to honor $(1 - (b + zq) + b \rightarrow 1 - zq)$. This scenario actually repeats Case 1 because the other condition, x at a value of $1 - b - z + zq$, does not actually change the outcomes. The government could offer higher values of x (in this case in place of $b + zq$, and, in Case 1, in place of 0), but, in both cases, if I assume that G will seek to maximize its share by offering the lowest possible value, none of these outcomes would occur. So, if $b + zq < 1$, $b \geq zq$, regardless of the relationship between $2b$ and $1 - z$, G will offer $x^\star = b + zq$, R will accept, G will renege, and R will honor.

I have not fully specified the off-the-equilibrium play, but I have shown in this proof that the government will not offer $x^\star$ such that it will honor in the final subgame when the rebel group reneges. Thus, the other outcome will always be fighting because the rebel group will reject the initial offer, and then this will be supported under certain conditions (those outlined above) as G will renege, R will honor, and, under the rest as G will renege, R will renege in the final subgame.

### Remarks

The basic result from the model is that neither side can commit in the last stage to honor if the other side is expected to honor. This is the commitment problem: neither side can credibly commit to not renege, even though both sides would benefit from such a commitment (Fearon 1995; Walter 2002). In addition to this result, the model also shows that, if the "sucker's" payoff is small relative to the destruction of resources caused by war, the government can offer the rebel group enough to make getting reneged on worth it. Sometimes the rebel group will benefit more from agreeing to a deal in which the rebel groups expects to be the "sucker," honoring while the other side reneges. Once the sucker's payoff is larger relative to the destruction of resources caused by war, fighting is the only possible outcome.

A final note on the model: I have modeled the "sucker" outcome as gaining some power relative to a peace agreement that is accepted and not broken (even by the side that is reneged on in the model). I could also model reneging as a return to fighting with a unilateral advantage for the reneging side. This is the way that others have modeled the commitment problem (usually based on the models in Walter 2002), and, indeed, it results in a standard prisoner's dilemma: each side would now have a payoff that is worse than what it can get from fighting if it honors and the other side reneges (which is $z(q - b)$ for the rebel group and $z(1 - q - b)$ for the government). But each side has a benefit from reneging (of $b$), so, in the absence of external enforcement, fighting is the equilibrium outcome. In many cases, this may be what both sides fear – one side will demobilize and be in a weak position, and then the other side will attack from a position of strength – but in some cases they appear to fear being reneged on further down the road – for example, perhaps a strong but short international force comes in to help both sides demobilize, but then the two sides will have to finish establishing the power-sharing deal without this outside assistance. Fears about reneging on a deal, even without a return to conflict, can be problematic too (for example, see Macedonia in Chapter 6 for a case in which these fears were pervasive). While in a limited number of cases, one side will accept getting reneged in this conception, the commitment problem still makes a peace agreement that both sides will honor impossible, even without a direct return to

|  | R honors | R reneges |
|---|---|---|
| G honors | $1-x$<br>$x$ | $1-x-b$<br>$x+b-c$ |
| G reneges | $1-x+b-c$<br>$x-b$ | $z(1-q)-c$<br>$z(q)-c$ |

Figure A.2  Civil Conflict Termination with International Involvement

fighting (and, indeed, such noncompliance may lead to a return to fighting down the road). The incredibility of a peace agreement with compliance by both sides is the most important aspect of either conception, and it is the commitment problem.

## Modified Model

I return to the formalization to show the impact of changing the cost-benefit analysis at the margins on whether both sides will honor the peace agreement. I model the cost imposed on the side that reneges as $c \in (0,1]$. I show just the normal form game that represents the final stage of the extensive form game (shown in Figure A.1), but what is clear is that, as long as $c \geq b$, there is no benefit from reneging for either side if the other side will honor. In order to get this outcome, of course, conflict must be costly enough for both sides. The rebel group will still reject the offer if $x < zq$, and the government will not make an acceptable offer if $1 - x < z(1 - q)$, but, otherwise, the outcome will be for both sides to honor the deal.

The main theoretical question that remains, then, is how to ensure that $c \geq b$. I identify a mechanism through which international actors can provide an effective $c$ efficiently in Chapter 2, and I also discuss mechanisms for decreasing the value of b through agreement design.

# Bibliography

"1990 Country Report on Human Rights Practices: Guatemala," 1990, September 7, Case ID 95122240, Document No. E1529, Guatemala Declassification Project, U.S. Department of State Freedom of Information Act, U.S. Department of State.

"Agreement on the Strengthening of Civilian Power and the Role of the Armed Forces in Democratic Society," 1996, September 19, Mexico City. Available from the Peace Accord Matrix: https://peaceaccords.nd.edu/accord/accord -firm-and-lasting-peace.

"Ambassador Calls on MOD and Discusses Topics Surrounding Military-to -Military Relationships," 1993, June 29, Case ID 951222H5, Document No. E3371, Guatemala Declassification Project, U.S. Department of State Freedom of Information Act, U.S. Department of State.

"Background Information for Mr. Lake's November 21 Meeting with Jennifer Harbury," 1994, November 18, Case ID 951222D0, Document No. E4777A, Guatemala Declassification Project, U.S. Department of State Freedom of Information Act, U.S. Department of State.

"Cerezo Nixes Dialogue with Guerrillas," 1986, November 4, Case ID 95122214, Document No. E5 [missing], Guatemala Declassification Project, U.S. Department of State Freedom of Information Act, U.S. Department of State, Guatemala City, Guatemala.

"Cocaine: A Supply Side Strategy," 1989, June 15, U.S. Department of State, Washington, D.C.

"Colombian Rebels Seek Status as Political Party," 1988, *The Globe and Mail* (Canada), December 20.

"El Salvador Elections," 1997, *The Washington Post*, March 17.

"En El 89, Washington Pensó En Enviar Tropas a Colombia," 2010, *El Tiempo*, May 16.

"FMLN Begins Destruction of Arms," 1992, December 1, Case ID F-2008–05748, Document No. C17582238, El Salvador Declassification Project, U.S. Department of State Freedom of Information Act, U.S. Department of State.

"FMLN Legalization – Contingent on Demobilization," 1992, October 29, Case ID F-2008–05748, Document No. C17582252, El Salvador Declassification Project, U.S. Department of State Freedom of Information Act, U.S. Department of State.

"Guatemala Human Rights Practices, 1995," 1996, March, Electronic Research Collections, U.S. Department of State and Federal Depository Library, Richard J. Daley Library, University of Illinois at Chicago.

"Guatemala Human Rights Report – 1991," 1991, January 1, Case ID 95122249, Document No. E1869, Guatemala Declassification Project, U.S. Department of State Freedom of Information Act, U.S. Department of State.

"Guatemala Meeting with President Ramiro de Leon Carpio," 1994, February 15, Case ID 95122295, Document No. E3698A, Guatemala Declassification Project, U.S. Department of State Freedom of Information Act, U.S. Department of State.

"Guatemala: Negotiating Peace to Foster Democracy," 1994, May 1, Case ID 951222H0, Document No. E6131, Guatemala Declassification Project, U.S. Department of State Freedom of Information Act, U.S. Department of State.

"Guatemalan Guerrillas Deny Issuing Truce Communique," 1986, *BBC Summary of World Broadcasts*, March 8.

"Guatemalan President Views Visit to Mexico," 1986, *BBC Summary of World Broadcasts*, July 4.

"Harbury/Bamaca Case: Supporting MINUGUA," 1994, January 4, Case ID 95122293, Document No. E3627, Guatemala Declassification Project, U.S. Department of State Freedom of Information Act, U.S. Department of State.

"Re: GOES/FMLN Talks," 1991, September 18, 7pp., Box No. CF00196B2, Latin American Directorate Files, Bush Presidential Records.

"Report in Spanish Re Michael Vernon Devine Case," 1990, June 9, Case ID 95122236, Document No. E1395, Guatemala Declassification Project, U.S. Department of State Freedom of Information Act, U.S. Department of State.

"Returning Exiles Test Guatemala's New 'Democracy'," 1993, *Guardian Weekly*, May 16.

"Review of Key Issues," 1992, November 14, Case ID 95122270, Document No. E2715, Guatemala Declassification Project, U.S. Department of State Freedom of Information Act, U.S. Department of State.

"US Policy toward Guatemala," 1994, February 24, Case ID 95122297, Document No. E3758, Guatemala Declassification Project, U.S. Department of State Freedom of Information Act, U.S. Department of State.

Abrahms, Max, 2008, "What Terrorists Really Want," *International Security*, 32: 78–105.

Acharya, Amitav, Pierre Lizée, and Sorpong Peou, eds., 1989, *Cambodia – The 1989 Paris Peace Conference* (Toronto: Centre for International and Strategic Studies).

Acosta, Benjamin, 2014. "From Bombs to Ballots: When Militant Organizations Transition to Political Parties," *The Journal of Politics*, 76, 3: 666–683.

Ake, Claude, 1996, "Rethinking African Democracy." In Larry Diamond and Marc F. Plattner, eds., *The Global Resurgence of Democracy*, Second Edition (Baltimore, M.D.: Johns Hopkins University Press): 63–75.

Alberts, Susan, Chris Warshaw, and Barry R. Weingast, 2012, "Democratization and Countermajoritarian Institutions: Power and Constitutional Design in Self-Enforcing Democracy." In Tom Ginsburg, ed., *Comparative Constitutional Design* (Cambridge, U.K.: Cambridge University Press): 69–100.

Alden, Chris, 2005, "China in Africa," *Survival*, 47, 3: 147–164.

Allison, Michael E., 2006a, "Leaving the Past Behind? A Study of the FMLN and URNG Transitions to Political Parties," Ph.D. dissertation, Florida State University.

Allison, Michael E., 2006b, "The Transition from Armed Opposition to Electoral Opposition in Central America," *Latin American Politics and Society*, 48, 4: 137–162.

Allison, Michael E., 2009, "Opportunity Lost: The Guatemalan National Revolutionary Unity (URNG)." In Bruce Dayton and Louise Kriesberg, eds., *Conflict Transformation and Peacebuilding: Moving from Violence to Sustainable Peace* (New York, N.Y.: Routledge): 188–203.

Álvarez, Alberto Martín, 2010a, "From Revolutionary War to Democratic Revolution: The Farabundo Martí National Liberation Front (FMLN) in El Salvador," No. 9. In Véronique Dudouet and Hans J. Giessmann, eds., *Berghof Transition Series: Resistance/Liberation Movements and Transition to Politics* (Berlin: Berghof Conflict Research).

Álvarez, Alberto Martín, 2010b, "Process of Change in Non-State Armed Groups: Learning from the Salvadorean Experience," Unpublished paper presented at the International Studies Association, New Orleans, L.A., February 17–20.

Alvarez, Enrique, 2002, "The Grand National Dialogue and the Oslo Consultations: Creating a Peace Agenda," *Accord*, 13: 44–47.

Amundsen, Inge, Cesaltina Abreu, and Laurinda Hoygaard, 2005, "Accountability on the Move: The Parliament of Angola," CMI Working Paper 11 (Bergen: Chr. Michelsen Institute).

Andrade Casama, Luis Evelis, 2009, Author Interview, Bogotá, Colombia, 10 December.

Angrist, Joshua D., and Jörn-Steffen Pischke, 2009, *Mostly Harmless Econometrics* (Princeton: Princeton University Press).

Annan, Kofi, 2003, "The Situation in Central America: Progress in Fashioning a Region of Peace, Freedom, Democracy and Development: United Nations Verification Mission in Guatemala, Report of the Secretary-General," United Nations General Assembly, A/58/267, August 11.

Antsee Margaret J., 1996, *Orphan of the Cold War: The Inside Story of the Collapse of the Angolan Peace Process, 1992–1993* (New York, N.Y.: St. Martin's Press).

Arnault, Jean, 2001, "Good Agreement? Bad Agreement? An Implementation Perspective," Center for International Studies, Woodrow Wilson School of Public and International Affairs, Princeton University, N.J., Unpublished paper.

Arnson, Cynthia, 2012, "Introduction: Conflict, Democratization, and the State." In Cynthia Arnson, ed., *In the Wake of War: Democratization and Internal Armed Conflict in Latin America* (Washington, D.C.: Woodrow Wilson Center Press): 1–34.

Ash, Timothy G., 2001, "Is There a Good Terrorist?," *New York Review of Books*, November 29.

Atlas, Pierre M. and Roy Licklider, 1999, "Conflict among Former Allies after Civil War Settlement: Sudan, Zimbabwe, Chad, and Lebanon," *Journal of Peace Research*, 36, 1: 35–54.

Azpuru, Dinorah, 1999, "Peace and Democratization in Guatemala: Two Parallel Processes." In Cynthia J. Arnson, ed., *Comparative Peace Processes in Latin America* (Stanford, CA: Stanford University Press): 97–126.

Azpuru, Dinorah, Carlos Mendoza, Evelyn Blanck, and Ligia Blanco, 2004, "Democracy Assistance to Post-Conflict Guatemala: Finding a Balance between Details and Determinants," CRU Working Paper 30 (The Hague: Clingendael Institute).

Azpuru, Dinorah, Steven E. Finkel, Aníbal Pérez-Liñán, and Mitchell A. Seligson, 2008, "What Has the United States Been Doing?," *Journal of Democracy*, 19, 2: 150–159.

Bagley, Bruce M, 1988, "Colombia and the War on Drugs," *Foreign Affairs* 67, 1: 70–92.

Balcells, Laia and Abbey Steele, 2016, "Warfare, Political Identities, and Displacement in Spain and Colombia," *Political Geography*, 51: 15–29.

Baloyra, Enrique A, 1998, "El Salvador: From Despotism to Partidocracia." In Krishna Kumar, ed., *Postconflict Elections, Democratization, and International Assistance* (Boulder, C.O.: Lynne Rienner Publishers): 15–37.

Barnett, Michael N., 2006, "Building a Republican Peace: Stabilizing States after War," *International Security*, 30, 4: 87–112.

Beardsley, Kyle, 2012, *The Mediation Dilemma* (Ithaca, N.Y.: Cornell University Press).

Beardsley, Kyle, 2013, "The UN at the Peacemaking-Peacebuilding Nexus," *Conflict Management and Peace Science*, 30, 4: 369–386.

Beaulieu, Emily, 2014, *Electoral Protest and Democracy in the Developing World* (New York, N.Y.: Cambridge University Press).

Bekoe, Dorina A., 2008, *Implementing Peace Agreements: Lessons from Mozambique, Angola, and Liberia* (New York, N.Y.: Palgrave Macmillan).

Bennett, Andrew and Jeffrey T. Checkel, eds., 2014, *Process Tracing: From Metaphor to Analytic Tool (Strategies for Social Inquiry)* (Cambridge, U.K.: Cambridge University Press).

Bentley, Kristina A. and Roger Southall, 2005, *An African Peace Process: Mandela, South Africa, and Burundi* (Cape Town: Human Sciences Research Council Press).

Betts, Richard K., 1994, "The Delusion of Impartial Intervention," *Foreign Affairs*, 73, 6: 20–33.

Birnir, Jóhanna Kristín, 2006, *Ethnicity and Electoral Politics* (Cambridge, U.K.: Cambridge University Press).

Bjornlund Eric C., 2004, *Beyond Free and Fair: Monitoring Elections and Building Democracy* (Baltimore, M.D.: Johns Hopkins University Press).

Blainey, Geoffrey, 1988, *The Causes of War* (New York, N.Y.: The Free Press).

Blaydes, Lisa, 2011, *Elections and Distributive Politics in Mubarak's Egypt* (New York, N.Y.: Cambridge University Press).

Boix, Carles and Milan W. Svolik, 2013, "The Foundations of Limited Authoritarian Government: Institutions, Commitment, and Power-Sharing in Dictatorships," *The Journal of Politics*, 75, 2: 300–316.

Boix, Carles and Susan Stokes, 2003, "Endogenous Democratization," *World Politics*, 55, 4: 517–549.

Borzyskowski, Inken von and Felicity Vabulas, 2014, "The Punishment Phase: IGO Suspensions after Political Backsliding," Unpublished paper presented at Political Economy of International Organizations (PEIO), Princeton, N.J., January 16–18.

Boucher, Richard, 1993, "Guatemala: Suspension of Congress, Courts," National Security Council, Office of Press and Communications, and Philip "PJ" Crowley, Clinton Digital Library, William J. Clinton Presidential Library and Museum, http://clinton.presidentiallibraries.us/items/show/48515.

Boulding, Carew and Susan D. Hyde, 2005, "Political Terror, Election Fraud, and Foreign Aid: When Do Donors Withdraw Aid to Promote Democracy?," Unpublished paper presented at the Midwest Political Science Association (MPSA) National Annual Conference, Chicago, I.L., April 6–10.

Box-Steffensmeier, Janet M. and Bradford S. Jones, 2004, *Event History Modeling: A Guide for Social Scientists* (New York: Cambridge University Press).

Brambor, Thomas, William Roberts Clark, and Matt Golder, 2006, "Understanding Interaction Models: Improving Empirical Analyses," *Political Analysis*, 14, 1: 63–82.

Brancati, Dawn and Jack Snyder, 2011, "Rushing to the Polls: The Causes of Premature Postconflict Elections," *Journal of Conflict Resolution*, 55, 3: 469–492.

Brancati, Dawn and Jack Snyder, 2013, "Time to Kill: The Impact of Election Timing and Sequencing on Post-Conflict Stability," *Journal of Conflict Resolution*, 57, 5: 822–853.

Brancati, Dawn, 2014, "Democratic Authoritarianism: Origins and Effects," *Annual Review of Political Science*, 17: 313–326.

Brooks, Stephen G. and William C. Wohlforth, 2000, "Power, Globalization, and the End of the Cold War: Reevaluating a Landmark Case for Ideas," *International Security*, 25, 3: 5–53.

Brooks, Stephen G. and William C. Wohlforth, 2005, "Hard Times for Soft Balancing," *International Security*, 30, 1: 72–108.

Brooks, Stephen G. and William C. Wohlforth, 2008, *World out of Balance: International Relations and the Challenge of American Primacy* (Princeton, N.J.: Princeton University Press).

Brown, Michael E., ed., 1996, *The International Dimensions of Internal Conflict* (Cambridge, M.A.: MIT Press).

Brownlee, Jason, 2007, *Authoritarianism in an Age of Democratization* (New York, N.Y.: Cambridge University Press).

Brownlee, Jason, 2012, *Democracy Prevention: The Politics of the US-Egyptian Alliance* (New York, N.Y.: Cambridge University Press).

Bush, Sarah Sunn, 2015, *The Taming of Democracy Assistance: Why Democracy Promotion Does Not Confront Dictators* (Cambridge, U.K.: Cambridge University Press).

Bush, Sarah Sunn and Lauren Prather, 2016, "Third Party Monitors and the Credibility of Political Processes," Unpublished paper presented at the International Studies Association Annual Convention, Atlanta, G.A., March 16.

Butenschøn, Nils A. and Kåre Vollan, 2011, "Electoral Quotas and the Challenges of Democratic Transition in Conflict-Ridden Societies:

A Nordem Special Report," The Norwegian Centre for Human Rights, University of Oslo, Oslo, Norway, September.

Büthe, Tim, 2002, "Taking Temporality Seriously: Modeling History and the Use of Narratives as Evidence," *American Political Science Review*, 96, 3: 481–493.

Call, Charles T., 2002, "Assessing El Salvador's Transition from Civil War to Peace." In Stephen J. Stedman, Donald Rothchild, and Elizabeth Cousens, eds., *Ending Civil Wars: The Implementation of Peace Agreements* (Boulder, C.O.: Lynne Rienner Publishers): 383–420.

Call, Charles T. with Vanessa Wyeth, eds., 2008, *Building States to Build Peace* (Boulder, C.O.: Lynne Rienner Publishers).

Carothers, Thomas, 1997, "The Observers Observed," *Journal of Democracy*, 8, 3: 17–31.

Carothers, Thomas, 1999, *Aiding Democracy Abroad: The Learning Curve* (Washington, D.C.: Carnegie Endowment for International Peace).

Carter, Brett L., 2016, "Why the Democratic Recession Will Be Brief: The View from Africa," *Journal of Democracy*, 27, 3: 36–50.

Cederman, Lars-Erik, Simon Hug, and Lutz F. Krebs, 2010, "Democratization and Civil War: Empirical Evidence," *Journal of Peace Research*, 47, 4: 377–394.

Cepeda Castro, Iván, 2006, "Genocidio Político: El Caso De La Unión Patriótica En Colombia," Published online on *Desaparecidos.org*, Originally published in *Revista Cetil*, No. 2, September.

Chafee, John H., 1991, "Letter to President George H.W. Bush," March 14, 2pp, Box No. CO046, 002807–094748. Bush Presidential Records.

Chayes, Abram and Antonia Handler Chayes, 1995, *The New Sovereignty: Compliance with International Regulatory Agreements* (Cambridge, M.A.: Harvard University Press).

Cheibub, José A. and Jude C. Hays, 2015, "Elections and Civil War in Africa," *Political Science Research and Methods*, FirstView: 1–22.

Chenoweth, Erica, 2010, "Democratic Competition and Terrorist Activity," *The Journal of Politics*, 72, 1: 16–30.

Chernick, Marc W., 1999, "Negotiating Peace amid Multiple Forms of Violence: The Protracted Search for a Settlement to the Armed Conflict in Colombia." In Cynthia J. Arnson, ed., *Comparative Peace Processes in Latin America* (Stanford, C.A.: Stanford University Press): 159–196.

Claude, Inis L., 1966, "Collective Legitimization as a Political Function of the United Nations," *International Organization*, 20, 33: 367–379.

Clayton, Govinda, 2013, "Relative Rebel Strength and the Onset and Outcome of Civil War Mediation," *Journal of Peace Research*, 50, 5: 609–622.

Clinton, William J., 1994, "State of the Union Address (Transcript)," Accessed through Charlottesville, V.A.: Miller Center: http://millercenter.org/president /clinton/speeches/speech-3437.

Collier, David, 2011, "Understanding Process Tracing," *PS: Political Science and Politics*, 44, 4: 823–830.

Collier, Paul, 2009, *Wars, Guns, and Votes: Democracy in Dangerous Places*, (New York, N.Y.: Harper Perennial).

Collier, Paul and Anke Hoeffler, 1999, *Justice-Seeking and Loot-Seeking in Civil War* (Washington, D.C.: World Bank).

Collier, Paul and Anke Hoeffler, 2004, "Aid, Policy and Growth in Post-Conflict Societies," *European Economic Review*, 48, 5: 1125–1145.

Collier, Paul, Anke Hoeffler, and Måns Söderbom, 2008, "Post-Conflict Risks," *Journal of Peace Research*, 45, 4: 461–478.

Collier, Paul, V. L. Elliott, Havard Hegre, Anke Hoeffler, Marta Reynal-Querol, and Nicholas Sambanis, 2003, *Breaking the Conflict Trap: Civil War and Development Policy, A World Bank Policy Research Report* (Washington, D.C.: World Bank and Oxford, U.K.: Oxford University Press).

Collier, Robert, 1995, "'An Enduring 'Nuisance'; Rebels Hang in against a Brutally Effective Army," *The Gazette*, 5 March.

Cornick, Tully, 2014, Author Interview (Telephone), Washington, D.C., May 7.

Cox, Gary W., Douglass C. North, and Barry Weingast, 2013, "The Violence Trap: A Political-Economic Approach to the Problems of Development," Unpublished paper presented at the CDDRL Special Director's Seminar, Stanford University, Stanford, C.A., June 10.

Cronin, Audrey Kurth, 2009, *How Terrorism Ends: Understanding the Decline and Demise of Terrorist Campaigns* (Princeton, N.J.: Princeton University Press).

Cunningham, David E., 2006, "Veto Players and Civil War Duration," *American Journal of Political Science*, 50, 4: 875–892.

Cunningham, David E., 2007, "Responding to Multi-Party Civil Wars: Designing Peace Processes That Make Peace More Likely," Paper presented at the American Political Science Association's Annual Meeting, Chicago, IL, August 30–September 2.

Cunningham, David E., Kristian Skrede Gleditsch, and Idean Salehyan, 2009, "It Takes Two: A Dyadic Analysis of Civil War Duration and Outcome," *Journal of Conflict Resolution*, 53, 4: 570–597.

Dafoe, Allan, 2013, "First Do No Harm: The Risk of Modeling Temporal Dependence." Unpublished paper presented at the 30th Annual Summer Meeting of the Society for Political Methodology, University of Virginia, Charlottesville, V.A., July 18–20.

Dahl, Robert A., 2003, "Democratic Polities in Advanced Countries: Success and Challenge." In Atilio Borón, ed., *New Worldwide Hegemony: Alternatives for Change and Social Movements* (Amsterdam: Transnational Institute Publishing): 51–50.

Davenport, Christian, 2004, "The Promise of Democratic Pacification: An Empirical Assessment," *International Studies Quarterly*, 48, 3: 539–560.

Daxecker, Ursula E., 2007, "Perilous Polities? An Assessment of the Democratization-Conflict Linkage," *European Journal of International Relations*, 13, 4: 527–553.

De Jonge Oudraat, Chantal, 1996, "The United Nations and Internal Conflict." In Michael E. Brown, ed., *The International Dimensions of Internal Conflict* (Cambridge, U.K.: MIT Press): 489–535.

De Soto, Alvaro, and Graciana del Castillo, 1994, "Obstacles to Peacebuilding," *Foreign Policy*, 94: 69–83.

De Zeeuw, Jeroen, 2005, "Projects Do Not Create Institutions: The Record of Democracy Assistance in Post-Conflict Societies," *Democratization*, 12, 4: 481–504.

De Zeeuw, Jeroen, 2008, "Understanding the Transformations of Rebel Movements." In Jeroen De Zeeuw, ed., *From Soldiers to Politicians: Transforming Rebel Movements after Civil War* (Boulder, C.O.: Lynne Rienner Publishers): 1–32.

De Zeeuw, Jeroen, ed., 2008, *From Soldiers to Politicians: Transforming Rebel Movements after Civil War* (Boulder, C.O.: Lynne Rienner Publishers).

De Zeeuw, Jeroen, and Krishna Kumar, 2006, *Promoting Democracy in Postconflict Societies* (Boulder, C.O.: Lynne Rienner Publishers).

Deonandan, Kalowatie, David Close, and Gary Prevost, eds., 2007, *From Revolutionary Movements to Political Parties* (New York, N.Y.: Palgrave Macmillan).

Dermota, Ken, 1990, "Barco Lambasted for Not Protecting Presidential Field," *The Washington Times*, April 30.

Derouen, Karl, Jenna Lea, and Peter Wallensteen, 2009, "The Duration of Civil War Peace Agreements," *Conflict Management and Peace Science*, 26, 4: 367–387.

Diamond, Larry, 2006, "Promoting Democracy in Post-Conflict and Failed States: Lessons and Challenges," *Taiwan Journal of Democracy*, 2, 2: 93–116.

Dobbins, James, 2003, *America's Role in Nation-Building: From Germany to Iraq* (Santa Monica, C.A.: RAND Corporation).

Dobbins, James, 2008, "Europe's Role in Nation Building," *Survival*, 50, 3: 83–110.

Dobbins, James, Seth G. Jones, Keith Crane, Andrew Rathmell, Brett Steele, Richard Teltschik, and Anga Timilsina, 2005, *The UN's Role in Nation-Building from the Congo to Iraq* (Santa Monica, C.A.: RAND Corporation).

Dobbins, James, Seth G. Jones, Keith Crane, and Beth Cole DeGrasse, 2007, *The Beginner's Guide to Nation-Building* (Santa Monica, C.A.: RAND Corporation).

Dobbins, James, Seth G. Jones, Keith Crane, Christopher S. Chivvis, Andrew Radin, F. Stephen Larrabee, Nora Bensahel, Brooke Stearns Lawson, and Benjamin W. Goldsmith, 2008, *Europe's Role in Nation-Building: From the Balkans to the Congo* (Santa Monica, C.A.: RAND Corporation).

Donno, Daniela, 2013, *Defending Democratic Norms: International Actors and the Politics of Electoral Misconduct* (Oxford, U.K.: Oxford University Press).

Downes, Alexander B., 2011, "To the Shores of Tripoli? Regime Change and Its Consequences," *Boston Review*, 36, 5: 429–436.

Downes, Alexander B. and Jonathan Monten, 2013, "Forced to Be Free: Why Foreign-Imposed Regime Change Rarely Leads to Democratization," *International Security*, 37, 4: 90–131.

Downes, Alexander B. and Lindsey A. O'Rourke, 2016, "You Can't Always Get What You Want: Foreign-Imposed Regime Change and Interstate Conflict," *International Security*, 41, 2: 43–89.

Downs, George W., David M. Rocke, and Peter N. Barsoom, 1996, "Is the Good News about Compliance Good News about Cooperation?," *International Organization*, 50, 3: 379–406.

Doyle, Michael W., "Authority and Elections in Cambodia: Keeping the Peace." In Michael W. Doyle, Ian Johnstone, and Robert C. Orr, eds., 1997, *Keeping the Peace: Multidimensional UN Operations in Cambodia and El Salvador* (Cambridge U.K.: Cambridge University Press): 134–164.

Doyle, Michael W. and Nicholas Sambanis, 2000, "International Peacebuilding: A Theoretical and Quantitative Analysis," *American Political Science Review*, 94, 4: 779–801.

Doyle, Michael W. and Nicholas Sambanis, 2006, *Making War and Building Peace: United Nations Peace Operations* (Princeton, N.J.: Princeton University Press).

Driscoll, Jesse, 2008, "Inside the Leviathan: Coup-Proofing after State Failure," Stanford University, Stanford, C.A., Unpublished paper.

Duarte, José Napoleón and Diana Page, 1986, *Duarte: My Story* (New York, N.Y.: G.P. Putnam's Sons).

Dudley, Steven S., 2004, *Walking Ghosts: Murder and Guerrilla Politics in Colombia* (New York, N.Y.: Routledge).

Dunning, Thad, 2004, "Conditioning the Effects of Aid: Cold War Politics, Donor Credibility, and Democracy in Africa," *International Organization*, 58, 2: 409–423.

Dunning, Thad, 2011, "Fighting and Voting: Violent Conflict and Electoral Politics," *Journal of Conflict Resolution*, 55, 3: 327–339.

Durant, T. Clark and Michael Weintraub, 2014, "How to Make Democracy Self-Enforcing after Civil War: Enabling Credible Yet Adaptable Elite Pacts," *Conflict Management and Peace Science*, 31, 5: 521–540.

Eaton, Kent, 2006, "The Downside of Decentralization: Armed Clientelism in Colombia," *Security Studies*, 15, 4: 533–562.

Eck, Kristine, 2009, "From Armed Conflict to War: Ethnic Mobilization and Conflict Intensification," *International Studies Quarterly*, 53, 2: 369–388.

Eder, James F. and Thomas M. McKenna, 2008, "Minorities in the Philippines: Ancestral Lands and Autonomy in Theory and Practice." In Christopher R. Duncan, ed., *Civilizing the Margins: Southeast Asian Government Policies for the Development of Minorities* (Singapore: National University of Singapore Press): 56–85.

Edwards, Aaron and Stephen Bloomer, 2004, "A Watching Brief? The Political Strategy of Progressive Loyalism since 1994," Conflict Transformation Papers 8 (Belfast, LINC Resource Centre).

Elkins, Zachery and Simmons, Beth A., 2005, "On Waves, Clusters and Diffusion: A Conceptual Framework," *Annals of the American Academy of Political and Social Science*, 598, 1: 33–51.

Elklit, Jorgen and Palle Svensson, 1997, "What Makes Elections Free and Fair?," *Journal of Democracy*, 8, 3: 32–46.

Emmanuel, Nikolas and Donald Rothchild, 2007, "Economic Aid and Peace Implementation: The African Experience," *Journal of Intervention and Statebuilding*, 1, 2: 171–188.

Evans, Gareth and Mohamed Sahnoun, 2002, "The Responsibility to Protect," *Foreign Affairs*, 81, 6: 99–110.

Evans, Michael, 2002, "Conditioning Security Assistance." In Evans, Michael, "War in Columbia: Guerrillas, Drugs and Human Rights in US-Colombia Policy, 1988–2002," National Security Archive Electronic Briefing Book No. 69, May 2.

Farah, Douglas, 1997, "Salvadorans Reminded of War's Polarization; Ex-Rebels Lead in Polls for Midterm Elections, Provoking Furious Reaction on Right," *The Washington Post*, February 23.

Farer, Tom J., 2004, "The Promotion of Democracy: International Law and Norms." In Roland Rich and Edward Newman, eds., *The UN Role in Promoting Democracy: Between Ideals and Reality* (Tokyo: United Nations University Press): 32–61.

Fazal, Tanisha, 2015, "Peace Treaties in Civil War." In *Wars of Law: Unintended Consequences in the Regulation of Armed Conflict*, University of Notre Dame, South Bend, I.N., Unpublished manuscript.

Fearon, James D., 1995, "Rationalist Explanations for War," *International Organization*, 49, 3: 379–414.

Fearon, James D., 2004, "Why Do Some Civil Wars Last So Much Longer Than Others?," *Journal of Peace Research*, 41, 3: 275–301.

Fearon, James D., 2007, "Fighting Rather Than Bargaining," Unpublished paper presented at 2007 Annual Meetings of the American Political Science Association, Chicago, I.L., August 30–September 2.

Fearon, James D., 2010, "Governance and Civil War Onset," World Development Report 2011 Background Paper, World Bank, Washington, D.C., August 31.

Fearon, James D., 2011, "Self-Enforcing Democracy," *The Quarterly Journal of Economics*, 126, 4: 1661–1708.

Fearon, James D. and David D. Laitin, 2003, "Ethnicity, Insurgency, and Civil War," *American Political Science Review*, 97, 1: 75–90.

Fearon, James D. and David D. Laitin, 2004, "Neotrusteeship and the Problem of Weak States," *International Security*, 28, 4: 5–43.

Fearon, James D. and David D. Laitin, 2007, "Civil War Termination," Unpublished paper presented at the Annual Meetings of the American Political Science Association, Chicago, I.L., August 30–September 1.

Félix, Walter, 2013, Author Interview, Guatemala City, Guatemala, August 20.

Feste, Karen A., 2003, *Intervention: Shaping the Global Order* (New York, N.Y.: Praeger).

Fine, Jason P., and Robert J. Gray, 1999, "A Proportional Hazards Model for the Subdistribution of a Competing Risk," *Journal of the American Statistical Association* 94, 446: 496–509.

Finkel, Steven E., Aníbal Pérez-Liñán, and Mitchell A. Seligson, 2007, "The Effects of US Foreign Assistance on Democracy Building, 1990–2003," *World Politics*, 59, 3: 404–439.

Finnemore, Martha, 1996, "Constructing Norms of Humanitarian Intervention." In Peter Katzenstein, ed., *The Culture of National Security: Norms and Identity in World Politics* (New York, N.Y.: Columbia University Press): 153–185.

Finnemore, Martha, 2003, *The Purpose of Intervention: Changing Beliefs about the Use of Force* (Ithaca, N.Y.: Cornell University Press).

Fish, Steven M. and Matthew Kroenig, 2006, "Diversity, Conflict and Democracy: Some Evidence from Eurasia and East Europe," *Democratization*, 13, 5: 828–842.

Flores, Thomas E. and Irfan Nooruddin, 2009a, "Democracy Under the Gun: Understanding Post-Conflict Recovery," *Journal of Conflict Resolution*, 53, 1: 3–29.

Flores, Thomas E. and Irfan Nooruddin, 2009b, "Financing the Peace: Evaluating World Bank Post-Conflict Assistance Programs," *Review of International Organizations*, 4, 1: 1–27.

Flores, Thomas E. and Irfan Nooruddin, 2012, "The Effect of Elections on Post-Conflict Peace and Reconstruction," *Journal of Politics*, 74, 2: 558–570.

Flórez, Enrique, 2010, Author Interview, Bogotá, Colombia, March 16.

Fortna, Virginia Page, 2004, "Does Peacekeeping Keep Peace? International Intervention and the Duration of Peace after Civil War," *International Studies Quarterly*, 48, 2: 269–292.

Fortna, Virginia Page, 2008, *Does Peacekeeping Work? Shaping Belligerents' Choices after Civil War* (Princeton, N.J.: Princeton University Press).

Fortna, Virginia Page, 2015, "Do Terrorists Win? Rebels' Use of Terrorism and Civil War Outcomes," *International Organization* 69, 3: 519–556.

Fortna, Virginia Page and Reyko Huang, 2012, "Democratization after Civil War: A Brush-Clearing Exercise," *International Studies Quarterly*, 56, 4: 801–808.

Fortna, Virginia Page and Lise Morjé Howard, 2008, "Pitfalls and Prospects in the Peacekeeping Literature," *Annual Review of Political Science* 11: 283–301.

Fowler, Robert R., 2000, "Letter Dated 10 March 2000 from the Chairman of the Security Council Committee Established Pursuant to Resolution 864 (1993) Concerning the Situation in Angola," United Nations Security Council, New York.

Franck, Thomas M., 1990, *The Power of Legitimacy among Nations* (New York, N.Y.: Oxford University Press).

Frerks, Georg, 2006, *The Use of Peace Conditionalities in Conflict and Post-Conflict Settings: A Conceptual Framework and a Checklist* (The Hague: Clingendael Institute).

Fuentes, Juan Alberto and Thomas Carothers, 1998, "Luces Y Sombras De La Cooperación Internacional." In International IDEA, ed., *Democracia En Guatemala: La Mision De Un Pueblo Entero* (Stockholm, International IDEA): 214–219.

Fukuyama, Francis and Michael McFaul, 2008, "Should Democracy Be Promoted or Demoted?," *The Washington Quarterly*, 31, 1: 23–45.

Gandhi, Jennifer, 2008, *Political Institutions under Dictatorship* (Cambridge, N.Y.: Cambridge University Press).

Gandhi, Jennifer and Ellen Lust-Okar, 2009, "Elections under Authoritarianism," *Annual Review of Political Science*, 12: 403–422.

Garbar, Larry, 1998, "Introduction." In Krishna Kuman, ed., *Postconflict Elections, Democratization, and International Assistance* (Boulder, C.O.: Lynne Rienner Publishers): 1–3.

García Durán, Mauricio, Vera Grabe Loewenherz, and Otty Patiño Hormaza, 2008, "M-19's Journey from Armed Struggle to Democratic Politics: Striving to Keep the Revolution Connected to the People," No. 1. In Véronique Dudouet and Hans J. Giessmann, eds., *Berghof Transition Series: Resistance/Liberation Movements and Transition to Politics*, Berghof Conflict Research, Berlin, Germany.

Garst, Rachel, 1995, "Guatemala: United State Policy and the Guatemalan Peace Process," WOLA Policy Brief, Washington Office on Latin America, Washington, D.C.

Geddes, Barbara, 2003, *Paradigms and Sand Castles: Theory Building and Research Design in Comparative Politics* (Ann Arbor, M.I.: University of Michigan Press).

Gellman, Barton, 1992, "Keeping the US First; Pentagon Would Preclude a Rival Superpower," *The Washington Post*, March 11.

Gent, Stephen E., 2011, "Relative Rebel Strength and Power Sharing in Intrastate Conflicts," *International Interactions*, 37, 2: 215–228.

Gerring, John, 2007, "Is There a (Viable) Crucial-Case Method?," *Comparative Political Studies*, 40, 3: 231–253.

Ghosh, Partha S., 1989, *Conflict and Cooperation in South Asia* (New Delhi: Manohar).

Gilligan, Michael J., Eric Mvukiyehe, and Cyrus Samii, 2013, "Reintegrating Rebels into Civilian Life: Quasi-Experimental Evidence from Burundi," *Journal of Conflict Resolution*, 57, 4: 598–626.

Gilligan, Michael J. and Ernest J. Sergenti, 2008, "Do UN Interventions Cause Peace? Using Matching to Improve Causal Inference," *Quarterly Journal of Political Science*, 3, 2: 89–122.

Gilligan, Michael J. and Stephen John Stedman, 2003, "Where Do the Peacekeepers Go?," *International Studies Review*, 5, 4: 37–54.

Girod, Desha M., 2011, "Effective Foreign Aid Following Civil War: The Nonstrategic-Desperation Hypothesis," *American Journal of Political Science*, 56, 1: 188–201.

Gleditsch, Kristian S. and Kyle Beardsley, 2004, "Nosy Neighbors: Third-Party Actors in Central American Conflicts," *Journal of Conflict Resolution*, 48, 3: 379–402.

Gleditsch, Kristian S., Idean Salehyan, and Kenneth Schultz, 2008, "Fighting at Home, Fighting Abroad," *Journal of Conflict Resolution*, 52, 4: 479–506.

Gleditsch, Kristian S. and Michael D. Ward, 2000, "War and Peace in Space and Time: The Role of Democratization," *International Studies Quarterly*, 44, 1: 1–29.

Gleditsch, Kristian S. and Michael D. Ward, 2006, "Diffusion and the International Context of Democratization," *International Organization*, 60, 4: 911–933.

Gleditsch, Nils P., Peter Wallensteen, Mikael Eriksson, Margareta Sollenberg, and Håvard Strand, 2002, "Armed Conflict 1946–2001: A New Dataset," *Journal of Peace Research*, 39, 5: 615–637.

Golan, Guy and Wayne Wanta, 2003, "International Elections on US Network News: An Examination of Factors Affecting Newsworthiness," *International Communication Gazette*, 65, 1: 25–39.

Grabe, Loewenherz Vera, 2009, Author Interview, Bogotá, Colombia, December 14.

Greene, Kenneth F., 2007, *Why Dominant Parties Lose: Mexico's Democratization in Comparative Perspective* (New York, N.Y.: Cambridge University Press).

Guilengue, Fredson, 2013, "Mozambique: Why Has RENAMO Gone Back to the Bush?," *All Africa Media*, November 28.

Guttieri, Karen, and Jessica Piombo, eds., 2007, *Interim Governments: Institutional Bridges to Peace and Democracy?* (Washington, D.C.: U.S. Institute of Peace Press).

Guzman, Andrew T., 2008, *How International Law Works: A Rational Choice Theory* (Oxford, U.K. and New York, N.Y.: Oxford University Press).

Hafner-Burton, Emilie M., 2005, "Trading Human Rights: How Preferential Trade Agreements Influence Government Repression," *International Organization*, 59, 3: 593–629.

Hafner-Burton, Emilie M., 2013, *Making Human Rights a Reality* (Princeton, N.J.: Princeton University Press).

Hamilton, John R., 1994, "Memo 'Your Meeting with Guatemalan Foreign Minister Maritza De Vielman' from John R. Hamilton (State) to Alexander F. Watson," September 20, Case ID 951222A9, Document No. E4104, Guatemala Declassification Project, U.S. Department of State Freedom of Information Act, U.S. Department of State.

Handel, Shafick Jorge, 1984, "Analisis De La Situacion Politico-Militar Hecho Por El Miembro De La Comandancia General Del FMLN," Box 3, El Salvador, Salvadoran Subject Collection (1976–1994), Hoover Institution Archives.

Handel, Schafik Jorge, 1988, "Salvadoran Guerrilla Letter to POTUS," December 8, 1 pp., Box No. CF00196B1, Latin American Directorate Files, Bush Presidential Records.

Hansen, Bertel Teilfeldt, 2014, "Ballots and Blue Helmets," Institut for Statskundskab, Copenhagen, Unpublished paper.

Happold, Tom, 2004, "Sinn Fein Leaders Face Pay Cuts," *The Guardian*, April 20.

Harbom, Lotta, Stina Högbladh, and Peter Wallensteen, 2006, "Armed Conflict and Peace Agreements," *Journal of Peace Research*, 43, 5: 617–631.

Harbom, Lotta and Peter Wallensteen, 2010, "Armed Conflict, 1946–2009," *Journal of Peace Research*, 47, 4: 501–509.

Harish, S.P., and Andrew T. Little, Forthcoming, "The Political Violence Cycle," *American Political Science Review*.

Hartlyn, Jonathan, and Jennifer L. McCoy, 2001, "Elections with 'Adjectives' in Contemporary Latin America: A Comparative Analysis," Unpublished paper presented at the Annual Meeting of the Latin American Studies Association, Washington D.C., September 6–8.

Hartzell, Caroline A., Matthew Hoddie, and Donald Rothchild, 2001, "Stabilizing the Peace after Civil War: An Investigation of Some Key Variables," *International Organization*, 55, 1: 183–208.

Hartzell, Caroline A., and Matthew Hoddie, 2003, "Institutionalizing Peace: Power Sharing and Post-Civil War Conflict Management," *American Journal of Political Science*, 47, 2: 318–332.

Hartzell, Caroline A. and Hoddie, Matthew, 2007, *Crafting Peace: Power-Sharing Institutions and the Negotiated Settlement of Civil Wars* (University Park, P.A.: Pennsylvania State University).

Hartzell, Caroline A., and Matthew Hoddie, 2015, "The Art of the Possible: Power Sharing and Post-Civil War Democracy," *World Politics*, 67, 1: 37–71.

Heard, John, 1999, "Guatemala Demobilization and Incorporation Program: An Evaluation Prepared for the Office of Transition Initiatives, Bureau for Humanitarian Response, US Agency for International Development," January.

Hegre, Havard, Havard Mokleiv Nygard, Havard Strand, Scott Gates, and Ranveig D. Flaten, 2011, "The Conflict Trap," Unpublished paper presented at the Annual Meeting of the American Political Science Association, Seattle, W.A., September 1–4.

Hernandez, Carolina G., 1996, "The Philippines in 1995: Growth Amid Challenges," *Asian Survey*, 36, 2: 142–151.

Hernandez, Carolina G, 1997, "The Philippines in 1996: A House Finally in Order?" *Asian Survey*, 37, 2: 204–211.

Heston, Alan, Robert Summers, and Bettina Aten, 2011, "Penn World Table," 7.0 edition, Center for International Comparisons of Production, Income and Prices, University of Pennsylvania.

Hillen, John, 2000, *Blue Helmets: The Strategy of UN Military Operations* (Dulles, V.A.: Potomac Books Inc.).

Hoddie, Matthew and Caroline A. Hartzell, 2003, "Civil War Settlements and the Implementation of Military Power-Sharing Arrangements," *Journal of Peace Research*, 40, 3: 303–320.

Högbladh, Stina, 2012, "Peace Agreements 1975–2011 – Updating the UCDP Peace Agreement Dataset." In Thérése Pettersson and Lotta Themnér, eds., *States in Armed Conflict 2011*, Department of Peace and Conflict Research Report 99, Uppsala University, Uppsala: 39–56.

Hopmann, P. Terrence, 1988, "Negotiating Peace in Central America," *Negotiation Journal*, 4, 4: 361–380.

Horowitz, Donald L., 1991, *A Democratic South Africa? Constitutional Engineering in a Divided Society* (Berkeley, C.A.: University of California Press).

Howard, Lise Morjé, 2008, *UN Peacekeeping in Civil Wars* (New York, N.Y.: Cambridge University Press).

Howard, Marc Morjé and Philip G. Roessler, 2006, "Liberalizing Electoral Outcomes in Competitive Authoritarian Regimes," *American Journal of Political Science*, 50, 2: 365–381.

Huang, Reyko, 2016, *The Wartime Origins of Democratization: Civil War, Rebel Governance, and Political Regimes* (Cambridge, U.K.: Cambridge University Press).

Hultquist, Philip, 2013, "Power Parity and Peace? The Role of Relative Power in Civil War Settlement," *Journal of Peace Research*, 50, 5: 623–634.

Hultman, Lisa, Jacob Kathman, and Megan Shannon, 2014, "Beyond Keeping Peace: United Nations Effectiveness in the Midst of Fighting," *American Political Science Review*, 108, 4: 737–753.

Hultman, Lisa, Jacob Kathman, and Megan Shannon, 2016, "United Nations Peacekeeping Dynamics and the Duration of Post-Civil Conflict Peace," *Conflict Management and Peace Science*, 33, 3: 231–249.

Human Rights Watch, 1994, "Human Rights Watch World Report 1994 – El Salvador," January 1.

Humphreys, Macartan and Jeremy M. Weinstein, 2007, "Demobilization and Reintegration," *Journal of Conflict Resolution*, 51, 4: 531–567.

Huntington, Samuel P., 1991, *The Third Wave: Democracy in the Late Twentieth Century* (Norman, O.K.: University of Oklahoma Press).

Hyde, Susan D., 2007, "The Observer Effect in International Politics: Evidence from a Natural Experiment," *World Politics*, 60, 1: 37–63.

Hyde, Susan D., 2010, "Experimenting in Democracy Promotion: International Observers and the 2004 Presidential Elections in Indonesia," *Perspectives on Politics*, 8, 2: 511–527.

Hyde, Susan D., 2011a, "Catch Us If You Can: Election Monitoring and International Norm Diffusion," *American Journal of Political Science*, 55, 2: 356–369.

Hyde, Susan D., 2011b, *The Pseudo-Democrat's Dilemma: Why Election Observation Became an International Norm* (Ithaca, N.Y.: Cornell University Press).

Hyde, Susan D. and Nikolay Marinov, 2012, "Which Elections Can Be Lost?," *Political Analysis*, 20, 2: 191–201.

Hyde, Susan D. and Nikolay Marinov, 2014, "Information and Self-Enforcing Democracy: The Role of International Election Observation," *International Organization*, 68, 2: 329–359.

Ikenberry, G. John, Michael Mastanduno, and William C. Wohlforth, eds., 2011, *International Relations Theory and the Consequences of Unipolarity* (Cambridge, U.K.: Cambridge University Press).

International Court of Justice, 1986, "Case Concerning the Military and Paramilitary Activities in and against Nicaragua (Nicaragua V. United States of America)," June 27.

InterPress Service, 1994, "URNG Asks for UN Participation in Peace Talks," January 26, Civil War, Society and Political Transition in Guatemala: The Guatemala News and Information Bureau Archive (1963–2000), Princeton University Digital Library, http://pudl.princeton.edu/objects/p5547s24n.

Inter-Parliamentary Union, 1995, "Guatemala: Parliamentary Chamber: Congreso de la República."

Irvin, Cynthia L., 1999, *Militant Nationalism: Between Movement and Party in Ireland and the Basque Country* (Minneapolis, M.N.: University of Minnesota Press).

Jakobsen, Peter Viggo, 1996, "National Interest, Humanitarianism or CNN: What Triggers UN Peace Enforcement after the Cold War?," *Journal of Peace Research* 33, 2: 205–215.

Jarstad, Anna K., 2006, "The Logic of Power Sharing after Civil War," Unpublished paper presented at the Power-sharing and Democratic Governance in Divided Society, Center for the Study of Civil War, PRIO, Oslo, August 21–22.

Jarstad, Anna K., 2008, "Dilemmas of War-to-Democracy Transitions: Theories and Concepts." In Anna K. Jarstad and Timothy D. Sisk, ed., *From War to Democracy: Dilemmas of Peacebuilding* (Cambridge, U.K.: Cambridge University Press): 17–36.

Johnson, Harold J., 1993, "El Salvador: Status of Reconstruction Activities One Year after the Peace Agreement, 1993," Statement before Subcommittee on Western Hemisphere Affairs, Committee on Foreign Affairs, U.S. House of Representatives, Washington, D.C., March 23.

Jonas, Susanne, 1996, "Dangerous Liaisons: The US In Guatemala," *Foreign Policy*, 103: 144–160.

Jonas, Susanne, 2000a, "Democratization through Peace: The Difficult Case of Guatemala," *Journal of Interamerican Studies and World Affairs*, 42, 4: 9–38.

Jonas, Susanne, 2000b, *Of Centaurs and Doves: Guatemala's Peace Process* (Boulder, C.O.: Westview Press).

Joshi, Madhav and T. David Mason, 2011, "Civil War Settlements, Size of Governing Coalition, and Durability of Peace in Post–Civil War States," *International Interactions*, 37, 4: 388–413.

Kalyvas, Stathis N. and Laia Balcells, 2010, "International System and Technologies of Rebellion: How the End of the Cold War Shaped Internal Conflict," *American Political Science Review*, 104, 3: 415–429.

Karl, Terry Lynn, 1985, "After La Palma: The Prospects for Democratization in El Salvador," *World Policy Journal*, 2, 2: 305–330.

Karl, Terry Lynn, 1990, "Dilemmas of Democratization in Latin America," *Comparative Politics*, 23, 1: 1–21.

Karl, Terry Lynn, 1992, "El Salvador's Negotiated Revolution," *Foreign Affairs*, 71, 2: 147–164.

Karl, Terry Lynn and Edward S. Herman, 1985, "El Salvador after La Palma," *World Policy Journal*, 2, 3: 587–592.

Katayanagi, Mari, 2002, *Human Rights Functions of United Nations Peacekeeping Operations* (The Hague: Martinus Nijhoff Publishers).

Kecskemeti, Paul, 1957, *Strategic Surrender: The Politics of Victory and Defeat* (Santa Monica, C.A.: RAND Corporation).

Kelley, Judith G., 2008, "Assessing the Complex Evolution of Norms: The Rise of International Election Monitoring," *International Organization*, 62, 2: 221–255.

Kelley, Judith G., 2009, "D-Minus Elections: The Politics and Norms of International Elections Observation," *International Organization*, 63, 4: 733–764.

Kelley, Judith G., 2012, *Monitoring Democracy: When International Election Observation Works, and Why It Often Fails* (Princeton, N.J.: Princeton University Press).

Keohane, Robert O., 1984, *After Hegemony: Cooperation and Discord in the World Political Economy* (Princeton, N.J.: Princeton University Press).

Kierkegaard, Ralph, 1994, "Confusion in the Jungle," *Guardian Weekly*, May 1.

Knack, Stephen, 2004, "Does Foreign Aid Promote Democracy?," *International Studies Quarterly*, 48, 1: 251–266.

Krasner, Stephen D., 2004, "Sharing Sovereignty: New Institutions for Collapsed and Failing States," *International Security*, 29, 2: 85–120.

Krasner, Stephen D. and Thomas Risse, 2014, "External Actors, State-Building, and Service Provision in Areas of Limited Statehood," *Governance*, 27, 4: 545–567.

Kreps, Sarah E., 2011, *Coalitions of Convenience: United States Military Interventions after the Cold War* (Oxford, U.K.: Oxford University Press).

Kreutz, Joakim, 2010, "How and When Armed Conflicts End: Introducing the UCDP Conflict Termination Dataset," *Journal of Peace Research*, 47, 2: 243–250.

Kumar, Krishna, ed., 1998, *Postconflict Elections, Democratization, and International Assistance* (Boulder, C.O.: Lynne Rienner Publishers).

Kydd, Andrew, 2003, "Which Side Are You On? Bias, Credibility, and Mediation," *American Journal of Political Science*, 47, 4: 597–611.

Kydd, Andrew and Barbara Walter, 2002, "Sabotaging the Peace: The Politics of Extremist Violence," *International Organization*, 56, 2: 263–296.

Lacina, Bethany and Nils Petter Gleditsch, 2005, "Monitoring Trends in Global Combat: A New Dataset of Battle Deaths," *European Journal of Population*, 21, 2: 145–166.

Lacina, Bethany, Nils Petter Gleditsch, and Bruce Russett, 2006, "The Declining Risk of Death in Battle," *International Studies Quarterly*, 50: 673–680.

Lafraie, Najibullah, 2011, "Insurgency and Democratisation: Taliban Real Winners of Elections in Afghanistan," *Global Society*, 25, 4: 469–489.

Lake, David A. and Christopher Fariss, 2014, "Why International Trusteeship Fails: The Politics of External Authority in Areas of Limited Statehood," *Governance*, 27, 4: 569–587.

Lake, David A. and Donald Rothchild, 2005, "Territorial Decentralization and Civil War Settlements." In Philip G. Roeder and Donald S. Rothchild, eds., *Sustainable Peace: Power and Democracy after Civil Wars* (Ithaca, N.Y.: Cornell University Press): 109–132.

Le Billon, Philippe, 2001, "Angola's Political Economy of War: The Role of Oil and Diamonds, 1975–2000," *African Affairs*, 100, 398: 55–80.

Lebovic, James H. and Erik Voeten, 2009, "The Cost of Shame: International Organizations and Foreign Aid in the Punishing of Human Rights Violators," *Journal of Peace Research*, 46, 1: 79–97.

Lebow, Richard N. and Thomas Risse, 1995, *International Relations Theory and the End of the Cold War* (New York, N.Y.: Columbia University Press).

Leffler, Melvyn P. and Jeffrey W. Legro, eds., 2011, *In Uncertain Times: American Foreign Policy after the Berlin Wall and 9/11* (Ithaca, N.Y.: Cornell University Press).

Legro, Jeffrey, 2005, *Rethinking the World: Great Power Strategies and International Order* (Ithaca, N.Y.: Cornell University Press).

Lehoucq, Fabrice Edouard, 1995, "The Election of 1994 in El Salvador," *Electoral Studies*, 14, 2: 178–183.

Leiras, Marcelo, Guadalupe Tuñón, and Agustina Giraudy, 2015, "Who Wants an Independent Court? Political Competition and Supreme Court Autonomy in the Argentine Provinces (1984-2008)," *The Journal of Politics*, 77, 1: 175–187.

LeMoyne, James, 1992, "Out of the Jungle – in El Salvador, Rebels with a New Cause," *New York Times*, February 9.

LeoGrande, William M., 1998, "Foreign Aid to Central America: Is the Era of Aid Over?." In Richard Grant and Jan Nijman, eds., *Global Crisis in Foreign Aid* (Syracuse, N.Y.: Syracuse University Press): 103–112.

LeVine, Mark, 1997, "Peacemaking in El Salvador." In Michael W. Doyle, Ian Johnstone, and Robert C. Orr, eds., *Keeping the Peace: Multidimensional UN Operations in Cambodia and El Salvador* (Cambridge, U.K.: Cambridge University Press): 227–255.

Levite, Ariel E., Bruce W. Jentleson, and Larry Berman, eds., 1992, *Foreign Military Intervention: The Dynamics of Protracted Conflict* (New York, N.Y.: Columbia University Press).

Levitsky, Steven and Lucan A. Way, 2010, *Competitive Authoritarianism: Hybrid Regimes after the Cold War* (Cambridge, U.K.: Cambridge University Press).

Licklider, Roy, 1995, "The Consequences of Negotiated Settlements in Civil Wars, 1945–1993," *American Political Science Review*, 89, 3: 681–690.

Licklider, Roy, 2006, "Democracy and the Renewal of Civil Wars." In Harvey Starr, ed., *Approaches, Levels and Methods of Analysis in International Politics: Crossing Boundaries* (Hampshire, U.K.: Palgrave Macmillan): 95–116.

Lijphart, Arend, 1968, *The Politics of Accommodation: Pluralism and Democracy in the Netherlands* (Berkeley, C.A.: University of California Press).

Lijphart, Arend, 1984, *Democracies: Patterns of Majoritarian and Consensus Government in Twenty-One Countries* (New Haven, CT: Yale University Press).

Lijphart, Arend, 1989, "Democratic Political Systems: Types, Cases, Causes, and Consequences," *Journal of Theoretical Politics*, 1, 1: 33–48.

Lindberg, Steffan I., 2006, *Democracy and Elections in Africa* (Baltimore, M.D.: The Johns Hopkins University Press).

Liotta, P.H. and Cindy Jebb, 2004, *Mapping Macedonia: Idea and Identity* (Westport, C.T.: Praeger Publishers).

Lo, Nigel, Barry Hashimoto, and Dan Reiter, 2008, "Ensuring Peace: Foreign-Imposed Regime Change and Postwar Peace Duration, 1914–2001," *International Organization*, 62, 4: 717–736.

Lujala, Päivi, Jan Ketil Rød, and Nadia Thieme, 2007, "Fighting over Oil: Introducing a New Dataset," *Conflict Management and Peace Science*, 24, 3: 239–256.

Lust-Okar, Ellen, 2005, *Structuring Conflict in the Arab World: Incumbents, Opponents, and Institutions* (New York, N.Y.: Cambridge University Press).

Lust-Okar, Ellen, 2008, "Competitive Clientalism in Jordanian Elections." In Ellen Lust-Okar and Saloua Zerhouni, eds., *Political Participation in the Middle East and North Africa* (Boulder, C.O.: Lynne Rienner Publishers): 75–94.

Lyons, Terrence, 2002a, "Postconflict Elections: War Termination, Democratization, and Demilitarizing Politics," Institute for Conflict Analysis and Resolution, George Mason University, Washington, D.C., Working Paper No. 2.

Lyons, Terrence, 2002b, "The Role of Postsettlement Elections." In Donald Rothchild, Stephen Stedman, and Elizabeth Cousens, eds., *Ending Civil Wars: The Implementation of Peace Agreements* (Boulder, C.O.: Lynne Rienner Publications): 215–236.

Lyons, Terrence, 2004, "Post-Conflict Elections and the Process of Demilitarizing Politics: The Role of Electoral Administration," *Democratization*, 11, 3: 36–62.

Lyons, Terrence, 2005, *Demilitarizing Politics: Elections on the Uncertain Road to Peace* (Boulder, C.O.: Lynne Rienner Publishers).

Lyons, Terrence, 2016, "The Importance of Winning: Victorious Insurgent Groups and Authoritarian Politics," *Comparative Politics*, 48, 2: 167–184.

Mack, Andrew, ed., 2014, *Human Security Report 2013: The Decline in Global Violence: Evidence, Explanation, and Contestation* (Vancouver, B.C.: Human Security Research Group).

Magaloni, Beatriz, 2008, *Voting for Autocracy: Hegemonic Party Survival and Its Demise in Mexico* (Cambridge, U.K.: Cambridge University Press).

Maharaj, Mac, 2008, "The ANC and South Africa's Negotiated Transition to Democracy and Peace." In Véronique Dudouet and Hans J. Giessmann, eds., *Berghof Transition Series: Resistance/Liberation Movements and Transition to Politics*, Berghof Conflict Research, Berlin, Germany.

Mahoney, James, 2010, "After KKV: The New Methodology of Qualitative Research," *World Politics* 62, 1: 120–147.

Manning, Carrie, 2004, "Armed Opposition Groups into Political Parties: Comparing Bosnia, Kosovo, and Mozambique," *Studies in Comparative International Development*, 39, 1: 54–76.

Manning, Carrie, 2008, *The Making of Democrats: Elections and Party Development in Postwar Bosnia, El Salvador, and Mozambique* (New York, N.Y.: Palgrave Macmillan).

Manning, Carrie and Monica Malbrough, 2010, "Bilateral Donors and Aid Conditionality in Post-Conflict Peacebuilding: The Case of Mozambique," *The Journal of Modern African Studies*, 48, 1: 143–169.

Manning, Carrie, and Ian Smith, 2016, "Political Party Formation by Former Armed Opposition Groups after Civil War," *Democratization* 23, 6: 972–989.

Mansfield, Edward D. and Jack Snyder, 1995, "Democratization and the Danger of War," *International Security*, 20, 1: 5–38.

Mansfield, Edward D. and Jack Snyder, 2002, "Incomplete Democratization and the Outbreak of Military Disputes," *International Studies Quarterly*, 46, 4: 529–549.

Mansfield, Edward D. and Jack Snyder, 2005, *Electing to Fight: Why Emerging Democracies Go to War* (Boston, M.A.: MIT Press).

Mansfield, Edward D., Helen V. Milner, and B. Peter Rosendorff, 2002, "Why Democracies Cooperate More: Electoral Control and International Trade," *International Organization*, 56, 3: 477–513.

Marinov, Nikolay, 2004, "Do Sanctions Help Democracy? The US and EU's Record, 1977–2004," Center for Democracy, Development and Rule of Law: Stanford Institute for International Studies, Working Paper no. 28, November 2.

Marinov, Nikolay, 2005, "Do Economic Sanctions Destabilize Country Leaders?," *American Journal of Political Science*, 49, 3: 564–576.

Marshall, Michael Christopher and John Ishiyama, 2016, "Does Political Inclusion of Rebel Parties Promote Peace after Civil Conflict?," *Democratization* 23, 6: 1009–1025.

Mason, T. David, Mehmet Gurses, Patrick T. Brandt, and Jason Michael Quinn, 2011, "When Civil Wars Recur: Conditions for Durable Peace after Civil Wars," *International Studies Perspectives*, 12, 2: 171–189.

Mason, T. David and Patrick J. Fett, 1996, "How Civil Wars End: A Rational Choice Approach," *Journal of Conflict Resolution*, 40, 4: 546–568.

Mastanduno, Michael, and Ethan B. Kapstein, eds., 1999, *Unipolar Politics: Realism and State Strategies after the Cold War* (New York, N.Y.: Columbia University Press).

Matanock, Aila M., 2012, "International Insurance: Why Militant Groups and Governments Compete with Ballots Instead of Bullets." Ph.D. dissertation, Stanford University.

Matanock, Aila M., 2014, "Governance Delegation Agreements: Shared Sovereignty as a Substitute for Limited Statehood," *Governance*, 27, 4: 589–612.

Matanock, Aila M., 2016a, "External Engagement: Explaining the Spread of Electoral Participation Provisions in Civil Conflict Settlements," University of California, Berkeley, Unpublished paper.

Matanock, Aila M., 2016b, "Using Violence, Seeking Votes: Introducing the rebel Group Electoral Participation (MGEP) Dataset," *Journal of Peace Research*, 53, 6: 845–853.

Matanock, Aila M., 2017, "Bullets for Ballots: Electoral Participation Provisions and Enduring Peace after Civil Conflict," *International Security*, 41, 4: 93–132.

Matanock, Aila M. and Natalia Garbiras-Díaz, 2016, "Running Candidates after Using Violence? Evidence on a Possible Path to Peace from a Survey Experiment in Colombia," University of California, Berkeley, Berkeley, C.A., Unpublished paper.

Matanock, Aila M. and Adam G. Lichtenheld, 2016, "How Does International Intervention Work? Mechanisms for Securing Settlements to Civil Conflicts," University of California, Berkeley, Berkeley, C.A., Unpublished paper.

Mattes, Michaela and Burcu Savun, 2009, "Fostering Peace after Civil War: Commitment Problems and Agreement Design," *International Studies Quarterly*, 53, 3: 737–759.

Mattes, Michaela and Burcu Savun, 2010, "Information, Agreement Design, and the Durability of Civil War Settlements," *American Journal of Political Science*, 54, 2: 511–524.

Mayall, James, ed., 1996, *The New Interventionism 1991–1994: United Nations Experience in Cambodia, Former Yugoslavia and Somalia* (Cambridge, U.K.: Cambridge University Press).

McAuley, Richard., 2009, Author Interview, Belfast, North Ireland, July 28.

McCleary, Rachel M., 1997, "Guatemala's Postwar Prospects," *Journal of Democracy*, 8, 2: 129–143.

McCormick, David H., 1997, "From Peacekeeping to Peacebuilding: Restructuring Military and Police Institutions in El Salvador." In Michael W. Doyle, Ian Johnstone, and Robert C. Orr, eds., *Keeping the Peace: Multidimensional UN Operations in Cambodia and El Salvador* (Cambridge, U.K.: Cambridge University Press): 282–311.

McCoy, Jennifer L., 1993, "Mediating Democracy: A New Role for International Actors?." In David Bruce, ed., *New World Order: Social and Economic Implications* (Atlanta, G.A.: Georgia State University Business Press): 129–140.

McCoy, Jennifer L., Larry Garbar, and Robert A. Pastor, 1991, "Pollwatching and Peacemaking," *Journal of Democracy*, 2, 4: 102–114.

McCullogh, G., 1990, "Assistant Secretary's Daily Activity Report," November 19, Case ID 95122244, Document No. E1714, Guatemala Declassification Project, U.S. Department of State Freedom of Information Act, U.S. Department of State.

McFaul Michael, 1989, "Rethinking the 'Reagan Doctrine' in Angola," *International Security*, 14, 3: 99–135.

McFaul, Michael, 2010, *Advancing Democracy Abroad: Why We Should and How We Can* (Stanford, C.A.: Hoover Institution and Lanham, M.D.: Rowman and Littlefield Publishers).

McGarry John, 1998, "Political Settlements in Northern Ireland and South Africa," *Political Studies*, 46, 5: 853–870.

Mejía, Carlos, 2013, Author Interview, Guatemala City, Guatemala, August 20.

Milner, Helen V. and Dustin H Tingley, 2016, *Sailing the Water's Edge: The Domestic Politics of American Foreign Policy* (Princeton, N.J.: Princeton University Press).

Mohsin, Amena, 2003, *The Chittagong Hill Tracts, Bangladesh: On the Difficult Road to Peace* (Boulder, C.O.: Lynne Rienner Publishers).

Montgomery, Tommie Sue, 1998, "International Elections, Observing Elections, and the Democratic Transition in El Salvador." In Kevin Middlebrook, ed., *Electoral Observation and Democratic Transitions in Latin America* (Boulder, C.O.: Lynne Rienner Publishers): 115–140.

Morrison, Daniel "Danny," 2009, Author Interview, Belfast, North Ireland, July 23.

Morrow, James D., 2007, "When Do States Follow the Laws of War?," *American Political Science Review*, 101, 3: 559–572.

Mukherjee, Bumba, 2006, "Why Political Power-Sharing Agreements Lead to Enduring Peaceful Resolution of Some Civil Wars, but Not Others?," *International Studies Quarterly*, 50, 2: 479–504.

Mullenbach, Mark J., and William Dixon. 2007, *Third-Party Peacekeeping Missions: 1946–2006, Version 2.1. Codebook* (Conway: University of Central Arkansas).

Mullins, Janet G., 1991, "Information Copy of a Direct Reply, Re: Urges the President to Uphold the Congressional Decision to Freeze Military Aid to El Salvador," September 10, 2pp., Box No. CO046, 101116–243988, Bush Presidential Records.

Munck, Gerardo L., 1993, "Beyond Electoralism in El Salvador: Conflict Resolution through Negotiated Compromise," *Third World Quarterly*, 14, 1: 75–93.

National Democratic Institute, 2002, "Macedonia: Parliamentary Elections, September 2002," Election Watch Report, Washington, D.C., August 15.

National Network in Solidarity with the People of Guatemala (U.S.), 1993, "Peace Process: Background and Current Status of Peace Negotiations," January 31, Civil War, Society and Political Transition in Guatemala: the Guatemala News and Information Bureau Archive (1963–2000), Princeton University Digital Library, http://pudl.princeton.edu/objects/w9505134d.

National Security Council, 1989a, "Andean Drug Summit." In Evans, Michael, "War in Columbia: Guerrillas, Drugs and Human Rights in US-Colombia Policy, 1988–2002," National Security Archive Electronic Briefing Book No. 69, November 1.

National Security Council, 1989b, "Interagency Working Group Draft: Security for Narcotics Control in the Andean Region." In Evans, Michael, "War in Columbia: Guerrillas, Drugs and Human Rights in US-Colombia Policy, 1988–2002," National Security Archive Electronic Briefing Book No. 69, June 30.

Natsios, Andrew S., 2006, "USAID Primer: What We Do and How We Do It," U.S. Aid Agency for International Development, Washington, D.C., June.

Navarro Wolff, Antonio, 2012, Author Interview (Telephone), July 9.

Navarro Wolff, Antonio, 2012, Author Interview (Email), 12 July.

Nielsen, Richard A., Michael G. Findley, Zachary S. Davis, Tara Candland, and Daniel L. Nielson, 2011, "Foreign Aid Shocks as a Cause of Violent Armed Conflict," *American Journal of Political Science*, 55, 2: 219–232.

Nielsen, Richard A. and Beth A. Simmons, 2015, "Rewards for Ratification: Payoffs for Participating in the International Human Rights Regime?," *International Studies Quarterly*, 59, 2: 197–208.

Niksch, Larry, 2002, "Abu Sayyaf: Target of Philippine-US Anti-Terrorism Cooperation." CRS Report for Congress, ed., Congressional Research Service, Washington, D.C., Order Code RL31265, January 25.

Nilsson, Desirée, 2008, "Partial Peace: Rebel Groups Inside and Outside of Civil War Settlements," *Journal of Peace Research*, 45, 4: 479–495.

Norris, Pippa, 2004, *Electoral Engineering: Voting Rules and Political Behavior* (Cambridge, U.K.: Cambridge University Press).

Norris, Pippa, 2008, *Driving Democracy: Do Power-Sharing Institutions Work?* (Cambridge, U.K.: Cambridge University Press).

Nuvunga, Adriano, 2007, *Post-War Reconstruction in Mozambique: The United Nations' Trust Fund to Assist the Former Rebel Movement RENAMO* (Maputo, Mozambique: Centro de Integridade Publica (CIP)).

O'Donnell, Guillermo, and Philippe C. Schmitter, 1986, *Transitions from Authoritarian Rule: Tentative Conclusions about Uncertain Democracies* (Baltimore, M.D.: Johns Hopkins University Press).

Ofuho, Cirino Hiteng, 2006, "Negotiating Peace: Restarting a Moribund Process," Issue 8. In Mark Simmons and Peter Dixon, eds., *Peace by Piece: Addressing Sudan's Conflict* (London, U.K.: Conciliation Resources): 20–21.

Organization for Security and Cooperation in Europe, 2010, "Bosnia and Herzegovina: General Elections, 3 October 2010," Office for Democratic Institutions and Human Rights, Warsaw, Poland, December 17.

Organization of American States, 1993, "The On-Site Visits of the IACHR to Colombia, 1990–1992," Inter-American Commission on Human Rights.

Ossa Escobar, Carlos, 1998, "El Gobierno Barco Revelo La Magnitud Del Conflicto Y La Dificultad De Lograr La Paz." In *Serie El Proceso De Paz En Colombia 1982–2002* (Bogotá: Fundación Cultura Democrática): Volume II.

Oswald, Bruce, Helen Durham, and Adrian Bates, 2010, *Documents on the Law of UN Peace Operations* (Oxford, U.K.: Oxford University Press).

O'Toole, Kathleen, 1997, "Why Peace Agreements Often Fail to End Civil Wars," Stanford Online Report, November 19.

Ottaway, Marina, 1997, "From Political Opening to Democratization?." In Marina Ottaway, ed., *Democracy in Africa. The Hard Road Ahead* (Boulder, C.O.: Lynne Rienner Publishers): 1–14.

Ottaway, Marina, 1998, "Angola's Failed Elections." In Krishna Kuman, ed., *Postconflict Elections, Democratization, and International Assistance* (Boulder, C.O.: Lynne Rienner Publishers): 133–151.

Ottaway, Marina, 2003, "Promoting Democracy after Conflict: The Difficult Choices," *International Studies Perspectives*, 4, 3: 314–322.

Pardew, James, 2011, Author Interview (Telephone), April 20.

Pardo Rueda, Rafael, 1998, "Política De Paz, Acuerdo Con El M-19 Y Reactivación De Los Diálogos." In *Serie El Proceso De Paz En Colombia 1982–2002* (Bogotá: Fundación Cultura Democrática): Volume 2.

Paris, Roland, 2004, *At War's End: Building Peace after Civil Conflict* (Cambridge, U.K.: Cambridge University Press).

Pascoe, William, 1987, "Mozambique Merits the Reagan Doctrine," Heritage Foundation, Washington, D.C., March 31.

Peceny, Mark and William Stanley, 2001, "Liberal Social Reconstruction and the Resolution of Civil Wars in Central America," *International Organization*, 55, 1: 149–182.

Peic, Goran and Dan Reiter, 2011, "Foreign-Imposed Regime Change, State Power and Civil War Onset, 1920–2004," *British Journal of Political Science*, 41, 3: 453–475.

Peñaranda, Ricardo, 1999, "De Rebeldes a Ciudadanos: El Caso del Movimiento Armado Quintín Lame." In Ricardo Peñaranda and Javier Guerrero, eds., *De las Armas a la Política* (Bogota: TM Editores): 75–131.

Peou, Sorpong, 2004, "The UN's Modest Impact on Cambodia's Democracy." In Roland Rich and Edward Newman, eds., *UN Role in Promoting Democracy: Between Ideals and Reality* (Tokyo: United Nations University Press): 258–281.

Pereira, Anthony W., 1994, "The Neglected Tragedy: The Return to War in Angola, 1992–3," *The Journal of Modern African Studies*, 32, 1: 1–28.

Pevehouse, Jon C., 2002, "Democracy from the Outside-In? International Organizations and Democratization," *International Organization*, 56, 3: 515–549.

Pevehouse, Jon C., 2005, *Democracy from Above? Regional Organizations and Democratization* (Cambridge, U.K.: Cambridge University Press).

Phillips, John, 2004, *Macedonia: Warlords and Rebels in the Balkans* (New Haven, CT: Yale University Press).

Pickering, Paula M., 2004, "Explaining Moderation in Post-Communist Ethnic Party Systems: A Cross-National Investigation in the Balkans," Unpublished paper presented at the Midwest Political Science Association Annual National Conference, Chicago, I.L., April 15–18.

Pop-Eleches, Grigore and Graeme B. Robertson, 2015, "Information, Elections, and Political Change," *Comparative Politics*, 47, 4: 459–495.

Powell, Robert, 2002, "Bargaining Theory and International Conflict," *Annual Review of Political Science* 5: 1–30.

Powell, Robert, 2006, "War as a Commitment Problem," *International Organization*, 60, 1: 169–204.

Prantl, Jochen, 2006, *The UN Security Council and Informal Groups of States* (Oxford, U.K.: Oxford University Press).

Prendergast, Kieran, 1997, "Guatemala," United Nations General Assembly, A/52/, October.

Prisk, Court and Max G. Manwaring, eds., 1988, *El Salvador at War: An Oral History of Conflict from the 1979 Insurrection to the Present* (Washington, D.C.: National Defense University Press).

Przeworski, Adam, 1991, *Democracy and the Market: Political and Economic Reforms in Eastern Europe and Latin America* (New York, N.Y.: Cambridge University Press).

Przeworski, Adam, 2006, "Self-Enforcing Democracy." In Donald Wittman and Barry Weingast, eds., *Oxford Handbook of Political Economy* (New York, N.Y.: Oxford University Press).

Purvis, Dawn, 2009, Author Interview, Belfast, North Ireland, July 28.

Quayle, Dan, 1989, "Vice President Quayle's Remarks to the ESAF," February 3, 5pp., Vice President Dan Quayle's Office, Chief of Staff's Office, Quayle Speech Files, Bush Presidential Records, White House Office of Records Management.

Quiroga, Jahel, 2009, Author Interview, Bogotá, Colombia, December 11.

Reid, Michael, 1992, "Award Spotlights Longest War: Talks between Government and Guerrillas in the Country Are Stalled," *The Guardian*, October 17.

Reid, Michael, 1993, "Guatemalan Army Opts for Democratic Dawn: A New Spirit of Consensus Shows That in Central America Regression to Dictatorship Is Not Inevitable," *The Guardian*, June 21.

Reilly, Benjamin, 2002, "Post-Conflict Elections: Constraints and Dangers," *International Peacekeeping*, 9, 2: 118–139.

Reilly, Benjamin and Andrew Reynolds, 1999, *Electoral Systems and Conflict in Divided Societies* (Washington, D.C.: National Academies Press).

Reilly, Benjamin and Per Nordlund, eds., 2008, *Political Parties in Conflict-Prone Societies: Regulation, Engineering and Democratic Development* (Tokyo: United Nations University Press).

Reiter, Dan, 2003, "Exploring the Bargaining Model of War," *Perspectives on Politics*, 1, 1: 27–43.

Rice, Condoleezza, 2013, Author Interview, Stanford University, Stanford, CA, May 28.

Riley, Kevin Jack, 1993, *The Implications of Colombian Drug Industry and Death Squad Political Violence for US Counternarcotics Policy* (Santa Monica, C.A.: RAND Corporation).

Robberson, Tod, 1993, "Vanguard of Guatemalan Refugees Returns from Exile," *The Washington Post*, January 21.

Roca, Roberto, Shafik Handal, Leonel González, Fermán Cienfuegos, and Joaquín Villalobos, 1989, "FMLN Proposal to Turn the Elections into a Contribution to Peace," *Envio*, January 24.

Rohter, Larry, 1997, "Salvador's Ex-Rebels Expect Gains in Vote Today," *The New York Times*, March 16, Section 1, Page 8.

Rojas Puyo, Alberto, 2009, Author Interview, Bogotá, Colombia, December 3.

Romero, P., 1990, "Assistant Secretary's Daily Activity Report," March 16, Case ID 95122234, Document No. E1290, Guatemala Declassification Project, U.S. Department of State Freedom of Information Act, U.S. Department of State.

Romero, P., 1991, "Tying ESF to Human Rights in Guatemala – Status and Possible Calls to the Hill," April 5, Case ID 96122251, Document No. E1972, Guatemala Declassification Project, U.S. Department of State Freedom of Information Act, U.S. Department of State.

Romero, Peter F., 1989. "Information Copy of a Direct Reply, Re: Writes Concerning Repression and Violation of Human Rights of El Salvador Women since March 19, 1989," May 17, 2pp., Box No. CO046, 002807–094748, Bush Presidential Records, White House Office of Records Management.

Rosa, Herman and Michael Foley, 2000, "El Salvador." In Shepard Forman and Stewart Patrick, eds., *Good Intentions: Pledges of Aid for Postconflict Recovery* (Boulder, C.O.: Lynne Rienner Publishers): 113–158.

Ross, Michael L., 2011, "Oil and Gas Production and Value, 1932–2009," http://hdl.handle.net/1902.1/15828, Harvard Dataverse, Version 4.

Rothchild, Donald and Caroline Hartzell, 1995, "Interstate and Intrastate Negotiations in Angola." In I. William Zartman, ed., *Elusive Peace: Negotiating an End to Civil Wars* (Washington D.C.: The Brookings Institution): 175–203.

Ruggeri, Andrea, Theodora-Ismene Gizelis, and Han Dorussen. 2013. "Managing Mistrust: An Analysis of Cooperation with U.N. Peacekeeping in Africa," *Journal of Conflict Resolution*, 57, 3: 387–409.

Roy, J. Stapleton, 1991, "J. Stapleton Roy to Brent Scowcroft, Re: Presidential Delegation for Elections in El Salvador," February 2, 2pp. Box No. 07004–069, Personnel Office, Katja Bullock Files, Bush Presidential Records.

Russett, Bruce M. and John R. Oneal, 1997, "The Classical Liberals Were Right: Democracy, Interdependence, and Conflict, 1950–1985," *International Studies Quarterly*, 41, 2: 267–293.

Russett, Bruce M. and John R. Oneal, 2000, *Triangulating Peace: Democracy, Interdependence, and International Organizations* (New York, N.Y.: Norton).

Salvesen, Hilde, 2002, "Guatemala: Five Years after the Peace Accords, The Challenges of Implementing Peace," A Report for the Norwegian Ministry of Foreign Affairs, International Peace Research Institute, Oslo, Norway, March.

Sambanis, Nicholas and Jonah Schulhofer-Wohl, 2007, "Evaluating Multilateral Interventions in Civil Wars: A Comparison of UN and Non-UN Peace Operations." In Dimitris Bourantonis, Kostas Ifantis, and Panayotis Tsakonas, eds., *Multilateralism and Security Institutions in an Era of Globalization* (London, U.K.: Routledge): 252–287.

Sambanis, Nicholas, 2000, "Partition as a Solution to Ethnic War: An Empirical Critique of the Theoretical Literature," *World Politics*, 52, 4: 437–483.

Sanders IV, Lewis, 2016, "EU Cuts Financial Aid to Burundi Government," *Deutsche Welle*, March 14.

Santa-Cruz, Arturo, 2005, "Constitutional Structures, Sovereignty, and the Emergence of Norms: The Case of International Election Monitoring," *International Organization*, 59, 3: 663–694.

Santa-Cruz, Arturo, 2013, *International Election Monitoring Sovereignty and the Western Hemisphere Idea: The Emergence of an International Norm* (New York, N.Y. and Oxford, U.K.: Routledge).

Santiso, Carlos, 2002, "Promoting Democratic Governance and Preventing the Recurrence of Conflict: The Role of the United Nations Development Programme in Post-Conflict Peace-Building," *Journal of Latin American Studies*, 34, 3: 555–586.

Schedler, Andreas, 2002, "The Menu of Manipulation," *Journal of Democracy*, 13, 2: 36–50.

Schelling, Thomas C., 1960, *The Strategy of Conflict* (Cambridge, M.A.: Harvard University Press).

Schelling, Thomas C., 1966, *Arms and Influence* (New Haven, CT: Yale University Press).

Schraeder, Peter J., Steven W. Hook, and Bruce Taylor, 1998, "Clarifying the Foreign Aid Puzzle: A Comparison of American, Japanese, French, and Swedish Aid Flows," *World Politics*, 50, 2: 294–323.

Schultz, Kenneth A., 2010, "The Enforcement Problem in Coercive Bargaining: Interstate Conflict over Rebel Support in Civil Wars," *International Organization*, 64, 2: 281–312.

Schumpeter, Joseph, 1942, *Capitalism, Socialism and Democracy* (New York, N.Y.: Harper).

Schwarz, Benjamin C., 1991, *American Counterinsurgency Doctrine and El Salvador: The Frustrations of Reform and the Illusion of Nation Building* (Santa Monica, C.A.: RAND Corporation).

Scott, James M. and Carie A. Steele, 2005, "Assisting Democrats or Resisting Dictators? The Nature and Impact of Democracy Support by the United States National Endowment for Democracy, 1990–99," *Democratization*, 12, 4: 439–460.

Scott, Kirsty, 1995, "Cry, the Benighted Country. Image Makers Mask Brutality," *The Herald*, November 4.

Sharpe, Kenneth E., 1986, "El Salvador Revisited: Why Duarte Is in Trouble," *World Policy Journal*, 3, 3: 473–494.

Shugart, Matthew Soberg, 1992, "Guerrillas and Elections: An Institutionalist Perspective on the Costs of Conflict and Competition," *International Studies Quarterly*, 36, 2: 121–151.

Sichar Moreno, Gonzalo, 1999, *Historia De Los Partidos Políticos Guatemaltecos: Distintas Siglas De (Casi) Una Misma Ideología* (Guatemala: Editorial Los Altos).

Simmons, Beth A., 1998, "Compliance with International Agreements," *American Political Science Review*, 1: 75–93.

Simmons, Beth A., 2009, *Mobilizing for Human Rights: International Law in Domestic Politics* (New York, N.Y.: Cambridge University Press).

Simmons, Beth A., 2010, "Treaty Compliance and Violation," *Annual Review of Political Science*, 13: 273–296.

Simmons, Beth A., Frank Dobbin, and Geoffrey Garrett, 2006, "Introduction: The International Diffusion of Liberalism," *International Organization*, 60, 4: 781–810.

Simmons, Beth A. and Zachary Elkins, 2004, "The Globalization of Liberalization: Policy Diffusion in the International Political Economy," *American Political Science Review*, 98, 1: 171–189.

Simpser, Alberto and Daniela Donno, 2012, "Can International Election Monitoring Harm Governance?," *The Journal of Politics*, 74, 2: 501–513.

Simpser, Alberto, 2013, *Why Governments and Parties Manipulate Elections: Theory, Practice, and Implications* (New York, N.Y.: Cambridge University Press).

Simpson Mark, 1993, "Foreign and Domestic Factors in the Transformation of Frelimo," *The Journal of Modern African Studies*, 31, 2: 309–337.

Singer, J. David, Stuart Bremer, and John Stuckey, 1972, "Capability Distribution, Uncertainty, and Major Power War, 1820–1965." In Bruce Russett, ed., *Peace, War, and Numbers* (Beverly Hills, C.A.: Sage): 19–48. Version 4.

Smale, Alison, 2014, "Roots of Bosnian Protests Lie in Peace Accords of 1995," *The New York Times*, February 14.

Snyder, Jack, 2000, *From Voting to Violence: Democratization and Nationalist Violence* (New York, N.Y.: W. W. Norton and Company).

Söderberg Kovacs, Mimmi, 2007, "From Rebellion to Politics: The Transformation of Rebel Groups to Political Parties in Civil War Peace Processes," Ph.D. dissertation, Uppsala University.

Söderberg Kovacs, Mimmi, 2008, "When Rebels Change Their Stripes: Armed Insurgents in Post-War Politics." In Anna Jarstad and Timothy Sisk, eds., *From War to Democracy: Dilemmas of Peacebuilding* (Cambridge, U.K.: Cambridge University Press): 134–156.

Söderberg Kovacs, Mimmi, and Sophia Hatz, 2016, "Rebel-to-Party Transformations in Civil War Peace Processes 1975–2011," *Democratization* 23, 6: 990–1008.

Spence, Jack, 2005, "Central America and Political Terrorism." In William J. Crotty, ed., *Democratic Development and Political Terrorism: The Global Perspective* (Lebanon, N.H.: University Press of New England): 473–498.

Staniland, Paul, 2015, "Armed Groups and Militarized Elections," *International Studies Quarterly*, 59, 4: 694–705.

Stanley, William and David Holiday, 1997, "Peace Mission Strategy and Domestic Actors: UN Mediation, Verification and Institution-Building in El Salvador," *International Peacekeeping*, 4, 2: 22–49.

Stanley, William and David Holiday, 2002, "Broad Participation, Diffuse Responsibility: Peace Implementation in Guatemala." In Donald Rothchild, Stephen J. Stedman, and Elizabeth M. Cousens, *Ending Civil Wars: The Implementation of Peace Agreement* (Boulder, C.O.: Lynne Rienner Publications): 1–54 in pre-publication PDF provided.

Stanley, William, 2013, *Enabling Peace in Guatemala: The Story of MINUGUA* (Boulder, C.O.: Lynne Rienner Publications).

Stedman, Stephen J., 1997, "Spoiler Problems in Peace Processes," *International Security*, 22, 2: 5–53.

Steele, Abbey, 2011, "Electing Displacement: Political Cleansing in Apartadó, Colombia," *Journal of Conflict Resolution*, 55, 3: 423–445.

Stewart, Steve, 1995, "Guatemala's Blood Is on US Hands," *The Vancouver Sun*, August 22.

Suhrke, Astri and Julia Buckmaster, 2005, "Post-War Aid: Patterns and Purposes," *Development in Practice*, 15, 6: 737–746.

Suhrke, Astri, Espen Villanger, and Susan L. Woodward, 2005, "Economic Aid to Post-Conflict Countries: A Methodological Critique of Collier and Hoeffler," *Conflict, Security and Development*, 5, 3: 329–361.

Sullivan, Joseph G., 1994, "How Peace Came to El Salvador," *Orbis*, 38, 1: 83–98.

Sumbeiywo Lazaro, 2006, "The Mediator's Perspective," Issue 8. In Mark Simmons and Peter Dixon, eds., *Peace by Piece: Addressing Sudan's Conflict, Accord: An International Review of Peace Initiatives*, Conciliation Resources, London, U.K.: 22–27.

Svensson, Isak, 2009, "Who Brings Which Peace?: Neutral versus Biased Mediation and Institutional Peace Arrangements in Civil Wars," *Journal of Conflict Resolution*, 53, 3: 446–469.

Svolik, Milan W., 2012, *The Politics of Authoritarian Rule* (Cambridge, U.K.: Cambridge University Press).

Themnér, Lotta and Peter Wallensteen, 2012, "Armed Conflicts, 1946–2011," *Journal of Peace Research*, 49, 4: 565–575.

Tierney, Michael J., Daniel L. Nielson, Darren G. Hawkins, J. Timmons Roberts, Michael G. Findley, Ryan M. Powers, Bradley Parks, Sven E. Wilson, and Robert L. Hicks, 2011, "More Dollars than Sense: Refining Our Knowledge of Development Finance Using AidData," *World Development*, 39, 11: 1891–1906.

Toft, Monica Duffy, 2009, *Securing the Peace: The Durable Settlement of Civil War* (Princeton, N.J.: Princeton University Press).

Toft, Monica Duffy, 2010, "Ending Civil Wars: A Case for Rebel Victory?," *International Security*, 34, 4: 7–36.

Tull, Denis M., 2006, "China's Engagement in Africa: Scope, Significance and Consequences," *The Journal of Modern African Studies*, 44, 3: 459–479.

Turner, J. Michael, Sue Nelson, and Kimberly Mahling-Clark, 1998, "Mozambique's Vote for Democratic Governance." In Krishna Kumar, ed., *Postconflict Elections, Democratization, and International Assistance* (Boulder, C.O.: Lynne Rienner Publishers): 153–175.

Tvedten Inge, 1992, "US Policy towards Angola since 1975," *The Journal of Modern African Studies*, 30, 1: 31–52.

UNDP, Undated, "A Handbook on Working with Political Parties," Democratic Governance Group, Bureau for Development Policy, United Nations Development Programme, New York, N.Y.

United Nations, 2006, *The Blue Helmets: A Review of United Nations Peacekeeping* (New York, N.Y.: United Nations Publications).

United Nations, 2008, *60 Years of United Nations Peacekeeping* (New York, N.Y.: United Nations Publications).

United Nations General Assembly, 1999, "The Situation in Central America: Procedures for the Establishment of a Firm and Lasting Peace and Progress in Fashioning a Region of Peace, Freedom, Democracy and Development: United Nations Verification Mission in Guatemala, Note by the Secretary-General," A/54/688, December 21.

United Nations General Assembly, 2003, "Resolution adopted by the General Assembly: United Nations Verification Mission in Guatemala," A/RES/57/161, January 28.

United Nations General Assembly, 2014, "Evaluation of the Implementation and Results of Protection of Civilians Mandates in United Nations Peacekeeping Operations," Report of the Office of Internal Oversight Services, A/68787, March 7.

Upegui, Mario, 2009, Author Interview, Bogotá, Colombia, December 15.

URNG, 1985, "URNG: To the Guatemalan People," September, Civil War, Society and Political Transition in Guatemala: the Guatemala News and Information Bureau Archive (1963–2000), Princeton University Digital Library, http://arks.princeton.edu/ark:/88435/v118rf32x.

URNG, 1986, "Message from the Guatemalan National Revolutionary Unity – URNG – to the 8th Summit Conference of the Non-Aligned Countries," August, Civil War, Society and Political Transition in Guatemala: The Guatemala News and Information Bureau Archive (1963–2000), Princeton University Digital Library, http://arks.princeton.edu/ark:/88435/bv73c119d.

URNG, 1987, "Proposal to the Guatemalan Government," October 11, Civil War, Society and Political Transition in Guatemala: the Guatemala News and Information Bureau Archive (1963–2000), Princeton University Digital Library, http://arks.princeton.edu/ark:/88435/3n203z869.

URNG, 1990a, "For a New Guatemala, for Genuine Democratization and Development, for Progress and Peace," August 25, Civil War, Society and Political Transition in Guatemala: the Guatemala News and Information Bureau Archive (1963–2000), Princeton University Digital Library, http://arks.princeton.edu/ark:/88435/w3763762j.

URNG, 1990b, "Statement about the Present Situation from the General Command of the URNG," October 15, Civil War, Society and Political Transition in Guatemala: the Guatemala News and Information Bureau Archive (1963–2000), Princeton University Digital Library, http://arks.princeton.edu/ark:/88435/1n79h508w.

URNG, 1991, "The Actual Situation in the Negotiations Regarding the Topic of Human Rights," December 9, Civil War, Society and Political Transition in Guatemala: the Guatemala News and Information Bureau Archive (1963–2000), Princeton University Digital Library, http://arks.princeton.edu/ark:/88435/9019s335t.

URNG, 1993a, "Making Room for the Truth in Guatemala: URNG High Command Briefing on the Current State of the Negotiations," May 8, Civil War, Society and Political Transition in Guatemala: the Guatemala News and

Information Bureau Archive (1963–2000), Princeton University Digital Library, http://arks.princeton.edu/ark:/88435/fb494919s.

URNG, 1993b, "Renew the Negotiations Process and Go Forward on the Basis of What Has Been Agreed To," May 8, Civil War, Society and Political Transition in Guatemala: the Guatemala News and Information Bureau Archive (1963–2000), Princeton University Digital Library, http://arks.princeton.edu/ark:/88435/z890rv14b.

URNG, 1994a, "In Order for the Negotiations to Continue, Compliance with the Accords is Indispensable: Declaration of the General Command of the URNG," August 12, Civil War, Society and Political Transition in Guatemala: the Guatemala News and Information Bureau Archive (1963–2000), Princeton University Digital Library, http://arks.princeton.edu/ark:/88435/t148fj080.

URNG, 1994b, "Vital Moment for Human Rights and the Negotiations Process," April 19, Civil War, Society and Political Transition in Guatemala: the Guatemala News and Information Bureau Archive (1963–2000), Princeton University Digital Library, http://arks.princeton.edu/ark:/88435/fn106z80n.

URNG, 1995, "Future Must be Forged with Struggle and Decisiveness: Political Declaration of the General Command of the URNG," October 31, Civil War, Society and Political Transition in Guatemala: the Guatemala News and Information Bureau Archive (1963–2000), Princeton University Digital Library, http://arks.princeton.edu/ark:/88435/br86b435r.

URNG, Undated, "International Communique," [possibly 1982 based on the context], Civil War, Society and Political Transition in Guatemala: the Guatemala News and Information Bureau Archive (1963–2000), Princeton University Digital Library, http://arks.princeton.edu/ark:/88435/76537211v.

USAID, 2009, "US Overseas Loans and Grants: Obligations and Loan Authorizations," U.S. Agency for International Development, Washington, D.C., CONG-R-0105, September 30.

Van Cott, Donna Lee, 2005, *From Movements to Parties Latin America: The Evolution of Ethnic Politics* (Cambridge, U.K.: Cambridge University Press).

Van Evera, Stephen, 1997, *Guide to Methods for Students of Political Science* (Ithaca, N.Y.: Cornell University Press).

Verstegen, Suzanne, 2000, "The Netherlands and Guatemala: Dutch Policies and Intervention in the Guatemalan Conflict and Peace," Clingendael Institute, Conflict Policy Research Unit, The Hague, the Netherlands, December 1.

Vickers, George, 1992, "El Salvador: A Negotiated Revolution," *NACLA Report on the Americas*, 25, 5: 4–8.

Villalobos, Joaquín, 1989, "A Democratic Revolution for El Salvador," *Foreign Policy*, 74: 103–122.

Vinegrad, Anna, 1998, "From Guerrillas to Politicians: The Transition of the Guatemalan Revolutionary Movement in Historical and Comparative Perspective." In Rachel Sieder, ed., *Guatemala after the Peace Accords* (London, U.K.: Institute of Latin American Studies, University of London): 207–227.

Vines, Alex, 1993, "One Hand Tied: Angola and the UN," CIIR Briefing Paper, Catholic Institute for International Relations, London, U.K., June.

Voeten, Erik, 2005, "The Political Origins of the UN Security Council's Ability to Legitimize the Use of Force," *International Organization*, 59, 3: 527–557.

Walker, William Graham, 1991, "Embassy, El Salvador to SECSTATE, Re: Cristiani Believes USG Meeting with FMLN Now Could Be Helpful," December 20, 3pp., Box No. CF00196B2, Latin American Directorate Files, Bush Presidential Records.

Walter, Barbara F., 1997, "The Critical Barrier to Civil War Settlement," *International Organization*, 51, 3: 335–364.

Walter, Barbara F., 1999, "Designing Transitions from Civil War: Demobilization, Democratization, and Commitments to Peace," *International Security*, 24, 1: 127–155.

Walter, Barbara F., 2002, *Committing to Peace: The Successful Settlement of Civil Wars* (Princeton, NJ: Princeton University Press).

Walter, Barbara F., 2004, "Does Conflict Beget Conflict? Explaining Recurring Civil War," *Journal of Peace Research*, 41, 3: 371–388.

Walter, Barbara F., 2015, "Why Bad Governance Leads to Repeat Civil War," *Journal of Conflict Resolution*, 59, 7: 1242–1272.

Wantchekon, Leonard, 2004, "The Paradox of 'Warlord' Democracy: A Theoretical Investigation," *American Political Science Review*, 98, 1: 17–33.

Watson, Alexander F., 1995, "United States Policy toward Guatemala," Testimony before the U.S. Senate Select Committee on Intelligence, 104th Congress, 1st Session, Hearing on Guatemala, Washington, D.C., April 5.

Washington Office on Latin America, 1990, "The Guatemalan Elections in Context," September 24, Case ID 95122241, Document No. E1583, Guatemala Declassification Project, U.S. Department of State Freedom of Information Act, U.S. Department of State.

Wedeen, Lisa, 2009, *Peripheral Visions: Publics, Power, and Performance in Yemen* (Chicago, I.L.: University of Chicago Press).

Weinberg, Leonard, Ami Pedahzur, and Arie Perliger, 2009, *Political Parties and Terrorist Groups*, 2nd ed. (New York, N.Y.: Routledge).

Weingast, Barry R., 1997, "The Political Foundations of Democracy and the Rule of Law," *American Political Science Review*, 91, 2: 245–263.

Weingast, Barry R., 1996, "Off-the-Path Behavior: A Game-Theoretic Approach to Counterfactuals and Its Implications for Political and Historical Analysis." In Philip E. Tetlock and Aaron Belkin, eds., *Counterfactual Thought Experiments in World Politics: Logical, Methodological, and Psychological Perspectives* (Princeton, N.J.: Princeton University Press): 230–243.

Werner, Suzanne, 1999, "The Precarious Nature of Peace: Resolving the Issues, Enforcing the Settlement, and Renegotiating the Terms," *American Journal of Political Science*, 43, 3: 912–934.

Whitehead, Laurence, 1991, "The Imposition of Democracy." In Abraham F. Lowenthal, ed., *Exporting Democracy: The United States and Latin America* (Baltimore, M.D.: The Johns Hopkins University Press): 356–382.

Wilkinson, Tracy, 1993a, "Guatemala Leader Seizes Total Power," *Los Angeles Times*, May 26.

Wilkinson, Tracy, 1993b, "More Salvador Officers Will Be Purged, Cristiani Says: Pressed from at Home and Abroad about Delays, the President Pledges to Fulfill Peace Pact," *Los Angeles Times*, January 5.

Willetts, Peter, ed., 1996, *"The Conscience of the World": The Influence of Non-Governmental Organizations in the UN System* (London, U.K.: Hurst).

Williams, Richard, 2012, "Using the Margins Command to Estimate and Interpret Adjusted Predictions and Marginal Effects," *The Stata Journal*, 12, 2: 308–331.

Willingham, P. and L. Kusnitz, 1994, "Guatemala: Peace Process," November 17, Case ID 951222D0, Document No. E4779, Guatemala Declassification Project, U.S. Department of State Freedom of Information Act, U.S. Department of State.

Wood, Elisabeth J., 1995, "Agrarian Social Relations and Democratization: The Negotiated Resolution of the Civil War in El Salvador," Ph.D. dissertation, Stanford University.

Wood Elisabeth J., 2000, *Forging Democracy from Below: Insurgent Transitions in South Africa and El Salvador* (New York, N.Y.: Cambridge University Press)

Wooldridge, Jeffrey M., 2002, *Introductory Econometrics: A Modern Approach*, 2nd ed (Cincinnati: Thomson/South-Western).

World Bank, 2011, *World Development Report 2011: Conflict, Security and Development* (Washington, D.C.: The World Bank).

Wright, Joseph, 2008, "Do Authoritarian Institutions Constrain? How Legislatures Affect Economic Growth and Investment," *American Journal of Political Science*, 52, 2: 322–343.

Wurst, Jim, 1994, "Mozambique: Peace and More," *World Policy Journal*, 11, 3: 78–82.

Young, John, 2007, "Sudan IGAD Peace Process: An Evaluation," *Sudan Tribune*, May 30.

Youngs, Richard, 2008, "What Has Europe Been Doing?," *Journal of Democracy*, 19, 2: 160–169.

Zahar, Marie-Joelle, 1999, "Fanatics, Mercenaries, Brigands . . . And Politicians: Militia Decision-Making and Civil Conflict Resolution," Ph.D. dissertation, McGill University.

Zartman, I. William, 1995, "Negotiating the South African Conflict." In I. William Zartman, *Elusive Peace: Negotiating an End to Civil Wars* (Washington D.C.: The Brookings Institution): 147–174.

Zartman, I. William, 1985, *Ripe for Resolution: Conflict and Intervention in Africa* (New York, N.Y.: Oxford University Press).

Zürcher, Christoph, 2011, "Building Democracy While Building Peace," *Journal of Democracy*, 22, 1: 81–95.

# Index

CPSIA information can be obtained
at www.ICGtesting.com
Printed in the USA
LVOW13s1713210518
577959LV00011B/105/P